ALLEN COUNTY PUBLIC LIBRARY
S0-BKX-480

Soviet Russia and Indian Communism

Soviet Russia and Indian Communism

1917 - 1947 With an Epilogue Covering the Situation Today

by

David N. Druhe, Ph.D.

BOOKMAN ASSOCIATES
New York

Library of Congress Catalog Card Number: 59-8397

MANUFACTURED IN THE UNITED STATES OF AMERICA BY
UNITED PRINTING SERVICES, INC.
NEW HAVEN, CONN.

To My Parents

Table of Contents

Introduction

The history of Russo-Indian relations may be divided into three basic periods. The first of these basic periods deals with the relations between Czarist Russia and India and may in turn be sub-divided into two sub-periods; namely, the relations between Russia and India of the pre-Mogul and Mogul periods, and between Czarist Russia and the British masters of India after the middle of the eighteenth century. The second of these periods treats on Soviet policies in regard to India from the Bolshevik Revolution of November, (so-called October) 1917 to August, 1947 when the peoples of India were liberated from foreign rule and came to live under the free Indian Union and free Pakistan. The third period is concerned with Soviet relations with India and Pakistan to the present day. This work endeavors to consider the second basic period in some detail.

As regards the first basic period, it may be noted that Russo-Indian relations in the cultural sense had their beginnings in the time of the purely unofficial mission of Athanasius Nikitin, a merchant of Tver (Kalinin) to India between the years 1466 and 1475. Nikitin preserved a record of his journey to the sub-continent in his journal which is known as "A Journey beyond the Three Seas." In this journal Nikitin rendered an interesting account of the mores and manners of India in the epoch prior to the Mogul period.

It was under the auspices of the Mogul Empire that the first effort to establish political relations between India and Russia was initiated. In September, 1532, the Government of Muscovy was astonished by the arrival of an Indian, Tausein Hozya by name, the envoy of Babur, the first Grand Mogul of India. Tausein Hozya bore a letter of recommendation from the Mogul in which the latter expressed the desire to live in "friendship and fraternity" with the ruler of Muscovy. The latter also proposed a trade agreement between Muscovy and the Mogul Empire. However, the Muscovite officials evinced no interest whatever in political and economic relations with so distant a land as India. Besides, Babur had died even before his emissary had arrived in Moscow and the former's successors evidenced no desire in establishing political relations with a land so far to the northwest of Hindustan.

In the seventeenth century Czar Alexis Michaelovich Romanov determined on opening political and economic relationship between Russia and the Mogul Empire. He sent out no fewer than four diplomatic missions to that Empire, all without fruition. These missions, however, resulted in the exploration of much of the intervening territory between European Russia and India in the area of Central Asia which was to prove valuable to the Russians in their future policy in respect to that region.

In 1694 during the reign of Peter the Great, under a merchant named Simon Malenki, a new mission was sent forth to inaugurate the desired political and economic relations. Traveling through Persia, the Russian mission arrived at the Mogul capital Delhi in December, 1696. The Great Mogul, Aurangzeb, treated the Muscovite mission with courtesy, but at the same time refused to make any arrangements for the definite establishment of Russo-Indian political or economic relations. The mission attempted to return to Russia by way of Persia on two ships, loaded with Indian goods, but disaster struck in the form of Arab pirates who attacked these vessels and seized the goods. While returning to Moscow, the empty-handed and chagrined Malenki died and only one member of his mission to India, who had held only a subordinate capacity in it, arrived in Moscow.

During the latter part of his reign, Czar Peter boldly determined to conquer the lands between Russia and India, just as his predecessors had won Siberia a century before. But his two expeditions to Central Asia ended in disaster and those parts of Northern Persia which he had seized were lost by his successors.

In 1791 a certain Frenchman, M. de St. Genie, drew up a plan for the consideration of Empress Catherine the Great which involved an invasion of India. This plan was not carried out, but her son and successor, Paul, the so-called "mad Czar," ardently espoused the idea of a Russian invasion of India. He proposed to Napoleon in 1800 a scheme for a Franco-Russian invasion of India. Upon Napoleon's refusal to collaborate in the proposed "Quixotic enterprise," Czar Paul determined to "go it alone." In January, 1801 he ordered the chief of the Don Cossacks, Orlov-Denisov, to invade India. Orlov-Denisov obeyed his Czar's instructions. In the depth of winter he managed somehow to assemble a force of 22,000 Cossack cavalrymen and two companies of horse artillery. His hastily organized and bewildered force of Cossacks set forth for the conquest of India from the Don River Valley on March 12, 1801. In spite of great privations, they had reached a point north of Lake Aral some 450 miles from the Don by April, when the news was received that the "mad Czar" had been assassinated the previous March 23rd. The "mad adventure" was abandoned, and the Cossacks straggled back to the Volga.

Several years later, in 1808, at the meeting of Emperors, Napoleon and Alexander at Tilsit, the question of a joint Franco-Russian march on India was considered. However, when the two Emperors fell out shortly thereafter the idea was naturally abandoned.

During the course of the Crimean War (1854-1856) three Russian Generals, Chickachev, Duhamel and Khrulev proposed that Russian forces should attack India through Persia and the Afghan principalities of Herat and Kabul. The defeat of Russia brought an end to these military speculations and Russia did nothing to encourage the leaders of the "Indian Mutiny" or "War of Indian Independence" in 1857. However, the Russian conquests of the native states of Central Asia, Bukhara in 1868, Khiva in 1873 and Kokand in 1875 gave the impression to certain apprehensive Britons that Russia was preparing a march on India.

On April 25, 1878 when war between Britain and Russia appeared inevitable as a result of the Russo-Turkish conflict, on order of Emperor Alexander II, three columns in Turkestan were actually alerted to undertake a march to India. However, the Treaty of Berlin, June 13, 1878, ended what would have, at best, been an extremely audacious military enterprise.

The consolidation of Russian power in Central Asia between 1879 and 1895 and the construction of strategic railways connecting this area with European Russia evoked fear in some English quarters for India's safety, but these apprehensions were dissipated by Russia's evident weakness in her war with Japan in the years 1904-1905. The result was the Agreement of 1907 by which Russia and Britain stabilized and recognized each other's rights in India's northern and western borderlands.

The First World War also reflected the more favorable relations between Britain and Czarist Russia in that the Russian consul-general in Calcutta was permitted to enjoy in New Delhi the same quasi-ambassadorial status as other Allied envoys; moreover Russian warships cooperated with those of Britain in the Indian Ocean. When Russia fell to the Communists in November, 1917 an abrupt change took place in the relations between Russia and India under British rule, and it is the story of this change which the writer will relate in some detail.

As to Russian designs on India in the Czarist era, it may be said that save for the "mad" Emperor Paul and for a portion of the reigns of Empress Catherine the Great and Emperors Alexander I and Alexander II, Russia had no design of invading India either to liberate the Indians or to substitute Russian for British rule in the Peninsula. The Russian conquests in Central Asia, rather, represented a fairly logical rounding out of the Czarist Empire in Asia at the expense of poorly organized states and turbulent tribesmen. These conquests also served to augment Russian bargaining power in respect to Britain as a consequence of the potential threat to India from the new Muscovite positions.

But so far as the Soviets were concerned, as the succeeding pages will show, it was an entirely different matter, or rather there was a return to the thinking of Czars Paul and Alexander I.

As applied to India, the plan of the world revolution meant nothing more nor less than the substitution of the British Raj by a disguised Russian Raj, ruled nominally by the Indian agents of the Soviet Union, operating as a radical Indian organization, the Communist Party of India. The Russian line and that of the Communists in India often changed between November, 1917 and August, 1947, as regards India, but those changes only reflected Russia's interests and not those of India.

An entirely new scope in Indo-Russian relations was afforded by the liberation of the peoples of the Indian Peninsula from the British Raj into the nations of the Indian Union and Pakistan. The relations of free India and Pakistan with Soviet Russia as well as the activities of the Communist Party of India (C.P.I.) and the Communist Party of Pakistan (C.P.P.) cannot be dealt with in detail in this work in that to do so would hinder an adequate presentation of the relations of the Soviet Union with India, when the latter was yet a colony, as well as with the foundation and development of the Communist movement in the sub-continent.

CHAPTER ONE

Early Soviet Designs on India

One week before the revolution which overthrew the ill-fated Provisional Government of Alexander Kerensky, the Russian Bolsheviks were manifesting an interest in India and the East. On October 31, 1917, a Communist agency, known as the "League for the Liberation of the East" called for the overthrow of "Western Imperialism in the East."[1] And, shortly afterwards, on November 24, 1917, the newly installed Council of People's Commissars called upon the Indians and the people of the Middle East to "Shake off the tyranny of those who for a hundred years have plundered your land."[2]

Several months later, in the late spring of 1918, the Bolshevik government published a so-called "Blue Book" on relations between Czarist Russia and India. This "Blue Book," edited by K. M. Troyanovsky, was a "Collection of Secret Documents Taken from the Archives of the Russian Ministry of Foreign Affairs." Of significance to us here is the introduction by Troyanovsky who expounded the first Soviet viewpoint as regards India.

Troyanovsky devoted a considerable amount of attention to the periodic famines which have beset the people of India and blamed these catastrophes upon ". . . the evil exploitative will of their mighty masters—the English Imperialists who for more than a century have drunk the blood of this unhappy country."[3] At the same time he eagerly charged that the British ruled the Indians by means of ruthless "material strength" in the form of their army and police and that they deprived the natives of the sub-continent of even the smallest share in the government of their own country. Besides, the British have been truly cruel, held this early Soviet expert on India, in that they have monopolized the Indian market and thereby prevented the development of native Indian industries.[4] Furthermore, the British have added insult to injury by forcing the Indians to pay for the support of "100,000 English bureaucrats annually about 14 million pounds sterling."[5]

In view of the ruin which the British have brought about to the "richest country of the world." its inhabitants were held to be yearning for liberation from "the hated yoke of the English" and so a liberation movement on the part of the people of India threatens the oppressive tyranny. But, argued Troyanovsky, Great Britain is determined to hang on to the land which is "the very basis of her existence as an imperialist power," a land which she is able "to milk as one milks a cow." Hence England has refused to grant even a modicum of autonomy to the Indians and has even brought about the World War to save her imperial holdings, specifically to check the German threat to India by way of the Turkish province of Mesopotamia.[6]

Troyanovsky then went on to maintain that India in rebellion would become a "natural ally" for Russia in her own struggle to avoid becoming a "colony of Western Europe." And this alliance would also be one which would aid and abet the cause of Bolshevism in India for

> . . . our revolutionary path in the not distant future will bring forth joy, not only on the plane of the struggle for national liberation from foreign domination, but also for the broader principle of the class struggle and for the Socialist order.[7]

At about the same that Troyanovsky was propounding this propaganda, the Moscow wireless telegraphy station in May, 1918, broadcast the report of an appeal for help said to have been received from a so-called "Indian delegation." During that same month, it was announced that Communist propaganda would be disseminated in India.[8]

Some months later, in March, 1919, the First Congress of the Communist (or Third) International took place. India was referred to in this conclave in Moscow. The line taken at the Congress was that the World War had been waged with the aid of the colonial peoples, of which the Indians were the first mentioned, whose reward would merely be to remain the "slaves" of the colonial powers. The Congress also held that "as to India, revolutionary ferment has not been absent there for a single day. The British Government took action with armoured cars in Bombay."[9]

The views expressed by Troyanovsky and the First Congress of the Communist International had actually been antedated by those of Marx, Engels and Lenin before the First World War while the Czars yet ruled. In their famous "Manifesto of the Communist Party" drawn up in January, 1848, Marx and Engels took note of India in the following words:

> The East Indian and Chinese markets, the colonisation of America, trade with the colonies, the increase in the means of exchange and in commodities generally, gave to commerce, to navigation, to industry, an impulse never before known, and thereby, to their evolutionary element in the tottering feudal society, a rapid development.[10]

Thus the markets of India facilitated the replacement of the feudal order by the capitalist order. Realizing this, Karl Marx devoted a considerable measure of attention to the sub-continent in his writings.

Marx charged that the British had shattered the traditional Indian agricultural and village economy, by downright looting during the course of the eighteenth century and the attendant transporting of the plunder from India to England, by the neglect by the British of vital Indian irrigation and public works projects, by the introduction of the English system of large private landholdings and by prohibitory duties on the imports of Indian manufactures, first into England, and later into the continent of Europe.[11] Somewhat later, in the first half of the nineteenth century, argued Marx, Indian economy was altogether smashed by the entrance into India of cheap British machine-produced goods which ruined the native artisans. At the same time England secured a monopoly for her own manufacturing interests and the exclusion of Indian manufactures from their own market.[12]

The British policy of destroying the economic basis of India has been supplemented by political tyranny, contended Marx, for the oppressed Indians are compelled to pay a tribute of five million pounds for a so-called "good government" which is not in their interest but rather in that of dividend-searching British capital.[13] As for the semi-autonomous Indian native states, Marx tartly remarked they were mere "vassals" of the British government.[14]

However, it should be noted that Marx did assert that British policy in India was in itself a "tool of history" which made for the "regeneration" of India in that it provided for political unity, a native army, a free property, the formation of an educated Indian class, regular and rapid communication with Europe by steamship and within India by railway, which factors would make for an Indian capitalism which would be a stage on the road from feudalism to socialism.[15] However, Marx was quick to add that the Indians could not "reap the fruit of the new elements of society" until either the British proletariat had overthrown their capitalist masters or the Indians themselves had been successful in throwing off the English yoke in its entirety.[16] And Marx was optimistic that this would occur, for he expressed the view that Britain's "bloodsucking" policy in India would lead to a "serious complication if not a general insurrection."[17]

In a letter written in 1882 to Karl Kautsky, a noted German Socialist, Friedrich Engels predicted that colonies occupied by persons of European blood, such as Canada and Australia, would all become "independent," but that India and other colonial countries inhabited by native peoples must be "taken over by the proletariat" of these countries in order that independence within them might be achieved. On the same occasion Engels confidently predicted a "probable" revolution in India against British rule there. It would be a destructive one, but averred

Engels lightly, "that sort of thing is inseparable from all revolutions."[18]

Prior to the Bolshevik revolution Vladimir Ilyitch Lenin also displayed interest in India. When in the year 1908, some of the cotton mill operatives in that land struck in protest against the incarceration of the Indian patriot, B. G. Tilak, the future master of Russia was prompted to remark that

> . . . also in India the proletariat has sufficiently matured to carry on an acknowledged mass political struggle—and once this is so, the swan-song of the English order in India will have been sung.[19]

Lenin also held that next to Czarist Russia, misery was greatest in "English India among other nations of the East."[20]

In the spring of 1919 there were two avenues open to the Soviets in the furtherance of their designs on India. The first was to utilize the strife between British India and Afghanistan, the strategic buffer state between Russian Turkestan and India. The second was to utilize the services of Indian revolutionaries both within and without the peninsula.

The sudden unprovoked attack of the Afghans upon British India on May 3, 1919 greatly encouraged the Bolsheviks. Prior to February 20th, 1919, Afghanistan had been ruled by Emir Habibullah, a ruler who had always been friendly to the British masters of India. But subsequent to the assassination of the latter Emir upon that date, a ruler of an entirely different character appeared on the Afghan scene—after a scuffle for power—named Amanullah. Motivated by the disturbances then going on within India as well as a belief that he would remove dissaffection towards his rule by means of a foreign war, Amanullah entered upon the disastrously daring step of his attack on India. Having launched this attack, the foolhardy Emir determined to effect a firm military alliance with Russia, and so he telegraphed Lenin a proposal that Soviet Russia and Afghanistan should initiate diplomatic relations, a proposal to which Lenin readily assented.[21]

To further his policy, Amanullah dispatched missions to

Moscow. The first of these missions arrived in the Soviet capital on May 9, 1919, according to the official Soviet wireless telegraph station. Early in June, 1919, a larger mission under General Mohammed Wali Khan entered the Communist stronghold and capital of Turkestan, Tashkent, which mission was most enthusiastically received by the local Soviet authorities.[22] The Afghan general asked the Red Governor-General of Turkestan for help in arms and men for the war against British India, especially in respect to artillery. The Communists offered sympathy, but no arms, for they were hard pressed in the spring of 1919 by various White Armies and anti-Russian Central Asian Muslim elements, and their position was, then, in Turkestan precarious, to say the least. However, the Soviets and the Afghans agreed that a Russian agent from Tashkent should be accredited to the Emir at Kabul.[23]

On June 14th, after a ten days' sojourn at Tashkent, the mission of General Mohammed Wali Khan left for Moscow, but was delayed by the Russian civil war, and was only able to proceed to Moscow after the Bolsheviks had opened the railroad line from Tashkent to Orenburg and Moscow. However, the mission succeeded in establishing formal diplomatic relations between Soviet Russia and Afghanistan so that the latter country received the doubtful distinction of being the first country to recognize the Communist regime in Moscow, and in turn, Russia was the first European country, outside of Great Britain, to recognize the full independence and sovereignty of Afghanistan.[24] Besides, the Soviet-Afghan relationship permitted the Communists to carry on propaganda in respect to India on the very borders of the sub-continent.

On June 14, 1919, the day the Afghan mission under General Mohammed Wali Khan had set out for Moscow, a Soviet mission under a man named Bravin proceeded to Afghanistan. This mission which brought with it a quantity of munitions, including artillery shells, had a reception in Kabul, the Afghan capital, which Bravin described as "pompous but without interest."[25] That Soviet war material was really used during the Third Anglo-Afghan war is claimed by a British source.[26] The supposed fact that they sent arms to the Afghans indicates their interest in having the British ousted from the sub-continent. Indirectly substantiating the British contention, Soviet organs of propaganda, especially those in Central Asia, extolled the Afghan cause, excoriated that of the British, claimed vast non-existent victories for the Afghan armies and went into considerable detail about a great revolution against British rule which was supposed to be sweeping across the sub-continent.[27] In Moscow, Stalin in his role as Commissar of Nationalities hailed the war as a "revolutionary struggle," even though it was being conducted under the auspices of an hereditary monarch.[28]

The war was, of course, an entirely uneven struggle owing to the vast technical supremacy of the British, particularly in aviation, their use of which utterly terrified the Afghans. Consequently the Afghans were content to agree to a virtual armistice at the end of June and to conclude a peace treaty with the British at Rawalpindi in the North-West Frontier Province on July 26, 1919, by which the latter suffered the Afghans to retain their independence and territorial integrity and indirectly permitted the Emir's government to establish diplomatic relations with governments other than the Anglo-Indian, a right previously denied to the Afghans.[29]

The conclusion of the Anglo-Afghan conflict did not deter the Soviets from endeavoring to carry on a policy of disseminating revolutionary propaganda into India. For this purpose Lenin utilized Indian revolutionaries. Emigré Indian revolutionary centers had been established since the turn of the century in London, Paris, San Francisco and Berlin, in which latter city a so-called "Provisional Government of India" had been set up by an "Indian Revolutionary Committee" during the years of the First World War.[30] These various emigré centers endeavored, in spite of rigorous British opposition, to maintain contact with revolutionary societies within India, notably in Bengal and the Punjab.[31] One of the agents of the "Provisional Government of India" was a certain emigré Indian revolutionary named Mahendra Pratep, a landowner from Uttar Pradesh (then known as the United Provinces). He was sent by his German superiors in 1916 on a mission to Afghanistan to induce that country to join the Central Powers, but under British and

Czarist pressure, the Afghans forced him to flee into Chinese Turkestan.[32]

With the defection of Russia from the Allied side, it became possible for Mahendra Pratep to return to Berlin and report to his Indian colleagues and Teutonic superiors. On his way to Germany, however, Mahendra Pratep conceived the idea that the new Russian regime might be interested in the liberation of India, so he had an interview with Leon Trotsky, the Commissar of War.[33] Apparently, the wireless telegraph message of the Bolsheviks of May, 1918, about an Indian delegation in Moscow referred to Mahendra Pratep's visit. The latter apparently found the Soviets less attractive patrons than the Germans, for he returned to the Reich and rejoined his comrades in Berlin until the end of the war.

With the defeat of Germany, Mahendra Pratep had only one course open if he were to receive foreign support for an insurrection in India. He had to go to the Soviets. Hence, once again, the Indian revolutionary proceeded to Moscow early in 1919 and there he engaged in several conversations with Lenin. The Indian candidly informed the Red leader that he was not a Communist, but rather a believer in the "Religion of Love," and presented Lenin a tract on this thesis. Lenin was obviously disgusted with the views of this seemingly eccentric revolutionary, but he nonetheless recognized Mahendra Pratep as one who was fervently anti-British and as such one who might prove a willing servant of Russian designs, if not of Communism, per se, as an ideology. Therefore, Lenin dispatched him to the border of India. However, not pleased at serving those peculiar godless Bolsheviks, Mahendra Pratep on his own responsibility, proceeded to the Khanate of Bukhara which had thrown off its former vassal status to Russia as a result of the revolutions of 1917. The Indian hoped to interest the Khan of that land in the cause of Indian independence, but in this he was unsuccessful. Consequently, making the best of a bad lot, Mahendra Pratep resumed service with the Bolsheviks.[34] He was joined by a certain Baraktullah, another agent of the Indian "Provisional Government" in Berlin, who by his own assertion had undertaken an unsuccessful mission to Japan to win support there for the Indian revolutionary cause.[35]

Late in 1919, accompanied by a small group of Red Army soldiers, Mahendra Pratep and Baraktullah traveled to Kabul where they joined the Soviet envoy, Bravin. The Indian revolutionaries were well received by Emir Amanullah and with his permission they founded a "Provisional Government of the People of India" at Kabul to replace the one in Berlin which had been dissolved upon Germany's defeat. Mahendra Pratep held the post of President and Baraktullah that of Foreign Minister in this shadow "government."[36] At about the same time, in November, 1919, the Soviets backed up their newly sponsored Indian "government" at Kabul with a show of force. In November, 1919, General Sokolnikov, the commander of the Red Army of Turkestan, ordered his forces to take up positions in the Pamirs area where the boundaries of Russia and India virtually touched, being separated by only a thin wisp of Afghan territory. Through the "Krasnaya Gazeta," a then influential Communist paper, Moscow declared this move was designed "to bring the British Government to its senses."[37]

Early in 1920 the Russians replaced Bravin as their chief envoy to Afghanistan, by a man named Suritz, Bravin remaining as the latter's assistant. However, the effort of the Soviets to disseminate propaganda into India from Afghanistan received a jolt when early in that year dissension broke out in the ranks of the Indian revolutionaries. At that time, a certain Acharya, who had been one of the Indians sent by the Berlin "Provisional Government of India" to carry on propaganda among the Indians, captured by German-Turkish forces on the Mesopotamian front, entered the picture. After the war, he had slipped into India. Subsequently, accompanied by an old Muslim Indian trader named Abdur Rab, Acharya repaired to Kabul. Acharya thereupon proclaimed himself a Communist and immediately ingratiated himself with the Soviet embassy, and induced it to stop supporting Mahendra Pratep and Baraktullah, with whom Acharya had fallen out almost at once. Suritz backed the professed Bolshevik as against the "Provisional Government" leaders who were no Communists. The result of all this was that the plans of the Bolsheviks for carrying on propaganda within India and ultimately Red revolution there were thrown into utmost confusion.[38] The Soviets needed above all an Indian revolutionary who would also be a Communist by conviction and not merely one by expediency, as appeared to be the case with Acharya. Such a man appeared in Moscow, in January, 1920. He called himself M. N. Roy.

Manabendra Nath Roy, né Manabendra Nath Bhattacharji, was born in Bengal in February, 1893 of the Brahmin caste.[39] In his early youth he was connected with the Bengali terrorist movement and upon the outbreak of the First World War, he became an agent of the "Berlin Committee" and in that capacity carried on anti-British activities throughout the Far East. In 1916 he arrived in San Francisco where he became affiliated with the Indian emigré revolutionary center there known as the Ghadr party.[40] On the campus of nearby Leland Stanford University, Roy met and married an American girl, Evelyn Trent, who had socialist sympathies and played a role in Roy's conversion to Communism.[41] She subsequently accompanied her husband in all of his travels.

Roy then proceeded to New York City where his socialist convictions were further bolstered by his reading the works of Marx, and his contact with the American radical, Jay Lovestone. Early in 1917 Roy was arrested on the campus of Columbia University, but "jumping" bail and armed with a letter of introduction from President David Starr Jordan of Stanford University to General Alvarado, the Governor of Yucatan, the Bengali fled to Mexico. In the land of the ancient Aztecs Roy got in touch with the revolutionary leaders, Obregón and Carranza, and the latter, then President of Mexico, gave Roy protection within that country and refused the request of the British legation there to have him handed over for extradition.[42]

Having now forsaken the cause of the "Berlin Committee," Roy plunged into the thick of the Mexican socialist movement and was one of the founders of the Mexican Socialist Party in 1918. By the summer of 1919 the Brahmin revolutionary was the General Secretary of the Mexican Socialist Party and the head of the incipient Mexican Communist movement. At that time there arrived in Mexico a personage almost as interesting as Roy himself, Michael Borodin, a Russian Jew who had resided in the United States and who was also known as Branntwein and Gruzenberg. Borodin's task was to found a Communist Party in Mexico, a land deemed fertile ground for the dissemination of Bolshevik propaganda by Moscow. While they were forming the Mexican Communist Party, Roy expressed the desire to Borodin, with whom he had struck a firm friendship, to work for the cause of Communism in his native land. Specifically, Roy offered his services for the furthering of Soviet Russia's aims in the great Indian sub-continent. Borodin agreed that, although Roy's work in Mexico had been effective, it would be well if the latter should go to Russia and work for the Indian revolution after a successor to Roy had been trained to carry on as the leader of the Communist Party of Mexico. Hence Roy left Mexico in November, 1919 and arrived two months later in Russia, having successfully eluded British agents who had sought to apprehend him.[43]

As a result of his being the leading organizer of the first Communist party in Latin America and one of the first outside Russia, Roy had interviews with the leading figures of Bolshevism in the early months of 1920. He was treated with considerable respect by Chicherin, the Commissar for Foreign Affairs and his deputy, Karakhan, the Assistant Commissar, by Madame Angelica Balabanova, "the matriarch of Bolshevism" and the first General Secretary of the Communist International, and by Lenin himself. They were impressed by the audacious approach of the young Indian in his zeal for revolution in the sub-continent. Lenin was struck and perhaps astonished by Roy's criticism of the then Communist line in regard to the peoples of the East.

Lenin maintained the view that Communist Russia should support the national liberation movements in Asian countries including India, regardless of their ideological bases. He held that since, according to Marxism, every stage of social revolution is historically determined, colonial countries like India should have their own bourgeois democratic revolution before the stage of proletarian revolution could be entered upon. It was the duty of Communists to help the colonial liberation movement under the leadership of the national bourgeoisie, regarding the latter as an objectively revolutionary power. As an example of this line of reasoning, Lenin held that the Pan-Islamic movement, certainly a non-Bolshevik movement, was revolutionary and thus merited the support of the world Communist movement; the success of Mustafa Kemal Pasha in Turkey being alluded to as one of ultimate benefit to Bolshevism.[44]

Roy boldly disagreed. He pointed out to Lenin that even in the most advaneed colonial countries, such as India, the bourgeoisie was not economically advanced nor socially differentiated from the ancient feudal orders in the Eastern countries. Hence a revolution by the bourgeoisie in the East, including India, would not at all mean a bourgeois democratic revolution. Hence Roy characterized the rising Gandhian movement in India as purely "reactionary" and argued that Gandhi was but a "religious and cultural revivalist" in contrast to Lenin who deemed him a "revolutionary." Roy took the view that the Indian revolution must originate from the workers and peasants on the Russian model, and cited the judgment of Plekhanov on the Russian Populist and Social Revolutionary movements to prove his points. Lenin's attitude was "very kind and tolerant" to the "Indian upstart," but as a matter of fact, the attitude of the Bolsheviks towards the East was plastic and uncertain early in 1920; it had not yet crystallized into a rigid "party line."[45]

Lenin's emphasis on "national revolution" was satisfactory to such non-Bolsheviks as Mahendra Pratep and Baraktullah and it was this line which poured forth from the "Provisional Government of the People of India" in Afghanistan and from the Bolsheviks in Turkestan. This propaganda stressed the excessive wealth of the British in India, the famines they supposedly engendered, the tyranny of British rule, the absolute lack of civil rights including restrictions on freedom of worship for Hindus and Muslims alike, the arbitrary imprisonment of thousands of Indians including Sir Rabindranath Tagore, "the Tolstoy of India," the forbidding of Indians to ride in tramcars in the towns and their being allowed to ride only on cattle-cars on the trains. Indian history was also oddly interpreted by this propaganda. Thus it was held that the

Sepoys of 1857 had formed soviets in precisely the same way as had the Russian Bolsheviks of 1917. Economic grievances were also mentioned—wretched wages were duly noted, but here again the emphasis was on the colonial exploiters and not on alleged wicked deeds of the native Indian bourgeoisie.[46] Moreover, Barak-tullah, as a Muslim, put a decided pan-Islamic slant into his propaganda which thereby simply represented a continuation of efforts along the same line that had earlier been made under German aegis.[47] The British, it may be noted, were somewhat worried by this propaganda and Colonel Etherton, the British consul at Kashgar, Chinese Turkestan, went to great pains to try and offset it by issuing a proclamation of the Sheikh-ul-Islam, the leading cleric of Islam next to the Caliph, in which the former rigorously attacked Bolshevism and all its works.[48]

The Second Congress of the Communist International held between July 19 and August 7, 1920, in Moscow, was the arena for a continuation of the friendly debate between Roy and Lenin on the subject of what the Communist propaganda line should be as regards India and other countries of the East. In his address before the delegates, Roy took the view that the Communist International should exclusively assist the formation and development of the Communist movement of India and that the Communist Party of India, when once formed, should be devoted exclusively to the "organisation of the broad popular masses" and for the class struggle. Roy held that world capitalism, and especially European capitalism, was securing its main resources and income from the colonies; hence, in order to destroy European capitalism, there must be a Communist revolution per se in the East. As for the national liberation movement, Roy argued that the popular masses, living in a state of utmost destitution are not interested in the nationalist movement, but only in questions of a socio-economic character. This was all the more reason why the masses should be indoctrinated exclusively in Communist principles. Roy admitted that the industrial proletariat in India was weak, but pointed out the vast size of the Indian agricultural proletariat—the depressed peasantry. He felt that from these elements a "strong Communist party" could be formed.[49] Roy delivered his address in English and claimed that he was applauded by the few delegates to the Congress who could understand that tongue.[50]

Lenin disputed Roy's position. He held that since the Russian Bolsheviks had supported the "liberal liberation movement" when it had opposed the Czar, so the Indian Communists should, by analogy, support the bourgeois-liberation movement without actually merging with it. Lenin also disputed Roy's view that the "destiny of the West" would be dependent upon the strength of the Revolution in the countries of the East. Supporting the then leader of world Communism, "Comrade Welch," a leading British Communist, added that Roy's thesis was defective in that the British government could easily "handle the purely Communistic propaganda . . . in the colonies" and could also "suppress the Communist movement there," but it would be harder for it "to defeat the national liberation movement in a colony."[51]

The second Congress produced two notable results. In the first place, a special bureau of the Communist International was set up, the "Central Asiatic Bureau" which was designed to further the dissemination of Communism, particularly in India, and in the borderlands of the sub-continent, Afghanistan, Persia, and Chinese Turkestan as well as in Russian Turkestan itself. This bureau was composed of M. N. Roy, who was not in any way censored for his heterodoxy, General Sokolnikov, the Commander in Chief of the Red Army in Central Asia, and Chairman of the Turkestan Commission of the Central Soviet Government, and a man named Safarov, known to be a "close follower" of Zinoviev who had recently become President of the Communist International. This new bureau, called the "Turk-Bureau" was to act in close collaboration with the Turkestan Commission of the Soviet government.[52]

The other important decision resulting from the Second Congress of the Comintern, affecting India, was the agreement to hold a conference composed of nations of the Near, Middle and Far East. The conference was to meet at the city of Baku in Azerbaijan which had been recently won by the Bolsheviks from the whilom anti-Communist independent state of Azerbaijan. The conference was to assemble at the important petroleum port on the west shore of the Caspian on September 1, 1920.[53]

The Congress of the Peoples of the East represented no fewer than 37 countries. The Indian delegation was a small one, as contrasted to the delegation from other Eastern countries. There were only 14 members representing India as compared to 235 Turks, 192 Persians and 157 Armenians present at the Congress. The Indian delegates consisted mainly of deserters from the Anglo-Indian forces which were still occupying the Iranian province of Khorasan.[54] They were mainly Pathans of Muslim faith (today such people are Pakistanis) who were not imbued with Bolshevism but only with the desire to support the Caliphate.[55] They had apparently been influenced by the pan-Islamic propaganda of the Communists which held that the aims of Communism and of pan-Islam were one. The leader of the Indian delegation was a man named Abani Mukherji, who was, however, a professed Communist. Roy refused to attend the Congress on the grounds that it could not, in itself, bring about the Bolshevik revolution in Asia and that, called as it was on short notice, it could be nothing more that a "glorified mass meeting."[56]

The leaders and organizers of the Congress naturally were non-Asians, the most important of whom were Zinoviev, the President of the Executive Council of the Comintern and Karl Radek, the General Secretary of the Comintern.[57]

Due attention was paid to India in the Congress and one of the full reports presented to it was that of Abani Mukherji. The latter in a pessimistic report indicated that the situation in India from the revolutionary and Communist point of view was almost the least promising of all the nations of the East. Although there had been a nationalist movement in Hindustan since the 'eighties of the past century, it had been confined to the middle classes and students and had found little approval amongst the Indian masses. Mukherji asserted that the land question had played a great role in India and had been characterized by the existence of huge landed estates, land hunger among the masses of the people and an unduly high export of foodstuffs from India in proportion to the population of that country. Consequently, famines were all too frequent in India. Delegate Mukherji also observed that the industrial proletariat in India was very small numerically and was poorly organized. He admitted that, as of 1920, there was no Communist party in India, although there existed a movement for the creation of one. However, remarked Mukherji, this potential Communist movement had made every effort to be isolated from the movement for national independence, looking upon the nationalist movement as one of bourgeois character. In this respect the Communist "leaders" of India had maintained a marked difference from and even opposition to the general policies of the Communist International in the East. Hence this attitude had weakened the position of the Comintern towards India.[58] Here Mukherji was evidently criticizing Roy. For at this time Mukherji was jealous of the position of Roy and desired to supplant him as leader of Indian Communism. Mukherji then held that the progress of Communism in India would be affected, although not directly, by events taking place in China. This progress would, however, be even more affected by the establishment of a center of propaganda in Afghanistan. In addition to the effect of Soviet propaganda from, and Russian diplomatic relations with, the Afghan state, Mukherji remarked darkly that a third weapon could be added to those just mentioned—the establishment there of armed forces which could be controlled and commanded directly from Moscow.[59]

The principal speeches of the Congress were made by Zinoviev and Radek. Zinoviev held that the example of Russia should be followed by revolutions throughout the entire East,[60] while Radek advocated a line of internal Communization in eastern countries coupled with a violent Anglophobia. The latter uttered the phrase that "there can be no permanent peace between the countries of labor and the countries of exploitation," that is between Communist and non-Communist countries, non-European as well as European. Indeed, Radek boldly deemed it the task of Communists to "create a new culture under the banner of Communism." Besides assuring the workers and peasants of India and other Eastern lands of Russian support, even to the extent of furnishing them with arms, Radek evoked the tradition of the Huns of Attila, and the Tartars of Genghis Khan and Tamerlane in calling for an end to the patient pacifism which had seemingly characterized the peoples of the East. The latter must strike as "a new wave of barbarism."[61] As a matter of fact, this emphasis on the need for Communism in the East alienated not a few non-Communist delegates who were hostile to European, and especially British imperialism, but were social and religious conservatives. However, the emphasis on the necessity for Bolshevizing the East was in line with the hopes and designs of M. N. Roy.

The Bengali Bolshevik now concocted a plan to bring a Russian army into Afghanistan, which with the connivance of Emir Amanullah—a connivance which Roy expected—would be expanded in size, trained and thoroughly equipped. Using the support of tribes of the northwestern Indian frontier who would be inflamed by Communist propaganda and who would, in addition, supply "mercenary support" to the Communist army, this "army of liberation" would then march into India. The force would occupy some Indian territory and set up a Communist government on Indian soil as soon as possible. It should immediately issue manifestoes calling upon the people of India to launch a great revolution and would outline a program of social reform which would be in conformity with the destruction of British rule in the sub-continent. At the same time "the entire adult population of the liberated territory would be armed," thereby augmenting the size of the Red forces. The social program which would be supposedly attractive to the Indian masses, a program, which presumably would involve the abolition of landlordism and the destruction of great capitalists as well as the elimination of British rule—would permit the Communist forces to advance well into India. As it advanced it was believed that "the masses would enthusiastically support the new regime." Roy was confident that Great Britain, weakened by the First World War, would be unable to meet the combined onslaught of the invasion of the Communist army and a popular uprising. Roy also felt that the Indian bourgeoisie who would conceivably support the British would be brushed aside by the uprising of the masses.[62] Roy indicated that the cooperation and support of Afghanistan was absolutely indispensable for this scheme to succeed, but since the Emir would conceivably like to avenge himself on the British who had so thoroughly trounced his army in 1919, there was reason to believe that he would permit the use of his country as the base for the Red invasion, if he did not actually join in the proposed invasion of India.

The scheme was a bold one and it was necessary to convince the leaders of Soviet Russia that it was a wise one and one potentially productive of success. Certain factors favored Roy. He was a member of the new, important Turkestan Bureau of the Communist International and in that capacity had been foremost in urging the successful occupation of the Khanate of Bukhara, which actually fell to the Bolsheviks by the middle of September, 1920. The success of the campaign against the Khanate must have added to Roy's prestige. This prestige was likewise enhanced when the Indian revolutionary revealed to Lenin and Chicherin the conversation he had had with the Turkish emigré, Enver Pasha, in which the latter had revealed his plans for the establishment of a great Central Asian empire at the Soviets' expense. This made the shock of Enver's eventual desertion of the Bolshevik cause not as disastrous to the Soviets as it might otherwise have been.[63] Besides, it was believed that in addition to being an allegedly easy target for Communist expansion, India was a very wealthy target. And further, it was at about that time that Lenin thought up his slogan that the road to London and Paris lay through Peking and Calcutta.[64]

Roy's very audacious plan was approved in the early autumn of 1920 by the Politburo of the Russian Communist Party and the Council of the People's Commissars. Although he approved of the scheme, Lenin observed that the connivance of Emir Amanullah of Afghanistan on whom the success of the whole project depended, was a doubtful one. Nonetheless, Lenin approved the whole scheme because he felt it was in the interest of the world revolution.[65]

Roy himself was placed at the head of the project, in which he was to be assisted by a new Russian envoy to Afghanistan, Fedor Raskolnikov, who would succeed Suritz at the Kabul post. Raskolnikov, the natural son of a court noble whose name he bore, had been a junior officer who had supported the "October" Communist revolution. During the Russian Civil War he had risen to the post of Commander of the Volga flotilla where he served the Red cause well. Raskolnikov was charged to win over Emir Amanullah to permit the Soviet forces to enter into and organize their strength in Afghanistan and, if possible, to induce him to renew his war with the British in conjunction with the Red army. At the same time, even though his treachery to them was now known, the Soviets permitted Enver Pasha to leave for Turkestan and Afghanistan. It was felt that his prestige, as one of the leaders of Turkey during the First World War, in the Muslim world might even facilitate the success of the projected invasion of India.[66]

Details for the project were worked out by the Revolutionary Military Council and shortly after the celebration of the Third Anniversary of the "October" Revolution, that is after November 7, 1920 (since Russia had adopted the Gregorian calendar in 1918) the projected expedition which was ultimately aimed against India got under way. It consisted of two trains, each of which was composed of 27 cars of the weight of 20 tons. One of the trains carried arms exclusively—light artillery, machine-guns, rifles, pistols, grenades and "adequate" military supplies and stores as well as field equipment which consisted of a number of wireless transmitters and receivers. The other train consisted of freight cars loaded with dismantled airplanes and the complete outfit of an air force battalion, the personnel of the latter, as well as the staff of a projected military training school or academy in Russian Turkestan. One "saloon car" was attached to this train for the personal use of Roy, the commander of this expedition. In addition, two of the freight cars of this train were loaded with gold bullion, pound and rupee notes. Also accompanying the expedition were two companies of crack Red Army soldiers who were commanded by an American Communist, a physical giant identified only as "Wobbly John." The trains were well guarded, as precautions against Kirghiz tribesmen and possible White guerrillas. These trains proceeding from Moscow by way of Orenburg (now Chkalov) arrived at Tashkent in one week—according to schedule and without incident. The latter city in Turkestan was designated as the rear base for the projected incursion into India.[67]

Before the expedition could proceed from Tashkent to India, four conditions had to be met. First—a number of Indians would have to be trained as zealous Communists and good soldiers, so that the invasion would look like a true "liberation" of India, and not a conquest by Russia. Secondly, all of the territories of the Czar's former domains in Central Asia must be placed under complete and absolute Soviet rule. Thirdly, Chinese Turkestan and Iran, flanking India to the north and west must be put under as much Soviet influence as possible—with their governing authorities amicably disposed to the proposed invasion and fourthly, Afghanistan must be won over as an ally in the invasion of India, to the extent at least of having the Soviet army, which would be a motley affair, composed of Russians, Central Asians and Indians, be aided by Afghan tribesmen if not by the regular Afghan army itself.

Roy immediately plunged into the work for the fulfillment of the first condition—the propagandizing and military training of Indians to serve as the nucleus of the projected Red invasion and subsequent government of the sub-continent. The propaganda school was not new. As early as January 15, 1920, when Roy was just arriving in Moscow, the British War Office had indicated that it was aware that the Communists had opened a school for propaganda in Tashkent in which Oriental languages were taught and agents were being trained to be sent into India as well as other countries.[68] However, the coming of Roy signified the intensification of the propaganda training.

Three groups of Indians were available for this training, Indian traders in Central Asia, deserters from the Indian armies stationed in the Khorasan area of Northeastern Iran, and the "Mujahirs," or Indian Muslim advocates of the Caliphate who sought to go to the assistance of the Caliph and Turkey against the forces of the British and the Greeks. They had heard that Russia was friendly to their movement, so that they had proceeded across Afghanistan into Turkestan,[69] where they were well received by the Russian authorities.[70]

The traders who were few in number made poor material for Communism, but the soldiers, who were more numerous, possibly a few hundred strong, and the Mujahirs whose numbers were calculated to be as high as 5,000 contained a considerable number of men who seemed to possess a potential aptitude for acquiring Communist principles. The men found in this category were lodged at the so-called "India House" where they were indoctrinated in Anglophobia and elementary Marxism. It was among the students of "India House" in Tashkent that the Communist Party of India was first formed early in 1921. It was planned to send the graduates of the propaganda school into India as agents to form the Communist party there. These students were held subsequently by one of them to have been "well treated at Tashkent and given a fair amount of freedom."[71]

Considerable emphasis was also placed upon the military training of the Indians, for they would form the nucleus of the Indian portion of the army of the "liberation" of India. Those Indians who were deserters from the Anglo-Indian Army were immediately put into Soviet service, becoming members of a kind of international brigade, since they were joined together with Russian Communists, some Persian revolutionaries and probably some former prisoners of the Austrian-Hungarian Army who had been converted to Communism. The Indians served the Soviet cause well, guarding the vital railroad from Krasnovodsk to Tashkent and they even engaged the British with some success along the Persian-Soviet frontier, so that it is claimed that the British troops were forced to abandon their advanced positions and had to retire to their base in Meshed. The Indian troops appear to have done well with machine-guns, weapons which at that time they were not allowed to employ in the Anglo-Indian Army. In fact, they so pleased their Russian commanders, that some of the Indians, who were Pathans from the North-West Frontier Province (now they would be classed as Pakistanis) were commissioned as officers of the Red Army, posts which they could not have held in the Anglo-Indian Army.[72]

To facilitate the military training of the Mujahirs as contrasted with the above-mentioned deserters from the Anglo-Indian army, a military school at Tashkent was founded with a flourish of inflammatory anti-British speeches by local Red dignitaries. The military academy was staffed by officers of the Soviet Army in Turkestan. One of them was none other than "Wobbly John," the erstwhile American radical.[73] The military school appeared to be effectively turning out cadres for the Indian portion of the international Communist army for the liberation of India, as the year, 1921, progressed.[74]

Two of the Mujahir cadets at the academy were to play an important role in the history of Communism in the Indian sub-continent. One of them, named Fazl-I-Ilani Qurban subsequently became one of the leaders of the Communist Party of Pakistan, while another, Shaukat Usmani, became one of the founders of the Communist Party of India. It may be noted that the latter mentioned that he had met Roy and described the latter as "sincere, frank and full of learning but unpractical."[75]

A boastful description of the activity of the Soviets among the Indians in Central Asia at this time was rendered by Commissar Eliawa of the Eastern Department of Propaganda at a Communist conference held in Bremen on December 26, 1920. He bragged that "John Bull knows this (activity) and already shows his teeth, powerless in the sight of the bridles we shall throw him in India."[76]

The second preparatory move of the Russians prior to a potential thrust into India was the complete conquest of Central Asia for Communism. This conquest had been effectuated by the defeat of anti-Communist Muslim armies in the Fergana area as well as the troops of the Khan of Bukhara in the closing months of 1920. Roy himself accompanied the expedition to Fergana which penetrated into the High Pamirs to within a few miles of India, separated by a thin strip of Afghan territory. From a high peak on the Pamirs the Bengali Bolshevik was able to survey his homeland, but a few miles away through his field-glasses and to dream that soon the forces of Communism would surge into Hindustan.[77]

The Communist authorities in Turkestan made no secret of

the significance of the conquest of the Pamir area to India. On October 10, 1920 during the course of the Pamir campaign, General Sokolnikov, the Chief Commissar of Turkestan and Roy's colleague on the Comintern's "Turk-Bureau" issued the following inflammatory communique which held in part:

> On this tableland, you, the signalers of the Revolution must hoist the Red Flag of the Army of Liberation. May the peoples of India who fight against their English oppressors soon know that friendly help is not far off.[78]

The third preparatory move of the Russians before the contemplated invasion of India involved the subversion and gaining of influence in the strategic areas of Chinese Turkestan, Iran and Afghanistan. Moves to attain this end in these regions were duly carried on. Indeed, as early as 1918 the Soviets attempted to secure influence in Chinese Turkestan.[79] Their prospects in this region were fairly promising in view of the extremely weak condition of China in the years following the First World War—years in which that ancient land was convulsed by internecine civil conflict. As a consequence of that conflict the local Chinese authorities in this large and strategic province of Sinkiang could expect little support from a central Chinese government. Indeed, the only resolute opposition the Soviets could expect in Chinese Turkestan appeared to emanate from the British consul-general at Kashgar, Colonel P. T. Etherton.

Bolshevik propects were even brighter in Persia than in Sinkiang. Here again it was only the British, the occupiers of much of the country from 1918 to the latter part of 1920 who were the principal barrier to Soviet expansion in the land of the Shahs. Indeed, a Soviet government had been formed in Ghilan Province in Northern Iran as early as 1918 under a Communist peasant leader, Kuchik Khan. Furthermore, an autonomous, although non-Communist government, had been established in 1919 in the province of Persian Azerbaijan, and, taking advantage of this circumstance, Soviet forces took possession of the city of Enzeli (now Pahlevi) in the vicinity of

Azerbaijan. In addition, the Soviets had officially inaugurated relations with the Iranian government in November, 1920 and were able to conclude a treaty with the latter government on February 26, 1921, the provisions of which opened Iran to Bolshevik penetration.[80] During this same month a new regime came into power in Persia headed by Riza Pahlevi and Seyyid Zia. The latter had been a resident of the Russian Caucasus area and the Kremlin apparently expected that he would lend support to the Bolshevik ukase, and the former was known to be an anti-British Persian nationalist. In addition, as an early manifestation of Communist fifth column tactics, the Persian Communists had formed a "National Bloc" which obtained fifteen seats in the Iranian Parliament and the Persian minions of Moscow had also secured a measure of control over the Persian labor movement, by the summer of 1920.[81]

By the late spring of 1921 the Soviets felt that in view of Communist control of much of Northern Persia and the Communist fifth column in the remainder of the country, they could seize control of all Persia. So in June of that year, Soviet troops were taking part with those of Kuchik Khan on a march to Tehran.[82] Were this operation to effectuate in Soviet control of Iran, India's strategic western borderland, the projected move by Roy's army against India would be vastly facilitated.

But the focal point of the possibility of an invasion of India by the Communists remained, above all, in Afghanistan. As the year 1921 got under way, prospects for the Soviets appeared bright, in that Ambassador Raskolnikov and his beautiful wife made a not inconsiderable impression on Emir Amanullah and his Queen.[83] In the meantime, the Afghan ambassador at Moscow, General Mohammed Wali Khan, as early as the winter of 1920, had been conducting preliminary arrangements for a treaty between Afghanistan and Soviet Russia.

This treaty was also the subject of negotiations between the Emir and Raskolnikov and, on February 28, 1921, it was signed in Moscow. It was extremely favorable to Russia. Making for a virtual alliance between the two countries, it pledged each of the two high contracting parties to refrain from entering into a political or military agreement with a third power to the detriment of the other signatory. This would seem to have ruled out a treaty by Afghanistan favorable to Britain and, correspondingly, unsatisfactory to Russia. At the same time Soviet Russia was permitted to establish consulates in Herat, Jalalabad, Maimana, Mazar-i-Sharif, Kandahar and Ghazni. These consulates, of course, would be nothing more nor less than propaganda centers aimed against British India. Furthermore, Afghanistan acknowledged the "independence of Khiva and Bukhara" regardless of the form of government obtaining in those erstwhile semi-autonomous Khanates of the Czarist era. Since those states were now under Communist rule, and were really unincorporated parts of Russia, this was tantamount to recognition of Soviet rule in these states. Other clauses were still more favorable to the Bolsheviks. They were permitted to establish a powerful radio station at Kabul, they might build a telegraph line between Kushk on the Russo-Afghan border to both Kabul and Kandahar, and Russian engineers were permitted to engage in road building which would, presumably, better connect Turkestan and Afghanistan and thus facilitate the advance of Roy's army. Russia was also given the right to send instructors to build an Afghan air force, and Soviet planes were to be bestowed as a free gift to the Afghans as the first step to inaugurate this force.[84]

In the summer of 1921 the Russo-Afghan treaty was formally ratified and the Soviets planned to send agents to the proposed consulates near the Indian border.[85] Furthermore, at that time a Soviet squadron made a spectacular flight across the Hindu Kush range from Turkestan to Kabul to implement the training of the Afghan Air Force, which was destined in the Russians' eyes to be employed against the Royal Air Force. This action was followed by the establishment of a regular air service between Tashkent and Kabul.[86] Also of a spectacular character was the disclosure that the Soviet government had been trying to persuade a notorious Indian anarchist, known as Dr. Hafiz, who had been studying processes of bomb manufacture in Vienna, to proceed to Afghanistan "to supervise" a bomb "depot" on the frontier of India and to facilitate the export of explosives into Hindustan. At the same time, it was alleged that Dr. Hafiz had been ordered by the Soviet government to undertake the manufacture of smokeless powder in Kabul for the bombs and it was further alleged that he had been granted a sum of money by the Soviet government to carry out this dark purpose.[87]

Thus in the summer of 1921, the time seemed to be ripe for a possible Soviet invasion of India through Afghanistan, since the connivance of the latter country in this scheme appeared likely. But no Communist force moved on India. Why then did this Soviet plan not come to pass?

In the first place, the Bolsheviks, in spite of their efforts, were not so successful in bringing about the formation of a nucleus of Indian revolutionaries in Central Asia as they had desired. Many of the Indian merchants in Central Asia were only interested in returning to India since Bolshevism threatened their livelihood, and as a matter of fact, many of them succeeded in effectuating this desire.[88] Moreover, many of the Mujahirs likewise proved to be useless from the Communist point of view, and consequently made poor scholars at the revolutionary school at Tashkent. After all, they could well perceive that atheistic Communism was incompatible with the Muslim faith for which they had been sacrificing so much in pursuance of their desire to save the spiritual head of Islam, the Caliph.[89]

Moreover, there was dissension among the Indian Communists. Acharya and Abdur Rab had arrived in Tashkent in the spring of 1921 and they appear to have resented Roy's authority in Central Asia. They and a minority of Mujahirs who had been converted to Communism in the Tashkent propaganda school advocated the immediate formation of the Communist Party of India. On the other hand, Roy himself thought the move a premature one and opposed it. However, the view of Acharya prevailed, undoubtedly because it had the support of the Russian authorities in Central Asia.[90] Hence Acharya and his follower, the old trader, Abdur Rab, rather than Roy, may be deemed the founders of the Communist Party of India. Mohammed Sadiq, a fairly well-educated young Muslim who had come to Tashkent from Kabul with Acharya and Abdur Rab, was named the first Secretary-General of the Communist Party of India.

In addition to his rivalry with Acharya, Roy likewise had difficulty with the Indian delegate at Baku, Abani Mukherji. The latter appeared early in 1921 in Tashkent where in Roy's view, he "had no business."[91] Like Acharya, Mukherji was an advocate of immediately developing and building up the Communist Party of India as contrasted with Roy's more cautious view that this step should be delayed.

A second reason for the abandonment of the scheme to invade India, was the failure of Soviet Russia on the borderlands of India, in Chinese Turkestan and Persia, and above all, in Afghanistan.

Between 1918 and 1921 the Soviets sent three missions to Chinese Turkestan, all of which completely failed to exert any influence whatsoever upon that territory. Their failure was due to the anti-Communist policy of the local Chinese authorities as well as that of the redoubtable British consul-general, Colonel Etherton.[92] It may be noted that the third of these Soviet missions carried out in the latter part of 1920, was headed by no less a personage than "President" Mahendra Pratep of the "Provisional Government of the People of India." The latter was accompanied by an Afghan sirdar (nobleman) and an escort of forty-six men, but this notwithstanding, his mission was a fiasco. Indeed, Mahendra Pratep was fortunate to escape from the British consul who had planned to seize him and have him sent to India where he was a very much wanted fugitive.[93] The Bolsheviks were furious at their failures in Chinese Turkestan, but they decided it would be the wiser policy not to arouse the Chinese and British governments by sending in armed forces to conquer Sinkiang.

The Soviets also failed in Iran. The Soviet-supported force of Kuchik Khan was not successful in its attempted march on Tehran in June, 1921, and the Soviets, in the circumstances, felt it best to honor their treaty of the previous February which had provided that Russian troops be withdrawn from Iran by the end of May, 1921. Hence Soviet forces were withdrawn from Northern Persia in September, 1921. As a result, Riza

Pahlevi, who had overthrown Seyyed Zia, his rival for power in Persia, and had assumed control of the Iranian government in May, 1921, was able to destroy the little Soviet state of Kuchik Khan in Ghilan (the autonomous state in the Azerbaijan area had already been dissolved by the Central Persian government in September, 1920) and to execute that Communist leader in the fall of 1921.[94] Having put down Bolshevism in Ghilan, Riza Pahlevi suppressed the Red-controlled "National Bloc" and the trade union confederation alike.[95] Iran, then, was no avenue for a successful Soviet invasion of India.

But the basic cause for the abandonment of the ambitious Soviet plan regarding India involved Afghanistan, the Emir of which, refused to cooperate with the Bolshevik scheme. Even in 1920 there were difficulties between Afghanistan and Soviet Russia. There was a dispute concerning the disposition of the strategic Penjdeh regime north of Herat[96] and conversations between members of an Afghan mission to India and a British diplomat, Sir Henry Dobbs, in the late spring and summer of 1920, although not resulting in any precise agreement, nonetheless indicated that the Emir was willing to deal with his erstwhile foes, a move hardly calculated to evoke joy in the Kremlin.[97]

In addition, at a "diplomatic dinner" given by M. N. Roy late in 1920 to which the Afghan envoy to the Soviet Central Asian capital at Tashkent, had been invited, the latter indicated that all Russian arms to be sent to Afghanistan for use in the eventual "liberation" of India could be transported only by the Afghan government, although he half-promised that they would be delivered to anti-British Indians on the Indian Northwest frontier. At the same time, the envoy indicated that the Afghans would agree to permit Roy and a number of Indian revolutionaries to enter Afghanistan, but they must be disarmed on their entry into that land and if armed at all, only later on the frontier of India. It was fairly apparent that the Soviets could not utilize Afghanistan for an invasion of India as it was clear that Afghanistan had no desire for any Soviet force to enter its territory and employ it as a base of operations for an invasion of India, and much less did the Afghans desire to participate in the operation itself.[98]

Prospects appeared no brighter for the Communists in Afghanistan early in 1921 when Bravin, the first Soviet envoy to Afghanistan, who had at one time even crossed into the North-West Frontier Province of India for a short distance, was assassinated at Ghazni. He had been one of the key Bolshevik agents in Afghanistan working under the aegis of Ambassador Raskolnikov.[99]

Although Soviet reverses in Afghanistan were seemingly more than offset by the Soviet-Afghan treaty of February 28, 1921, which has already been noted, the fact was that the very success of the Soviets in this matter actually led to the downfall of their influence in Afghanistan, for the British were now roused to take counter-measures against this alliance, so threatening to their position in India.

Indeed, this Russo-Afghan treaty resulted in a stern British note to the Russians on March 17, 1921, which indicated that Great Britain was quite aware of Soviet intrigues in Afghanistan up to the date of the signing of the Russo-Afghan treaty, which intrigues were specifically detailed. The note referred to the activity of the Russian embassy in Kabul, especially in respect to the Soviets' shipping arms and ammunition to the turbulent tribesmen on the Indian Northwestern frontier.[100] The note concluded with the blunt warning that "Soviet activities must cease."[101]

Not wishing to antagonize the thoroughly aroused British by seeming to support Soviet designs on India's Northwestern frontiers and recognizing in this context the relative impotence of Soviet Russia as contrasted to the might of the British Empire, Emir Amanullah assumed a clearly hostile attitude towards the Soviets in the late summer of 1921 and after. Although the Soviet-Afghan treaty was actually confirmed in that summer, it turned out to be but a paper confirmation, because Afghanistan refused to allow the Soviets to establish consulates at Kandahar, Ghazni and Jalalabad as was provided by the treaty of February 28, 1921, and now the Afghans decided to ban free transit of Bolshevik agents across Afghan soil.[102] Furthermore, in the autumn of 1921, the Afghan government ordered the "Indian Provisional Government" and its leaders, "President" Mahendra Pratep, "Prime Minister" Maulana Obeidullah, and "Foreign Minister" Baraktullah, to leave Afghan soil forthwith. The crestfallen Indians were compelled to return to Soviet soil. All these anti-British yet non-Communist agents soon thereafter left Soviet service. However, it may be noted that Mahendra Pratep subsequently returned to Afghanistan, but as a free anti-British agent and not as a Soviet agitator.[103]

The drift of the Afghan government towards a pro-British and anti-Soviet stand, was further accentuated by a very strong note sent by Great Britain to the Soviet government on September 26, 1921 (which Britain recognized de facto but not de jure) which devoted a considerable amount of attention to Russian intrigues in Afghanistan previous to the eviction of the Soviet agents in the "Provisional Government of the People of India." This note, which once again made it clear that Britain was fully aware of Soviet intrigues in Afghanistan directed against her Indian Empire and that she would not tolerate them,[104] had the dual effects of decelerating Soviet intrigue in Afghanistan—for the Communists now had come to recognize they could not risk war with the British Empire—and of inducing Amanullah to assume a pro-British policy, for he now saw who was the master of the situation.

The denouement of the drift of Afghanistan towards the British was that a delegation of the Anglo-Indian government made progress in negotiations with the Afghans in the autumn in 1921 in conversations with the government of Emir Amanullah in Kabul, which resulted in the signing of an Anglo-Afghan treaty of November 22, 1921. By the terms of this treaty Britain and Afghanistan reciprocally recognized each other's territories and confirmed the existing Indo-Afghan boundary (that is the one established by the Durand line of 1893) subject to slight modification in the area around the Khyber Pass, and the two nations agreed mutually to establish diplomatic relations. At the same time, provisions were made for the facilitation of the exchange of goods between the two countries.[105] News of this treaty evoked no joy in Moscow,[106] for the Soviets now knew that not only could the land of Emir Amanullah not be used as the base of operations for an invasion of India, but that to a measurable extent it had reverted to a British sphere of influence.

The diplomacy of the British in Afghanistan was not the only means by which they endeavored to thwart the Soviet design on India at this time. Thus in the spring of 1921 the British sent an agent known as "Maulana X," a Pathan, to Tashkent to disrupt the military and propaganda schools there. The spy was detected by the Turkestan agents of the Cheka. The affair is interesting in that Vyacheslav Molotov, then the Secretary of the Turkestan Commission and the liaison man between this body and the Turkestan Bureau of the Communist International, of which Roy was a most important member, interceded vainly for the Indian who was executed. Molotov felt it was a horrible thing to kill an "Indian comrade," even thought he might well be a possible spy, for such a deed would alienate the Russians in the eyes of all Indians.[107]

Another cause for the decision of the Communists not to invade India lay in the discord which resulted from the clashes between the Bolsheviks and the Central Asian Muslim peoples. The action of the Communists in destroying the Muslim Khanates of Khiva and Bukhara, and of ruthlessly suppressing other Muslim elements in Central Asia from 1918 to 1920,[108] and later (in 1922) their effective suppression of the Basmachi Rebellion of the fabulous Turk, Enver Pasha, led Muslims throughout the Middle East and in Britain's Indian Empire, to recognize that Soviet Russia was no friend of Islam.[109] It may be noted that the Emir of Afghanistan gave a measure of moral support and perhaps even some material assistance to the man who hoped to re-create the Empire of Tamerlane, but, of course, such assistance was of no avail.[110] Furthermore, increasing Russo-Turkish discord, which followed the conclusion of the Russo-Turkish pact of March 16, 1921, the treaty notwithstanding, added fuel to the flames of Muslim animosity towards the Bolshevik regime.[111]

On the other hand while Russian prestige among the Muslims of India and the Middle East sank, that of Britain rose. The improvement of British relations with Afghanistan, an improvement which Communist sources attributed to bribery,[112] and a like improvement of English relations with the Turkey of Mustafa Kemal,[113] made a favorable impression among the followers of the Prophet.

Finally, we may observe that a cause for the failure by Russia to carry out the scheme for an invasion of India lay in conditions within Russia herself. During the summer of 1921 there was a marked increase in the domestic difficulties within Soviet Russia. European Russia was racked by famine and pestilence[114] and there was still sympathy in many quarters for the Whites, whose armies had been but recently defeated. These internal difficulties help to explain the conciliatory nature of the reply of the Soviet government to the strong British note of September 26, 1921, which among other matters, had so bitterly excoriated Russian intrigues against India. The Soviet note in reply, sent to London in the first week of October, 1921, falsely declared, that the Soviet government, since the conclusion of the Anglo-Soviet Trade Agreement of the previous March, had had no dealings whatever with Indian revolutionaries. More truthfully, however, it declared that there was no propaganda school in Tashkent, for, by October, 1921, such activities had been transferred to Moscow.[115] This note was reasonably satisfactory to the British government which continued to maintain its de facto relationship with the Soviet government.

This Soviet note coincides with the renunciation of the Soviet scheme to intervene directly in India. The new Soviet plan which will now be considered was not to attempt an armed intrusion into Britain's Indian Empire but rather to launch a Soviet fifth column in India through the instrumentality of a Communist Party within India.

CHAPTER TWO

Moscow Launches the Indian Communist Movement

During the summer of 1921 at the very time that the Soviet government was beginning to recognize that a Red invasion of India was no longer practicable, the Third Congress of the Communist International was held. Paradoxically, the number of Indians present was greater than at any previous Communist meeting. On hand at this conference in Moscow were not only M. N. Roy and Abani Mukherji, but also the leading members of the German-sponsored "Indian Provisional Government." Since the termination of the First World War these Indians who had been divested of their "rank," had been cooling their heels in the German capital hoping to find a patron who would assist them in their aspirations of liberating India from the British yoke. At first they refused to admit Soviet Russia as such a patron. They were shocked by Roy who had accepted the godless creed of Bolshevism, and unlike Mahendra Pratep and Baraktullah, they felt they could not even serve the Communist movement, while not actually becoming Communists themselves.

But by the spring of 1921 their views had changed. No patron other than Soviet Russia was in sight, and so these Indians felt they should undertake a mission to Moscow by which they hoped they would receive full Soviet backing for their designs against the British Raj. They received encouragement for this from M. Kopp, the Soviet envoy to Germany, and so, in May,

1921, there was a delegation of Indians from Berlin in Moscow.[1] The delegation included no fewer than fourteen persons encompassing the leadership of the old "Berlin Committee": Virendranath Chattopadhyaya, Bhupendranath Dutta, Virendranath Das Gupta, Ghulam Khan Luhani and Nalini Gupta.[2] But the "driving force" of the delegation was an American radical, Miss Agnes Smedley, who like Evelyn Roy had fallen in with the members of the Indian revolutionary center in San Francisco. Miss Smedley had been inclined to anarchism in the United States, and had gone to Berlin after the First World War to join the Indian revolutionaries there for whom she evinced a great amount of sympathy.[3] In addition, it may be mentioned that a Pathan from the Northwestern Frontier of India and a delegate from Afghanistan were also supposed to have been present at the Congress which met from June 22nd to July 12th, 1921.[4]

The Indians from Berlin immediately demanded interviews with Chairman of the People's Commissars Lenin, Foreign Commissar Chicherin, and Comintern Secretary Radek, to demand of these Soviet leaders that Russia give them a position similar to that which they had enjoyed under the Kaiser, but without being committed to Communism as an ideology. The Soviet leaders were polite but non-committal to the Indian revolutionaries. This disinterestedness on the part of the rulers of Bolshevism filled the Indians with wrath and many of them left Soviet Russia forthwith.[5] However, the leaders of the old "Berlin Committee," Chattopadhyaya, Dutta, Luhani and Nalini Gupta stayed on in Moscow. In addition to trying to induce the Soviets to give them more support in their own plans for the eviction of the British in India, the Berlin Indians endeavored to have the Soviets remove M. N. Roy as the leader of the Indian revolutionaries in Russia. They despised Roy because he had espoused Communism as an ideology, and even more, they were jealous of the Bengali because he had succeeded in obtaining the favor of Lenin and held a high place in the Communist hierarchy.[6]

In view of the inharmonious relations between Roy and his

fellow Indians, the Communist International decided to set up a commission composed of August Thalheimer, the then leader of the German Communist Party, Tom Quelch of the British Communist Party and Borodin to hear the case of the Indian revolutionaries from Berlin (and also Roy) as well as to examine the situation in India from the Communist and revolutionary point of view. In the hearings before this commission, the Indian revolutionaries from Berlin through their spokesmen Chattopadhyaya and Luhani hurled an ultimatum to the effect that if the Communist Party of India were not dissolved, "they would leave Moscow."[7] When the Comintern refused to comply with this demand, most of the Berlin Indians remaining in Moscow carried out their threat, "fully convinced that Indian revolutionaries could not count on any help" from Soviet Russia.[8]

However, two Indian revolutionaries remained in Moscow and actually embraced Communism, Ghulam Khan Luhani and Nalini Gupta. The former became a worker in the Information Department of the Comintern and never became a Communist of significance, but the latter became a trusted assistant of Roy and played an important role in the early history of Communism in India.[9] Moreover, other Indian revolutionaries—members of the "Indian Provisional Government" which had been compelled to leave Kabul, notably a man named Zahiara and another named Mohammed Ali—and also Acharya and Abdur Rab from Tashkent—arrived in Moscow in the autumn of 1921. These personages formed the nucleus of the Indian Communist movement under the leadership of M. N. Roy.[10]

Meanwhile, in the thesis of the Third Congress of the Communist International, the view was taken that the bourgeoisie of "the Eastern Countries" was bound closely to foreign capital and had thus become a "very important weapon of capitalist domination." At the same time greater emphasis than heretofore was placed on the Communist Party, for it was held that "the great masses of the peasants of the Oriental countries, look upon the Communist vanguard as their real revolutionary leader." The thesis went on to hold that

> the revolutionary national movement in India and in other colonies is to-day an essential component part of the world revolution to the same extent as the uprising of the proletariat in the capitalist countries of the old and new world.[11]

This part of the Communist thesis is interesting in that it indicates partial acceptance, at least, by the leaders of the Soviet Union, of Roy's view that the national bourgeoise could not be utilized by the Communists, but rather that Communist parties, per se, must carry on their revolutionary task. It also reflects the breaking down of the unnatural flirtation between the Pan-Islamic movement and international Communism. The Communists were beginning to show their true colors.[12]

One decision which followed the wake of the Third World Congress, was that of the abolition of the Turkestan Bureau of the Communist International and the opening in its stead of an Eastern Section of the Comintern in its headquarters at Moscow which would take charge of the Communist revolutionary movement in the East and guide its course. Since the attempt to establish contact with revolutionary movements in India and other Eastern countries from the base in Central Asia had proved fruitless, it was also decided that in the future the Communist parties in the "imperialist countries" should be charged to carry on subversive work in the colonies controlled by their countries.[13] This meant that in the case of India, the British Communist party would collaborate with the Eastern Section of the Executive Committee of the Comintern in promoting the Communist Party of India, but would be, of course, subordinate to the latter. M. N. Roy has asserted that he was offered the post as chairman of the Eastern Section of the Communist International, so as to continue his work initially begun in Central Asia. However, he turned the plan down because, influenced by Nalini Gupta who was now a strong Communist, Roy felt that he should proceed to Western Europe and there establish a base to carry on propaganda and develop a Communist revolutionary movement in Hindustan.[14]

A second decision taken after the Third Congress of the Communist International was the disbandment of the Communist propaganda school and the military training school in Tashkent and their removal to Moscow. This would, the Soviet leaders believed, modify the hostile fear of Great Britain towards the new Russia. But in the place of the schools at Tashkent, it was proposed that a Moscow training center for propaganda should be set up, the University of the Toilers of the East, which would carry out the work of the earlier propaganda school in Turkestan but would be less liable to produce apprehension in, and stern notes from, London than the school in Tashkent.[15]

In connection with these decisions, Roy was ordered to return to Central Asia to "wind up the Turkestan Bureau of the Communist International" and to disband the Indian propaganda and military schools, and to have those Indian Mujahir students at the Tashkent military and political academies be brought to Moscow who were believed to be potentially loyal Communists. At the same time Roy was charged to assist in the closing down of the agency of the Soviet Commissariat of Foreign Affairs in Turkestan which had cooperated with the Soviet Bureau of the Communist International, since the former agency, like the latter, no longer served a useful purpose.[16]

Having carried out his commission in regard to the closing down of the Red schools, Roy returned to Moscow in the autumn of 1921, which city he temporarily made his headquarters, and there assisted in the foundation of the Communist University of the Toilers of the East. To this college of propaganda, 22 Mujahirs were brought by Roy's secretary-interpreter, a certain Russian Jew named Tivil or Levit.[17] Other Mujahirs entered the Soviet armed forces including the Red Air Force.[18] But the majority of the Indians who had attended the propaganda and military schools were conducted to the frontiers of Persia and Afghanistan where Soviet border guards put them across these borders.[19]

In the summer of 1921 when news of the non-cooperation movement in India which had grown out of Indian disappointment at Britain's failure to grant autonomy after the First World War, and which had been officially inaugurated at the Nagpur session of the Indian National Congress in December,

1920, trickled into Moscow, it was decided to carry on a program of intensive Communist propaganda within India. Believing that the Congress might sanction the outbreak of a new Indian Mutiny, Roy conceived of the idea of sending an appeal to the Congress when it should meet at Ahmadabad in December, 1921. Consequently the appeal, signed by Roy and Mukherji was drawn up in the name of the Communist Party of India.[20] The manifesto called on the National Congress to support the trade unions and peasant organizations so that the former body might then "lead the revolution, which is shaking India to the very foundation."[21]

In order to disseminate copies of the manifesto in India, to lay the foundation of a Communist party within India and to contact Mr. C. R. Das, believed to be the most radical of the then Congress leaders, Roy dispatched Nalini Gupta to India. Since Gupta was an acquaintance of Das, Gupta's mission appeared to be a promising, albeit dangerous, one.[22]

Gupta succeeded in arriving in Hindustan loaded down "with the large bundle of the appeal" and had copies of them "broadcast throughout the country" just prior to the meeting of the Ahmadabad Congress in December. The appearance of this Communist manifesto in India created a certain amount of sensation and it was actually published in a "number" of Indian newspapers. Unfortunately for Gupta, however, he could not contact Das who had been arrested shortly before the session at Ahmadabad. Nonetheless, the appeal did get into the hands of some of the more radical Congress delegates. Indeed, two of them had the document clandestinely reprinted under their own signatures and it was said that this Communist manifesto induced a prominent Congress delegate, Maulana Hasrat Mohani, to move a resolution for the complete independence of India which was the first time that this radical idea had ever been broached at a session of the National Congress. Although this radical resolution was rejected, the Congress did approve a program of mass disobedience which had the sanction of its revered leader, Mahatma Gandhi. Thus to the extent that non-cooperation became a mass movement through non-payment of taxes and other peaceful means, the Communist demand had been, in part, fulfilled.[23]

Roy and his followers had also reason to be pleased by a resolution voted in the second session of the All-India Trade Union Congress at this time which expressed a resolution of sympathy for Soviet Russia as well as by a speech by Mr. Chaman Lal, the secretary of the organization who stated that if the condition of the Indian working class were not to be improved, this would signal "the coming of Bolshevism to India," and that if labor were to receive no concessions, workers "would take matters into their own hands."[24] It may be noted here that taking cognizance of the incipient Indian labor movement, on October 27, 1921, the Red International of Labour Unions, the labor section of the Comintern, invited the A.I.T.U.C. to join it in the great world movement for international labor solidarity.[25]

In spite of the suspension of the Indian non-cooperation movement in 1922 owing to the firm British policies of repression, Roy persevered in his endeavor to introduce Communism into India. He put out a book in the spring of 1922 entitled "India in Transition" a few copies of the English language edition of which were smuggled into India. The book is held to have helped pave the way for the appearance of an Indian Communist party.[26]

During the closing months of 1921 and the opening months of 1922 M. N. Roy was among those who supervised the operations of the Communist University of the Toilers of the East. In a large four-story structure in the center of Moscow, some 600 students from all parts of Asia, including the erstwhile Indian Mujahirs, studied the principles of Marxism, and various foreign languages.[27]

The Indian section, numbering only 22 members, was small in comparison to the Chinese section which formed "the large majority of the students and the Korean which held second place." The Indians were told that in order to initiate the revolution in India as elsewhere in the East, the propagandizing activity of the Communists must be secretly conducted and they were also informed that since the "Indo-Afghan border did not offer a very safe or convenient method of approach to India," links from Russia to India should be maintained through the countries of Western Europe.[28]

Above all, the professors of the Communist University made it clear to their Indian pupils that all countries of the world must follow Russia's example of establishing a Communist state and that for the proper operation of Communism within Russia itself "a world revolution was indispensable."[29]

Having been duly instructed in Communist ideology, the quondam Mujahirs were sent to Chinese Turkestan by way of Tashkent. From Sinkiang they crossed the mountainous border into India where they were to act as missionaries of Bolshevism. However, British border authorities had got wind of the plot and succeeded in arresting no fewer than eight of the would-be agents at the Northwest Frontier outpost town of Chitral.[30] Other agents, however, did elude the British; notably Mohammed Sadiq and Shaukat Usmani. The captured Red agents were immediately subjected to trial in a case referred to as the "Moscow Conspiracy Case." The Indians received lenient treatment, at least one of them, Abdul Qadir Khan, being acquitted outright. The Anglo-Indian authorities apparently felt that the "Red agents" were, after all, merely "creatures of circumstance" whose conversion to Communism had been a purely fortuitous event.[31] This affair was significant in that it made the Anglo-Indian authorities alert to the danger of Moscow's agents penetrating into India.

In the spring of 1922 with the permission and support of his Russian masters, M. N. Roy decided to transfer his activities from Moscow to Berlin. He chose Berlin because he felt Germany "was the country of great revolutionary promise,"[32] its Communist party being second only to Russia's in strength and influence. At the same time, Roy felt he could win over the Indian revolutionaries in Berlin to the cause of Communism.

Having arrived in Berlin, Roy with the aid of the German Communists started the publication of an English-language periodical called the "Vanguard of Indian Independence" and proselytized the Indians of Berlin with Communist ideology.

This publication which boastfully proclaimed itself the organ of the Communist Party of India assailed British imperialism in the sub-continent in the political, economic and social spheres, condemned Gandhi and the former non-cooperationists as preachers of counter-revolution at a time when "mass revolt is at flow tide," and praised radical and insurrectionary peasant movements such as that of the Akali Sikhs in the Punjab and the Mophlah Muslims of the Malabar coast. Needless to say, paeans of praise for the Soviet Union prominently featured this publication's propaganda.[33]

This publication was supplemented by a manifesto to the All-India Congress Committee on July 15, 1922, in which Roy complained that "the tactics of militant non-cooperation . . . has not required courage and determination," and argued that

> the Congress should at once launch a programme advocating the fight for higher wages . . . an eight-hour day, better housing, recognition of Unions, right of strike, equal pay for equal work, abolition of landlordism, reduction of rents and taxes . . . abolition of usury. These demands should be forced by mass action, strikes, demonstrations, peasant revolts.[34]

Roy was remarkably successful in his proselytization of the Indians in Berlin in that he won over the two former leaders of the former Berlin "Provisional Government of India," Virendranath Chattopadhyaya and Dr. Ferozdin Mansoor. The latter had not attended the Third Congress of the Comintern and as we have noted, the former had left Moscow in disgust. Both men, apparently convinced that only through Communism could India be freed, repaired to Moscow where Mansoor attended the Communist University of the Toilers of the East and Chattopadhyaya became a worker for the Comintern.[35] They joined the little Indian colony of Mukherji, Acharya and Abdur Rab whose numbers had been augmented by a number of members of the Punjabi Ghadr party, a terrorist organization who having made good their escape from British custody in India, had successfully fled to Russia.[36] This colony was not as significant as the Berlin headquarters of Roy in furthering Communism in the Peninsula.

In the year 1922, Roy sent his chief assistant, Gupta, to India "to establish centres" for the reception of Communist propaganda and to arrange for its underground circulation.[37]

Gupta found a fertile field in which to work. Many Indians, particularly the young intellectuals, were discouraged and disgruntled by the collapse of the non-cooperation movement and were reading extensively about the Communist experiment in Russia with interest.[38] Some of them became converts to Communism.

Communist propaganda likewise found a certain response among the former adherents of the Ghadr Party of the Punjab, the terroristic revolutionaries of Bengal whose ideology had been tinged with anarchism, the left-wing leaders of the nascent labor movement in Bombay and Calcutta, and even among the more radical followers of the late Indian leader, Tilak, in the Maharashtra area of Central India.[39]

Communist propaganda resulted in the establishment of no fewer than five Communist centers in India by the fall of 1922 in the following places: Calcutta under the leadership of Muzaffar Ahmad, Bombay under Shripat A. Dange, Cawnpore in Uttar Pradesh (then the United Provinces) under Shaukat Usmani, Madras under Singaravelu-Chettiar and Lahore (the Punjab) under Mohammed Sadiq.[40] The first two mentioned individuals have remained important leaders of the Communist Party of India to the present day.

An event of significance to the cause of Communism in India was the holding of the Fourth Congress of the Comintern in Moscow from November 7th to December 3rd, 1922. Of course, M. N. Roy, who had achieved the "honor" during that year of being named a member of the Presidium of the Comintern was present at the Congress. Also attending the conference were two Indian delegates who represented the Ghadr Party of California which was being revived, Rattan Singh and Santokh Singh.[41]

Addressing the Congress, Roy advocated that Communist parties in various Eastern countries should take their place "in the organization of a United Front against Imperialism" in which the Communists, of course, would become the leaders of "a united anti-Imperialist Front." This "front" would then liberate the masses from the leadership of "the timid and hesitating bourgeoisie."[42]

India was alluded to in the speeches of various delegates to the Congress of the Third International. Thus the delegate of Iran, Nik Bin, argued that

> Communists had not done much in connection with the great trade union movement in India and the large number of strikes, which convulsed the country.[43]

Furthermore, the weakness of India's Communists was brought forth in the report of the Credentials Committee of the Congress which disclosed that only four delegates from India had been invited to the Fourth Congress and that only "one" (Roy) had been admitted to the Congress with the right to vote.[44] This signified that other potential delegates such as Mukherji and Acharya were so jealous of Roy that they would not collaborate with him, which made for all the greater weakness among India's Communists. On the other hand, however, Zinoviev, the then head of the Comintern, hailed the formation of a Communist party within India and especially noted the entrance of Communists into Indian trade unions and newspapers.[45]

Just prior to his leaving for the Fourth Comintern Congress, Roy on November 7th, 1922, dispatched to India a pamphlet entitled "What Do We Want" along with a leaflet captioned "A Programme for the Indian National Congress." In the leaflet, which constituted a greeting to the Congress, Roy stressed the need for the elimination of British rule in India by means of "a sanguinary revolutionary struggle." This declaration was followed by demands for the election of a National Assembly by universal suffrage and the establishment of a "federated Republic" of India. As to economic measures, Roy's program called for the "abolition of landlordism" but it otherwise presented only a mild platform of social reform—specifically urging such reforms as "an eight-hour day," "profit-sharing in all big industries," a minimum wage, old age and sickness benefit, and the legalization of trade unions and the right to strike.[46] Why was this program so mild? In the first place it was in line with the Leninist thesis that Communists should collaborate with the national bourgeoisie as against the imperialists, and secondly, Roy and his Soviet masters hoped that by this moderation the petty and middle bourgeoisie of India as represented in the National Congress would become friendly to the Indian Communists.

This program, incidentally, was given a considerable measure of publicity by Reuter's News Agency and the British press which resulted in the Communist program being given not a little amount of corresponding publicity in India. Commenting on the program, the conservative and pro-government "Times Of India" (Bombay) of December 22, 1922, editorially growled that Reuter's agency had given Roy's program

> a publicity . . . seldom accorded even to a Prime Ministers' most serious utterance. Why should it have been thought worth-while to cable three columns of Bolshevist delirium to this country?[47]

On the other hand, the pro-Nationalist Calcutta "Amrita Bazar Patrika's" issue of December 27, 1922, expressed a favorable criticism for Roy's plan.[48]

Roy was pleased to hear that at the Gaya session of the Congress, that recent convert to Communism, Singaravelu-Chettiar had boldly arisen and spoken out as a representative of world Communism which through him was conveying greetings to the workers of India. He implored the Congress to pledge itself to the cause of the toilers and held that the Communists would support the Congress were the latter to support the workers' cause. Singaravelu-Chettiar concluded with an admonition to the Indian bourgeoisie that Indian workers had awakened and would fight for their rights.[49]

In addition to his pronouncements, Roy stepped up his contacts with Communist comrades in India by means of an extensive correspondence with the leaders of the comrades in India. However, the Criminal Investigation Division (C.I.D.)

of the Anglo-Indian government, recognizing full well the Soviet designs on India, was successful in intercepting much of this correspondence. The first of these letters was written on November 2, 1922 by Roy to Shripat A. Dange, the leader of the Communist group in Bombay. In this letter, Roy informed the latter that he was in charge of the "Eastern Section" of the Comintern and that the question of Communism in the East was to be one of the principal problems to be discussed in the forthcoming Comintern Congress. Roy informed Dange that "the organization of a mass party" in India had been discussed by the leaders of the Third International, that it was considered an indispensable move and that since the previous May (when Roy had arrived in Berlin) the groundwork for such a party was being prepared "through our paper," (the "Vanguard of Indian Independence," later the "Advance Guard,") and through other media of propaganda. This mass party would, held Roy, embrace "all the truly revolutionary elements" in India. It would be based upon the workers and peasants of India. The control of this party would be in the hands of the Communists. It would be a legal organization, whereas its Communist leadership would operate underground as such and rule this "front party." This "front party," explained Roy to Dange, would liberate the masses of India from the control of the "conciliatory leadership in the National Congress."[50]

Having returned to Berlin following the conclusion of the Fourth Comintern Congress, Roy intensified his efforts of building up the Communist movement in India. On December 12, 1922 he wrote letters to Dange and to Singaravelu-Chettiar, the Communist leader of Madras, in which he urged that an all-India leftist conference to be dominated and controlled by the Communists should be convened, not later than the end of January, 1923. Moreover, Roy held it was indispensable that some one from the All-India Trade Union Congress should be present at this conference.[51] But all this Communist-sponsored activity should be seemingly legal so as not to attract the suspicion of British authorities. Thus in a letter written by Roy to a certain Sharma, an Indian Communist who carried on his activities from Pondicherry in French India, the former summarily rejected the latter's request for pistols. Roy insisted that the Communist movement in India should eschew "individual terrorism," since it was, rather, a mass movement.[52]

As the year 1923 opened, Roy intensified his efforts at establishing a puissant Communist movement within India from his headquarters in Berlin. At that time he put out a so-called "open letter" to the people of India which pointed out that the Indian people faced two alternatives—either submission to British rule through "constitutional" processes with the consequent continued rule of the British and their agents, or the adoption of "more revolutionary methods" which could lead to Indian freedom. This meant first of all, that in India there should be created "a revolutionary mass party."[53]

Roy desired that Congressmen (members of the National Congress) should join his proposed mass party, and in a letter written to C. R. Das on January 6, 1923, he expressed positive support for the Congress—if it should adopt a really revolutionary policy.[54] But the Congress certainly could not endure the sentiments of an "open letter" written by Roy to Das on February 4, 1923, in which the Bolshevik Brahmin averred: "We Communists stand for the abolition of classes and consequently of class struggle, but classes cannot disappear unless private property is abolished."[55] No wonder the Communists did not secure the services of Das, although they did find a patron in the Congress in a certain Vithalbhai who was not a very influential Congressman.[56]

Roy also continued his correspondence with Indian Communists. On March 19, 1923, he urged Shaukat Usmani, the Communist leader in Uttar Pradesh "not to lose time in organizing the nucleus of a Communist Party wherever possible." In addition, Roy urged two other steps: "A preliminary conference of (Communist) pioneers for all provinces at Berlin," where they would meet with Roy and receive orders from him and his Soviet masters. The other step proposed by Roy to Usmani was the calling of a "National Convention" after the Berlin meeting of an Indian mass party.[57] The theme of establishing the "People's Party" was brought out even more sharply in a letter by Roy to Muzaffar Ahmad, the Communist leader in Calcutta, dated May 13, 1923. Roy wrote the latter that the "People's Party" should forthwith be formed in India, which party would be, of course, under the leadership of the Communists and which would "gradually" be transformed into an "open Communist Party."[58] Muzaffar Ahmad was likewise charged to carry on Communist propaganda among the workers of Calcutta, notably amongst the jute mill and tramway workers. At the same time, Muzaffar Ahmad was ordered to get busy and publish Bolshevik pamphlets. The Calcutta Communist was likewise informed how he might receive funds supplied from Moscow through Roy's propaganda centers in Western Europe.[59]

By May, 1923, Roy's efforts (in spite of the interception of some of his letters) began to bear fruit. The five Communist sections were actively functioning. Two of them, that of Bombay and that of Lahore, put out publications known, respectively, as "the Socialist," in English, edited by Dange and a Punjabi journal known as "Inquilab" (Revolution) edited in Lahore by Mohammed Sadiq.[60] These journals spread the doctrines of Bolshevism as did a number of their pamphlets.[61] Moreover, probably influenced by this propaganda, certain elements in Bengal, formerly sympathetic to the pre-war terroristic revolutionary sentiments, were now indulging in "academic Bolshevism."[62] This indigenous Communist propaganda was supplemented by copies of the "Advance Guard" and other material put out by the international Communist conspiracy relative to India. Much of the smuggling, as before, was done by Nalini Gupta.[63] He was assisted in this task by R. C. L. Sharma, the Communist agent in Pondicherry, French India, to which town Communist literature was mailed and whence it was smuggled across the land boundary into British India.[64]

This propaganda was actually beginning to take effect. At this time, in 1923, there was founded by the Communist center in Bombay under S. A. Dange, the Girni Kamgar (Mill Workers') Union, often called the "Red Flag" Union which was to play an important role, subsequently, in the history of Communism in India.[65] This move, hoped the Communists, would signal their imminent conquest of Indian labor.

Enthused by the incipient founding of their movement, the

Communists of India prepared to meet in Lucknow, in June, 1923, to organize an all-Indian Workers' and Peasants' Party which would operate as a not-too-veiled front for the Communists. Singaravelu-Chettiar, the Madras Communist leader, was designated to be the leader of the party since it was felt that he would be less obnoxious to the Anglo-Indian authorities than the other Communist leaders.

Likewise encouraged by the coming founding of this party, the Executive Committee of the Communist International (Known as E.C.C.I. or I.K.K.I.) on June 4, 1923, sent a memorandum to the Workers' and Peasants' Party which urged that this party be dedicated to two purposes, secession from the British Empire and "the establishment of a democratic (sic) republic." This memorandum is also interesting in that it denounced Abani Mukherji; manifestly, we hear no more in our story of Roy's would-be rival.[66]

The apparent progress of Indian Communism also attracted the attention of that rising member of the Soviet hierarchy, Joseph Stalin. Speaking at the Twelfth Congress of the Russian Communist Party on April 23, 1923, the future dictator opined:

> Great Britain is now ruling India exactly the same way (as Austria once ruled her subject peoples). In order to make it easier from the point of view of bureaucracy to deal with the nationalities and tribes of India, Great Britain has divided India into British India—240 millions and native India—72 millions. Why? Because Great Britain wanted to pick out one group of nations and grant it privileges in order to rule the remaining nationalities.[67]

This increased Soviet and Comintern interest in India as well as the formation of Communist groups within the sub-continent did not escape the attention of the British Raj which took action against the apparent menace. Within India the Criminal Investigation Division (C.I.D.) intercepted the correspondence between Roy and his Indian comrades and early in May, 1923 arrested the Uttar Pradesh leader of the Communists, Shaukat Usmani. This event thwarted the Communist conference which had been scheduled to take place in Lucknow.[68] Outside of

India the British undertook two diplomatic moves. In the spring of 1923 the British Embassy in Berlin put heavy pressure on the German Government to cease permitting Roy to remain in the German capital, and the latter, fearing that the German Government, which was then hard pressed by France on the Reparations question, might seek to please Britain by handing him over to the English agents, fled to Zürich.[69] Roy set up his headquarters in the Swiss city in May, 1923, but this obviously represented a set-back to the cause of Indian Communism, for Roy could no longer utilize the services of the puissant German Communist party. The second diplomatic move came in the form of a virtual ultimatum, dispatched on May 2, 1923 by Foreign Secretary Lord Curzon, in which the anti-British activity of Soviet agents in India, Afghanistan and Iran was excoriated. The Soviet envoys, Raskolnikov in Afghanistan and Shumiatsky in Iran were the particular targets of the British Foreign Minister. Raskolnikov was accused of having endeavored to foment insurrection in the North-West Frontier Province of India and of having requested the Moscow government for 5,000 rubles and ten cartons of cartridges to aid fanatical Waziri tribesmen. The blistering British note also charged that through M. N. Roy, the Indian Communists were receiving subsidies from the Soviets.[70] Unwilling to submit to a break in its de facto relations with England, the Soviets after an exchange of correspondence evinced a disposition to conciliate the British, and Raskolnikov, but not Shumiatsky, was dismissed from his post.[71]

As a consequence of these British actions there was a marked lessening of Soviet and Comintern interest in India in the second half of 1923 and a corresponding deterioration in the position of the budding Indian Communist movement. Intercepted correspondence between Roy and Indian Red leaders indicated that the latter were becoming disappointed by a lack of interest in Hindustan in the Communist movement (they had apparently optimistically felt that once the idea was introduced—Communism would sweep the country), and by the effective surveillance of their movement by the Anglo-Indian authorities and they were disappointed with the work of Roy in Europe.[72] By the end of 1923, the Indian Communists who earlier in that year had been so intent on launching their grandiose all-Indian Workers' and Peasants' Party were now begging Roy to have the Comintern in Moscow send them funds to keep their two publications, "The Socialist" and "Inquilab" going, and were demanding that these funds should be sent on a "regular" and not on a "sporadic" basis as heretofore.[73]

However the assumption to power of the Liberal-supported Labour ministry of Ramsay MacDonald and its prompt de jure recognition of Soviet Russia[74] prompted the Soviets to take a bolder course in regard to India. This is reflected by an address at Sverdlov University in Moscow, early in 1924 in which the ever-rising Stalin (who was taking advantage of the death of Lenin in January, 1924) averred:

> Where will the (imperialist) chain break in near future? Again, where it is weakest. It is not precluded that the chain may break, say in India. Why? Because that country has a young, militant revolutionary proletariat, which has such an ally as the national-liberation movement—an undoubtedly powerful and undoubtedly important ally. Because there the revolution is opposed by such a well-known foe as foreign imperialism which lacks all moral credit and is deservedly hated by the oppressed and exploited masses of India.[75]

Taking his cue from his masters in Moscow, M. N. Roy became more active. On January 23, 1924, the Bolshevik Brahmin urged Singaravelu-Chettiar to see to it that the Communists should at once get control of the Indian labor movement.[76] But if Moscow and its Indian agents thought the new British government would condone open Red activity in India, they were sadly mistaken. For, only a few weeks later, in March, 1924, the Anglo-Indian authorities arrested the leaders of Indian Communism, S. A. Dange in Bombay, Muzaffar Ahmad in Calcutta, Singaravelu-Chettiar in Madras and Roy's immediate agent, Nalini Gupta.[77] It was apparent the new British ministry was just as wary as had been the case with the preceding Tory cabinet, of the danger of Soviet Russia to India and was just as determined to halt the insidious development of a Russian fifth column within Hindustan in the form of the Communist party of India.

On March 18, 1924, the Director of Central Intelligence of the Anglo-Indian government, Colonel Kaye preferred charges in the Magistrate's Court of Quarter Sessions at Cawnpore against the several Communist conspirators. They were charged with endeavoring to deprive the King-Emperor of his sovereignty in India.[78] One month later on April 24th, the trial—referred to as the "Cawnpore Conspiracy Trial"—actually got under way. In the prisoners' dock were Dange, Muzaffar Ahmad, Usmani and Gupta.[79] Proceedings against Singaravelu-Chettiar had been suspended owing to his ill-health and charges against one Ghulam Hussain, another alleged Communist, had been dropped, apparently for want of evidence.[80] Charged in absentia were M. N. Roy, then resident in Switzerland and R. C. L. Sharma, a resident of Pondicherry, French India.[81]

The trial was featured by testimony by Colonel Kaye which made use of the captured correspondence between Roy and his Indian agents and by the vigorous presentation of the case for the Crown by Mr. Ross Alston, the public prosecutor. On the other hand, the defense attorneys for the accused, the so-called Indian "vikils" could not disprove the connection between the Indian Communists and the Communist International. The defense was sufficiently effective to convince the three Indian assessors who served as advisory judges to hold in their separate opinions that one or more of the defendants were not guilty. However, since Indian assessors were really only advisory judges, their verdict actually had no legal force.[82] The judgment rested exclusively with Mr. H. E. Holme, the Sessions Judge at Cawnpore and he found all the defendents guilty and so he sentenced them to four years' imprisonment at hard labor for daring to conspire against the King-Emperor's sovereignty in India.[83]

British reaction to the trial and its outcome, except on the extreme left was either indifferent to, or favorable to the conviction of the Communists.[84] Reasonable Indian opinion likewise showed little sympathy for the incarcerated Communists. Some months after the conclusion of the trial, in November,

1924, the All-Parties Conference of prominent Indian leaders including Gandhi, Das, Pandit Motilal Nehru and Mrs. Annie Besant, repudiated the Third International in a specific reference to the Cawnpore trial. The attitude of the people of India towards the trial is uncertain. It is true that there was a strike of mill workers in Cawnpore during the time of the trial that at one time resulted in a riot and all this may have been connected with the trial.[85] It is possible that the Communist leaders, prior to their apprehension, had disseminated some of their pamphlets among these and other workers throughout India and that these had, therefore, a special sympathy for the convicted Communists. The workers would, at all events, have sympathy for any sort of anti-British political prisoners. However, it is probably safe to say that in the year 1924 the Communist movement was so weak among the masses of India that the arrest and condemnation of the Communist leaders were, on the whole, greeted with a profound indifference.

But the attitude of M. N. Roy was anything but indifferent. Writing from the safety of Zürich, Roy addressed an open letter to Prime Minister MacDonald which appeared in the then organ of the British Communist party, the "Communist Review" of July, 1924. Roy charged that the trial was designed to destroy the working class organization in India. He made much of the argument that contrary to the allegations of the prosecution "no overt act was alleged." Roy then denied that the propaganda of the Communists or his own letters to the Indian comrades contained material hostile to the laws of India, and hence he maintained the arrest and condemnation of the prisoners was based on "an unconstitutional and undemocratic charge."[86] Because of this, held Roy, the trial had been only a "mockery of justice," especially since "all the witnesses, with one exception, were police officers and Government hirelings," and that one exception, he charged, was really a "police spy."[87]

Well might Roy fulminate against the decision of the Anglo-Indian court at Cawnpore, for it deprived the Communists in India of effective leadership. But his appeal to MacDonald, of course, had no effect whatsoever.

The Communist International also took note of the prosecution of its Indian adherents. In their report of its Executive Committee which surveyed Communist activities throughout the world from November, 1922, to June, 1924, it was declared:

> The severe persecution by the British Government which realizes the magnitude of the Communist peril, makes any activities of our young party extremely difficult. Not only are Communist organisations and publications prohibited in India, but even any kind of contact between individuals and the Communist International is a punishable offence while expression of opinion in a Communist spirit is a crime.[88]

However, manifesting blustering Bolshevik bravado, the Executive Committee of the Comintern claimed that four factors were making for an impetus to Communist activities in the sub-continent, namely, the disintegration of the national mass movement, the continuation of agrarian unrest in the North, especially among the Sikhs, a more militant attitude on the part of Indian labor manifested by its demands for economic concessions and the discrediting of the reformist nationalists in the eyes of the working class which had become disgusted by the former's policy of compromise with the British.[89]

The Executive Committee held that in the circumstances the following should be the tasks of the Communist Party of India: the development of the national-liberation movement on a revolutionary basis, the formation of a National People's party which would comprise the urban petty-bourgeoisie, the "pauperised" intellectuals and "small clerks" as well as workers and peasants, and the establishment of an exclusively Communist Party in India as well. The Indian Communists were also charged to get control of the Indian labor movement, reorganize it on a "class basis" and purge it of hostile (i.e., anti-Communist) elements.[90]

The "persecution" so bemoaned by the E.C.C.I. was further manifested on November 10, 1924 when the Indian High Court of Judicature at Allahabad peremptorily rejected the appeal of the Cawnpore conspirators and in so doing praised Colonel

Kaye "and the remarkable efficiency of his department (which) frustrated and hampered them at every turn."[91]

The "Cawnpore Conspiracy Case" evinced the weakness of native Communism in India in 1924. The fact that the British knew all about the Communist movement, and that they were easily able to quash it, indicated that this attempt by the Soviets to penetrate India by internal subversion was no more successful than their earlier plan to effectuate a successful external invasion of the sub-continent from Soviet Turkestan by way of Afghanistan. Thus, once again Soviet designs on India had hit a snag.

CHAPTER THREE

Communist Intrigue in India

In spite of their initial failures, the Soviets and their Indian minions boldly determined to increase the influence of Bolshevism in the sub-continent. At the Fifth Congress of the Communist International which met from June 17 to July 8, 1924, in Moscow, Comrade Zinoviev in his capacity as Secretary-General of that organization asserted that "the Achilles Heel of the British Empire is India . . . and we must therefore make every effort to develop all possible lines of advance there."[1] Taking his cue from this Soviet leader, M. N. Roy also made a bold front at the Congress. The emigré leader of the Indian Communists not only attacked the upper and middle classes of India, but also the petty bourgeoisie as well for collaborating with the British. However, the Bolshevik Brahmin held that if "we organise the peasantry and the workers, they will force the pace for the petty bourgeoisie, who are now ready to compromise with imperialism" and so make them "bolder and less inclined to compromise" with the British masters of India.[2] Roy also praised the greater class consciousness of the Indian workers, hailing a strike of a large number of textile workers for three months in Bombay, an event occurring earlier in 1924, as a manifestation of the growing class struggle in India.[3]

Of greatest significance, however, was Roy's appeal that the British Communist party recognize that its "task . . . transcends the boundaries of the British Isles."[4] This, in effect, meant that the leaders of the international Communist movement were beginning to realize that Roy's work in Western

Europe had not produced the desired results in India and that the task of furthering Soviet aims in Hindustan would be best carried out through the instrumentality of the British Communist party. Indeed, the task of the Communist Party of Great Britain (C.P.G.B.) in regard to India had already been foreshadowed in a declaration rendered by the Executive Committee of the Communist International over two years before on March 4, 1922 by which the British Communist Party was specifically ordered "to launch a well-organised and continued action with a view of supporting the revolutionary movement in India and Egypt."[5] In accordance with this mandate, a British Communist named Ashley was sent to India in the autumn of 1922 where he came into special contact with the Communist center in Calcutta which was under the direction of Muzaffar Ahmad. Moreover, it was in line with this policy that at the Fifth Congress it was a British Communist named MacManus who read a "protest against the persecution of revolutionaries in India by the British Labour Government."[6]

Soon after the Fifth Congress, the British Communists decided on making their activities empire-wide. The British party set up a Colonial Department to exercise leadership of the Communist movement in India as well as in other British colonies.[7]

At the beginning of 1925, the leadership of that party decided to send an emissary in the person of a certain Percy Gladding (alias Richard Cochrane) to India "in order to establish real connections of a healthy character" with the Communist movement there.[8] Gladding was also charged to encourage those Communist leaders, still at liberty, to reform their incipient party and report his findings to his superiors in the C.P.G.B. who in turn would relay them to the Kremlin. Gladding surreptitiously sneaked into India under the name of Cochrane on January 30, 1925 and remained there until April 10th of that year. During his brief visit he was able to make contacts with the representatives of the All-India Trade Union Congress and even of the National Congress.[9]

The C.P.G.B. evinced pleasure over Gladding's visit. Its Colonial Department commented:

> This visit was extremely useful indeed. Our representative was able to attend the All-India Trade Union Congress and held many conversations with the representatives there.[10]

Also of significance was the Pan-Pacific Labour Conference held under the auspices of the Red International of Labour Unions at Canton in June, 1924. This meeting decided on forming a bureau in China for the Red Eastern Labour Unions which would have representation from British India as well as from other countries in the Far East. The conference also put forth a thesis holding the view that the gaining control of trade unions, especially transport unions, was absolutely vital for the success of Red revolution in the Orient.

During the years 1924-1925, new leaders were emerging in India to take the place of the convicted Cawnpore conspirators, notably Satya Bhakta and S. V. Ghate. Bhakta, an odd character, was really a non-Marxist and a pacifist and apparently had been drawn to Communism out of a purely idealistic motivation.[11] Ghate, on the other hand, was a militant labor organizer and readily absorbed the doctrines of Bolshevism.[12] The latter became the General Secretary of the clandestine Communist party. He and other Communist agitators such as K. N. Joglekar and a certain Iyengar undoubtedly had done their best to help foment a textile workers' strike in Bombay in which 150,000 to 180,000 workers participated early in 1924.[13] Moreover, in an official report the Comintern claimed that Communists had participated in the 1924 Congress of the All-India Trade Union Congress (A.I.T.U.C.) and noted that in a number of trade unions the Indian Communists held "influential positions."[14]

During the course of 1925, Ghate and other Communist leaders followed the then official line and endeavored to form front workers' and peasants' parties. The first such party was formed on November 1, 1925 in Calcutta and bore the imposing name of the "Labour Swaraj Party of the Indian National Congress."[15] The mentioning of the National Congress is significant, for the Communists were beginning to feel they might be able to infiltrate into that organization which would supplement their organizing workers' and peasants' parties.

In an official statement, this Bengali Communist "front" party declared that since other means for having attained Indian independence had failed, the party would seek Indian self-rule by organization of the workers and peasants who constituted 80 per cent of the population "so that they may wrest freedom from the hands of vested interests by their own might and for their own interests."[16] In spite of its supposed connection with the National Congress, the party proposed "to send its own members into the legislatures."[17] The nominal founders of the party were Bengalis named Quazi Navrul Islam, Shamsuddin Hussain and Hemant Sarkar.[18] Behind them, however, were the Communist leaders of India and most notably S. V. Ghate. As its mouthpiece, the Labour Swaraj Party put out a journal called "Langal" (Plow) on December 16, 1925.[19]

The Communists also made surprising progress in the labor movement in India during 1925. Indeed, at the fifth All-India Trade Union Congress session of Bombay in that year, a convert to Communism, D. R. Thengdi was actually elected the President of the A.I.T.U.C. at that session. Thengdi evinced his Communist ideology in his presidential address by advocating a nation-wide strike movement in India, and indeed Thengdi's appeal was heeded in the form of a strike by workers of the North-West Indian Railway in the spring of 1925 and a renewed strike by some 130,000 textile mill operatives in Bombay in the autumn of that year.[20] The latter strike was particularly interesting in that the All-Russian Textile Union sent financial assistance to the embattled workers.[21] It is claimed that in 1925 the strike wave hit a then record for India.[22]

However, in the latter part of 1925 the gains made by the Indian Communists were more than offset by a schism in their ranks. One group which was led by S. V. Ghate followed the orthodox views of Moscow and aided in the formation of the Labour Swaraj Party of Bengal and planned the further founding of workers' and peasants' parties of that type in other parts of India, which process would be culminated in the foundation of an all-Indian Workers' and Peasants' Party in which the Communist element, while maintaining its secret identity as such, would be the dominating factor. Another group was led by Satya Bhakta. The latter group desired the Communist Party in India to act openly under its own name, to carry on, by constitutional means, agitation of a Marxist nature and to be independent of the Kremlin.

Bhakta indicated his views in two manifestos appearing on July 16th and October 21st, 1925 entitled respectively "The Future Programme of the Communist Party" and "The First Indian Communist Conference." In these documents Bhakta presented the thesis that the transition from capitalism to Communism might be achieved without injustice or violence, a view which naturally subjected him to vigorous criticism from Communists outside his own circle.[23] This notwithstanding, Bhakta won over to his peaceful and nationalist Communist views, Singaravelu-Chettiar and Maulani Hasrat Mohani, a leader of the former Caliphate movement, who had irked Gandhi when, as we have already noted in connection with the Ahmadabad Congress, he had argued that Swaraj or Indian self-government be defined by the Congress as "complete independence, free from all foreign control."[24]

In an apparent effort to heal the breach in the Communist movement in India, the pro-Comintern Communists led by Ghate and Joglekar and the independent Communists led by Bhakta and Singaravelu-Chettiar met in the First Conference of the Communist Party of India in Cawnpore on December 26, 1925.[25] That this meeting did not have the blessing of Moscow, in view of the prominent position of the dissident Communists participating in it, is attested by the fact that the Communist press throughout the world ignored it. It also would seem to explain why the British suffered the meeting to be held at all.

The dissident Communists dominated the preceedings. The nominal president of the conference was Mohani, but Bhakta and Singaravelu-Chettiar dominated it from behind the scenes. In his presidential address Mohani declared it was the aim of the Communists "to establish Swaraj or complete independence by all fair means and after establishing Swaraj to see that it takes the form of a Soviet republic.[26] To attain this end Mohani argued that Indian Communists should not accept the Gandhist precept of non-violence as a "fixed principle," but on the other hand the Indian Communist party should also deny that the party "necessarily stands for bloodshed and terrorism" in the attainment of its goal. Mohani also insisted that the Communist party was purely Indian in that "at least for the present the work of our party will be restricted to India alone" and that as for the Third International

> we are only fellow-travellers on their path, and not their subordinates. Neither do we give them any practical help, nor do they extend any financial aid to us.[27]

Singaravelu-Chettiar, who had assumed the presidency of the Indian Communist party, surpassed Mohani in disavowing any foreign influence on the policies and program of the Indian Communist party, averred:

> Indian Communism is not Bolshevism, for Bolshevism is a form of Communism which the Russians have adopted in their country. We are not Russians. Bolsheviks and Bolshevism may not be needed in India.[28]

Angered by these statements, Ghate, Joglekar and their followers on December 28, 1925, irrevocably parted company with the group of Bhakta, Mohani and Singaravelu-Chettiar and moved their headquarters from Cawnpore to Bombay.[29]

During the years 1926 and 1927 the Communist party of Great Britain did its utmost to carry out the task which had been devolved upon it by the Fifth Congress of the Communist International in the summer of 1924, that of furthering a revolution in India for the benefit of Soviet Russia. Interestingly enough, the leading Communists in Britain in charge of the hoped-for Bolshevization of the sub-continent were themselves of Indian blood, the brothers Rajani Palme and Clemens Palme Dutt and Shapurji Saklatvala, the latter having been elected a member of the House of Commons from a working class constituency in London. Such leaders of the British Communist party as Harry Pollitt, and R. Page Arnot also took an active interest in Indian affairs. Work in regard to India was dealt with by the C.P.G.B.'s colonial bureau.[30] The British Communists were, of course, under the over-all supervision of the Executive Committee of the Comintern.

The British Communist party furthered its policy in regard to India on six different fronts. The first front involved the propagandizing of Indian students attending Oxford and Cambridge Universities so as to make them emissaries of Communism upon their return to India. This Communist activity was fully confirmed by an investigation by the Chancellor and Proctors of Oxford University in 1926. As a result of this investigation, as an alternative to expulsion from the University, the Indian students were obliged to sign a written pledge that they would refrain from any association with Communists and would not disseminate "Communist ideas" in the future.[31] Thus Communist advance on this front was balked.

The second front concerned the winning over of prominent Indian personages who should be visiting England, to Communism. Three such Indians who visited London early in 1926 were N. M. Joshi, the President of the All-India Trade Union Congress and a member of the Indian Legislative Assembly and his fellow legislators, the labor leader Chaman Lal and a certain Goswami. The comrades of the C.P.G.B. attempted to convince these Indians that they should participate in an "Oriental Convention" which would be Communist dominated. Although Lal displayed definite interest in this scheme, his fellow visitors were averse to thus being made into puppets of Bolshevism, so that this plan fell through. Nonetheless, the fact that Chaman Lal, a fairly prominent left-wing member of the Congress had been won over to an apparently fellow-traveling position, was encouraging to the British Communists.[32]

The third front involved the activity of a Communist-front organization in England known as the "Labour Research Department," the task of which, among others, was to send Communist literature into India.[33] The principal Indian participant in this organization was a certain M. G. Desai who subsequently returned to India toward the end of 1926 bringing a large mass of Communist propaganda with him.[34]

The fourth front had as its concern an attempt to convert

Indian seamen on the docks of London to Communism. However, this maneuver had little success.[35] In this connection, we may note that Indian Communist couriers between Europe and India traveled in the guise of sailors.

The fifth front was the literary front—the attempt to formulate a specific Communist party line on India and was carried out by R. Palme Dutt in his book entitled "Modern India" which appeared late in 1926. This book was a fairly thorough review of Indian conditions from the Marxist and Communist point of view.

Dutt held that "imperialist domination" had drained the life-blood out of India,[36] argued that the Indian upper classes existed "under the protection of the British bourgeois" as subordinate shareholders of the spoils,[37] contended that the Indian bourgeoisie as a whole "cannot be trusted" and that fear of insurrection makes it "hasten to the side of the British,"[38] and charged that the political arm of the Congress, the Swarajist Party, was following a policy of "surrender to imperialism."[39]

In his political program Dutt maintained that India must enjoy "complete independence,"[40] and to attain that end a "People's Party" should be organized combining workers and peasants—this being analogous to the projected all-Indian Workers' and Peasants' party.[41] In the free India there would be complete civil rights—notably freedom of speech and assembly.[42]

In his economic program Dutt advocated the "expropriation of the big landowners and the nationalisation of land," and in industry a program for the amelioration of labor conditions by raising of wages, workmen's compensation on European standards and reforms of a like sort.[43]

Thus with the exception of the provision on land tenure, Dutt's program was a mild one, a program in line with the view that Communists should collaborate to an extent with non-proletarian elements, and thus was a continuation of the Lenin line of 1920.

The sixth and most important front dealt with the sending of emissaries of the C.P.G.B. to India. We have already noted the sending of Gladding alias Cochrane to Hindustan in 1925. Early in 1926 the leaders of British Bolshevism decided to send another agent to India, one who stood higher in the party hierarchy than Gladding. The man selected for this mission was George Allison who was to travel to India under the false passport of Donald Campbell. Allison was a high-ranking British Communist who had previously attended a session of the E.C.C.I. in Moscow.[44] He was instructed to organize a small illegal Communist Party and a large legal party—the Workers' and Peasants' Party which, it was hoped, would operate on an All-India scale, but, of course, would be Communist-dominated. Allison was likewise charged to induce Communists to enter the National Congress and the All-India Trade Union Congress with the ultimate hope that these organizations might be captured by the Communists.[45]

Allison whose funds for his mission were supplied from the "Continent," meaning Moscow, arrived in Bombay on April 30, 1926 and remained there until November of that year when he betook himself to Calcutta and carried on his Communist activities in the Bengali metropolis.[46]

During the year, 1926, the workers' and peasants' parties were maintained as fronts for Communism. In February of that year the Labour Swaraj Party of Bengal changed its name to the Workers' and Peasants' Party[47] and conducted "an All-Bengal Tenants' Conference."[48] During the course of the year the party published its party organ known at first as "Langal," (the Plow) and later as "Ganavani," (The Voice of the People).[49] The arrival of Allison in Bengal spurred this party's activity at the end of that year.

Allison also was largely instrumental in founding the so-called Congress Labour party of Bombay in the spring of 1926 shortly after his arrival in India.[50] The Communists also founded a Workers' and Peasants' Party in Lahore, the Punjab, in the spring of 1926 and they were laying plans in the latter part of the year of forming similar parties in other parts of India as well, with the hope that these separate parties might serve as the foundation stones for an All-India Workers' and Peasants' Party.

The programs of these Red-front parties in 1926 stressed the need for national independence, demanded the organization on class lines of the workers and peasants, and insisted that "direct action" by the workers and peasants would be the best means of attaining independence. The economic demands of these parties resembled those of R. P. Dutt.[51] Their relative moderation indicated that the Communists were not determined on alienating the Indian bourgeoisie as a whole, particularly that part which vigorously aspired towards national freedom.

It may be noted that the Congress Labour Party of Bombay succeeded in 1926 in rejuvenating the revolutionary Girni Kamgar textile workers' union which had been founded in 1923[52] but which had failed to gain numbers and influence after 1924. The revivification of this union played an important role in spreading Communism among the workers of Bombay and encouraged the dissemination of Communist ideological notions thoughout India as well.[53] The fact that Communist precepts were spreading in India out from Bombay was evinced by the the fact that in 1926 the Punjabi Workers' and Peasants' Party put forth the first May Day demonstration in Indian history in Lahore.[54]

Besides setting up front organizations in the form of workers' and peasants' parties and trade unions, the Communists in India endeavored to build up the organization of their own, illegal, secret party during the year, 1926. They were definitely interested in attracting members of former terrorist societies to their clandestine party organization and they were highly pleased when they recruited the services of Dharani Goswami, former member of the "Anushilan Society," a terrorist organization in Bengal. Goswami was instrumental in converting many of his former terrorist accomplices to Communism.[55] It was felt the terrorists would be most useful to the clandestine Communist Party when the day of Red revolution should arrive. The entry of the terrorists compensated for the defection of the "independent" Communists, led by Bhakta, Singaravelu-Chettiar and Mohani. As a matter of fact these dissident Communists disappeared into obscurity during the years 1926 and 1927.

In November, 1926 the Third International issued the following instruction to the Indian Communists in regard to workers' (w) and peasants' (p) parties:

> The W & PP of Bengal should call a conference to organise the W & PP of India. To this conference will be invited all organisations which now belong to the C.P. as well as other revolutionary working class or socialistic organisations that sympathise with us . . . . This conference will be entirely controlled by us and the W and PP of India will remain under our leadership. The Central Committee will easily be composed of conscious Communists.[56]

In order to implement this directive the C.P.G.B. sent out a trusted agent to India named Philip Spratt, a genuinely talented young Englishman who was a graduate of Cambridge University. While attending that university, he had been converted to Communism. Upon his graduation, Spratt worked in the Labour Research Department, a front for British Communism, in which post he directed not a little propaganda to India.[57] Simultaneously he was also a member of a Communist-controlled agency known as the National Minorities movement. Indeed, the view that "his profession in England was Communism" was most apt.[58]

Philip Spratt's arrival in Bombay on December, 1926 in the capacity of a "humble bookseller" for a firm known as Birrell and Carrott, itself a Communist front, was to prove a "philip" to the Communist movement in India.[59] For, immediately after his arrival, Spratt effectively reorganized the Congress Labour Party under the new name of the Workers' and Peasants' Party of Bombay. In this capacity he did his utmost to educate Indian radicals in the mores and precepts of international Communism, teaching them duly to hold demonstrations on "Lenin Day," May Day, the anniversary of the Bolshevik revolution and even to protest violently over the execution of the American radicals, Sacco and Vanzetti.[60]

Spratt and his Indian comrades conducted an important meeting in Bombay on May 31, 1927 which made an earnest attempt to clarify the relationship of Indian Communism to the Comintern. Hence a declaration was put forth to the effect that

> the CPI (Communist Party of India) looks up to the CP's of the world as well as the (Third) International for lead and guidance in the work undertaken by this Party in this country.[61]

The party specified that only those subscribing to the policies of the Comintern would be eligible for membership. The meeting also approved the policy of the formation of workers' and peasants' parties, the activities of which would be open in contrast to the clandestine activities of the C.P.I. per se.[62]

In this session, the leadership of S. V. Ghate was confirmed in his being "elected" General Secretary,[63] although Spratt as chief emissary of the C.P.G.B., the tutor of India's Communists had, in fact, probably even more influence.

The latter, it may be noted, conducted an extensive correspondence with his comrades in London, which correspondence, as had earlier been the case with that of M. N. Roy, was intercepted by the alert officers of the Indian C.I.D. This correspondence, mainly between Spratt and Clemens P. Dutt or R. Page Arnot, was in cipher and invisible ink in the proper "cloak and dagger style."[64]

On the basis of its knowledge of the affairs of Indian Communism, the C.P.G.B. decided to spur on the cause of Communism in India by sending new agents, to wit, Benjamin (Ben) F. Bradley and Shapurji Saklatvala. The former, an active worker in another of that party's front organizations, the Workers' Welfare League of India of London, arrived in Hindustan on September 23, 1927, which arrival was heralded by the cryptic message: "Engineer will shortly go to Glasgow," Glasgow here meaning Bombay.[65] Having joined Spratt in the latter city, Bradley immediately plunged into Communist activity, specializing, it seems, exclusively in trying to win over Indian trade union leaders to Bolshevism.[66]

Saklatvala, taking advantage of the prestige he enjoyed as a British M.P., boldly visited "many important centres in India" where "he delivered a number of speeches, the substance of which received wide publicity in the Press."[67] He audaciously attended the Delhi session of the All-India Trade Union Congress in the spring of 1927 and the Cawnpore session of that body in the autumn of that year.[68] On being praised by the All-India Congress Committee on October 26, 1927 for his seemingly pro-Indian policies,[69] Saklatvala replied by sending a message to the plenary session of the Congress assembled in

Madras which called on the Congress to "awaken our working masses, (and) organise our teeming peasants" and to carry on a boycott against British goods, "not of a picturesque political kind but of an economic character."[70] However, Saklatvala really injured the Communist cause by his own "autocratic manner"; indeed, at one time he even refused to attend a secret conference of the Communist Party of India "because it was not officially affiliated with the Communist International."[71] From the British standpoint Saklatvala's conduct was so obnoxious that his passport was cancelled and he had to return ignominously to England.[72]

All this activity by Spratt, Bradley, Saklatvala and their Indian accomplices did make for progress in the workers' and peasants' parties during 1927. Thus, that of Bombay came to control during that year to a large extent the organized labor movement of that city and it was even able to establish itself as the official "opposition" to the Swarajist party there.[73] As a symptom of its growth, two publications appeared under its aegis, one in the Marathi language boldly called "Kranti" (Revolution) and another being denominated the "Spark," the same name as the first pre-revolution clandestine Russian Bolshevik newspaper.[74] As the premier Communist-controlled party in India, the Workers' and Peasants' Party of Bombay by the end of 1927 maintained liaison not only with the Communist International and the C.P.G.B., but also with the Red International of Labour Unions, the U.S.S.R. Society for Cultural Relations with Foreign Countries and other Communist-controlled and sponsored groups.[75]

The Workers' and Peasants' Party of Bengal likewise became more active in 1927 although not to the extent of its sister party in Bombay. In Bengal, under its General Secretary, S. N. Tagore, the Workers' and Peasants' Party expanded its activities, which were featured by the second conference of the party in Calcutta in February, 1927. It had received a veritable rejuvenation towards the close of 1926 when Allison had come to Bengal and had reorganized its lagging ranks. The party continued to gain strength during the course of 1927 until at the beginning of 1928 it claimed an "affiliated membership" of "over 10,000," probably an exaggerated figure.[76] It continued to disseminate Marxist propaganda through its journal, now called "Jagaran."[77] Especially important to this party was the work of Dharani Goswami, the erstwhile terrorist, who was one of the founders of the "Young Comrades' League," the first Indian Communist organization aimed specially at attracting the youth of India to Communism.[78]

But the spread of Communism in the Peninsula was not limited to India's two greatest metropolitan communities in 1927. Under the leadership of U. N. Mukerji and Puran Chandra Joshi, the United Provinces Workers' and Peasants' Party became active in that year.[79] The Punjab also had its Workers' and Peasants' Party by the end of 1927 headed by its General Secretary Abdul Majid. Majid had been one of the Mujahirs who had been successfully indoctrinated in Communist ideology at the Bolshevik "political academy" in Tashkent and in the University of the Toilers of the East in Moscow. He subsequently had returned to India eluding British frontier guards on the way.[80] This Punjabi party was particularly active in that it put out three journals and in that its agents were known to be in touch with Communists in China.[81] Another Workers' and Peasants' party was also established in Ajmer in Rajputana in 1927.[82]

At the end of 1927 the Communist Party of India as such was still little more than a secret society composed of the real (and sometimes nominal as well) leaders of the several workers' and peasants' parties.[83] However, it could hardly have remained otherwise, for the British would surely not have permitted a Communist party, per se, to operate boldly in the open. Besides, the workers and peasants appeared to be well serving the Bolshevik cause in India, by attracting elements which could be controlled by the Communists in a "united front" type of party, but which elements would not have desired to be enrolled as members of an out-and-out Communist party.

In 1928 the several workers' and peasants' parties became even more active. That party in Bombay was visibly strengthened in that year by the release from imprisonment of the Cawnpore conspirator, S. A. Dange. The latter immediately furthered the

Communist cause in the Girni Kamgar textile workers' union, in which organization he became General Secretary,[84] while simultaneously he made inflammatory addresses, the contents of which were not unnoticed by the British authorities.[85] It was Dange who became the principle correspondent of Clemens P. Dutt, the British Communist, who supervised the activities of Indian Communists from London. But it was Dange's colleague in Bombay, the Indian Communist R. S. Nimbkar, who was in direct contact with the Comintern in Moscow, which agency also supervised Dutt in London.[86] The Bombay Workers' and Peasants' Party was particularly active in the labor organizations of that city and took an important role during the great textile strike in the Bombay area of which we shall presently take note.

The Workers' and Peasants' Party in Bengal was strongly bolstered in March, 1928 by the arrival of Spratt from Bombay. Soon after the arrival of that British Communist, who immediately inaugurated a program of extensive agitation amongst the workers of Bengal,[87] especially the railway workers, the third annual conference of this party took place on the thirty-first of March. At this meeting the current line of the workers' and peasants' parties, and hence that of the Indian Communists, was expounded. The "Soviet Republics" which were held to be "menaced" by Britain were lauded,[88] the policy of British "Imperialism" was thoroughly denounced[89] although it was stated that imperialism was in "a very serious position," the "Indian bourgeoisie" was denounced for its alleged "position of subordination to British capital" which resulted in its "treachery and desertion" from the Indian national movement,[90] and the Indian petty bourgeoisie was held either to be (in its "upper strata") "following the bourgeoisie" or else (its "lower strata") "falling into indifference or a radical policy." On the other hand, in keeping with the then Communist line, the National Congress was not denounced as such, but rather, the comrades in Bengal were urged to "become members of the provincial and All-Indian Congress Committee" and in the Congress to take "active part in such work as leads towards the development of mass movement."[91] The followers of the Workers' and Peasants' Party of Bengal were informed also that it should have its "alliance . . . with the petty bourgeoisie" consolidated on the basis of direct action for "complete independence"[92]—a manifestation of the tactic of the "popular front."

The political program of the Bengal Workers' and Peasants' Party was defined in terms of proximate and ultimate goals. The ultimate political aims of the party were held to be those of "complete national independence of India" and the convocation of a Constituent Assembly to be elected by universal suffrage. Another ultimate goal was to be the "abolition of native states." The proximate political policy of the party would have as its goal the boycotting of the Simon Commission, then touring India, and in the international sphere, the adherents of the party were called upon to support the Russian "revolution," "particularly in view of the danger of war," presumably to be waged by the British against Soviet Russia.[93]

In order to carry out these political tasks, it was urged that party workers should organize not only geographically in "Towns, Districts, Divisions, and Villages" but also functionally by means of "groups" which would be "set up in Factories, Railways, Mines . . ." The party was also to organize "definite Youth organisations" and "women's sections."[94]

In the economic field both proximate and ultimate demands were also put forth. In the domain of agriculture, although the final goal was held to be the "abolition" of the "landlord system," immediate reforms such as "substantial reduction in rent" were stressed.[95] In the field of industry immediate aims of a reformist nature such as an "eight hour day" and the "abolition of child labour" were emphasized to the exclusion of the radical prescription of the nationalization of industry.[96] It was evinced by the mildness of the program, typical of workers' and peasants' parties in 1928, that the Communists hoped to entice many Indian liberals into these parties in order to utilize them all the better as fronts for the Communists.

It may be noted that Muzaffar Ahmad, another recently released Cawnpore conspirator and the former terrorist, Dharani Goswami, played an important role in this Bengali conference and were ordered by it "to form a sub-committee to represent the party in making arrangements to form a united Party (of Workers' and Peasants') and to hold an All-India Conference in December next."[97] The Workers' and Peasants' Party of Bengal increased both in size and in influence during the year 1928 and by the time that the All-India Workers' and Peasants' Party held its conference in December of that year, the leadership of Spratt, Muzaffar Ahmad and Goswami had made the Workers' and Peasants' Party of Bengal nearly the equal of the like organization in Bombay.

During the course of 1928 the Workers' and Peasants' Party of the United Provinces, the activities of which centered in the town of Meerut, likewise were extended in scope.[98] This party was ever more falling under the control of P. C. Joshi, a young law student. The Punjabi party under Mohammed Abdul Majid was likewise active and its principal organ, the "Kirti" (Worker) was unusually vituperative and candid for a Workers' and Peasants' party publication. This journal with temerity displayed the Hammer and Sickle on its front page, and it did not shirk from asserting, in connection with a potential Anglo-Soviet war, that "the Russian Government is the toilers' Government and it encourages us to fight."[99]

In 1927 and 1928 under cover of a policy of "friendship" for the National Congress[100] the Communists really endeavored to infiltrate that body so as ultimately to control it. At that time a number of out-and-out Communists were elected to the All-India Congress Committee, the large executive Committee of the Congress, and about this time a pro-Communist was elected to the Presidency of the Punjab Provincial Congress Committee.[101] Besides, such Communists as Spratt and Joglekar who also attended the Madras Congress of December, 1927 played an important part in the proceedings of the Bombay Provincial Congress Committee which resolved to organize group agitation against the Simon Commission,[102] which on the basis of its investigations was to report on whether India might or might not secure more autonomy.

In those years the Communists secured marked influence within individual unions and in the All-India Trade Union Congress. The expressed intention of the Communists, through their workers' and peasants' parties was to base the trade union movement in India on the principle of the class struggle and to draw the workers into the nationalist struggle by means of a program of national independence which could be secured by "direct action," especially involving the political strike as a weapon.[103]

A manifestation of the growing Communist influence in the Indian labor movement occurred at Delhi on March 12 and 13, 1927 at the seventh annual session of the All-India Trade Union Congress (A.I.T.U.C.). At that session "hearty greetings and welcome" were extended to Saklatvala who very officiously participated in the meeting.[104] This session of the A.I.T.U.C. furthermore passed not only a resolution of welcome to the Indian Communist member of Britain's Parliament, but also adopted resolutions praising the revolution in China and condemning the sending of Indian troops to that land, which resolutions were in line with the Comintern policies.[105]

Even more than in the case with the Delhi session, did the Cawnpore Congress of the A.I.T.U.C. evince the growth of Communist influence in the Indian labor movement. At this session, held in November, 1927, a number of resolutions again were carried which were in conformity with the Comintern line.[106] They included resolutions affiliating the A.I.T.U.C. with that international Communist front, the League Against Imperialism,[107] and congratulating Soviet Russia on the tenth anniversary of the "October" Revolution.[108] In addition to penetrating existing unions the Communists in 1927 also busily bolstered their own union of textile workers in Bombay, the Girni Kamgar Union, and organized their own Indian Seamen's Union.[109] In addition, where they could, the Communists aided and abetted the strike movement, most notably in the strike on the Bengal Nagpur Railway's workshops at Kharagpur near Calcutta in the early spring of 1927 and in a walk-out of the weavers of Bombay in the summer of that year.[110]

The Communists made considerable progress in 1928 in securing influence in the Indian labor movement, especially in the Bengal and Bombay areas. Among unions they came to control were those of four Indian railway systems, which gave them the opportunity of potentially partially paralyzing the commerce of India.[111] At the same time the Communists worked assiduously to augment their sphere of influence in the A.I.T.U.C. In the annual conference of the A.I.T.U.C. in Jharia in December, 1928, the Communists succeeded in having resolutions enacted reaffirming the affiliation of the A.I.T.U.C. to the League Against Imperialism and opposing any affiliation with the anti-Comintern International Federation of Trade Unions. In addition, Communist leaders K. N. Joglekar and D. R. Thengdi were assigned to be the A.I.T.U.C. representatives at a forthcoming conference of the League Against Imperialism. Although at this session, the moderate element in the organization secured the election of Jawaharlal Nehru to the Presidency of the body, the Communists were compensated by the election of their men, Muzzafar Ahmad, Mohammed Majid and D. B. Kulkarni as Vice-Presidents and Secretary of that organization.[112]

The growth of the strike movement also featured Red activity in Indian labor in 1928. Communist inspired and supported strikes broke out in all parts of the country. Involved were the steel workers at Tata's mills in Bengal where 18,000 men struck[113] the tin plate workers in the same province,[114] the jute mill workers of Calcutta of whom 200,000 walked out,[115] the operatives of the cotton mills of Sholapur, the woolen mills' workers of Cawnpore and even the garbage collectors of Calcutta.[116] Of serious potential were the strikes of rail workers in Bengal and Southern India, the latter region having been previously immune from the Communist virus.[117]

But the most important strike centered in Bombay and involved the textile operatives of that city. The workers had had a legitimate grievance in the early part of 1928 when the management of the mills endeavored to put into effect a scheme of standardization which resulted in reduced wages, double work for each operative and a large measure of unemployment.[118] The strike which involved over 60,000 workers was unique in the annals of Indian labor for its duration—six months—the strike lasting from April 28th to October 4th,

1928.[119] The walkout also saw the rise to prominence of the Red textile workers' union, the Girni Kamgar Union, and the Bombay Communist leaders, particularly S. A. Dange and R. S. Nimbkar, played an important role in furthering this strike which was successful in that the management of the textile mills agreed to abandon their standardization scheme and restored the old system of wages and working conditions.[120] In England, R. Palme Dutt hailed the walkout as "the greatest strike in Indian history,"[121] but on the other hand, non-Communist Britons and Indians recognized that the strike had resulted in the "grave unsettlement of the working classes" there.[122] Communist activity in the textile strike was fully appreciated by the British authorities who also noted Red instigation of other strikes in India during the course of the year, 1928.[123] Thus a C.I.D. report at the end of the year stated that "there was hardly a public utility service or industry which had not been affected in whole or in part by the wave of communism which swept the country during the year."[124]

The grave character of the strike wave in 1928 was attested to by figures showing that 506,851 workers were involved in them and that no fewer than 31,647,404 working days were lost; statistics which registered the unprecedented extent of the largely Communist-inspired labor unrest.[125] It may also be noted that the workers, in addition to their strike activities, were all the more indoctrinated in Communism by political demonstrations such as that against the Simon Commission. Their participation in routine Red rituals, notably May Day demonstrations,[126] also contributed to their indoctrination into the ideology of Communism.

In addition to their activity among the workers, the Communists through their workers' and peasants' parties endeavored arduously to win over the Indian peasantry to the cause of Moscow. This was particularly the case in Uttar Pradesh (United Provinces).[127] There were in 1928 a number of peasants' strikes in scattered parts of India which had, particularly in Uttar Pradesh, been instigated by the Communists.[128] However, in general the Communists made little progress among the peasantry as compared to that which they had made among the workers in the year, 1928.[129]

The Indian Communists and their advisers of the C.P.G.B. were highly desirous of winning support from the educated youth. Facilitating their purpose was Lester Hutchinson, a young, British, free-lance journalist who arrived in India in September, 1928. Besides engaging in the activities of the Workers' and Peasants' Party of Bombay, Hutchinson established "study circles" for young Indian intellectuals who read "proscribed books" such as Stalin's volume on Lenin, Bukharin's "A.B.C. of Communism" and like samples of Red literature.[130] It may also be noted that Spratt endeavored to establish Communist-controlled "Youth Leagues" in his travels from "province to province" during the course of 1928.[131]

In addition to winning over a number of impressionable educated Indian youths to Communism, the ideology of Communism made a profound impression upon a number of great Indian intellectuals who had nothing whatever to do with the clandestine Communist Party of India or its workers' and peasants' parties. Among them was the renowned Bengali poet, Sir Rabindranath Tagore, who, in spite of his profound individualism, admired what he deemed were the great achievements of the Bolshevik Revolution, particularly in the development of educational and health facilities and over-all cultural progress in the Soviet Union, as well as the growth of an alleged spirit of equality in Russia.[132] Moreover, the most famous Indian Muslim intellectual at this time, Sir Muhammed Iqbal, also evinced sympathy for Communism. In his writings he evidenced a hatred for Western capitalism, composed many "socialist" poems and even employed at times the notions of Marx in his condemnation of the West. At one time, Iqbal even averred that Soviet Russia was already, to a certain extent, doing "God's work," albeit unconsciously. However, Iqbal appears not to have known precisely what "Socialism" really meant.[133] Furthermore, Jawaharlal Nehru, son of Motilal Nehru, the then principal leader of the National Congress attended the "Congress of Oppressed Nationalities," in Brussels of February, 1927, which founded the "League Against Imperialism."[134] It may also be noted that in a journey with his father, the "younger Nehru" visited the Soviet Union in November, 1927. Upon his return to India he had a book published which praised the domestic accomplishments of the Soviet Union; for example, Nehru noted that the Soviet government had "practically" abolished illiteracy in urban areas.[135] In foreign relations, Nehru insisted that Soviet Russia had no designs upon India whatsoever, but held by contrast that British foreign policy was designed to "crush" the Soviet Union.[136] It was with this thought in mind that Nehru, besides sponsoring the well-known independence of India resolution at the Madras session of the National Congress of December, 1927,[137] also was the probable principle framer of a resolution which stated

> that in the event of the British Government embarking on any warlike adventure and endeavoring to exploit India in it for the furtherance of their imperialist aim, it will be the duty of the people of India to refuse to take part in such a war, or cooperate with them in any way whatsoever.[138]

Jawaharlal Nehru held this resolution indicated that the Indian people would not support an aggressive British war against the Soviet Union.[139]

* * * * *

We have now seen that it was the Communist Party of Great Britain which was the dominant agent for Moscow in the establishment of a growing Communist movement in India from 1924 to 1928. In this circumstance, the C.P.G.B. had virtually eclipsed M. N. Roy. However, the latter tried his best—subject to the overriding will of the Kremlin—to maintain a kind of none-too-friendly competition with the London comrades in the aim of winning India to Communism.

Thus in July, 1924, after the close of the Fifth Congress of the Comintern, Roy repaired to Paris which he felt might make a good Continental European headquarters for his plans in regard to India.[140] However, his hopes in this regard were rudely shattered when on January 30, 1925, he was summarily hustled out of France and thrust across the Luxembourg frontier,[141] a manifestation of sudden French hostility to Indian exiles which was also evinced in in Pondicherry, French India, by the internment of R. C. L. Sharma, the Communist leader there a few months before Roy's expulsion.[142] It is likely that both these moves were undertaken by the French at British suggestion.

However, Roy's ruffled feelings over the ascendancy of the C.P.G.B. in Indian affairs and his expulsion from France were somewhat assuaged by his being appointed in February, 1925 as one of the four directors of the Far Eastern Bureau of the Communist International. At that time Roy and his fellow directors of the Far Eastern Bureau put forth a pompous manifesto calling for a British-empire wide revolution.[143]

In the mean time, the Bengali Bolshevik's devoted wife, Evelyn Roy, who had remained behind after the expulsion from there of her husband, boldly formed an organization in Paris known as "le comité pro-Hindu (or Indian League), the ostensible purpose of which was to aid the cause of Indian independence and to secure the "fulfillment of the pledges made (to India) during the Great War."[144] Actually it was just a front to further the spread of Communism in India. The society published a number of bulletins which, incidentally, complained bitterly about Roy's expulsion from France.[145]

A showdown between the two competitive sets of fomenters of Communism in India occurred at a Communist colonial conference in Amsterdam on July 11-12, 1925. Representing the C.P.G.B. were Messrs. Clemens P. Dutt, R. W. Robson and Gladding, the latter just returned from his mission to India. The meeting resulted in a most acrimonious exchange of heated remarks between these British gentlemen and the Roys over who "should have the right to control Communist work in the British colonies." The chasm between the British Communist Party and the Roys' Indian bureau remained as gaping as ever.[146]

M. N. Roy then endeavored to re-establish his influence over the Indian Communist movement through his writing a book, which appeared in the spring of 1926, entitled, "The Future of Indian Politics." As in the work of his Communist competitor, R. Palme Dutt's "Modern India," that of Roy's dilated on how British capitalism had robbed the Indian people,[147] complained about the alleged bent of "the nationalist bourgeoisie" to join hands with the "imperialists" against the "revolutionary masses,"[148] demanded "complete independence for India," and called for the creation of a national workers' and peasants' party, a revolutionary nationalist party, "which would unite" the "petty bourgeoisie and the peasantry" in a "democratic coalition" under "the leadership of the proletariat."[149] This party would be known, held Roy (as with Dutt) as "the People's Party." However, to a greater extent than in the case of Dutt, Roy insisted that besides this "People's Party," the proletariat would "have its own party—the Communist party."[150]

In 1926 Roy organized a Western European group of Communist Indians, leading members of which were men named Sepassi (Roy's principal lieutenant), Haidar Khan and Upadhaya, which group maintained an unsuccessful competition with the C.B.G.B. of being the Kremlin's principal instrumentality in fomenting Bolshevism in India. Early in 1927 Roy was assigned by Stalin to assist in furthering the cause of Communism in China, and so, along with Borodin and General Blücher, he became one of the principal Communist agents who endeavored to further Communism in the erstwhile Celestial Empire.[151]

In China, Roy also conducted activities for the purpose of furthering Communism in India. In the spring of 1927, operating from Canton and Hankow, Roy supervised the sending of propaganda into India which assailed in the sharpest tones the Anglo-Indian government of the sub-continent.[152] On the anticipation that China would go Communist, Roy's propaganda featured the slogan "follow China's lead." This propaganda appears to have been smuggled into India, at least in part, from across the seemingly inaccessible Tibetan-Assam frontier.[153] Roy also employed this route to foment strikes among the tea plantation workers of Assam, who, being poorly paid and living under miserable conditions, were felt to be likely converts to Communism.[154] Besides, Roy disseminated Communist propaganda among certain "notoriously disaffected" Indians in China, notably certain Sikhs.[155] Some of these were men who had served under Mahendra Pratep earlier in the decade. Their venomous hatred for all things British was reflected in their literature which was of a "violently inflammatory nature" in both the English and Gurmukhi (a dialect of Punjabi, spoken by the Sikhs) languages. Contemporaneously, Roy endeavored to get into contact with the Sikhs in Western North America, and to convert them into supporters for Red revolt in India.[156]

However with the suppression of the Communists in China in the summer of 1927 Roy was compelled to give up these sundry activities and return to Europe. From there, on December 30th of that year, Roy sent a long letter to the Indian Communists which was obviously an attempt on his part to regain his leadership of Indian Communism which had been lost to the emissaries of the British Communist party. The letter, which was intercepted by British authorities, chided the Communists for allowing conservative elements to enter the workers' and peasants' parties. For example, Roy argued that both the then president and a former president of the Bengal Workers' and Peasants' Party were landlords.[157]

Roy made it clear in his letter that his "centres" in Berlin and not the British Communists should act as Moscow's lieutenants in furthering Communism in India by stating that

> the centres in Berlin are the agencies of the C.I. (Communist International) to look after the Indian affairs . . . The C.P. of India will have its relations with the C.I. through these centres and not through London.[158]

A tentative effort was made early in 1928 by the Comintern to heal the breach between Roy's group in Berlin, which was now putting out its own organ, "Masses of India," as successor to the "Advance Guard," and Moscow's principal lieutenant in Indian affairs, the C.P.G.B. To this end instructions were sent forth for the creation of a "three-man" Foreign Bureau, the members of which would be Roy, Sepassi and Allison, the latter representing the C.P.G.B. which group would foment

Communist subversion in India.[159] But in practice, the British Communists maintained their control, and Roy vented his displeasure by not attending the Sixth Congress of the Comintern, held between July and September, 1928, but instead sulked in his tent in Berlin.

* * * * *

The British Communist Party, M. N. Roy and his "centres" and the Indian Communists themselves were not the sole instruments of Moscow's designs on India. The leaders of the Soviets, were capable of publicly laying down the policies to be followed by international Communism towards India. Thus on May 18, 1925, Stalin, now emerging as Russia's dictator, noted in the case of India that the "national bourgeoisie had split into a revolutionary and a conciliatory party" and held the latter group had come to terms with British imperialism because

> fearing revolution more than imperialism, more concerned about its moneybags than the interest of its own motherland, this part of the bourgeoisie, the wealthiest and most influential, has both feet in the camp of the irreconcilable enemies of the revolution (and) forms a coalition with imperialism against the workers and peasants of its own country.[160]

As a result, held Stalin, "the revolution cannot be successful unless this coalition is broken." To break it a revolutionary bloc must be formed led by the proletariat in general and the Communists in particular. This bloc could take the form of a single "workers' and peasants' party, which would embody an alliance of the proletariat led by the Communists, and the 'revolutionary' section of the bourgeoisie," which alliance would, of course, really be dominated by the proletariat and, above all, by its "vanguard," the Communists.[161]

This policy which was substantially that which Roy had been trying to carry out since 1922, and which as we have seen was the policy of the Communists in India during the years 1925-1928, would seem to be one of alarm to the British since it had been enunciated by Russia's emerging top man. To sooth British nerves Foreign Minister Chicherin in an official statement declared "all the legends put out about the alleged interference of our Government in India are based on simple invention."[162]

Speeches by Stalin were not the only means of direct Soviet intervention in Indian matters. Thus, not only did the General Secretary of the Red International of Labour Unions, Comrade Lozovsky, commend the "aid" of his Soviet-sponsored organization to the Cawnpore Congress of the A.I.T.U.C. in November, 1927,[163] but the Soviet trade union system itself intervened in the large-scale strike of Bombay textile workers a few months later. According to the admission from a Communist source, the sums of Rs. 20,917 and 14,101 in two consignments were sent by the Central Committee of the Russian Textile Union to the Joint Strike Committee of the Bombay textile workers which enabled the latter to provide sustenance for the strikers.[164] It may be noted that the first consignment was not directed to Communist unionists but rather to N. M. Joshi, a conservative Indian labor leader, much to the chagrin of the former. However, the receipt of "bolshevik gold" did not embarrass Joshi and he even remarked that this was "not the first time that such help has come but the third time" and added that "there is nothing harmful in accepting money from Moscow or anywhere else for the support of the strike."[165] In this context one may remark that a responsible observer of the history of Indian trade unionism has declared that Soviet "assistance" to India from the years 1925 to 1932 amounted to Rs. 46,408 in addition to 25,000 rubles.[166]

In addition to this tangible support the Soviets saw fit to bolster the Communist cause in India in 1928 by moral support from their controlled press, notably from a periodical entitled "Novii Vostok" ("New East") and also from the official party newspaper, "Pravda." Indeed, following the failure of the Chinese Communist revolution of 1927, Soviet attention was all the more directed towards India, and it was constantly repeated in the Russian press that the errors of the Communists in China should be carefully analyzed so that they would not again be repeated in India.[167] It may be added, that the Russian Communists secretly sent an agent of their own to India, a certain Indian named Fazal Illahi, who had been trained in Moscow, probably at the Communist University of the Toilers of the East.[168] This indicates that Moscow was not willing to yield the field of promoting Communism in India entirely to the Communist Party of Great Britain or to Roy, for that matter.

In the summer of 1928 Moscow ordered a most significant change in policies of the Indian Communists. In the report of the Communist International prepared for the Sixth Congress of that organization, the whole concept of having the Indian Communists utilize the service of a workers' and peasants' party to further the Communist cause was challenged. The report held:

> . . . (The) weak point of the Workers' and Peasants' Party is, that, in practice, it is acting more as a Left wing of the Congress than as an independent political Party . . . It is entirely out of the question that the Workers' and Peasants' Party should be a substitute for the Communist Party, the organisation of which is absolutely necessary.[169]

The Sixth Congress of the Third International was duly held between July 17 and August 28, 1928. Representing the Indian Communists at this Moscow conference were four men, "Sikander Sur," and three individuals known as Raza, Mahmoud and Narayan. "Sikander Sur" was none other than Shaukat Usmani who upon his release from prison had once more plunged into Communist work. He "slipped out of India,"[170] at the end of June in order to attend the Sixth Congress. Also present at the Congress was R. Palme Dutt who really directed the Indian delegation.

As the principal Indian delegate Usmani stated what India's Reds' role would be in event of an Anglo-Soviet war:

> We have already concrete plans to deal blows in the rear if Imperialism adopts the offensive. We (shall) get the enemy between two fires, and his plans on Turkestan will be destroyed. India is the most vulnerable spot from which it is possible to deliver British Imperialism a mortal blow.

> Every section of the Comintern must co-operate with us, and each in his own country must facilitate our work. With such co-operation, the day is not distant when we shall hurl British Imperialism into the Indian Ocean.[171]

Delegate Raza dealt with the question of the workers' and peasants' parties in respect to the Communist Party of India. He noted with some concern that in his official report to the Executive Committee of the Comintern, Bukharin, a leading Soviet delegate, had showed his distaste (and that of the E.C.C.I.) for these parties by not even mentioning them in it. Raza affirmed that the "W.P.P.'s" had "so far been the organisers, of the workers in the present struggle against the bourgeoisie—a fact "which cannot be overlooked," and added "in this struggle every credit must be given to our comrades who are influencing the whole movement through the Workers' and Peasants' Parties."[172] But Raza quickly added his approval to the necessity for the development of a strong Communist Party in India.[173]

Reference to India was made by the well-known Finnish Comintern leader, Kuusinen, who affirmed that India would be the area of the next serious revolutionary outburst. Consequently, held Kuusinen, the Communist International should "focus its attention" there and should thus strengthen the Communists in India "to handle the coming revolutionary situation."[174]

India likewise was duly considered in the "Thesis on the Revolutionary Movement in the Colonies and semi-Colonies" adopted by the Sixth Congress.[175] The thesis which presented a Communist interpretation of Indian history from 1914 to 1928, excoriated "British imperialism" in the usual severe terms. The "national bourgeoisie" was also castigated.[176] But, unlike the case in Stalin's speech of May, 1925, (it appears the dictator had changed his mind) there was no differentiation between the "conciliatory" and the "revolutionary" wings of this bourgeoisie, the latter wing being of such a nature the Communists could collaborate with it. The thesis only stated the "national bourgeoisie" merely "exerts a breaking, retarding influence on the development of the revolutionary movement." Hence, Communists should reject "the formation of any kind of bloc between the Communist Party and the national-reformist opposition," although merely "temporary agreements" with them might be in order.[177] For in India and other colonies "Communist Parties" must "demarcate themselves in the most clear-cut fashion both politically and organisationally from all the petty bourgeois groups and parties."[178]

Referring again only to India it was stated that

> the basic tasks of the Indian Communists consist in a struggle against British Imperialism for the emancipation of the country, for the destruction of all relics of feudalism, for the agrarian revolution and for establishment of the dictatorship of the proletariat and peasantry in the form of a Soviet Republic.[179]

In order to carry out this program there must be a "union of all Communist groups and individual Communists scattered throughout the country into a single, illegal, independent and centralised party" and so the effectuation of this union "represents the first task of the Indian Communists."[180] As for the Communist-controlled workers' and peasants' parties and the proposed All-India Workers' and Peasants' Party the thesis warned the Indian comrades that "Communists are not recommended to organise such parties" because they "can too easily . . . be converted into ordinary petty bourgeois parties;" hence the Indian "Communist Party can never build its organisation on the basis of a fusion of two classes," the workers and the peasants.[181]

The thesis of the Sixth Congress of the Communist International, therefore, established a new party line for the Indian Communists by its emphasis on the need for the thorough establishment and independent isolation of the Communist party, per se, with a corresponding virtual abandonment of the workers' and peasants' parties. The thesis likewise abandoned the tactic of a united front against "imperialism," a tactic that had been evinced by the participation of Communists in the National Congress itself and its tacit approval of the Congress resultant from that body's Madras resolution on Indian independence. The thesis was manifestly also featured by its violent advocacy of "armed insurrection" as the ultimate aim of Communist activity in India. On this basis the thesis was conducive to the weakening of the Communists' position among potential fellow travelers of the non-Communist left who would be frightened by this new expressly violent approach. Moreover, the emphasis on the building up of a strong Communist party as such in India was somewhat assinine in that no overtly Communist party would possibly be permitted to exist openly by the Anglo-Indian authorities. In the year, 1928, the Communist Party of India as an illegal organization could only, in fact, exist, as a necessarily small body, completely obscured from the glare of publicity. Consequently, the decisions of the Sixth Congress of the Comintern as manifested in its thesis represented a reverse to Indian Communism. That it did so in the eyes of the C.P.G.B. is indicated by the following notation from R. P. Dutt commenting on the new unfriendly line of the Comintern towards the workers' and peasants' parties as represented in the thesis:

> The question of the Workers' and Peasants' Parties cannot be dismissed with a phrase of this sort . . . (their uselessness). The characteristic feature of the Workers' and Peasants' Parties in the present stage of development in India is that they are forming an important route through which the Communists are finding their way to the masses.[182]

In apparent defiance of the will of the Kremlin, the Indian Communists and their British mentors continued to work with the Workers' and Peasants' party. Indeed, the already-scheduled First Conference of the All-India Workers' and Peasants' Party which conference united delegates from the various parties of that name throughout India, was held in Calcutta in December, 1928.[183] This conference was an open one and was tolerated by the British authorities.

But this was not the only conference to be held in the capital of Bengal. The other was a conference of the Communist Party of India, a meeting designed to discuss the new lines which the Communist Party of India should take in view of the decision taken at the Sixth Congress of the Communist International. This Conference, it may be remarked, was a strictly clandestine meeting of Communist bosses.

As with other Communist and Communist-controlled conferences, that of the All-India Workers' and Peasants' Party in Calcutta duly presented an elaborate thesis which violently assailed the "provocative and apparently stupid policy of British imperialism,"[184] and severely castigated the "Indian bourgeoisie" for its alleged policy of "retreat."[185]

As to its program, the thesis came out for complete national independence for India, the expropriation of the zamindars (landlords), the nationalization of key industries, and reforms in industry such as that of the eight-hour day.[186]

International questions, it may be added, were also not absent in the thesis of this puppet party. Its members were informed that "a campaign of propaganda must be conducted against the war danger, and particularly against the war preparations against Soviet Russia," while at the same time

> the international nature of the revolutionary nationalist and working-class movement must be emphasized in a concrete manner and examples from current politics brought before the masses, particularly the workers.[187]

But while speeches were uttered and resolutions were drawn up at the conference of the Workers' and Peasants' party of December, 1928, in another part of Calcutta the entirely secret meeting of the real leaders of the Workers' and Peasants' party took place on 121A Circular Road.[188] There, acting upon the directives of the Communist International which had been reinforced by a letter from M. N. Roy in the preceding September,[189] the Red leaders of India decided that the Communist party which had previously not functioned as such and was only at most a small secret society, must "come out into the open," since their "objective," a "revolutionary situation, was there." The conspirators also agreed that their party should apply for formal affiliation to the Communist International as one of its sections. It was agreed that every effort should be made to overthrow the rule of the Anglo-Indian government and to destroy the economic power of the Indian bourgeoisie.[190] At the same time a constitution for the party specifically denominated as the Communist Party of India, was drawn up and its executive committee was selected. The members of this executive committee, who fancied that their operations were concealed from the Anglo-Indian authorities, busily furthered their plans for revolution, which plans were discussed at a special meeting held in Bombay on March 17-19, 1929.[191] But before that meeting was held, the British Communists undoubtedly received orders from the Comintern that their Indian protegés must abandon the workers' and peasants' parties forthwith, and on this occasion the almighty will of the Kremlin was meekly obeyed. Hence, reflecting obedience to this command, R. P. Dutt declared: "I think that there is a very real danger of the petty bourgeois elements getting hold of the W.P.P.'s."[192] As a consequence, just one month after the session of its All-India Congress, the workers' and peasants' party movement was abandoned by the British Communists and their Indian charges loyally followed suit. Henceforth, in the publications of the Comintern, the workers' and peasants' parties were treated with savage scorn and harsh hostility.[193]

At the meeting of the Communist leaders in Bombay between March 17th and 19th, 1929, the new course the Communist Party should take, was discussed. At this meeting Dr. G. M. Adhikari who, while he was in Berlin obtaining a Doctorate in Chemistry, had been converted to Communism by Roy's "centre" in the German capital, presented concrete proposals for the organization of the party. By his plan the Indian Communist party was to be organized into five departments, dealing with trade unions, the peasantry, propaganda, organizational development and political control—the details for the formulation of which were to be formulated by a sub-committee. This program for a hoped for puissant Communist party was accepted in theory.[194] The meeting undoubtedly also studied a memorandum of violent character issued by the Communist International which called for a revolution in India. After having called for "militant support for a revolution in India," this manifesto from Moscow concluded with the dramatic words: "Long live the Soviet Republic of India."[195]

This represented a challenge by Moscow to Britain's rule in India and the British were determined to meet it. British authorities in London and New Delhi alike had been by no means ignorant of Russia's fifth column inside India. Scotland Yard and the C.I.D. of India were generally aware of the movements of British and Indian Communists, and, as we have noted, much of the correspondence which passed between Communists in India and their colleagues in Britain was duly intercepted. British officialdom was thus cognizant of the Communist threat to India and important officials periodically indicated that knowledge publicly. For example, on May 15, 1925, the Home Secretary of the Conservative Ministry of Stanley Baldwin, Sir William Joynson-Hicks made the flat declaration that "India is one of the first objectives of the Bolshevik campaign. The East is the main endeavour of the world revolution."[196]

Certain prominent Indians were also aware of the Red threat. Thus Shiva Rao, the Chairman of the Executive Committee of the A.I.T.U.C. and foe of the Communists in that body averred in May, 1928:

> The time has come . . . when the trade union movement in India should weed out of its organisation, mischief makers. A warning is all the more necessary because there are certain individuals who go about preaching the gospel of strike.[197]

Moreover, the saintly Gandhi, spiritual leader of the Congress[198] and the leadership of the Muslim League had no sympathy for the Communists.

The Anglo-Indian government was determined, in the words of Shiva Rao to "weed out" the Communist "mischief makers" of India. As early as the close of 1924 and January, 1925, the Anglo-Indian police conducted a series of raids on Communist and pro-Communist organizations which culminated on January 30th in the closing down of a clandestine newspaper in Cawnpore called "The Revolutionary." This paper had claimed that it was following in the footsteps simultaneously of the glorious Indian rishis (sages) of the past and "Bolshevist Russia (of) today."[199] In January, 1927, George Allison, alias Donald Campbell was arrested by the Anglo-Indian police while organizing the Bengal Workers' and Peasants' Party. He received a prison sentence of eighteen months the following March and was then deported to England.[200]

On August 25, 1928, the Anglo-Indian government requested the Indian Legislative Assembly to enact legislation permitting the deportation of subversive agents who were not British-Indian subjects or subjects of Indian states. Such agents could either be other subjects of Great Britain or nationals of other countries.[201] Manifestly, non-Indian Communist agitators were the persons aimed at by the proposed law.

The bill was opposed by Indian Nationalists, both in their press and by their representatives in the Assembly, on the ground that the measure could be employed "against all foreigners who show or act in sympathy with Indian aspirations, economic and political."[202] As a result, in spite of the fact that the bill was supported by most Muslim representatives and the "Europeans," it suffered defeat in the Assembly on September 25, 1928 by the tie-breaking vote of the speaker of the Assembly, the Congress leader, Vithalbhai Patel.[203]

The government of the Viceroy, Lord Irwin (now Lord Halifax) re-introduced this measure, known as the Public Safety Bill on January 21, 1929 with hopes that the manifestly growing influence of the Communist party as indicated by the audacious convention of the All-India Workers' and Peasants' Party in December, 1928, would have created such apprehension as to secure its enactment.[204]

To facilitate the bill's passage, Lord Irwin addressed the Assembly and declared that for him the disquieting spread of Communism had been "causing an anxiety" and he argued that all classes of Indian society were endangered by the dissemination of Communist doctrines. He also contended that both Bombay and Calcutta had suffered from Communist-instigated strikes.[205]

Once again the Congress forces in the Assembly, led as in

the previous year by Motilal Nehru, fought the bill on the floor of that body with all the parliamentary dexterity of which they were capable.[206] Consequently, the Anglo-Indian government determined to act without waiting for Assembly action. Striking suddenly and swiftly in the latter part of March, 1929, police swept down on the Communists' headquarters and the headquarters of their front organizations, in Bombay and Poona in the West, in Calcutta and Dacca in the East, and in Lucknow, Allahabad and Lahore in the North. Hundreds of houses were searched and much Communistic literature in English and vernacular tongues, examples of which bore such titles as "What is Communism" and "What is Bolshevism," were seized.[207] At the same time, many arrests were made throughout India which involved all Moscow's important minions in the subcontinent. In Bombay, S. A. Dange, Shaukat Usmani, (who had sneaked back into India after his visit to the Sixth Congress of the Comintern) S. V. Ghate, R. S. Nimbkar, S. S. Mirajkar and G. M. Adhikari were apprehended as was Ben Bradley, their British Communist mentor. In Calcutta those arrested included Muzaffar Ahmad, Dharani Goswami, and R. R. Mitra, the leading Indian leaders of Communism in Bengal and their British adviser, Phillip Spratt. P. C. Joshi and Abdul Majid, the Communist leaders, in the United Provinces and the Punjab respectively, were likewise taken into custody.[208] Shortly afterwards, the young Britisher, Lester Hutchinson, editor of the newly formed pro-Communist journal, "New Spark," was also arrested.[209] In all, no fewer than thirty-two leading Indian leftists together with their three British tutors were arrested under the authority of Section 121A of the Indian penal code which legalized the imprisonment of those who would "deprive the King of the sovereignty of British India," the same provision which had been utilized in the Cawnpore Conspiracy case. Not all of those arrested were Communists, but even these had been fellow travelers who had supported the Communist cause in varying degrees. The arrests broke the back, for a time, of the Communist conspiracy in India. The arrests likewise dealt a severe blow to the over-all labor movement in India, many unions there, especially in Bombay and Calcutta, losing their leaders. This fact manifestly testified to the extent to which the Communists had been able to penetrate into the Indian labor movement in the spring of 1929.[210]

Further emphasizing its determination to stamp out Communist activity, the Viceroy proclaimed the Public Safety Bill as law on April 13, 1929 by vice-regal ordinance which was his prerogative under the British Indian Constitution of 1919,[211] and in the same month the Legislative Assembly enacted a "Trades Disputes" Act which like the Public Safety Bill, was passed for a duration of five years. The former act, which was evidently aimed against Communist labor organizers, barred certain types of strikes in public utility services, and sympathy strikes and also granted the authorities the right to ban strikes which the latter deemed would endanger the public interest.[212]

Thus Communism in India had suffered severe reverses. By Moscow's ukase they had been compelled to abandon their collaboration with the Congress and the formation of a broad front of workers, peasants and petty bourgeoisie in an All-Indian Workers' and Peasants' Party. By the Public Safety Act, they could no longer legally receive open support and advice from British Communists within India itself, by the Trades Union Act their activities in the Indian labor movement were bound to be curtailed and by the arrest of their leaders, the Communist movement in the sub-continent was veritably paralyzed and thereby the designs of Moscow on India were once again thwarted.

CHAPTER FOUR

Underground Communism in India

After having arrested the leaders of the Communist Party of India, the Anglo-Indian Government sent them to the town of Meerut in the United Provinces (Uttar Pradesh) to be tried for conspiracy against the rule of the King-Emperor in India.[1] The reason for the selection of Meerut, a relatively small provincial town as the venue of the trial was the fact that the Workers' and Peasants' Party of the United Province had been organized there even though this branch of the Communist conspiracy in India was small as compared to the Communist groups in the metropolitan areas of Bombay and Calcutta.[2] On the other hand, Communists complained that Meerut had been selected as the venue of the trial to "smash" the revolutionary movement. For example, Meerut was designed "to deter European Communists from giving any help to the revolutionary movement in India."[3]

Of the thirty-three men (the journalist, Lester Hutchinson was arrested several weeks after the detention of his comrades) arrested, twenty were Communists, by membership or conviction, including the Britons, Spratt, and Bradley. The remaining were in varying degrees, "fellow travelers" of the Communist Party of India.[4] All the prisoners, Communist and "fellow travelers" alike, were sternly refused bail by the British authorities.[5]

Owing to the peculiar importance of the case, a special preliminary trial, known as the Magisterial Enquiry was carried on in Meerut against the Communists under Special Magistrate Milner White, and Langford James was the chief prosecutor for the Crown.[6] As a result of the efforts of a special committee set up by the All-India Congress Committee, a fairly imposing staff of Indian attorneys were brought together to defend the prisoners.[7]

The arrests, needless to say, provoked bitter reaction not only from the Communists of Russia who were naturally angered by the severe blow administered to their agents in India, and from the British Communists, and radical elements in Indian labor, but also from non-Communist radicals in England and from the leaders of the Indian National Congress as well.

Moscow was manifestly furious that the promising Communist movement in India had been so suddenly decimated. Russian fury was reflected in an unusually violent manifesto from the Communist International which appeared early in April, 1929, a few weeks after the arrests. In the manifesto, "British imperialists" were branded as "the plunderers and hangmen of India" and the Swarajists and other bourgeois parties were assailed as "traitors to the Indian National Revolution." The Legislative Assembly was referred to as "this Diet of a handful of corrupted plutocrats," while the Simon Commission was denounced as "a gang of spies roving about India." This was in line with the assumption that "imperialism is hurling itself with all the force of military terror against the toilers of India." This "terror" was supposed to be correlated with hostile designs of Great Britain upon the Soviet Union, for the manifesto argued:

> The plans of British imperialism for the coming world slaughter are set by its aim to hold fast its monopoly in the plunder of India without having to share out its profits with other imperialist robbers. Subjugated, exhausted, losing millions of her sons through starvation, India must also provide cannon fodder for the British war machine.[8]

The notion that India would play a role in an imaginary British attack upon Russia was further alluded to in the expression: "The threads of imperialist war now being plotted are stretched out to India," for, relying on India as a base, "British imperialism" is preparing to carry out its long cherished plan of a "strategic assault" on the Soviet Union, presumably across Afghanistan and into Russian Central Asia.[9] In addition, the manifesto bluntly maintained that "only a . . . proletarian revolution will destroy imperialism and (its) bourgeois allies" and that "here in India meet the paths of the growing world revolution, marching into war against imperialism."[10] Thus the manifesto gave vent to Moscow's feeling of enraged frustration on the sudden disaster to befall the Communist movement in India.[11] The manifesto is also interesting in its savage assault on the Indian bourgeoisie which was in furtherance of the line dating to the Comintern's Sixth Congress that no popular front should be established between the proletariat, which the Communists hoped to control, and those bourgeois elements seeking autonomy or even complete independence for India.[12]

Another blast from the Moscow Comintern issued on April 7, 1929 specifically dealt with the Meerut arrests stating:

> Imperialism is hurling itself with all the force of military terror against the toilers of India. Their trade union leaders, their newspaper editors and the participants of open conference of workers and peasants are threatened with execution or with hard labour in prisons. Justice must be meted in the colonial chamber of torture without even the farce of a sworn jury or the staging of a trial. It is to open a new chapter in the bloody oppressions of the country with its 300,000,000 people.[13]

Outside of the Communists, the non-Communist but leftist Independent Labour Party of Britain was also bitterly critical of the arrest of the Indian radicals, and evinced considerable sympathy for them.[14] However, the Labour Party as well as the British Trades Union movement's leadership condoned the arrests.[15] Indeed, it was not until 1933, when the Labour Party (which was in office from 1929 to 1931) was again in opposition, that criticism was expressed by leading Labourites on the trial of the radical agitators of India.[16]

The news of the arrest of the Communists and their fellow travelers engendered much excitement throughout India, particularly in Bombay. There, on March 28, 1929 some 3,000 workers, belonging mainly to the Red-controlled G.I.P. (Great Indian Peninsula) Railwaymen's union staged a "procession" of protest which was broken up by a "baton charge" by the police when the "men refused to disperse."[17] Simultaneously, fourteen textile mills were struck in protest by workers whose Red Girni Kamgar Union had been especially decimated by the arrest of its leaders.[18] However, pressure by the authorities made this strike a short one. The fact that in Bombay a number of Anglo-Indian infantry units were mobilized as well as squadrons of well-armed police prevented the demonstration in that city from becoming more serious.

The news of the arrests had surprisingly strong repercussions in the National Congress and its political arm, the Swarajist Party. A Central Defence Committee, consisting chiefly of important Congressmen was formed to aid the accused. On March 23, 1929 this committee, which had been set up by the Congress Working Committee, "contrary to its usual practice," made a grant of Rs. 1,500 towards the defense.[19] In addition, an appeal was made to the public over the signature of Pandit Motilal Nehru and other Congress leaders to support the defense fund of the prisoners.[20]

The fact that a number of the accused were persons holding important rank in the Congress undoubtedly contributed to the solicitude of the leaders of that organization for the welfare of those, who had they been able, would surely have carried out policies detrimental to the National Congress.[21] It may also be noted that the Meerut convicts received sympathetic attention from a considerable portion of the Indian press.[22]

Among noted Indians taking an interest in the cause of the imprisoned radicals was Pandit Jawaharlal Nehru. In his autobiography he remarks that he became a member of the Meerut Conspiracy Case Central Defence Committee. In this capacity, Nehru observes that he and his colleagues had no easy time in dealing with the accused since there was a complete lack of harmony between them,[23] thus indicating a split between the outright Communists and the erstwhile fellow-travellers who now felt that they had taken the wrong road in their collaboration with the minions of Moscow.

It may be noted that Jawaharlal Nehru himself was not at that time beyond suspicion in regard to the Meerut conspiracy case. His visit to Moscow in 1927 and the resulting praise he had bestowed on the Soviet Union must have engendered a measure of suspicion towards him on the part of the British authorities. This suspicion was all the more brought forth during the course of the trial when one of the exhibits was revealed as a letter from the Communist Party of India to Jawaharlal Nehru which stated:

> If you are organisationally prepared, you will be able to strike a blow just as Gandhi was able to do in 1921. But I hope that this time there will be no sentimental nonsense about the shedding of a few litres of blood and that the revolutionary movement will be on purely materialistic lines.[24]

Indeed, at one time, the prosecution actually called on Nehru to produce other letters written to him by the Communists; however he was able to escape interrogation by the Crown counsel.[25]

Mahatma Gandhi also visited the Meerut prisoners in the autumn of 1929, but he was not particularly active in their behalf. Convict Hutchinson claimed that "he (Gandhi) had washed his hands of us."[26]

During the course of the Magisterial Inquiry and the formal trial in the Sessions Court which followed, the attorneys for the Crown stressed the relationship of the Indian Communists with the Comintern of Moscow. Accordingly, in the opening phase of the Magisterial Inquiry, the chief prosecutor for the Crown, Langford James, emphasized the role of Moscow in carrying on Communist propaganda in India and among Indian students residing in various British universities.[27] Besides, another attorney for the Crown, J. P. Mitter, specifically argued that the conspiracy "was conceived in Europe, primarily in Moscow and had been throughout fomented, directed and financed from there."[28] In addition, the prosecution pointed out the relationship of various Moscow-controlled and directed front agencies such as the Red International of Labour Unions, the National Minorities Movement and the League Against Imperialism to the furtherance of Communism in India.[29]

Besides stressing the subversive character of the Comintern to the entire non-Communist world Chief Crown Counsel James also emphasized the view that the Communists who in Russia harshly oppressed their own people,[30] were bent on annihilating the social structure of India, notably the so-called national bourgeoisie.[31]

Anticipating a defense argument to the effect that since there was technically no Indian Communist party which was formally a branch of the Communist International and that therefore Indian Communists were not officially members of the Comintern, Prosecutor James held that it was sufficient to show the Indian Communists were acting "at the behest of the Third International" to warrant the conviction of the Indian conspirators.[32]

For the Crown Counsel, the activity of the Communists in the Indian labor movement was a valid case in point. He noted, they had made an all-out effort to secure control of unions engaged in vital and indispensable public services and indeed "they boasted of having captured and controlled most of the big trade unions."[33] The immediate purpose of all of this Communist activity, held James, was to bring about a general strike on an extensive scale on the First of May, 1929.[34] Indeed, the Indian Communists were engaged in vigorous planning upon this ambitious task when they were arrested in March of that year.[35]

Another valid instance of Comintern-inspired activity in India involved efforts by the Communists to subvert young Indian intellectuals. For this aim, noted the Crown Counsel, Communist-controlled associations such as the Calcutta Socialist Youth Conference were founded and "study circles were started," to effectuate the dissemination of Communism.[36]

Realizing that the seizure of the Indian radicals was unpopular, to say the least, among influential Indians, notably in Congress circles, Prosecutor James stressed those features of Communism which he felt were utterly distasteful to the Indian

Nationalists. Thus he stated:

> Now . . . to be a Bolshevik, of unimpeachable character . . . you do not love your country, you are anti-country, you are anti-God and you are anti-family. In fact . . . it is fair to say that a Bolshevik, of unimpeachable character is anti-everything which the normal man can consider decent.[37]

Chief Prosecutor James went on to lay great stress upon the anti-patriotic and anti-religious character of Indian Communists.[38] However, he made it clear that the case was not directed against non-Communist trade unionists nor against Indian Nationalists. It was directed exclusively against the Communist conspiracy which was hatched in Moscow.[39]

As rebuttal, the Indian attorneys for the defense presented a bewildering variety of arguments. The senior Defence Counsel, Mr. D. P. Sinha, maintained that the case represented the first systematic prosecution of the Anglo-Indian Government of a number of men for "holding certain ideals and cherishing certain beliefs," even though their actions had really not been illegal.[40] Another defense attorney, K. C. Chakravarty argued that "the only law which applied to such a conspiracy was the Law of Nations." Hence a "municipal tribunal" such as that of Meerut had no true jurisdiction over the case.[41] He also contended, apparently in earnest, that the charge of depriving the King-Emperor of sovereignty in India was an invalid one, because "if anyone should successfully deprive the King of sovereignty, laws promulgated by His Majesty would cease to exist." As a result, the person or persons depriving him of sovereignty "would frame new laws and establish their own courts" and so "it would not be possible to prosecute them in their own courts." Hence, "the act of such depriving was no offence."[42]

While opposing counsel were presenting these arguments, certain of the prisoners boldly manifested their loyalty to Communism. On July 18, 1929 some of the conspirators audaciously sang the "Internationale" and on the following September 15th, the sedate court was startled by shouts of some defendants of "Down with the White Terror and the British Government," and the singing of the "Red Flag."[43] In addition, certain of the accused boldly admitted Communist precepts. Muzaffar Ahmad stated, "I am a revolutionary Communist,"[44] Dange audaciously asserted that "the aim of the Communist is the overthrow of imperialism and capitalism and (the) immediate aim of the Communist in India is the overthrow of British imperialism,"[45] while Nimbkar noted that "we have no objection to help by the Russian Working Class; in fact, we consider that India should welcome such help."[46]

In the latter part of September, 1929, certain of the Communist conspirators, emulating the methods of Gandhi, engaged in a fast on the ground they were ill-treated in jail.[47] By the fifth day of the strike, the prisoners were suffering discomfort, and they were pleased to suspend it on the excuse that the All-India Congress Committee (a bourgeois-dominated organ at that!) had passed a resolution calling on the Meerut prisoners to abandon their fast since it was "no longer necessary."[48]

The first phase of the Meerut Conspiracy Case, the Magisterial Inquiry, lasted seven months, from the middle of May to December 15, 1929. On January 13, 1930 the Committal Order by which the accused were formally ordered to be tried by the Court of Special Sessions, was rendered. All the prisoners except Dharamvir Singh, who was released, were committed to stand trial in the formal process.[49]

The formal trial of the Indian Communists and their fellow-travelers, the second phase of the conspiracy case, got under way before Judge R. L. Yorke in the Court of Special Sessions in Meerut on January 31, 1930 in spite of efforts by the defense to effect a change of venue and institute trial by jury.[50] The trial then dragged duly and dully along, featured by the defendants' dilatory tactics in their exercise of their right to cross-examine the numerous witnesses for the Crown.[51] On March 17, 1931 after no fewer than 281 witnesses were examined, the prosecution concluded its case. This was followed by the rendering of the formal statements of the accused. The Communists took advantage of this occasion to proclaim audaciously and defiantly their ideology.[52] Late in January, 1932, the formal defense of the accused was inaugurated. Although attorneys D. P. Sinha, Sheo Prasad and Pandit P. L. Sharma served as defense counsel at this time, some of the accused chose to plead their own cases.[53]

During the proceedings involving the formal defense of the accused, which was five months in duration,[54] the non-Communist accused availed themselves of the services of thirty-six witnesses, the most notable of these being N. M. Joshi, the then principal leader of the Indian labor movement. The Communist accused endeavored to call witnesses from abroad, but when this request was denied by the court, the Indian comrades decided to call no witnesses at all to their defense, by way of a protest.[55]

The trial reached its closing phase on June 16, 1932 when the special prosecutor for the Crown, M. I. Kemp, renewed the prosecution's case against the defendants. In conformity with Indian legal procedure, four Indian assessors—advisory judges—rendered their verdicts on August 17, 1932, which had no binding force whatever. It is noteworthy, however, that they found most of the Communists guilty and many of the non-Communists not guilty.[56] The court was now adjourned for judgment.

It may be noted that in the period of over three years in which the trial had taken place, during both the Magisterial Inquiry and the Court of Sessions proceedings, no fewer than 637 witnesses (nearly all were witnesses for the Crown) were examined and some 2,600 documents covering 10,000 printed pages were adduced as evidence.[57] So great was the strain on the prosecution in presenting this mammoth amount of evidence that several members of the prosecution staff broke down and Langford James, the Chief Crown Counsel died in May, 1930, his place being taken, as noted, by M. I. Kemp.[58]

After a delay of several months, the Sessions Judge R. L. Yorke, on January 17, 1933 delivered his verdict, which was binding but subject to appeal to the High Court at Allahabad. He sentenced the Bengal Communist, Muzaffar Ahmad to transportation for life, presumably to the Andaman Islands, the Devil's Island of India. Other leading Indian Communists, S. A.

Dange, S. V. Ghate, K. N. Joglekar and R. S. Nimbkar and their British mentor, Philip Spratt, were sentenced to twelve years' transportation. Moreover, the other most prominent Communists, Shaukat Usmani and the British Bolshevik, Ben Bradley, were sentenced to ten years' transportation. Other admittedly Communist accused, as well as non-Communists, received sentences of "transportation" and of "rigorous imprisonment" from three to seven years. Three defendants who had at one time been associated with the Communists, but who now vigorously evidenced opposition to them, were acquitted altogether.[59]

The judgment provoked a violent cry of wrath in the Communist press throughout the world. For instance, a writer in an official Comintern publication screamed that "the sentences are savage."[60] One can perceive the cause of Red rage, for the sentenced represented the flower of Indian Bolshevism whose members had been influential in the growing Indian labor movement.[61] It may be noted that a relatively recent Indian Communist explanation of the conspiracy case has held that

> general elections to (the British) parliament were scheduled to take place in May, 1929. The March, 1929 arrests in India as well as the opening of the political trial was designed by the Conservative Government of Baldwin to play up the 'Communist danger' which was allegedly threatening the entire capitalist world. It was intended to use the trial for preparing the ideological ground for a new anti-Soviet intervention.[62]

The sentences not only produced reaction from Communists in India but anti-Communists as well. Influential Indian journals waxed indignant over the sentences. Thus the "Tribune" of Lahore held that the "utter indefensibleness" of these "severe sentences" was borne out by the fact that "the Judge himself did not find that the accused were members of the Communist International,"[63] and the "Mahratta" of Poona registered wrath over "the savage and shocking sentences" and added that "we pray for good luck and sound health to them in jail."[64]

The Meerut trial sentences likewise produced a surprisingly

sharp reaction in England, and on the Continent. Protests on the severity of the sentences were rendered by such notables as Dr. Albert Einstein, Romain Rolland, H. G. Wells, R. H. Tawney, and Professor Harold Laski.[65] Furthermore, the National Joint Council of the Trades Union Congress and the Labour Party issued a brochure which stated that "the whole of the proceedings from beginning to end are utterly indefensible and constitute something in the nature of a judicial scandal."[66] The Independent Labour party reiterated its earlier sharp criticism of the Meerut case.[67] On the other hand, however, in its official leader on the "Meerut Trial," the "Times" approved of the trial and its results holding the process had been "conducted with exemplary fairness, and with the most meticulous compliance with Indian law."[68]

While the mild furor was going on within and without India about the verdict of Judge Yorke,[69] the wheels of justice continued to turn in India. In February, 1933, it was revealed that a formal appeal for review of the case to the High Court at Allahabad had been made, and in April the appeal was officially considered by that court and simultaneously, some of the professedly non-Communist prisoners were released on bail.[70] In July, 1933 the case was officially resumed by the High Court, and as it deliberated, in Westminster Labour and Independent Labour MP's argued on behalf of the Indian radicals.[71]

On August 4, 1933, judgment was rendered by Chief Justice Sulaiman and Justice Young which drastically reduced the sentences of the conspirators. No sentences more severe than three years incarceration were rendered, such sentences being given to the leading Communists, Dange, Muzzafar Ahmad and Usmani. Other Communists escaped with sentences ranging from seven months to two years.[72] At the same time, all the non-Communists were released outright. Some of the latter were formally acquitted while others were simply released on the ground that their detention during the trial was sufficient punishment. Among those acquitted outright were the alleged Communists, the Indian R. R. Mitra, and the Briton, Lester Hutchinson.[73] Indeed, later in the year, 1933, only four Communists were still in detention.[74]

In spite of their leniency, however, the justices of the High Court "held the prosecution was justified and complimented the police." They argued that severe sentences had been necessary, "but held that four years' detention" during the course of the trial "was sufficient and that that there was ground for reduction" of sentences.[75]

Grim satisfaction over the release of the prisoners was registered by international Communism, the reaction of which may be epitomized in the following terse statement by A. M. Dyakov, a contemporary Soviet "expert" on India who held:

> Under the pressure of a mass protest in India as well as beyond its frontiers, the English government was obliged to release them before the expiration of their sentences.[76]

Like grim satisfaction was expressed in the Indian nationalist press,[77] and Liberal and Labour publications in Great Britain.[78]

* * * * *

While the Meerut case was dragging tediously along, important events were occurring in the Peninsula. On January 26, 1930, India was proclaimed as "independent" by the Congress, and shortly thereafter the latter sponsored a program of civil disobedience to convert the fictional "independence" into reality. The British Raj responded with repression, including the incarceration of the revered Gandhi. The crisis was not resolved by the First Round Table Conference in London from November 12th, 1930 to January 31st, 1931, in which the Congress was not represented. Although an agreement between the Congress and the British (the Gandhi-Lord Irwin agreement or Delhi Pact) in March, 1931 temporarily eased the crisis, the failure of the Second London Round Table Conference held from September 7th to December 1st, 1931 led to the renewal of civil disobedience, in turn resulting in the imprisonment of tens of thousands of Indians including Gandhi and the banning of the Congress. Bowing to British power, the Indian Nationalists abandoned civil disobedience with the personal exception of Gandhi in May, 1934 and the Congress was again legalized in the following month and its imprisoned leaders released. From the summer of 1934 till the opening of the year, 1936, there was little militant nationalist activity in India.[79]

But in spite of the advice of Gandhi, the civil disobedience movement was not an altogether peaceful one. In May, 1930 Nationalists briefly seized control of the industrial town of Sholapur in the Bombay Presidency and in April and May of the same year they also temporarily secured possession of the capital of the North-West Frontier Province, Peshawar. The insurrectionary seizures of Sholapur[80] and Peshawar[81] evoked paeons of praise in the official journal of the Comintern, as did a peasant revolt in the princely state of Kashmir in 1931 against the autocratic rule of the Maharajah which was suppressed with the aid of troops from British India.[82]

In addition to this insurrectionary activity, there was the greatest outburst of terroristic activity in the history of British India, between the years 1929 and 1934. The terroristic outrages which were concentrated in Bengal were decried by the Congress but were approved of in the Comintern press.[83] By the summer of the latter year as a result of thorough British repression, terrorism had become a negligible factor in Bengal and had vanished from other parts of India.[84] The terrorist movement is of significance, for many of the leading terrorists, upon their release from prison, became ardent members of the Communist Party of India.

* * * * *

Between the years 1929 and 1936 that party was subjected to competition on the part of various left-wing movements which refused to obey the ukase of the Kremlin. Such a movement, operating on a strictly regional level, was the "Red Shirt" or Khuda-i-Khadmatgaram ("Servants of God") movement of the North-West Frontier Province, led by Abdul Ghaffer Khan. This movement was much more innocuous than the then beshirted movements of Europe in that it placed its emphasis solely on the need for social and economic reforms and on the rights of the Pathans of the Northwest Frontier area. In

June, 1930 the "Red Shirts," had a following of some 25,000 men.[85]Suspecting that his movement was insurrectionary, the British authorities jailed Abdul Ghaffer Khan, but he was released in March, 1931 as a result of the Delhi Pact.[86] Upon his release, he spoke out sharply against British rule and advocated the partial non-payment of taxes.[87] Consequently, in December, 1931 British authorities again incarcerated Abdul Ghaffer Khan and banned his movement, which by March, 1932, was completely crushed.

Certain British sources claimed that the '"Red Shirt" movement was Soviet inspired, the color of its members' uniforms, among other reasons being cited as proof of this alleged fact.[88] However, important leaders of the National Congress have refuted this charge. Thus they have pointed out that "the Red Shirt Volunteers . . . were Congress volunteers and had nothing to do with the Communist Party,"[89] and "as a matter of fact, they . . . were perfectly non-violent."[90] Hence the sobriquet of Abdul Ghaffer Khan as the "Frontier Gandhi" was justified. Besides, it was held that "a great achievement was wrought when the Kudai Khidmatagars were made a part of the Congress organisation" in 1931.[91] A further refutation of the view that the "Red Shirts" were the agents of Moscow is evinced by the fact that during his long career as a leader of the Pathans from 1930 to the present day, Abdul Ghaffer Khan has demonstrated no specific evidence of special sympathy for Soviet Russia. On the other hand, however, it must be admitted that the Comintern's press did not shower the kind of abuse on the "Red Shirts" which it so freely bestowed on other non-Communist left-wing Indian groups.[92]

The Red Shirt movement, then, as an affiliate of the Congress and an organization which sponsored social reform of a vaguely socialist character may be considered as a movement, competitive to the Communists in winning the favor of the masses of the North-West Frontier Province, although a certain measure of Communist infiltration into the ranks of that movement may well have taken place.

A more serious source of Socialist competition for the Indian minions of Moscow during the period under review came from none other than M. N. Roy himself! How did this surprising circumstance come to pass?

In 1927, the secret OGPU representative in Berlin was a man named Goldstein who, in addition to furthering the interest of Communism in the Weimar Republic, "kept a very close eye" on the Communist Indians of Berlin who were under the direction of Roy. Goldstein had an Indian assistant named Farouki whose task it was to recruit Soviet agents "for service in the East," and it may be noted that two such agents were sent out from Berlin in the winter of 1929, one to Bengal and the other to the Punjab.[93] It is certain that they had the intention of assisting the Indian Communists and their British advisers whose plans for expanding the scope of Communism had been hampered by the arrest of the Meerut conspirators. Farouki also maintained relations with the Brothers Ali who had led the Caliphate movement, which movement had disappeared in the mid-twenties owing to the abolition of the Caliphate in modern Turkey. There is no evidence, however, that the Ali Brothers were converted to Communism.

Farouki suggested to his Comintern superiors that Evelyn Roy was really a British agent and this suggestion appears to have been taken seriously by them.[94] Roy also was out of favor with the Comintern owing to his failure in China, his non-attendance at the Sixth Comintern Congress, and the fact that, unlike R. Palme Dutt, he had refused to bow down to the Comintern's policy of isolationism as the rule for Indian Communist policy, for the Brahmin Bolshevik maintained that Indian Communists should "prepare the masses for national liberation," which would be a necessary prerequisite to the establishment of a Socialist society in the Peninsula. This was a policy which involved a measure of cooperation with other elements in India which were avidly seeking "national liberation," even the "national bourgeoisie."[95] Thus, interestingly enough, Roy had swung over to the position which Lenin held in 1920 whereas the Comintern had adopted Roy's former policy of Communist exclusiveness. In addition, Roy held a theory of decolonization to the effect that the British bourgeoisie was transferring power to their Indian counterparts, which was contrary to the Comintern's view and was specifically repudiated by Bukharin in his report to the Sixth Comintern Congress.[96]

As a consequence of his divergence from the party line, Roy was secretly expelled from the Communist Party of India, and the Comintern as well, at the tenth "plenum" of the Executive Committee of the Communist International held in July, 1929, although the formal announcement from Comintern headquarters on Roy's expulsion was withheld until the following 4th of December.[97]

The charges against Roy were five-fold. First, he misled the Indian Communists by asking them to form workers' and peasants' parties. Secondly, his instruction that Communists should work within the National Congress "was calculated to make them a tool in the hands of the compromising and betraying bourgeoisie." Thirdly, Roy had expounded his theory of "decolonization," contrary to the will of the Comintern. Fourthly, he had betrayed the revolutionary movement in China, Fifthly, Roy had associated himself with men who had broken with the Comintern, notably Heinrich Brandler of Germany.[98] This latter charge was really true for Roy had allied himself with such outstanding anti-Comintern German Communists as Brandler and August Thalheimer in opposing the Comintern's policies in the Reich.[99] In this connection Roy contributed articles to publications operated by these dissidents in the course of 1929. Roy himself confirmed this connection when he later stated he opposed the Kremlin at this time "for opposing the adventurist policy in Germany which helped the rise of Fascism."[100]

The expulsion of Roy, which was naturally justified by the organs of the Comintern,[101] constituted the second terrific blow suffered by the Indian Communist movement during the course of 1929. Coming not long after the arrest of the leading Indian Communists and their British Bolshevik tutors, it deprived the Kremlin of the services of its best known Indian agent and destroyed the Indian Communist center in Germany. Moreover, it is claimed that a majority of Communists in India, no doubt disgusted by the servile dependency of their party immediately on the British Communist party and ultimately on Moscow, saw fit to break their allegiance with the Comintern and serve under M. N. Roy.[102] The latter and Evelyn Roy, escaped the undoubted fate which would have been theirs in Russia, by virtue of their being in Germany in the summer of 1929.

Having been expelled from the ranks of the Third International, Roy joined forces with the leaders of the so-called "International Communist Opposition" whose leaders at the beginning of 1930 were Thalheimer and the American dissident Communist, Jay Lovestone. In Germany, in that year, Roy issued a bold manifesto in which he urged members of the revolutionary trade union movement in India to organize and prepare for a "revolutionary party of the Indian working class" to engage upon a "relentless agitation" for the election of a "National Constituent Assembly" which would serve as the "sovereign authority of the oppressed and exploited classes."[103]

Roy established the best contacts he could with his adherents in India and these followers formed organizations in a number of Indian cities. The Anglo-Indian police were no more amicably disposed to the dissidents than they were to the orthodox Communists, and, on one occasion, acting on a rumor that Roy had arrived in India, the Anglo-Indian police, out of nervousness, arrested a number of persons in Bombay, Calcutta and other Indian towns suspecting that each of the arrested individuals was the wanted Bengali.[104]

The police were really justified, however, for Roy actually did determine to return to India, on the soil of which he had last stood in the year,1915. He was dissatisfied at running his own personally-directed Communist conspiracy in India from Berlin. Accordingly, he returned to India and was arrested on July 21, 1931 in Bombay by the Anglo-Indian police.[105]

Roy's arrest brought about quite a ripple of excitement in India. Leaders of the Royist Communists were rounded up so that this dissident Communist movement was severely shaken, just as the orthodox Communist movement had been rocked some two years previously;[106] thousands demonstrated before the police station where Roy was initially detained, and mass meetings were held on an India-wide basis with committees for his defense being set up throughout the land. Jawaharlal Nehru, and R. S. Ruikar, then President of the A.I.T.U.C. also protested against the allegedly "barbarous" treatment meted out to Roy.[107] Moreover, Roy's arrest caused a marked reaction abroad, especially in Germany. According to a dispatch to the Bombay "Chronicle" of October 2, 1931 a large mass meeting was held in Hamburg in which the release of Roy was demanded in a resolution which took the form of a letter addressed to the British consulate in that city demanding Roy's release. Various letters of protest on Roy's arrest which had been sent to the Second Round Table Conference, then in session, written by many distinguished men in Germany, among them one from Dr. Albert Einstein, were likewise read at the Hamburg meeting.[108]

In contrast to the Meerut process, then going on, Roy's trial was a swift one beginning on November 3, 1931 at the Court of Sessions in Cawnpore and terminating on January 9, 1932 when the Court sentenced him to twelve years' transportation,[109] but in fact, he was sent to the Bareilly Central Prison rather than to the Andaman Islands.[110]

In spite of the arrest of Roy, his followers carried on his dissident Indian Communist Party. Such labor leaders as V. N. Joshi, A. B. Kandalkar and others made the Royist Communist movement a powerful one within the ranks of the Indian labor movement and his party was at least as influential as the orthodox Communist Party in the early thirties.[111] As regards its policies the Royist Communists or "Royists," unlike the orthodox Communists, gave a measure of support to the National movement and refrained from indulging in harsh criticism of the left wing of the Congress.

There were also a number of other non-Communist radical parties espousing socialist ideology operating upon a regional basis in India between 1929 and 1936. These included the Bengal Labour party and two parties in the Punjab, the Punjab Socialist Party and the Punjab Kirti Kisan (Workers' and Peasants') Party.[112]

It was the founding of the Congress Socialist movement, however, which brought about the organization of the most important left-wing competitor to the orthodox Indian Communists. In the early 'thirties, a left wing was arising in the Congress as a cohesive group.[113] This group was galvanized into a definite organization, largely through the efforts of an individual of unusual character and ability, Jay Prakash Narayan. Born in a village in Bihar Province, Narayan as a youth succeeded in scraping up enough funds for a passage to the United States where he worked on farm and factory, attended several universities and was converted to Communism.[114] Upon his return to India, he joined the Communists, but in spite of his falling out with them[115]—perhaps he was opposed to their "sectarian" stand at that time—he was apprehended and incarcerated in Nasik Jail. There he came into contact with two young intellectuals, Ashoka Mehta and Achuyt Patwardhan who had been highly interested in Marxism, although it seems they had not, like Narayan, actually joined the Communist party.[116] On their release from prison Narayan and his friends founded the All-India Congress Socialist party at Patna on May 17, 1934, with Narayan being elected as the Organizing Secretary, thus the de facto leader of the party.[117] At Patna it was decided to make this party a group within the National Congress rather than a separate party altogether, because the leaders of the Socialists believed that as a portion of the great All-Indian national organization, they could popularize socialist policies. They also hoped to give a "mass basis" to the Congress which they felt it had hitherto lacked and at the same time they desired to convert the Congress into an outright socialist organization.[118]

Although the Congress Socialists, as they came to be known, had a tendency to shift their goals—especially their economic program—in general, it may be said that they stood for the nationalization of basic industries and likewise the nationalization of the land, although not necessarily involving a system of collectivized agriculture.[119] These economic aims were held to be in conformity with the over-all aim of leading the Indian National Movement in the direction of socialism.[120]

Besides the goal of the complete independence of India, the political end of the Congress Socialists was embodied in their demand that there be an all-Indian Constituent Assembly, elected on the basis of adult suffrage which would draw up the constitution of a socialist government.[121] The Congress Socialists also opposed council-entry, that is, the entry of the Congress, or its political agent, the Swarajist Party, into the provincial or national legislative assemblies.[122]

The founding of the Congress Socialist Party was generally welcomed in liberal political circles, inside and outside the Congress, it being pointed out that the Congress as a whole was not committed to defend "the present economic order."[123] However, Congress conservatives, including Mahatma Gandhi, objected to the Socialists' policy of class warfare and confiscation of property, as that implied violence.[124] This view was expressed in a formal statement made by the Congress Working Committee which was dominated by conservatives.[125]

Friction was also to develop between the majority of the Congressmen and the Congress Socialists after 1935 over the questions of council entry and the allegedly "soft" policy pursued by Congress towards the sectarian Muslim League.[126]

Almost immediately after the formation of the party, it opened branches in various provinces. The Congress Socialists took especial interest in the labor, peasant and student movements. They gave their support to the A.I.T.U.C. and in a "short time they had succeeded in practically capturing that organization," and the presidents of that body came to be the nominees of the Congress Socialist Party.[127] At the same time during the years, 1934 and 1935, the Congress Socialists formed peasant unions known as "kisan sabhas," which grew in scope and influence as well as students' organizations. All of these groups, naturally, were permeated with the Socialists' but not Communist ideology.[128]

A few months after its founding, the greater part of the "Royists" joined the Congress Socialist Party. But during the course of 1935 the "Royists" and Congress Socialists fell out over the question of the relations of the Congress Socialist Party to the National Congress, the former holding the view that the Congress Socialist Party should be dissolved and should instead form just the left wing of the Congress, whereas the latter insisted that the party maintain its identity as such.

Besides, the "Royists" appeared anxious to seize control of the Congress Socialist Party from Narayan and others of their leaders.[129] Therefore, at the end of 1935, the "Royists" unable to capture the Congress Socialist Party, withdrew from it and resumed their course as a strictly independent left-wing movement.

* * * * *

But what of the orthodox Communists of India against whom the above-mentioned groups were competitors, in the years, 1929-1936?

With the leaders of the Communist movement behind the bars of Meerut prison, the Comintern had to find new men to carry on its subversive work in India. Two men who met the Kremlin's standard of unconditional loyalty to the Third International and at the same time showed a measure of ability, came to the fore as leaders of the Communist movement in India in the spring of 1929. They were S. V. Deshpande and B. T. Ranadive.

Deshpande was a genuinely able man. A brilliant student, he had joined the non-cooperation movement of the early 'twenties as an ardent adherent of the National movement. At this time Deshpande was a member of the religious-nationalist Arya-Swaraj movement. However, during the course of the year 1928, he underwent a complete ideological metamorphosis. Influenced by the fervor of the Communist-led strikers in the Bombay textile mills strike of 1928, Deshpande forsook his traditional Hindu-Indian ideology and accepted wholeheartedly in its place that of Communist Russia.[130] In spite of the brevity of duration of his membership in the Communist movement, Deshpande's ability and the influential standing which he had gained among the workers of Bombay, induced the Comintern to make him its principal agent in India.

Deshpande's chief colleague, B. T. Ranadive had also been an active leader in the labor movement of Bombay and was connected with the textile workers' Girni Kamgar union.[131]

The basic task for Deshpande and his colleagues to fulfill,

during the period in which the Meerut trial was dragging along, was laid down as follows by the Comintern:

> The First fundamental task of the Communist Party, which is linked up with all its other tasks, is to convert itself into a mass, all-Indian Communist Party. This task is being tackled now, but has not yet been accomplished. Everywhere and on all occasions, the first thought of the Indian Communists must be directed towards the creation of party organisations on every hand. In all towns, in all workshops, factories, railway repair shops, plantations and mines—the Communist Party of India must have its organisations.[132]

Above all, the Indian comrades were made to realize that "the creation of an illegal Communist Party is the prerequisite for the establishment of the hegemony of the working class in the Indian revolution."[133]

Although the working class was to have "hegemony," the allegedly increasing "class-conscious activities of the agricultural proletariat" should also be taken advantage of; therefore the peasants and landless agricultural workers also should be induced to join the ranks of the Communist Party of India. The Communists were, then, deciding to place greater stress than had been hitherto been the case on winning over the peasantry.[134]

In spite of the arrests of their leaders, the Communists remaining at large maintained a bold front. Thus on May 19, 1929, the official and yet unbanned Communist journal of Bombay, "Kranti" defiantly declared that

> the fight of the Red Flag is not dependent on the leaders, but will continue as long as capitalism is in existence . . . The agitation which has been started by the workers suffering under repression of capitalism and imperialism, not only of India but of the whole world, cannot be stopped by one or many governments . . . The Red Flag has never submitted before any government.[135]

At this time the Communists in India could count on support from the C.P.G.B.,[136] its front, the Workers' Welfare League of India, and the League Against Imperialism[137] which after

1929 had become completely dominated by the Communists, a fact which was testified to by the expulsion of non-Communist Jawaharlal Nehru from that body.[138] But above all Indian Communists remained under control of the Comintern. This control was manifested in the publication of a "Draft Platform of Action of the Communist Party of India" in that Comintern journal, "International Press Correspondence" of December 18, 1930.

This manifesto which was almost certainly made in Moscow declared that the following were the goals of India's Communists.

1. The complete independence of India by the violent overthrow of British rule. The cancellation of all debts. The confiscation and nationalisation of all British factories, banks, railways, sea and river transport and plantations.
2. Establishment of a Soviet Government. The realisation of the right of national minorities to self-determination including separation. Abolition of the native states, the creation of an Indian Workers' and Peasants' Soviet Republic.
3. The confiscation without compensation of all the lands, forests and other property of the landlords, ruling princes, churches, the British Government, officials and moneylenders and handing them over for use to the toiling peasantry. Cancellation of all agreements and all the indebtedness of the peasantry to moneylenders and banks.[139]

In addition to this candid exposition of Communist policy, the "draft platform" stridently stated that

> the Communist Party of India declares with pride that it considers itself a party of the organised world Communist movement, a Section of the Communist International. The Communist Party of India calls upon all advanced workers and revolutionaries devoted to the cause of the working class to join the ranks of the Communist Party now being built,

> in order to fight to carry out the historic tasks of the Indian Revolution.[140]

Therefore, for the first time, the "honor" of being formally a section of the Communist International was bestowed upon the Communist Party of India.

But the progress of this newly launched section of the Comintern during the course of the year and a half subsequent to December, 1930 was evidently not satisfactory to Moscow. Hence orders were sent by the Comintern to the Indian comrades in the form of an "Open Letter to the Indian Communists," allegedly jointly written by the "Central Committee of the Communist Parties of China, Great Britain and Germany" and published in an official organ of the Comintern, the "Communist International" of June 1, 1932. Although the real authorship of this "Open Letter" very likely lay in the Kremlin, the alleged authorship of the missive was significant in that the Chinese was then (as now) the leading Communist party of Asia and the German held a corresponding position in Europe (next to the Russian) whereas, as before, the Communist Party of Great Britain was the basic link between Moscow and the Indian comrades. The "open letter" held:

> The general picture of the Communist movement is not satisfactory. On the one hand there is a tremendous unprecendented development of the working class movement. On the other hand, the Communist Party still consists of a small number . . . of weak groups, often isolated from the masses, discontented with each other, (and) not politically united. . .[141]

Much stress was laid on the theme that the Indian Communists had been pursuing a policy of "self-isolation" which was, as a mater of fact, perfectly true.[142] It was held that "self-isolation from the anti-imperialist struggle" had left the struggle in the hands of the National Congress and so "aids the work of all the agents of imperialism . . ."[143]

But did this mean that the Communists would adopt the view that they should cooperate with, or at least not be markedly uncooperative with, the leaders of the National Liberation Movement, the National Congress and other elements in India which desired independence? Not at all. The "Bourgeois National Congress," its left wing led by Jawaharlal Nehru[144] and Subhas C. Bose,[145] and, of course, the "Roy group," then led by V. N. Joshi and A. B. Kandalkar,[146] were subjected to scathing denunciations.

The "open letter" instructed the Indian comrades to differentiate between the petty bourgeoisie and the bourgeoisie, the latter, naturally, remaining, as before, the enemy of the proletariat. Hence, Indian Communists should not excoriate the petty bourgeoisie, but rather carry out the "mobilisation" of its "revolutionary strata." On the other hand Indian comrades must not in any way "join with or follow" the petty bourgeoisie in view of its "waverings and hesitations," since this would lead to "subordinating the proletariat to the leadership of the national bourgeoisie."[147]

An equivocal line analogous to that dealing with the petty bourgeoisie was laid down in respect to the peasantry by the "open letter." India's Communists were informed that "fighting in alliance with the peasantry" was a proper policy, but this should not cause the working class which the Communists hoped to control, to lose its "independence." The supremacy of the working class must be at all times stressed, so that the peasants would never be considered more than very dependent allies at best.[148]

The "open letter" ordered the Indian Communists to further "the development of the strike movement," to organize "trade unions" on an "all-Indian level" as well as "factory committees"[149] and above all to form an All-Indian Communist Party composed of workers and "revolutionary intellectuals," a party which would have a legal and an illegal press, particularly a "central party paper."[150]

Finally, the "open letter" insisted that Indian comrades obey and execute the Comintern's orders, a circumstance necessitated by the activities of imperialist countries, notably Great Britain, the United States and Japan, which were plotting to wage "war against the U.S.S.R."[151]

This "open letter" culminated a series of articles coming

forth from the publications of the Comintern, as well as from the British Communist press and even that of Russia, since the time of the arrest of the Meerut conspirators in 1929. These articles monotonously assailed the British—invariably referred to as "imperialists" who oppressed the Indian masses and particularly the labor movement[152]—as well as the bourgeoisie of India who were held to be trying to win over the working class and peasantry while seeking to effect "conciliation" with the British.[153] In this connection Gandhi was singled out for especial abuse.[154] Also excoriated were the left-wingers of the National Congress, notably Jawaharlal Nehru and Subhas C. Bose who were deemed the worst kind of "national reformists," as well as the Congress itself which was considered a mere tool of the bourgeoisie in the execution of that class' designs on the helpless toilers.[155] Perhaps the most severe vituperation fell upon Roy's dissident Communist party,[156] but even small leftist groups, such as the Punjab Socialist Party, which groups were competitors of the Communists in winning the allegiance of the proletariat, did not escape the Comintern's wrath.[157] On the other hand, the terrorists and especially the insurrectionists who had seized Peshawar and Sholapur in the spring of 1930 were granted fulsome praise.[158]

In the year, 1929, in spite of the detention of their leaders at Meerut, the Communists actually gained influence in the Indian labor movement. Reasons for this included, the clever leadership of Deshpande and Ranadive, the widespread surge of nationalist sentiment in India in 1929 which was receptive to the Communists' extreme pro-strike policy, the genuine amount of sympathy in labor circles for the Communists and fellow-travelers being tried at Meerut, and the marked disapproval in the ranks of Indian labor at the mission of a Royal Commission on Indian Labour or the Whitley Commission, it being felt that instead of finding means for improving the lot of the Indian worker, the Commission merely was a scheme whereby the "imperialists" sought to hoodwink the economic and nationalist aspirations of Indian workers.[159]

A showdown between the right and the left in Indian labor took place at the annual convention of the A.I.T.U.C. in the town of Nagpur, in November and December, 1929, the result of which was the splitting of the Indian labor movement into two groups, a new body which seceded from the A.I.T.U.C. known as the All-India Trade Union Federation (A.I.T.U.F.) which was conservative and which promptly became affiliated with the anti-Comintern, International Federation of Trade Unions of Amsterdam,[160] whereas the A.I.T.U.C. remained an uneasy combination of Communists and left-wing Congressmen, headed in that organization's post of General Secretary by Red boss S. V. Deshpande.[161]

Deshpande and Ranadive, bosses of the Girni Kamgar Union in 1929, utilized their power in that union to call a strike in April, 1929 in which the textile mill operatives, 150,000 strong, struck ostensibly because their wage demands were not met. For a time the walkout appeared "a great success" and "showed that there was considerable organising behind it,"[162] but the employers held firm and the strike ended in the following September.[163] Other strikes in India in 1929 in which the Communists at least, in part, directed, were those which involved thousands of workers in such varied enterprises as the Tata iron and steel works at Jamshedpur, the jute mills of Bengal, the woolen mills of Cawnpore, the East India Railway and the South India Railway and even the scavengers and street-sweepers of Calcutta.[164] Indeed, 1929 was a record strike year with no fewer than 153,059 workers involved in walkouts as contrasted to only 131,655 in 1927. The trade union movement in India also reached its peak in 1929.[165] The Communists were especially pleased that in 1929 "a very large number of strikes took place on the railways, particularly in the railway workshops."[166] This indicated they might be able to paralyze the Indian railroad system in connection with a revolutionary rising.

The Communists, then had at least held their own in the Indian labor movement in 1929 in spite of the arrest of their principal leaders in March of that year. This testifies to the ability of the new Red leaders, Deshpande and Ranadive. But the second great blow which Indian Communists received during the course of that year, the defection of M. N. Roy, was completely to alter the picture and reverse the drift of Indian labor towards orthodox Communism. The followers of Roy actually got control of the Girni Kamgar Union early in 1930, which evoked an anguished howl from the Comintern press. The latter admitted that the enemies of Communism had been able to "break" that textile workers' union so that it was declining in numbers and influence.[167]

The culminating blow to the position of the Communists in the Indian labor movement at this time came with the meeting of the A.I.T.U.C. in Calcutta in the late summer of 1931. At the convention a combination of "Royists" and left-wing Congressmen led by Bose secured control and furiously, the wrathful Reds "withdrew from the Congress after creating a lot of disturbance."[168]

Following their secession from the A.I.T.U.C., the Communists formed their own frankly Communist trade union federation, candidly denominated, the Red Trade Union Congress. This federation up to 1934 "had not shown much sign of activity except occasionally in Bombay and in Calcutta."[169] This notwithstanding, the Comintern did its utmost to encourage the growth of Red unionism in India. Thus in June, 1931, the Indian comrades were called upon "to strengthen the existing Red Trade Unions and to form new ones" as well as "to build up revolutionary opposition in the reformist trade unions."[170]

The strike wave definitely declined between 1930 and 1933, in spite of the growth of national unrest in those years. This decline was a concomitant of the decline of the Communists' influence in the Indian labor movement. This decline also produced wrathful fulminations by the Comintern's press over the alleged betrayal of the strike movement by the bourgeoisie and their supposed agents, the "Royists."[171]

The Communists made no progress in gaining influence among the peasants between 1929 and 1936. Their workers' and peasants' parties which were quietly buried had had little contact with the villages, but the Communists, acting exclusively under their own name since 1929 had even less to do with the peasants' movement in spite of verbose attention given to the agrarian situation in Comintern documents. A belated attempt to rectify this situation was made by the Provisional Central Committee of the party, meeting clandestinely, at the end of 1934. It laid down the thesis that one of the basic tasks of the Communist party in the near future would be the formation of peasant committees in rural areas. But by this time the Congress Socialists had the lead in the peasant movement and the Communists, harried by the Anglo-Indian authorities, could make but little headway in this movement.[172]

The Communists also sought to infiltrate the Indian students' movement. In March, 1932, a draft program of "The Young Communist League of India" appeared in the "International Press Correspondence," which program, besides stating demands for freedom of speech, assembly and press also asked for free education and the "free right to choose principals and professors."[173] The program castigated Jawaharlal Nehru and Bose, holding them to be "the most dangerous enemies in the struggle for independence," because they were "dulling the consciousness of the youth through their revolutionary phrases."[174] However, this Y.C.L. of India manifested little activity.

Two years later, in March, 1934, an authoritative Comintern spokesman claimed that the situation with respect to the Indian student youth was comparable to that of Russia before 1905, the year of the first abortive Russian Revolution. He held, however, that students "under no circumstances" should be allowed to join the Indian Communist Party "on a large scale" although selected ones might be brought into the party so that the student movement might be utilized in India as it had been utilized in Russia at the turn of the century.[175] However, the stern anti-Communist measures of Anglo-Indian authorities, as well as the successful competitive activity among Indian youths by the Congress Socialists, made this phase of the Communist program as futile as had been its activities among the peasantry in the years from 1929 to 1936.

Seventeen months after the "open letter" of the three Communist parties had been received by the Indian Communists, another "open letter," this time signed only by the Central Committee of the Chinese Communist Party was produced in the official Comintern press. The theme of the "open letter" was that

> there is no doubt that the chief and decisive question is the formation of a militant MASS INDIAN COMMUNIST PARTY . . . This Party must be a model of Bolshevik organisation and discipline, it must stand up against conciliation and adaption to the oppressors and the bourgeoisie; it is not a peaceful Party, but a militant, bold, revolutionary Party.[176]

As in the previous "open letter," this missive from Mao Tse-tung, or more likely Moscow, again vigorously declared that the Indian Communists must not be an isolated group; they must "participate in the struggle," and apply the "tactics of the united front," so as to form the "united front of workers, peasants and urban petty bourgeoisie."

This policy was held by the Red Chinese "open letter" to be all the more necessary in that

> British imperialism is trying to rally together the forces of counter-revolution against the Indian people, and PREPARE FOR A NEW INTERNATIONAL WAR AND ABOVE ALL INTERVENTION AGAINST THE U.S.S.R.[177]

Did this indicate a change in Communist policy towards a greater degree of collaboration with the partisans of Indian freedom? Again, not at all, for the National Congress, its left wing led by Jawaharlal Nehru and Bose, and of course, Roy, the "renegade," were excoriated, just as they had been since 1929. The fundamental fact remained that the Comintern still wanted in practice, although not in theory, a separate, "sectarian" Communist Party in India. The "united front" referred to was to be a "united front from below," i.e., a coalition of forces to be dominated entirely by the Communists.[178]

Galvanized into these orders by Mao (or Moscow), a meeting was held in Calcutta in November, 1933, the same month of the publication of this latest "open letter," at which it was decided that a Provisional Central Committee of the Communist Party of India should be set up. At this meeting plans were made to reorganize the local units of the party and increase their membership. Actually, modest goals were set up for this end—thus the huge province of Bengal was to furnish a membership of 50 Communists within six months, whereas smaller Indian provinces were to form "kernels" of five or six "whole-hearted workers."[179]

Another fact which aided the Communists at this time was the release shortly before and after the holding of the Communist conference in Calcutta, of many of the minions of Moscow who had been tried at Meerut and who immediately plunged into Communist activities with the same zeal and dispatch they had evinced prior to their incarceration.[180] Working under the leadership of Deshpande and Ranadive they sought to breathe life into the almost moribund Communist movement. As a result, early in 1934, that movement for the first time since 1929 began to show signs of growth. Thus in certain provinces several Communist provincial organizations came into being.[181] It has even been claimed that the Communist Party of India (C.P.I.) had two thousand members towards the end of the first half of 1934,[182] probably an exaggeration.

Nonetheless, the Indian Communists were making progress and, encouraged by this progress, the Central Committee laid down its official "Political Thesis of the Central Committee of the Communist Party of India," which publicly appeared on July 20, 1934. Here again, it is more than likely that this "political thesis," like the "open letters," was of Muscovite origin.

The "political thesis" opened by attacking "British imperialism" in India with the succinct statement:

> A hundred and fifty years of British imperialist rule has reduced the millions of Indian toiling masses to unspeakable poverty and abject slavery.[183]

It then duly attacked the Indian "National bourgeoisie" as "betrayers," and collaborators of the "imperialists," although with the modification that there was an error in "mechanically placing . . . the bourgeoisie completely in the camp of the imperialists." At the same time, the ideology of Mahatma Gandhi was bitterly attacked as an "anti-revolutionary ideology of the Nationalist bourgeoisie." The emphasis in Gandhi's philosophy on "love, meekness, modesty and hard-working existence," was held to be merely a means to divert the masses from their true revolutionary goals.[184]

The usual vigorous abuse was heaped on the "left reformism" of Jawaharlal Nehru and Bose and their followers as well as upon the "Royists" who "posed as Communists" but really were the latter's enemies.[185]

The thesis dilated freely on the usual tasks of the party, "the complete independence of India by the overthrow of British rule," and the like overthrow of the rule of the native princes. The creation of an "Indian Federal Workers' and Peasants' Soviet Republic" was demanded which naturally, would be accompanied by the nationalization of all important industries and the confiscation of landlords' land.[186]

Even more fully and frankly than in the 1930 "draft platform," the 1934 "political thesis" pointed out that " the structure of the state," when the revolution should have succeeded would be on the Soviet model "built on the councils (soviets) of representatives elected in every area, on the basis of the units of production." This mode of government, it was argued, "ensures the drawing of all the toilers in the task of governing."[187] It was also the form of government of the Soviet Union in July, 1934.

In elaborating on the "Revolution in India—a Soviet Revolution and its present task," the "political thesis" assailed with acerbity the slogan of "the Constituent Assembly as used by the Royists," advocating in its place the watchword, "The Indian Federative Soviet Workers' and Peasants' Republic."[188] At the same time the thesis called for a "united and anti-imperialist front under proletarian leadership." It was suggested that "one of the forms of broad anti-imperialistic movement can be (an) anti-Imperialist League."[189] However, it was indicated that such a League or other front would obviously be controlled outright by and would form a very thin mask for the C.P.I.

The thesis also deemed it a "task" to win the terrorists from the path of useless individual revolutionary activity to that of mass revolutionary activity which would really accomplish the terrorists' goal—the violent overthrow of the British and feudal order in India.[190]

The very fact that the Communists seemed in the year, 1934 to be making some headway led to very serious blows being applied against them. The first blow was struck against the growing Red menace in the spring of 1934 by the arrest of two of the leading Communists, P. C. Joshi—newly released from prison—and B. T. Ranadive who had heretofore escaped incarceration. Joshi was summarily (in contrast to the long-drawn out Meerut process) sentenced to three years' rigorous improvement and Ranadive to a term of two years. The charge against both men had been that of making inflammatory speeches.[191] The culminating blow against the Communists occurred on July 27, 1934 when the Anglo-Indian Central Government, through a notification in the official "Gazette of India" announced that under the terms of the Indian Criminal Law Act, the Communist Party of India and all its committees and other branches were declared illegal because their objective constituted a danger to public peace.[192] Contemporaneously, a dozen formerly legal registered trade unions which were under Communist influence or control, as well as the Young Workers' League were likewise outlawed.[193]

The banning of the C.P.I. obviously engendered extreme ire in the Comintern. A spokesman for that body sulkily stated that the powers employed by the Anglo-Indian Government against the Communists

> are to be used, not merely against the Communist Party of India, but also against the Trade Unions, Strike Committees . . . and to crush any movement to defend or improve economic conditions in the struggle for independence.[194]

The formal suppression of the Communists evoked a different response from non-Communist Indians as compared to the reactions upon the Meerut arrests of March, 1929. Little attention was paid to the affair in the Indian press, Nationalist or moderate. It would seem that with the repression of the national movement, that of the Communists was a small matter.

Praise for the ban on the C.P.I. was registered by the influential "Times of India" in a leading article of July 31, 1934 which simultaneously attacked the Congress as veiled Communists, subtly carrying on the work of the Communists themselves.[195] On the other hand the pro-Congress journal, the "Mahratta," expressed fear that the suppression of the Communists was but "prelude to the more vigorous repression of the labour movement."[196]

In Britain, Conservative opinion naturally sided with the formal statement of Sir Samuel Hoare, Secretary of State for India, who emphasized the danger to the administration of law and order in India as posed by the Communists.[197] Except for the independent Labourites, this statement went unchallenged.[198]

In spite of this setback, the international Communist movement kept up a drumfire of propaganda on behalf of the Indian Communists, thereby evidencing continued interest in India. Subsequent to, as well as prior to, the formal banning of the Communist Party of India, a voluminous and verbose barrage of propaganda was laid down condemning the British "imperialists" who were supposed to be threatening to attack Russia as well as ruling India with a tyrannical hand. Also vigorously and often viciously assailed were the Indian bourgeoisie,[199] the National Congress, and the "lefts" of that body, Jawaharlal Nehru being especially singled out for attack as a "left Gandhist and a bogus Socialist."[200] Also subject to abuse, as always, were the left-wing competitors of the Communists, most especially the Congress Socialists who replaced the declinging "Royists" as the leading left-wing target for Communist castigation.[201] However, as a portent of things to come, a Comintern spokesman instructed the Indian comrades to join "Trade Unions associations" and "youth groups" which latter bodies were actually affiliated with the National Congress.[202]

The spokesmen of the Comintern evinced an interest in the terrorists at this time. The individual character of their deeds, the lack of a "mass basis of their activities, as well as the petty bourgeois character of terrorist groups were factors which were noted and criticized, but it was inferred that in their violent ways, the terrorists were on the right road to the elimination of

British rule. As a matter of fact, many of the terrorists of the early 'thirties including many of the known members of the Bengal terrorist movements, the "Anushilan" and "Jugantar" societies, became Communist, many of them having learned the principles of Communism from fellow prisoners in jail in the Andaman Islands of all places,[203] a fact subsequently admitted by the leadership of the C.P.I.[204]

After its banning in July, 1934, the Indian Communist Party was handicapped by a want of effective leadership. As we have noted, both Ranadive and Joshi were imprisoned in the spring of 1934 and the most effective Communist leaders of the 'twenties such as S. A. Dange and Muzzafar Ahmad were still serving sentences for their part in the Meerut Conspiracy Case. The crushing blow for the Communists in this connection came in June, 1935 with the death of S. V. Deshpande, the principal and most effective leader of the C.P.I.[205]

A further blow against the minions of Moscow was struck when the Anglo-Indian Government followed up its official ban on the C.P.I. by sundry moves of a repressive character. During the course of 1935, the Communist press was silenced[206] and in September of that year widespread raids were conducted by the C.I.D. against the Communists.[207]

These raids were the prelude to the introduction by the Anglo-Indian Government of a bill amending the Criminal Law which provided for strict legal procedures against suspected Communists. Upon the passage of this law, the Viceroy, Lord Willingdon in a dispatch on November 28, 1935 justified the measure by stating it was aimed against the "avowed aim of Communism in India" which "is to bring about an armed revolution as quickly as possible."[208]

Prior to the ban of the C.P.I., the fortunes of the Communists had improved in respect to their position in the labor movement. They arranged a temporary truce between their Red Trade Union Congress and the Royist-Left Wing Congress A.I.T.U.C. in November, 1933 so that the two groups might carry on a successful strike movement in Bombay.[209] This and subsequent moves of a joint character between the two leftist labor federations resulted in a new strike of considerable proportions by the Bombay textile workers in April, 1934.[210] This strike lasted only until June of that year, thanks to effective and thorough means of repression carried out by Anglo-Indian authorities including the arrest of the Strike Committee of Action on the first day of the walkout.[211] Although the strike was unsuccessful this walkout and others that occurred in 1934, represented the greatest wave of strikes in India since 1928 and 1929, and testified to the effectiveness of the de facto alliance of the Communists with other left-wing groups.[212] The denouement of this alliance was "the great united front meeting on February the 7th (1935) in Bombay" and similar meetings in all parts of India which brought about the merger of the Red Trade Union Congress and the A.I.T.U.C. in that year.[213] This presaged that new course in Communist policy in India we shall review below. However, Communists were now in a much less advantageous position in the latter organization than they were when they had left it, thus indicating their weaker position in the labor movement as compared to 1928 and 1929.

Therefore, on the whole the Communists had less influence amongst the masses of India at the end of 1935 than they had at the commencement of 1929. A combination of vigorous repression of the Communist movement by the Anglo-Indian authorities combined with the rise of left-wing organizations competitive to the Communists, particularly the "Royists" and the Congress Socialists, as well as the Communists' own self-isolationist policies had definitely brought about a deterioration of the position of the minions of Moscow and thereby foiled at this time the designs of Soviet Russia on India.

CHAPTER FIVE

The United Front

In the year 1935 Soviet foreign policy and the policy of Communist parties throughout the world definitely changed. In Soviet foreign policy a definite seeming orientation towards the democracies was observed and the various Communist parties spoke of joining with various radical and liberal forces in "popular fronts" and "united fronts." This change in Soviet policy was not occasioned by a renunciation of the ultimate goal of that policy—world revolution—but rather by the rise of Fascism. In addition, Nazi Germany and militarist Japan threatened the Soviet Union as a nation and Fascist or pro-Fascist parties threatened the existence of the Communists in democratic countries. Hence arose the basis of the Soviet change in policy.

India and other colonial countries were included in the scope of the Soviet change in policy. Its application to India was clearly evidenced in the Seventh Congress of the Communist International which took place in Moscow from July 25 to August 20, 1935. Enunciating the line which the Indian comrades must follow in the future was Wang Ming, a delegate of the Chinese Communists. This fact is noteworthy for two reasons. In the first place it indicated there was no Indian Communist of sufficient importance in the eyes of Moscow (as compared to M. N. Roy when he was a loyal adherent of the Comintern) to lay down the correct party line for the Indian comrades. In the second place, once again, we see the Chinese Communist party, the most puissant Communist party of the

East, as the specific mouthpiece of Moscow in laying down the correct line for the Indian Communists.

In his address to the Congress, Wang declared:

> Our comrades in India suffered for a long time from 'left' sectarian errors; they did not participate in the mass demonstrations organised by the National Congress and organisations affiliated with it. At the same time the Indian Communists did not possess sufficient forces independently to organise a really powerful and mass anti-imperialist movement.[1]

Wang went on to criticize the Indian Communists for using wrong slogans such as "an Indian Workers' and Peasants' Soviet Republic," "confiscation of lands belonging to the zemindars (landlords) without compensation," "a general strike as the only effective programme of action" and the like. Wang held that

> such demands on the part of our Indian comrades can serve as an example of how not to carry on the tactics of the anti-imperialist united front.[2]

Of course, we may note here that these very slogans, now condemned, had been formulated in Moscow and the Indian Communists had only been carrying out the orders of the Kremlin in uttering them. Hence the latter were really being scolded for having carried out their previous orders.

As for the new orders of the Communist International, Wang held that it was incumbent for the Indian Communists

> to strive with all their power and all the means of their disposal for the establishment of a united anti-imperialist front of the broad masses of the people both within and without the National Congress, to strive for the active participation of Communists and their supporters in all mass anti-imperialist demonstrations, irrespective of who calls them, in order to show the people by deeds that the Communists are really the vanguard of the people of India in the struggle for national emancipation—this is now the main task of the Indian comrades.[3]

Georgi Dimitrov, the head of the Communist International in his capacity as its General Secretary authoritatively added:

> In India the Communists have to support, extend and participate in all anti-imperialist mass activities, not excluding those which are under national reformist leadership.[4]

This, then, represented a return to the line first propounded by Lenin and opposed by Roy, which was enunciated in the pronouncement of the Second Congress of the Communist International in 1920 and it was also the line which Roy himself had come to favor in 1928 and 1929, but which the Comintern then spurned in favor of the view that colonial Communist parties should stand boldly alone as candidly insurrectionary bodies hostile to the colonial "imperialists" and the "national bourgeoisie" alike.

As a consequence of the decision of the Seventh Comintern Congress, the line was stressed that the masses of India should participate in the United Front[5] alongside the brave peoples of Ethiopia, and China,[6] then fighting foreign aggressors. In order that this might be brought about, there must be a unity of all Indian patriots in "the anti-imperialist People's Front," a front which would checkmate the schemes of "the cunning British rulers" and their policy of "divide and rule."[7] It was further argued that the "mass character" of the united front should be its greatest feature and for this "mass character" to be properly made use of, the Communist program should be of such a nature as to meet the "vital demands of workers, peasants and middle classes,"[8] the latter a new addition. It was also held that the "situation in India is particularly favorable for the organisation of a United Anti-Imperialist Front,"[9] and that the Communists in India were actually "helping to mould the workers, peasants and middle class in such a way as to deal a smashing blow" to imperialistic British rule.[10] This would be in keeping with "the main task confronting the anti-imperialist front," which was "the liberation of the Indian people and the introduction of a democratic regime."[11]

Besides workers, peasants and the "middle classes," this "anti-imperialist united front" would comprise in the first place such local leftist parties as the Socialist and Radical League Parties of the Punjab and the Labour and Socialist parties of Bengal, and also the Congress Socialist Party. In fact, in calling for the "consolidation of the left wing" the spokesmen of the Comintern specified that this meant by necessity "that all-Left-Wing elements in Congress" as well as outside that body should be brought into the united front.[12] No leftist group, not even the "Royists" were specifically excluded. This was the manifestation of the "united front from above" strategy by which through cooperation with nationalist, socialist and liberal elements, the Communists sought to maneuver themselves into position to play an important—although not immediately a dominating role—in a broad anti-imperialist coalition. But ultimately, under this strategy, the Communists would seek to control the coalition. As noted above, a modified form of the "united front from above" strategy had been followed by the Communists from 1925 to 1928, and subsequently abandoned.

In the second place, trade unions, peasant unions (kisan sabhas) and youth organizations were held to be groups which should join the Communists in a "national front." On the basis of this "national front" it was held "a minimum programme of anti-imperialist struggle" could be drawn up.[13]

In the third place, the National Congress itself was to be brought into the united front. As a result, it was held that "the National Congress had undoubtedly achieved a gigantic task in uniting wide forces of the Indian people for the national struggle" so that "the National Congress can play a great part and a foremost part in the work of realising the anti-imperialist People's Front."[14] The Communists thereby diametrically reversed their position towards the formerly abhorred Congress. Indeed, Comintern propagandists between the years 1936 and 1939 saw fit to praise the actions of the National Congress both in regard to its domestic and its foreign policies. Thus in the summer of 1936 a very modest agricultural reform plan by a "Congress Committee," a program advocating such generalities as "a just and fair relief of agricultural indebtedness" was duly praised.[15] Furthermore, we find Ben Bradley, the whilom Meerut conspirator in April, 1939, praising the Congress for its reiteration of the "national demands," that is not only the need for Indian independence but also the election of a Constituent Assembly (a policy formerly so bitterly assailed) to implement that independence.[16]

The foreign policy of the Congress was also praised by the Comintern's agents, particularly the stand taken by the Congress in its plenary session at Haripura in February, 1938, which stand was held to be an anti-Fascist one, and was favorably contrasted with the allegedly imperialist policies of the British Government.[17]

The C.P.I. even saw fit during the period under survey to "greet" the plenary sessions of the Congress, while at the same time, expounding its views. Thus in their manifesto of "greeting" to the Haripura Congress, as prepared by fourteen leading Indian Communists it was stated:

> We shall stand for the overthrow of the Constitution, the convening of a Constituent Assembly with the participation of the representatives of the States' people to determine the Constitution of the free and united India, the freedom of the basic economic and political demands of the people, worked out in agreement with labour and States' People's Organisations and the representatives of the National Minorities.[18]

It may be noted that the leader of the British Communist Party, Harry Pollitt, along with Ben Bradley and R. Palme Dutt, saw fit to "greet" the Haripura Congress[19] and the Executive Committee of the C.P.G.B. also sent a message of "greeting" to the Tripuri Congress of March, 1939.[20] These messages again served to demonstrate the tutelage of the Indian Communists in respect to the British Communist Party.

A feature of the Communists' now pro-Congress policy was their "discovery" of Jawaharlal Nehru, who since his father Motilal Nehru's death in February, 1931 had become with Gandhi, the co-leader of Congress. Previously castigated as a "reformist" of the worst type, the Communist press now discovered him to be a great friend of Indian liberty. Nehru's statement made in December, 1933 that he believed the choice before the world lay between Communism and Fascism and that he chose the former, was duly noted.[21] Besides, Nehru's "presidential addresses" to the plenary sessions of the National Congress at Lucknow in April, 1936 and at Faizpur in December of that year, were officiously reproduced in the "Labour Monthly," that British Communist organ edited by R. Palme Dutt.[22] Furthermore, an interview by Nehru granted to the "International Press Correspondence," in March, 1936[23] was conspicuously featured in that Comintern journal and on June 27, 1936 a writer in that same publication referred to the Indian leader as "Comrade Nehru."[24] In addition, the British Communists were pleased to publish in the "Labour Monthly" of August, 1938 an article by Nehru entitled "Nationalism and the Mass Struggle in India." The article was a reasonably dispassionate review of the Indian national movement, not at all radical in its reference to social and economic matters. However, the theme of the article was the need for unity in the Indian national movement, a theme which was paralleled in the writings of the Communists of that time.[25]

Certain Congress leaders, however, did not receive a like laudation from the Kremlin's agents. Among them was Mahatma Gandhi who was acidly referred to as the leader of the Congress "right wing."[26]

At this time the spokesmen of the Comintern held that a program should be formulated which would be attractive to the needs of the masses of India which program would include:

(1) The aim of complete independence for India.
(2) Freedom of speech, press, organisation, assembly, strikes and picketing.
(3) Repeal of all exceptional and repressive laws, Criminal Amendment Act, Press Acts, etc.
(4) Release of all political prisoners, detenus and internees.
(5) Against reduction of wages and dismissal of workers; for an adequate minimum wage and eight hour day; for 50 per cent reduction in rents and against the seizure of peasant land for debt by imperialists, native princes, zemindars (landlords) and moneylenders.[27]

The moderation of this program as compared to the programs formulated by the Communists in their previous "platforms" and "theses" is startling, for gone now are references to armed insurrections, confiscations of land and the formation of a Soviet India.

The Comintern's propagandists urged the National Congress to participate in Indian national elections on the basis of an anti-imperialist bloc in such a way that there would be "no splitting of the vote for the benefit of the reactionary right wing outside the Congress."[28] When these provincial elections of 1937, held under the new Indian Constitution of 1935, a document based on the report of the Simon Commission which had been made public in June, 1930 and which was designed to replace the Constitution of 1919 and which also gave a measure of autonomy to Indians in provincial affairs,[29] resulted largely in Congress triumphs, (the Congress campaigning under its own name—not that of Swarajist as formerly) these triumphs were duly praised by the Comintern's spokesmen.[30]

One demand which the latter held the Congress should agree to, was entirely contrary to the best Indian traditions and one which would never have been agreed to under any condition by the vast majority of Congressmen. This was the demand that in "the tactics of mass struggle" the "dogma" of "non-violence" should be "omitted." However, this view was qualified by the assertion that 'this issue should not be allowed to split the national front.'[31]

The spokesmen of the Comintern also advocated policies which could be far more palatable to the Indian Congress than the abandonment of non-violence, namely that of opposing spiritedly the "war preparations" alleged to be carried on by the British Government and that of expressing solidarity for the struggles of peoples against imperialist aggression, notably struggles of the Ethopians against the Italians and the Chinese against the Japanese.[32] Such condemnation of imperalist aggression outside of India had been a prominent feature of the sessions of the Indian National Congress in the years from 1936 to 1939 inclusive.

Although the Communists had silenced their abusive criticism of the Congress and of the "national reformist" bourgeoisie, other elements in Indian life were still assailed. The British were still castigated, just as before–regardless of the possibility of an Anglo-Russian rapprochement on the over-all international political scene. Indeed, the new Red line was designed all the more to further "the popular struggle against imperialism,"[33] and the Indian Constitution of 1935 was particularly assailed by the international Communist press.[34]

This violent hostility to the British put the Communists in India in a rather potentially ticklish position in the event of a war in which Great Britain and Russia would be allies against the Axis Powers, an event which seemed possible in the years from 1936 till the Russo-German pact of August 23, 1939. In event of such an Anglo-Russian alliance the Indian Communists would, it might seem, have to withdraw, at least in part, their strong hostility to the "imperialists." When asked about this ticklish question, the Indian Communists between 1936 and 1939 answered with the claim that even were the Soviet Union to fight on the side of England and France, it would still be in their eyes "an imperialist war."[35] Thus the Communists implied they would in such a circumstance still oppose the British in India and thus directly hamper the latter's war effort, but indirectly they would simultaneously hamper the war effort of the U.S.S.R. as well. However, in practice, the Indian Communists would never act in any way contrary to the interest of Moscow and this, as we shall see, subsequently proved to be the case.

In addition to the British, the princes and their states were also subject to Communist abuse during the period under survey. The princely states were called "hotbeds of reaction" and the governments of these states were denominated as government by "feudal autocracy." The princely states were bitterly assailed in that they were held to be propped up by the British.[36]

As before, the Communists within and without India continued to make much over the hard lot, real and alleged, of the Indian masses. In this respect the tendency was to put the blame for this misery on British capitalists, for example an exposé which discussed with seemingly righteous wrath the conditions of the miners of the British-owned mines of Bihar blamed British industrialists more than on their Indian equivalents.[37] However, the Indian capitalists were not exonerated by the Communists from the alleged guilt of making for the hard lot of the Indian masses, a misery which the Communists did their utmost to exploit for their own subversive purposes.[38]

Entering the Congress in strength in 1936 Communists plunged into the work of that body feigning that they were good Congressmen. They even donned khaddar, the costume of the Congressmen and are said even to have preached "humanitarian uplift" in line with Gandhist ideology.[39] This, of course, was pure deception, They were only behaving like good Congressmen in order to gain influence and power in that organization. And, in this respect, the Communists were markedly successful, considering how bitterly they had criticized the Congress between 1929 to 1935.[40] Communists were elected to high posts in the provincial Congress organizations and some Communists were even elected to the All-India Congress Committee.[41] Prominent Communists who were serving on the latter body in 1939 included R. D. Bhardwaj, the leader of the Communists in the United Provinces, Sardar S. S. Joshi, a former Meerut convict, and a leader of the Communists in the Punjab and S. G. Patkar, a Red leader of Bombay.[42] Communists were also prominent on several provincial Congress Committees; indeed, in the Punjab, Communist Mlan Iftikharuddin was elected President of the Provincial Congress Committee.[43] In conformity with their newly adopted pro-Congress policy, Communists supported the Congress candidates in the election of the spring of 1937.[44] However, in one constituency, the Communists opposed the Congress "only to show their own importance and to blow their own little trumpet."[45] Communist policy within the Congress was based ostensibly upon uniting the left wing elements within it, but in practice it was premised upon a desire to be popular with all segments of that body while carrying on a "boring from within" campaign inside of it. Hence, when the Communists found that their policy of having the Congress accept taking over ministries in the provinces in 1937, was opposed by the Congress Socialists, and generally, by the left-wingers of Congress, they quickly veered around to the latter's position.[46]

But when the Congress finally decided to form provincial ministries the Communists "went along" with this policy.

An even more noteworthy example of this Communist course concerned Subhas C. Bose. The Communists approved the election of this left-wing Congress leader to the Presidency of the National Congress in the spring of 1938 and, according to A. K. Ghosh, the present leader of the C.P.I. (as its General Secretary) the Communists backed his policies before the Tripuri Congress of March, 1939.[47] They also supported the re-election of Bose at this plenary session of the Congress. However, subsequent thereto, when the dominant right wing of the Congress Working Committee urged Bose to resign, the Communists remained silent, in effect thereby assisting the right-wing, whereas the Congress Socialists had boldly advised Bose to remain at his post.[48] This would seem to indicate that the Communists were pursuing a purely opportunistic policy devoid of ideological considerations, simply to make themselves appear "respectable" in the "eyes of right-wing Congressmen and thus prevent themselves from being isolated."[49] The policy of "unity" which the Communists spoke of so passionately at the Tripuri Congress[50] was also in line with this policy.

The Communists also invaded the Congress Socialist Party in considerable force during the year 1936 and after. We have already seen that a kind of semi-truce had existed between the Communists and certain non-Communist leftists in connection with the Bombay textile mills strike of 1934. Furthermore, during the latter part of 1934 and the early part of 1935, prior to the Seventh Comintern Congress, in spite of public Communist abuse of the Congress Socialists, and the fact that at its first plenary session, its first Congress in Bombay, the Congress Socialist Party had gone on record that no Communists could be admitted into its membership, there was actually contact between the Congress Socialists and the Communists. Thus the General Secretary of the Congress Socialist Party, Jay Prakash Narayan and other important members of the Executive Committee of that party "kept up . . . constant contacts with the leaders of the Communist party," contacts which were held to have been "useful from the (Congress Socialist) Party's point of view."[51] Furthermore, the Congress Socialists sent an emissary to the Communists in the summer of 1935, the summer of the Comintern Congress, in the person of M. R. Masani one of the leaders of the party.[52] In September, 1935 Masani came into contact with the leaders of British Communism and the mentors of the Indian Communist party, Messrs. Harry Pollitt, R. Palme Dutt and Ben Bradley (recently released from prison). These gentlemen admitted to Masani that the Indian Communist party had erred in its "left sectarian" policy and held that now the Indian Communists should participate in a "broad anti-imperialist front" which would operate both within and without the National Congress. Masani then asked, why should not the Communist Party in India be dissolved altogether and the Socialist field in India be left exclusively to the Congress Socialists? Very well, answered the British Communists, if the Congress Socialist Party would accept affiliation with the Comintern and in effect become the Communist Party of India they would agree to this. On Masani's insistence that the Congress Socialist Party must maintain its independence, the British Communist leaders indicated that the Comintern must have its own party in India.[53]

Nonetheless, a new era in the relationship between the Congress Socialist party, as the leading left-wing group and the Indian Communists, was about to begin. Masani's mission had apparently convinced the Congress Socialists that they could collaborate with the Communists, for in January, 1936 at the second plenary session of the Congress Socialist Party at Meerut it was decided that in the interest of "socialist unity" the Communists might join their party, although under the stipulation they could be brought in only with the specific consent of the Executive Committee of the party and would be put under "supervision" once in the party.[54] But in May, 1936 at the time of the Lucknow session of the National Congress, the Congress Socialist party and the Communist party (which was now following the proper party line) signed an agreement, the "Lucknow Agreement," in which both parties recognized each other as bona fide socialist parties and in which it was declared they would cooperate with each other with a view to an eventual merger.[55]

Following the "Lucknow Agreement" Communists joined the Congress Socialist Party in considerable numbers and the provision that the Executive Committee of the latter party should approve their entry, was not observed. The Communists immediately took advantage of the circumstance and by the early part of 1937 they were working hard to capture the Congress Socialist local organizations in various parts of India. The Communists were particularly active in the Congress Socialist party in the industrial areas of Bombay, Calcutta and Cawnpore, and in that party's organization in the district of Andhra, an area located to the east of the princely state of Hyderabad and covering the north of Madras Province.[56] It was at this time, therefore, that the Communist story of intrigue and lust for power in this region had its inception. Furthermore, the Communists in many parts of India were themselves taking over the task of organizing the peasants and particularly the workers, nominally in the name of the Congress Socialist Party, and leaving the true Congress Socialists somewhat isolated at the top.[57] And even the top leadership of this party was successfully infiltrated by the Reds, for four Communists secured membership in the Executive Committee of the Congress Socialist Party.[58]

The leaders of the Congress Socialist Party (C.S.P.) became aware of the dangers to their movement from Communist infiltration when a secret statement of the C.P.I. was brought to their attention which declared it was the Communists' purpose to utilize their party as a "platform of left unity," a platform to be "dominated by the Communist party."[59] The Executive Committee of the Congress Socialist Party thereupon unanimously (even the Communists voted with the majority so as not to betray their identity) passed a decree, known as the Patna Decision, which forbade Communists to enter the Congress Socialist Party. However, no action was taken against Communists already in the party.[60] At the plenary conference of the C.S.P. in Lahore, April, 1938, the Chairman of that conference, M. R. Masani, demanded the expulsion of the Communists, but his demand was not agreed to.[61] However, the Executive Committee of the C.S.P. did authorize General Secretary Narayan to expel the Communists, but he refused to do so, hoping that by not so doing he could continue friendly relations between the C.S.P. and the C.P.I.[62]

The connection with the Congress Socialists was a useful one for the Communists in that it was through Congress Socialist votes that Communists were elected to important posts on provincial Congress committees and even to the All-India Congress Committee.[63] For example, it explains the victory of the Communists in the spring of 1939 in elections to the Bombay Provincial Congress Committee in which the Communists received the highest number of votes of any of the candidates in that city, and also in the Bombay municipal election, held at that time, in which the four Communist candidates who ran for election "topped the polls."[64]

The "Royists" were still in existence during the period under survey, but they were declining, both in numbers and in influence. There is no concrete evidence that the Communists did try to infiltrate their ranks; neither is there any definite evidence that they did not try to infiltrate the ranks of this group. Although Roy was released from prison in 1936,[65] he and his group failed to make a great stir in Indian politics. Under his direction the "Royists" joined the Congress party and like the Communists came out for Congreess unity. After the defeat of Bose following the Tripuri session of the Congress, the "Royists" formed a separate group called the League of Radical Congressmen which maintained a relationship within the Congross in the same autonomous way as did the Congress Socialists.[66] This "Royist" group was a small group and of little importance.

The Communists were also busy carrying on subversive activities inside the Indian labor movement during the years from 1936 to 1939.

When the Indian Communists adopted the line of the "united front," they did their utmost to advocate a merger between the two great Indian labor federations, the A.I.T.U.C. in which since 1935 they were a constituent and the National Federation of Trade Unions (N.F.T.U.) formerly known as the All-India Trade Union Federation (A.I.T.U.F.). Their policy, after a number of unsuccessful efforts finally achieved fruition in 1938. In January of that year the A.I.T.U.C. meeting at Delhi, ratified an agreement providing for provisional unity with the N.F.T.U. According to a Comintern source, the terms for the amalgamation were "considered favourable to the N.F.T.U." but "all the same" added this source, "it is to the credit of the executive of the A.I.T.U.C. as well as the progressive elements within the N.F.T.U. that this much needed unity has been practically achieved."[67] It may be noted that, at the time of amalgamation, the N.F.T.U. was the larger organization with a membership of 83,000 in sixty-two unions whereas the Communist-infiltrated A.I.T.U.C. had only 46,000 members in ninety-eight unions.[68]

This provisional unification was confirmed at a joint session of the two bodies at Nagpur where it was decided that the representation of the Joint General Council of the amalgamated trade union federation would be divided evenly between representatives of the A.I.T.U.C. and the N.F.T.U. and that there would be no affiliation with any foreign organization. This meant there would be no affiliation either with the Comintern's R.F.L.U. nor with the Socialist labor union international of Amsterdam. It is also interesting to note that the red flag, but without the hammer and sickle, was adopted as the official emblem of the new organization which retained the name of the All-India Trade Union Congress. It is noteworthy that the treasurer of the new organization was R. S. Nimbkar, the erstwhile Meerut convict.[69] However, the other officers were not Communists. The actual formal amalgamation of the A.I.T.U.C. and the N.F.T.U. did not occur until 1940, but in practice union between them had been achieved at the Nagpur session of 1938. The amalgamated trade union federation definitely prospered in that in 1939 it had a total membership of 354,000 with 191 affiliated unions.[70] The numerical position of the Communists in it was smaller, both in relative and in absolute terms, than it had been in the older, smaller A.I.T.U.C., for the N.F.T.U. had been free of Red influence. However, the

Communists had now a wider field to carry on their subversive tactics of infiltration. Of course, the Communists faced continued competition in the new organization not only from conservative labor elements but also from elements affiliated with the Congress Socialists and the "Royists." In addition there were two labor associations which remained independent of the new combined trade union federation over which the Communists had no influence, the Ahmadabad Labour Association, composed of 30,000 workers in 1939 which was under the influence of Mahatma Gandhi, and the unions of the Railwaymen's Federation, which did not include the Communist influenced union of the G.I.P. railwaymen.[71]

Before and after the amalgamation of the A.I.T.U.C. and the N.F.T.U., the Communists did their best to encourage the strike movement. Indeed, between the years 1935 and 1937 there was a startling increase in the number of strikes in India. In the latter year there were no fewer than 647,801 workers on strike with 8,982,000 working days lost, the greatest strike wave up till then in the history of India.[72] The strike wave covered all segments of Indian industry; thus in 1937, 225,000 workers struck in the Bengal jute industry, the greatest single strike in Indian labor history. Other Indian enterprises, notably the railways and textile mills as well as such miscellaneous industries as the Swedish-owned matchworks of Bombay were subjected to walkouts. At the same time, the strike movement spread to "geographically backward provinces," and the princely states, and vocationally, to handicraft workers.[73] Comintern spokesmen expressed pleasure at the "tenacity" of the strikers and the "new forms" of their struggle, notably the stay-in strike which was utilized in strikes in Cawnpore and Madras, as well as in Pondicherry, French India.[74] It is more than likely that the Indian workers learned this new technique from Communist agents.

The strike movement continued to convulse Indian labor-management relations in the years 1938 and 1939 up to the outbreak of the Second World War. Some 650,000 workers were on strike in 1938, which strike movements convulsed the large industrial centers of Calcutta, Cawnpore, Bombay, Allahabad, Ahmadabad (where even the "Gandhist" unions were affected), Madras and Sholapur. It is claimed by a Communist source that the workers, in contrast to previous years were now winning their strikes. The most important of these strikes was at Cawnpore, where after a walkout of fifty days' duration, the workers won their demands.[75] This strike was also noteworthy in that the Congress Inquiry Committee of the United Provinces supported the strike, thus making for "Congress-Labour unity" and in so far as the strikers were influenced by the Communists, Congress-Communist unity.[76]

Another dramatic strike was of short duration—one day—but it attracted a considerable amount of attention. This was the one day strike of protest on November 7, 1938 against the enactment of the Bombay Province Trades Disputes Bill which had been put forth by the Bombay Congress Ministry. This was a measure which hampered militant trade union activity by imposing a compulsory conciliation period of four months' duration as a "cooling off" period during which no strike action might be taken and by imposing regulations on the registration of unions in such a way as would seem to discriminate against militant trade unions in favor of "company unions."[77] This strike of November 7, 1938, was hailed by Ben Bradley as "the greatest independent political action by the proletariat in this country," (India).[78] It may also be noted that the specific day for this strike was on the anniversary of the Bolshevik Revolution in Russia.

The Communists were also active in the peasant movement between 1936 and 1939. That movement had been greatly bolstered by the holding of the first All-India Kisan (Peasant) Congress in 1936. This conference, which organized the All-India Kisan Sabha (All-India Peasants' Union) drew up a charter of fundamental demands which held as ultimate goals the abolition of the landlord system and the cancellation of debts and as immediate goals demanded the abolition of feudal dues and forced labor, a five year moratorium on all agricultural indebtedness and development of irrigation and credit facilities. We may note that the red flag was adopted as the official emblem of the All-India Kisan Sabha.[79]

This adoption of the red banner did not mean however, that the Communists controlled this first India-wide union of peasants. On the "Organisational Committee" of the new body, the controlling group of the organization, only one of the eleven members was a Communist, a man named Bankin Mukherjee who represented Bengal, although two others on the committee, Sajjad Zaheer and E. M. S. Namboodripad, subsequently became very important Communists.[80] Other Communists holding important positions in the All-India Kisan Sabha included Dr. Z. A. Ahmed, Dr. M. Ashraf, A. K. Gopalan, P. Sundarayya, P. Ramamurti and P. Jeevanandam.[81]

The peasants' movement in India, which was spurred on by the peasants' genuine misery as a result of the growth of rural indebtedness after 1929 owing to the great world depression,[82] became an important feature in Indian life after 1936. Throughout the length and breadth of India "peasant conferences" were held, schools were set up "to train peasant workers" and the peasants began a "disciplined struggle" to force a reduction of rent to landlords, interest to moneylenders and revenue to the government to abolish "forced labour" for the landlords' benefit and to retain possession of their lands. The methods employed by the peasant unions (kisan sabhas) were non-violent, consisting of meetings, demonstrations, marches, rent strikes and satyagraha or passive resistance. By this means they endeavored to break down the former isolation of the peasants, to promote active cooperation among them for the redress of their grievances and to draw them into the struggle against British rule.[83]

The peasants' movement encompassed by the All-India Kisan Sabha was led by true Congress Socialists and not by Communists at the top, but many of the organizers at the base were Communists. Hence, the movement in a number of areas came to be dominated by the Communists at the grass roots level.[84] In addition, as we have noted, the Communists were successful in infiltrating the Congress Socialist party, so that in so far they had succeeded in securing influence in that party, they gained ground in the peasants' movement. The position of the Communists in the peasants' movement in Bengal was particularly strong. Mukherjee and Muzaffar Ahmad, upon his release from prison, were the leaders of the Bengal peasant movement, and under their auspices a militant movement bordering on insurrection was organized.[85] The Communists were also influential among the peasants in other parts of India, notably in the rural part of Bombay Province, where there was a peasant movement bordering on revolt,[86] as well as in Bihar, the Punjab, Andhra and the United Provinces.[87] These "uprisings" in Bengal and Bombay Province just referred to consisted of attempts to "oust landlords" as well as refusal to pay taxes, rents and interests. It may also be noted that the Communists were also influential in the peasant movement of certain princely states, notably in the Travancore and Cochin states in the South and in the Telengana area of Hyderabad.[88] This last-mentioned region, alongside the adjoining Andhra region of British India, was to become the greatest Red hotbed in India.

In the Communist-controlled kisan sahbas (peasant unions) it is interesting to note that the red flag and the hammer and sickle were frequently displayed at meetings and demonstrations, and cultivators even refused to pay rent saying "Lenin Sahib has told us not to pay" although they had no knowledge whatever of the identity of the one-time Soviet leader. At the same time the shibboleths of European Communism were duly repeated by the indoctrinated kisans although it is unlikely that these illiterate peasants had any idea of what they were saying.[89] In some places, as in Bihar, the peasants under Communist stimulus would shout "long live the revolution" and "down with British imperialism,"[90] slogans which were at least intelligible to the Indian peasantry.

It may also be noted that the policies of the All-India Kisan Sabha were very far to the left of the National Congress and, indeed, disputes occurred between the Congress ministries and the peasants. The breach between the Congress and the All-India Kisan Sabha which had come to the surface as early as 1937, widened during the following two years.[91] In fact, in 1939, in an official statement, the National Congress stated:

> Kisans . . . have a right to organise Kisan Sabhas, but

> the Congress cannot associate itself with such of its activities as are incompatible with its basic principles and tend to create a hostile and inauspicious atmosphere against its policy.[92]

This indicates that the Communists' activity in the peasants' unions was often contrary to Congress' interest, in spite of the formal support of the former for the latter.

The Communists were also busy carrying on subversive activities among the Indian youth between 1935 and 1939. A Communist controlled Workers' Youth League in Bombay came into being in 1937 when a former ban against it had been lifted by the Congress Government of Bombay Province.[93] This group thereupon went busily about disseminating propaganda among the working class youth of Bombay, the Indian city where the Communists had the most influence. Furthermore, the Indian Students' Federation which had previously been dominated by Nationalists now contained a large and ever-growing segment of enthusiastic Communists.[94]

The organization of the Communists between 1935 and 1939 showed a distinct improvement over that prior to the Seventh Comintern Congress in Moscow. For one thing, by the end of 1938 all Communists who had been imprisoned at Meerut as well as those arrested in 1934, who were important leaders of the party, were now released from prison and were free to carry on their subversive activities. This meant that the ablest Communist leaders, men like S. A. Dange, Muzaffar Ahmad, S. V. Ghate and P. C. Joshi were able to take up the leadership of the movement, and fill the gap caused by the death of Deshpande in 1935. The leader of the Communists from 1935 to 1939 was Joshi. Describing his leadership during this period, Harry Pollitt, Joshi's mentor, averred in 1942:

> With the most harsh repression going on, hunted by the police day and night, without a home, living on a few shillings a month, Joshi along with other leaders of the Communist Party, built up the Communist Party from a small fighting organisation to the great mass political force that it is today, basing it firmly upon the working classes of Bombay and Calcutta and Cawnpore; establishing firm al-

liance with the organised Peasant movement; and winning over to their side the youth of the country.[95]

Besides Joshi, the leading Communists during this period were B. T. Ranadive and P. Sundarayya. As noted above, Ranadive had been, along with Deshpande, the principal Communist leader from 1929 to 1934 when he was imprisoned. Sundarayya was a native of the district of Andhra and it was under his influence that this agricultural region even by the end of the year 1939, had a strong Communist movement.

It must be noted, however, that the Communist Party was a strictly illegal organization between the years 1935 and 1939 and in the words of a Comintern commentator it was "carrying on the struggle deep underground."[96] Indeed, the British carried on an active anti-Communist policy. Thus towards the end of January, 1936, raids in Bombay led to the arrest of five Communists and the seizure of a sum of 4,000 rupees. A little later, on February 5th, raids were conducted by C.I.D. agents in Lucknow, Cawnpore, Allahabad and Benares, and it was announced that this was "one of the most sensational Communist conspiracies of recent years." The raids involved the premises of trade union offices, and interestingly enough, in both Benares and Allahabad they were carried on against students, indicating the spread of Communist propaganda among them.[97] Commenting on the searches and the seizures of large quantities of Communist literature which resulted, the Bombay "Chronicle" of February 6, 1936 noted:

> The searches were carried out with a thoroughness that showed the authorities are working on prepared plans. . . The raids were made with a view to finding out the headquarters and principles of these organisations. Suggestions that these bodies are being subsidised with Moscow gold have been made in certain quarters which claim that there is a network of secret Communist organisations in the country working under a Control Board.[98]

Attention to the Communist menace in India was also drawn in the Indian Legislative Assembly in February, 1936. At that time, a pro-Government member, Sir Mohammed Yakub, held that Communist propaganda was being distributed among Sikh soldiers[99] and further attention was turned towards the Communists in June, 1936 with the conviction in Calcutta of three Communist agitators to sentences of two years' rigorous imprisonment, that is, at hard labor for "being members of an unlawful organization—namely, the Communist Party of India —and of assisting it in conducting its activities and of issuing unauthorised newssheets."[100]

At this trial it was brought out that Indian Communism was being "carried on by underground propaganda" which propaganda showed that "its objects were the overthrow of British rule in India."[101]

Further evidences of the Red conspiracy in India were brought out in the trial of a Communist, Sheo Singh, in October, 1936 in Cawnpore. At that trial a special Investigation Officer named Rai Sahib Tika Ram testified that papers were found on the person of Sheo Singh which stated that "one of the objects of the Communist Party was to combine the scattered groups of Communists in India."[102]

It was further adduced that the C.P.I. had planned to pay its unemployed members 15 rupees per month and—in order to conceal the Communists' subversive activities within them —provincial secretaries were threatened with expulsion if they mentioned the names of legal bodies with whom the C.P.I. had entered into agreement.[103] This trial was an instance of strict British repression of the Communist movement in the second half of 1936, a repression which elicited cries of rage from the Comintern's press.[104]

During the year, 1937, the British Raj continued to maintain a stringent attitude towards the Indian Communists. On this subject, Ben Bradley complained in September, 1937 that "in every province in India, the Communist Party of India is illegal," and this was true, also in those provinces in which Congress Governments had been elected that year. Thus in the Congress-controlled Province of

Bombay alone the following organisations are among those

> still under the ban: Communist Party, the Marxist League (of) Bombay, the Young Workers' League, . . . Girni Kamgar Union and Mill Mazdur Union (of) Ahmadabad while a number of labour leaders are at present under order of deportation or whose personal liberties are restricted.[105]

In December, 1937, another Comintern spokesman complained bitterly about the alleged fact that "the police in many provinces are continuing to arrest people for political activities" and that searches and seizures, particularly in Bengal (which was not under a Congress Ministry) were being carried on.[106] British repression of the Communists in 1938 and in 1939 up to the outbreak of the war, slackened, but the Communist Party remained illegal.

In spite of this repression, by operating within legal organizations such as the A.I.T.U.C., the All-India Kisan Sabha, the Congress Socialist Party and even in the National Congress itself, the C.P.I. was able to extend its influence. The C.P.I. was especially able to do so in view of the fact that its then line of a united front against "imperialism" was genuinely attractive to wide strata of the Indian public.

The Communist press also made a reappearance in the years under survey. This was a direct product of a measure of leniency by the Congress ministries. Thus in Bombay there appeared in 1937 a weekly in English, entitled the "National Front," which paper has been held to have "played a great role in unifying the Communist movement and developing it in new areas."[107] In addition, in Bombay, the "Kranti" was revived as a Marathi publication, and in the Malabar area, at about this time, there appeared a paper called "Prabahatam," in Andhra, a paper called "Pabasakthi" (in Telegu) came forth and in Tamilnad (the Madras area) appeared a journal "Janasakthi."[108] The circulation of these journals did much to assist the dissemination of Communist propaganda in line with the Communist campaign in the furtherance of their utilization of the tactics of the "united front."

* * * * *

During the 'thirties the Communists were assisted by a friendly interest in India in Socialism and Communism as ideologies and their practical manifestation in Russia. Thus Sir Rabindranath Tagore visited the U.S.S.R. in 1930 and expressed a not inconsiderable amount of praise for the Soviet experiment. He emphasized that Soviet Russia had made considerable progress in education, indeed greater progress in eight years than India had made under British rule in 166 years. Tagore was also impressed by the alleged fact that education in Russia was applied equally to all Russian subjects "irrespective of class and race."[109] He also stated the view that the Soviet regime had been beneficent in that in modern Russia "greed of individual or party power and of money is absent."[110]

In Moscow, on September 24, 1930 the great poet declared: "I have envied you in all the great opportunities you have in this country,"[111] and on the following day in an interview with "Izvestia" he added:

> Before leaving your country let me once again assure you that I am struck with admiration for all that you are doing to free those who are in slavery, to raise those who were lowly and oppressed, and to bring help to those who were utterly helpless, reminding them that the source of their salvation lies in a proper education and their power to combine their human resources.[112]

Tagore was an admirer of, but not an adherent of Communism. He held that Communism had arisen from the "inhuman background of modern civilization," the greed of modern society and was a kind of "medical treatment" for it. As a "medical treatment" Communism was only a socio-economic system which was transitionary to an economy in which "co-operation in the production and control of wealth would prevail."[113]

Jawaharlal Nehru remained amicably disposed towards Socialism and the Soviet Union during the 'thirties. Just prior to the dawn of this decade, at the Lahore Congress of December, 1929 he personally proclaimed himself a "socialist."[114] It was thus under his influence that the next plenary session of the Congress at Karachi in December, 1931, included in its "Fundamental Rights of the Indian People" a provision that "the State shall own or control key industries and services, mineral resources, railways, waterways, shipping and other means of public transport."[115]

Nehru's boldest pronouncement regarding Communism and Socialism occurred in December, 1933 in which besides holding that the choice before the world lay between Communism and Fascism and of the two he chose the former, Nehru held in regard to the ideal of Communism:

> In regard to the method and approach to this ideal, I may not agree with everything that the orthodox Communists have done. I think that these methods will have to adapt themselves to changing conditions and may vary in different countries. But I do think that the basic ideology of Communism and its scientific interpretation of history is sound.[116]

These remarks caused some to feel that Nehru was playing the game of Moscow. It was humorously stated that "vodka has gone to his head"[117] and fear was expressed that such a socialist approach endangered Indian nationalism in that this stressed concept of the class struggle, whereas the need for India was "'co-operation among Nationalists of all strata of life to make their country free and independent."[118]

Nehru also followed the leftist line in his official "presidential address" to the Lucknow plenary session of the National Congress in which he maintained that "two rival economic and political systems," the capitalist and the socialist "faced each other in the world"; the first "prepared feverishly for war" whereas

> the other was the new socialist order of the U.S.S.R. which went from progress to progress though at a terrible cost, and where the problems of the capitalist world had ceased to exist.[119]

From this Nehru went on to add:

> Capitalism in its difficulties took to Fascism with its brutal suppression of what Western civilisation had ap-

parently stood for; it became even in some of its homelands, what its imperialist counterparts had long been in the subject colonial countries.[120]

Referring again to Russia Nehru noted that although there were things in the land of the Soviets which "pained" him and to which he "had to disagree," nonetheless, in the U.S.S.R. there was being founded a "new order and a new civilisation" and that

> if the future is full of hope, it is largely because of Soviet Russia and what it has done, and I am convinced that if some world catastrophe does not intervene, this new civilisation will spread to other lands and put an end to the wars and conflicts on which capitalism feeds.[121]

It was no surprise, then, that this address was hailed by a clandestine Indian Communist journal, "The Communist" as "a clearer anti-imperialist call than has ever been made from the Congress chair."[122]

But did this pro-Soviet and anti-capitalist attitude mean that Nehru favored that Socialism be pressed forward in India at all cost? Nehru answered by stating in the same address:

> Much as I wish for the advancement to socialism in this country, I have no desire to force the issue in the Congress and thereby create difficulties in the way of our struggle for independence.[123]

In his address as President of the Congress delivered in December, 1936 at the plenary session of the Congress in Faizpur, Nehru was more restrained in his utterances on Russia and Socialism than at Lucknow, but he did state that "backward Russia with one mighty jump has established a Soviet Socialist state and an economic order which has resulted in tremendous progress in all directions."[124] And as for the Congress and Socialism, he simply stated that "the Congress stands to-day for full democracy in India and fights for a democratic state, not for socialism."[125]

It may also be noted that in his writings between 1936 and 1939 he approved of the foreign policy of the Soviet Union and the British Communist Party in regard to such pressing matters as the Spanish Civil War and the Czechoslovakian or Sudeten question and he even held the view that the British and French "ruling classes" would rather endanger their empires than "engage in co-operation" with Soviet Russia for the "defence of democracy" as this policy might threaten their "privileged position." This, held Nehru, explains why the British and French governments "ignored Russia" at the time of the Munich crisis of September, 1938.[126]

Nehru held in these writings that Marxism appealed to him in a broad sense and helped him understand the processes of history. He stated further that class struggles are inherent in the present-day capitalist system, particularly since the "ruling or owning classes" resist all attempts to change the socio-economic state of their lands. Nehru denied that Marxism or Socialism envisioned violence, although like capitalism itself, Nehru felt that Socialism envisages the "possibility" of violence.[127] It may be noted in this connection that a "National Planning Committee" was set up under Congress' auspices under Nehru's direction. A "majority" of this Committee believed that "key industries" should be state-owned and the Committee decided that agricultural land also "must vest in the people of India collectively."[128]

Although in his writings during the years 1936 to 1939 Nehru continued to express satisfaction in the "progress" of Russian economy and the "advancing standards" of the Soviet people, there is evidence of doubt setting in. Hence, Nehru noted with apprehension the "purge" trials in the U.S.S.R., and although he believed the trials were generally "bona fide" and that there had been a "definite conspiracy" against the Soviet Government (contentions which are doubted today outside the Communist part of the world) Nehru nonetheless felt that all this might betoken "ill health" in the Soviet body politic which required, therefore, the employment of "violence" as a remedy.[129]

As to the Indian Communists, Nehru noted that the Indian Socialists (and presumably also the Communists) had not "reacted sufficiently to changing conditions," although he felt that the Communists "in Europe" might change "under the compulsion of events." But he specifically declared that such a change would not apply to the Indian Communists.[130] There is no reason whatsoever to feel that Nehru had any special inclination to the Indian Communist Party during the period under review in spite of his good words for Soviet Communism and for "Socialism," nor for that matter, his article in the British Communist publication, the "Labour Monthly."

It may be observed that the various resolutions on foreign affairs condemning "fascist aggression" and the "fascist powers," "Rebel Spain" and the Munich Pact, and "British imperialism" while approving of "collective security" against the Fascist menace probably written by Nehru and approved at the plenary sessions of the National Congress at Faizpur, December, 1936,[131] Haripura,[132] February, 1938 and Tripuri in March 1939,[133] were not at all dissimilar to the Comintern line.

The Congress Socialist Party also registered sympathy for Soviet Russia. Thus an official statement of the Socialists urged the National Congress at the time of the Faizpur Congress that "the Congress declare that the solidarity of the Indian people is with . . . the people of the U.S.S.R."[134]

The Congress Socialists further manifested sympathy for the Soviet Union in their party Conference at Lahore of April, 1938. A resolution of the party stated "that (the) U.S.S.R. is the only major Power working for peace" and in contrast argued that "the foreign policy of Great Britain is pro-fascist and is encouraging the forces of reaction and war." The resolution also went on to call for "support to the U.S.S.R."[135]

The Indian Communists were also assisted by certain articles in the Indian periodical press during the 'thirties which lauded the alleged ethics of Communism as practiced in Soviet Russia in the supposed freeing of the Russian people from the greed for money,[136] for improving morals in the Soviet Union in the advocacy of temperance and the abolition of prostitution "not by law . . . but by practice,"[137] by furthering child welfare and cultivating the fine arts,[138] as well as carrying on a "successful battle for the liquidation of illiteracy."[139] The progress of

Soviet economy was duly commented upon and praised,[140] the advantages present in young Indian technicians proceeding to Russia and securing work were pointed out,[141] and the progress of Soviet agriculture was extolled.[142] At the same time Indian writers refused to deem Soviet Russia a menace to India but even criticized British writers who spoke of that menace, and instead, lauded the alleged fact that Russia had "denounced the imperialist policy of the Tsars" and had instead recognized the right of the nations of Asia, notably China, Turkey, Iran and Afghanistan "to self-determination."[143]

However, right-wing elements in India naturally expressed disapproval of socialism, Soviet Russia and those favorable to them. Thus, an editorial in the "Feudatory and Zamindary Review" the ultra-conservative spokesman for India's princes and great landlords, referring to Nehru, in 1936 averred:

> The New President of the Congress will be satisfied with nothing less than Socialism all-round whatever that term may mean . . . The model of Pandit Jawaharlal is admittedly Soviet Russia. The socialism of India, according to him, means the sovietisation of the country.[144]

The leader of the Muslim League, Mohammed Ali Jinnah, likewise expressed his disapproval of the leftist tendencies of Nehru. At his Presidential address to the All-India Muslim League in October, 1937, Jinnah indicated marked distaste for that kind of public utterance which "is intended to lead the people towards socialistic and communistic ideas for which India is far from prepared."[145]

Mahatma Gandhi represented a bulwark for traditional Indian thought in the Congress and resisted pressures which would draw the Indian national movement into a materialistic Marxist direction. In November, 1921 he categorically stated "India does not want Bolshevism."[146] Three years later he added, of Communism that ". . . in so far as it is based on violence and denial of God, it repels me."[147] Hence, it is no wonder that when early in 1927, the Communist M. P. Shapurji Saklatvala clumsily attempted to induce Gandhi to "put on an ordinary pair of khaddar trousers and work with us in an ordinary way,"[148] his suggestion was most coolly and definitely rejected by the Mahatma in a lengthy correspondence.[149]

A few years later, on March 17, 1931 having been jeered in a public appearance by Communists, the Mahatma rebuked them by stating: "You claim to be communist, but you do not seem to live the life of communism."[150]

The passage of time did not induce Gandhi to evince great friendship for Soviet Communists. In February, 1937 Gandhi maintained that "Communism of the Russian type, that is, communism which is imposed on the people would be repugnant to India."[151]

Moreover, two years later, in January, 1939 referring to Soviet Communism, the Mahatma wrote:

> As I look to Russia, where the apotheosis of industrialisation has been reached, the life there does not appeal to me. To use the language of the Bible: 'What shall it avail a man if he gain the whole world and lose his soul?' In modern terms, it is beneath human dignity to lose one's individuality and become a mere cog in the machine. I want every individual to become a full-blooded, full-developed member of the society.[152]

However, this did not mean the Mahatma was a mere reactionary. Thus on March 26, 1931 the saintly Indian leader wrote:

> The Swaraj of my dream is the poor man's Swaraj. The necessaries of life should be enjoyed by you (the common people) in common with those enjoyed by moneyed men.[153]

Furthermore, Gandhi was not averse to Communism, taken as an idealistic concept. Hence, he stated in February, 1937:

> I believe in non-violent . . . communism . . . If communism came without any violence, it would be welcome. For then no property would be held by anybody except on behalf of the people and for the people.[154]

But what did "communism" mean to Gandhi in the final analysis? In March, 1937, he endeavored to answer this question by averring:

> What does communism mean in the last analysis? It means a classless society, an ideal that is worth striving for. Only I part company with it when force is called to aid for achieving it. We are all born equal, but we have all these centuries resisted the will of God. The idea of inequality of 'high and low' is an evil, but I do not believe in eradicating evil from the human breast at the point of the bayonet.[155]

Hence Gandhi believed in Communism as an ethical ideal, but opposed its practical manifestation in Russia, especially in its anti-religious manifestations. These manifestations were incidentally generally soft-pedalled by Indian Communists, although as an ultimate goal it was held by them "necessary to fight religion in India"[156] and to do so by joining religious organizations so as "to destroy such organisations from within."[157]

Gandhi distinctly discounted any Soviet threat to India. On July 2, 1932 he held that "it is a gratuitous assumption that Russia is to pounce upon India and is an insult to Russia,"[158] and on another occasion when asked "Are you not afraid of Bolshevik propaganda spreading into India," the Mahatma replied: "I do not think the Indian people are so gullible."[159]

Interestingly enough, one of the critics of a pro-Soviet policy was Motilal Nehru who, probably aiming his remarks at his son, declared that though "the example of the Russian revolution is trotted in and out of season," the Soviet Union was no terrestrial paradise. The elder Nehru observed there was really no equality there and all the elementary rights of free citizens were denied subjects of the Kremlin. Even advocates of freedom in Russia, held the present Indian premier's father, "were rotting in prison."[160]

Influenced by the right wing of Congress, some of the Congress ministries notably those of the Bombay Presidency and the Madras Presidency maintained a hostile attitude towards the Communists,[161] although, by contrast, that of the United Provinces refused to take action against them even though specifically requested to do so by the Employers' Association of Northern India.[162] The anti-Communist activities of certain of the ministries naturally evoked an aggrieved complaint from the Comintern's propagandists, that this "could only have extremely serious repercussions in relation to the United National Front in India."[163] However, by no means did this alter the Communists' policy in relation to the "united front." For this "united front" policy, in giving the Communists renewed access to the Indian labor movement, and opening up to them, as never before, access to the peasants' movement, in spite of continued British repression, had paid rich dividends to the Indian Communists and had thereby facilitated the designs of Soviet Russia on India.

CHAPTER SIX

Soviet Intrigues on India's Frontiers

Before taking up the story of the vicissitudes of the Communist Party of India during the years of the Second World War, we shall examine Soviet intrigue on the borderlands from the time that the projected incursion into India was abandoned, till the outbreak of that conflict. We shall also examine Soviet policy in relation to India which was affected both by the activities of the Bolsheviks in the borderlands and by the machinations of the Soviet fifth column, the C.P.I. within India.

Soviet maneuvers in the western and northern borderlands of India: Afghanistan, Iran, Chinese Turkestan and Tibet were of significance, for if the Soviets could obtain effective control of these lands, they would be in a position effectively to propagandize the sub-continent and dispatch agents into it to establish liaison with the C.P.I. and thus further the Communist conspiracy in India. Besides, Soviet control of Iran and Afghanistan, or of either country would make it possible for the Soviets, if they should risk such a daring policy, to emulate Alexander the Great and Tamerlane and effect an invasion of India.

We have seen that after a flirtation with Soviet Russia, between the years 1919 to 1921, Emir Amanullah of Afghanistan had resumed his father's policy of friendship for Britain. This policy was culminated by the appointment of an Afghan minister at the Court of St. James's in 1922 and the simultaneous appointment of a British minister to the Court of Kabul,[1] and by the successful negotiation of an Anglo-Afghan trade convention in June, 1923.[2]

Meanwhile, in spite of the fact that he was losing ground since the early part of 1921 when he had successfully negotiated the Soviet-Afghan treaty, the wily Soviet ambassador, Fedor Raskolnikov did his best to carry on intrigues in the court of the Emir. That his intrigues, albeit unsuccessful, were annoying to the English was evinced by the specific demand of the British Foreign Office under Lord Curzon of May 2, 1923, that Raskolnikov be removed from his post, which request was granted.[3]

Moscow was temporarily excited in December 1923 when the British sent a strong note to Kabul demanding that Afghanistan put a stop forthwith to disturbing incidents on the Indo-Afghan frontier.[4] Foreign Minister Chicherin in a press conference on December 19th held that in this "ultimatum" the British had demanded that Afghanistan should "sever all her relations with Russia" and that this "ultimatum" consequently resulted in the "danger of new complications in Anglo-Russian relations." This was all the more the case since the Soviet Union had close relations with the Emir's government.[5] The British foreign office "flatly contradicted" the Soviet notion that the note to Kabul was an "ultimatum"[6] and it added "no mention was made of Russia at any time" in the discussions with the Afghans.[7]

In March, 1924, an insurrection known as the "Khost Rebellion" broke out among the turbulent tribesmen of Southern Afghanistan. In this circumstance the Soviets felt they would gain the greatest measure of influence by supporting Emir Amanullah. Hence they accused the British of furnishing "money and arms" in order "to overthrow the liberal Emir."[8] In addition, at the end of April, 1924, they organized the most elaborate embassy they had yet sent to the land of the Afghans. The new embassy was headed by Leonid Stark, who, like Raskolnikov, was of non-proletarian origin, being the son of a Czarist admiral. This non-proletarian origin notwithstanding, Stark had joined the Bolsheviks in 1905 and "enjoyed great consideration in the Party." Among the members of Stark's embassy was a trusted agent of the O.G.P.U. named Georgi Agabekov. Besides the goal of bolstering Russia's position in

Afghanistan and taking advantage of the "Khost Rebellion," for furthering this aim, a very important purpose of Stark's embassy was to further the dissemination of Communist propaganda from Central Asia into India, particularly amongst the restless tribesmen of the North-West Frontier Province.[9]

In the summer of 1924, Stark's embassy, which had been greeted at the Afghan-Soviet frontier with the "highest honors" was ensconced in Kabul, and Agabekov immediately set to work in organizing a Soviet spy network to conduct operations in both Afghanistan and India.[10] Under the direction of Agabekov and another Soviet agent named Marhov, who had come from England to Russia and had studied at the Institute of Oriental Languages in Moscow, where he had specialized in Indian languages, the Soviets in Kabul gathered together a considerable number of spies to carry on espionage and further subversive activity in India. Among the agents utilized at this time by the Soviets was a certain Indian Muslim named Tchitzala who had "extensive relations" with the volatile tribesmen of the Afghan-Indian frontier and it was through him that the Soviet embassy in Kabul came into contact "with two famous chiefs of those tribes (who) became our (Soviet) agents."[11] The chiefs were named Moulk Bachir and Padcha Goulem and the former was paid a subsidy by the Soviets of no less than £500 every month to make mischief on the frontier.[12]

Another agent who was then utilized by the Soviets in their efforts to disseminate the seeds of Communist sedition into India from Afghanistan, was a certain Moustefi who was supposed to have been well-informed of the doings of the Muslims of India. He had also been "commissioned by Amanullah himself to tie up with the principal Indian Muslims," so that he was in the position to play the dual role of spying on behalf of the Soviets in fact as well as ostensibly on behalf of the Emir, on the leaders of the Indian Muslim community. He also spied on the Emir himself. Moustefi is held to have "executed his commission well" from the Soviet standpoint.[13]

In order to facilitate Red propaganda operations in Afghanistan and India, in August, 1924, the Executive Committee of the Comintern issued instructions to officials in Tashkent that a new propaganda base in Northern Afghanistan should be established at Mazar-i-Sharif. This action was followed by an increase in the number of Russians entering Afghanistan.[14]

In the beginning of 1925, the Russian agents in Afghanistan had a seemingly great opportunity. The influential old Sheik Ul Islam, an important power on the Northwest Frontier, proposed through his sons, an alliance with the Soviets in which he would conduct a wide-scale "partisan war" on the Indo-Afghan frontier if the Russians in turn would furnish him with 100,000 rubles, 5,000 rifles, and a hundred cartridges per rifle. This matter was reported to Moscow without delay by the Soviet embassy, but the response from there was negative, as the Kremlin refused to send the rifles. The reasons given by Moscow were that the transport of the arms to the Indian border would be too dangerous, and should news of such a provocative shipment of arms "leak out, diplomatic complications with Britain and Afghanistan might follow."[15] That such "complications" would have followed in respect to Britain is obvious, particularly since an anti-Soviet Conservative ministry now held office. The bellicose old Sheik was disappointed at not receiving the weapons, but he and his sons continued during the course of 1925 to supply the Soviets in Kabul with information.[16]

However, towards the close of that year the Russian position in Afghanistan deteriorated. In the first place, a serious quarrel developed between Stark and Agabekov which resulted in Agabekov's leaving Afghanistan in March, 1926. Agabekov's disappearance from the Afghan scene disrupted the espionage network of the Soviets. This circumstance from the Soviet standpoint had been further aggravated when Agabekov's able collaborator in intrigue, Marhov, had returned to Russia in August, 1925, and had been replaced by a certain Frantzevich whom Agabekov deemed a nincompoop. Frantzevich wrote wildly to Moscow of ways "to organize a revolt in India" while actually letting the Soviet network of agents in Afghanistan and India seriously deteriorate. Stark thought so little of Frantzevich's views on India that he did not even bother to forward them to Moscow.[17]

In the second place, the "Khost Rebellion," the outbreak of which in March, 1924 has so encouraged the Soviets, had been suppressed by January, 1925, largely through British aid, including the dispatch for the Afghans' use of military aircraft which actually were flown by German pilots.[18] The result was that in the year 1925 Emir Amanullah was more amicably disposed than ever towards the British, a situation obviously contrary to the desire of the intriguing Soviets.[19]

In the third place, an incident involving a clash over an island on the Oxus River which formed the Soviet-Afghan boundary in December, 1925, aroused an intense measure of Afghan ire and even caused some concern to the British who felt that the clash, which had been initiated by the Soviets, indicated the first step on a possible march to India. The incident was ended when the Soviets evacuated the disputed island, thereby backing down completely.[20]

Soviet influence in Afghanistan again rose in the summer of the year 1926 and even attained the highest point it had held since the spring of 1921. One great cause for this, in addition to Russia's backing down in the island crisis, was the fact that in the summer of 1926 Soviet planes manned by officers of the Soviet air force "vigorously" bombed certain unruly elements which had again revolted against the Afghan government.[21] It may be noted that the presence of some twenty Soviet military planes and pilots in Afghanistan, along with 100 Communist "Europeans" was reported in Afghanistan as early as March, 1926.[22] As a result of the presence of these planes in Afghanistan in 1926, the wily Stark conceived the idea of creating in the land of the Emir an advanced Soviet air base which would manifestly prove very valuable were the Soviets to undertake "an offensive against India."[23] The planes with their pilots and mechanics were nominally at the disposition of the Afghans, but in effect, their presence in Afghanistan already made for a "strategic base" for the Russians in Amanullah's domain.[24] It was also in 1926 that there were reports that the Soviets had been surveying the route for a strategic railway from the Soviet frontier to the city of Kabul.[25] Simultaneously, the Soviets were building up their network of agents under the direction of

Agabekov's successor, a man named Skijali Weiss, alias Schmidt, nominally an attaché of the embassy.[26]

During the summer of 1926 the Soviets, encouraged by this favorable turn of events for them, entered into negotiations with the Afghans, the result of which was a Russo-Afghan Treaty of Mutual Neutrality and Non-Aggression, concluded on August 31, 1926, which provided for the mutual neutrality of the two contracting parties in case either power was engaged in war with another power or other powers and provided also for mutual non-aggression and mutual non-interference in each other's affairs.[27]

Although the treaty was apparently an innocuous one, there was concern in unofficial British quarters that there was more in it than met the eye.[28] A different view, however, was taken by Tory Foreign Minister, Sir Austen Chamberlain, who answered a question in Parliament on November 19, 1926 by saying that he saw "no reason to suppose that the treaty would have any prejudicial effects on British-Indian interests."[29]

The reason for this apparent equanimity of the British Government lay, no doubt, in its belief that what was involved was simply Amanullah's policy of playing Britain off against Russia by granting favors at one time to the one power, and then, after a period of time had elapsed, of granting favor to the other while simultaneously cooling relations with the previously favored power.

This view was borne out in 1927. Quietly and without fanfare, King (the title had been changed from Emir in 1926) Amanullah made no effort to strengthen his bonds with Russia during that year. Indeed, during the spring of 1927 he undertook an ostentatious tour of Afghan Turkestan or Northern Afghanistan, the area adjacent to Soviet Central Asia—like the latter area populated by Uzbeks and Tajiks—where Communist influence was greatest, in which region he definitely counteracted to a measurable extent, Red intrigues.[30] Nothing more was heard of Soviet aircraft or Russian engineers surveying strategic railroad lines and it would seem that quiet Afghan pressure, which had British approval and support, had been utilized to compel the Soviets to curtail their intrigues in Amanullah's

Kingdom. Furthermore, Soviet intrigues there were further weakened by a quarrel which broke out between the ambassador, Stark, and the O.G.P.U. agent, Skijali Weiss, a quarrel which ended in the recall of the latter.[31] Indeed, the deterioration of Soviet-Afghan relations is shown by the fact that in March, 1928, angered at this deterioration of their position in Afghanistan, the Soviets refused to remit transit charges on Afghan goods passing through Soviet territory.[32]

King Amanullah undertook an extensive and expensive tour of Europe in the spring of 1928, visiting among other countries, Great Britain and Russia. In the latter country, the King received a royal reception, President Kalinin and Foreign Minister Chicherin greeting him officiously with the words "Your Majesty," strange words for Bolsheviks.[33] At the same time the Afghan ruler and his country were duly lauded in the Soviet press.[34] However, in order to protect him and to spy on him, King Amanullah was "surrounded" during his fortnightly visit to the "workers' paradise" in May, 1928, by agents of the O.G.P.U. These agents reported to their superiors that in spite of the lavish entertainment he had been receiving from the Russians, the Afghan monarch was no longer disposed to support the Soviets but rather "was inclined to favor the Occidental countries."[35]

On November 14, 1928, the important Shinwari tribe of Southeastern Afghanistan rose in rebellion against King Amanullah on account of the latter's efforts to effect the occidentalization of his feudal realm.[36] This revolt was followed by another insurrection led by an "illiterate bandit" of Tajik, rather than Afghan nationality, named Bakao-i-Sakao (meaning "Son of the Water Carrier"). Caught between two fires, King Amanullah, who had lost hope of successfully defending Kabul, abdicated his throne in favor of his elder brother, Sirdar Inayabullah, and fled by plane to Kandahar.[37] The "Son of the Water Carrier" immediately took possession of Kabul and proclaimed himself King of Afghanistan with the title of Habibullah Khan which means Beloved of God.[38]

The situation in Afghanistan evoked considerable interest in the Kremlin. The fact that three parties were contending for power in Afghanistan, the Shinwaris, the partisans of Bakao-i-Sakao and the royalists under Amanullah and Inayabullah, appeared to present a golden opportunity for the Russians to fish in the troubled waters of the most important borderland of India. A dispute immediately ensued among the highest echelons of Soviet officialdom in regards to which group the Soviets should support. The OGPU argued that the Soviet government should actively support Bakao-i-Sakao, because he had "sprung from the people," and because "his power was based on the peasants whose champion he was." Through him important steps to the "Sovietization" of Afghanistan might be carried out. On the other hand the Soviet Commissariat of Foreign Affairs (the "Narkomindel") held that the cause of Amanullah and Inayabullah should be supported on the ground that since Bakao-i-Sakao was supported only by the nationalities of Northern Afghanistan, the Uzbeks and Tajiks, he might desire to extend his influence into Soviet Central Asia, a region heavily populated by these peoples. On the other hand, argued the "Narkomindel," the clan of Amanullah, being Afghans or Pathans would rather be expected to divert any aggressive attitude on their part to their kinsmen in the North-West Frontier Province of British India. Besides, it was held Bakao-i-Sakao would hardly be able to hold power for long.[39]

The quarrel between the OGPU and the Foreign Commissariat over which Afghan party to support, was carried over to the Soviet Politburo itself and the latter (which undoubtedly meant Stalin) decided in favor of the "Narkomindel" and the clan of Amanullah. Thus the Bolsheviks placed themselves on the side of that segment of the Afghan landlords who favored the cause of Amanullah as against the "proletarian," Bakao-i-Sakao, who was actually carrying on a program of expropriating Afghan landlords.[40] Therefore, this was an example of cynical Soviet opportunism.

The Soviets now determined to go to considerable lengths to aid Amanullah who, having arrived at Kandahar, had revoked his abdication and was gathering a force to march back to Kabul.[41] In a conference one night in which Stalin was present, it was decided, or most likely Stalin decided, that a Soviet force disguised as Afghans, to be led by a certain Primakov, the Soviet military attaché in Afghanistan who had returned to Russia, would invade that country and march to Kabul. The nominal leader of the expedition would be Ghulam Wali Khan, the Afghan ambassador to Soviet Russia.[42]

Although the force was small—about 800 men only—thanks to its vastly superior military technology, it successfully penetrated Afghan Turkestan and in two engagements whipped very much larger forces of the partisans of the "Son of the Water Carrier." The road to Kabul was open to the Soviets.[43] But they were not destined to cross the Hindu Kush and set up a puppet regime on the borders of India.

Why did the Soviets abandon their plan? In the first place, Amanullah, for whom the campaign was nominally being undertaken, had been completely routed in the South in the middle of April by the adherents of Bakao-i-Sakao so that he ignominiously fled to India on May 23, 1929 whence he proceeded to Italy where he obtained asylum.[44]

In the second place the advance of the Russians was "the talk not only of the foreign legations at Kabul, but also of the European press,"[45] in which the claim was made that Soviet Russia was seeking to Bolshevize Afghanistan.[46]

Such reports of Soviet designs and intrigues in Afghanistan certainly were not conducive to an improvement in Anglo-Soviet relations. It should be noted that it was in the late spring of 1929 that the Soviets began their negotiations with the newly elected Liberal-supported Labour Cabinet of Ramsay MacDonald for the resumption of Anglo-Soviet diplomatic relations which had been broken off two years previously. Manifestly, the Soviet threat to control Afghanistan through a restored puppet ruler, not to speak of the establishment of a Communist state in Afghanistan would, to say the least, be prejudicial to the restoration and maintenance of tolerable Anglo-Soviet relations. Should the Soviets definitely commit themselves to an openly aggressive policy in Afghanistan, war with Great Britain, even with a Labour Government in office, might ensue. In the circumstances, therefore, the Soviet government saw fit to order the recall of its expeditionary force in Afghanistan in the late spring of 1929.[47] However, the Soviet press, outspokenly continued to vent its spleen on the role of the British in the Afghan crisis during the course of the year, 1929. The British were accused of having designs on Soviet Central Asia as well as on Afghanistan.[48]

In the meantime, in strife-torn Afghanistan, the rule of the "Son of the Water Carrier" was overthrown by the forces of Amanullah's brother, Nadir Khan, the former Afghan minister to France who had returned from that country. The latter captured Kabul on October 12, 1929, and was proclaimed King Nadir Shah on October 16th, while the hapless Habibullah was forthwith executed.[49]

The accession to power of Nadir Khan brought no joy to the Kremlin. He was regarded by the Soviets as an "adversary to be reckoned with."[50] Nonetheless, when it became evident that Nadir Khan would seize power, the Soviets adopted an amicable attitude towards him, perhaps hoping that he would manifest interest chiefly in the south of Afghanistan and that he might carry on an anti-British policy. In addition, the Afghan embassy in Moscow urged Soviet support for Nadir Shah which appears to have had some effect.[51] But when the new Afghan ruler consolidated his power in the Southern part of his realm, the Soviet authorities decided on carrying out a new intervention in Afghanistan. Hence the Soviets "with a considerable force" invaded Afghanistan in June, 1930 and advanced some forty miles south of the Soviet frontier. Their excuse for this act of aggression was that an anti-Soviet Central Asian insurrectionist known as Ibrahim Beg was utilizing Afghan territory for forays against Soviet Central Asia.[52] However, it would seem that through this invasion the Soviets hoped to prevent King Nadir Shah from seizing control of Afghan Turkestan which was still in a state of anarchy. However, this aggressive act had the diametrically opposite effect on Nadir Shah. Having suppressed all forces hostile to him in the South and West of Afghanistan, this redoubtable ruler sent his brother, Sardar Shah Mahmoud, Commander-in-Chief of the Afghan army, across the Hindu Kush range into Afghan Turkestan in December, 1930.[53] The Soviets, not wishing to provoke Nadir Shah and behind him Britain (which through the proceedings of the Meerut Conspiracy Case, then in progress, was aware of Soviet designs on India) had already evacuated Afghan Turkestan and did nothing to impede Sardar Shah Mahmoud's advance. By April, 1931 Afghan Turkestan was firmly under the rule of Nadir Shah, who proved an able ruler.[54] He avoided Amanullah's error in trying to force "occidentalization" too rapidly on a people steeped in its age-old conservative Muslim culture, while at the same time, he strengthened his country's economic and military position.[55]

On November 8, 1933, King Mohammed Nadir Shah was assassinated by a fanatical student.[56] He was succeeded by his 19-year old son who took the title of Mohammed Zahir Shah. But the real power behind the throne lay with his three able uncles, brothers of Nadir Shah and Amanullah: Hashin Khan, the Prime Minister, Shah Mahmoud Khan, the Minister of War, and Shah Ghulam Wali Khan.[57] They determined the domestic policies of Mohammed Zahir Shah[58] In their conduct of Afghan foreign affairs during the years 1933 to 1939, they continued the policy of Nadir Shah in maintaining correct relations with Soviet Russia as well as Great Britain, without in any way subordinating Afghanistan to either. They encouraged the nationals of several Western European countries to develop the resources of Afghanistan,[59] a policy begun as early as 1922 by Amanullah.[60] Under their rule as well as under that of Nadir Shah the Russians were far-less in evidence in Afghanistan than they had been during the reign of Amanullah. In addition the Soviet press paid far less attention to Afghanistan between 1933 and 1939 than it had hitherto, which indicated that the Soviets were forced to recognize the independent status of that vital border state between themselves and British India.

The Soviets also maintained intrigues against India from Iran in spite of the anti-Communist policy towards Persian Communists of that country's ruler, Riza Pahlevi, who had ascended the Peacock Throne of the Shahs in 1924. On October 1, 1927, however, Soviet Russia was able to conclude a non-aggression pact with Iran as a consequence of which the Soviet

Union was able to extend its commercial influence in that land to such an extent that by the early 'thirties, the U.S.S.R. stood as the leading nation in Persia's foreign trade, a situation which permitted the Soviet Union to engage in "dumping" her products on the Iranian market.[61]

Between 1926 and 1929 Soviet agents were active in Iran, particularly in the strategic northeastern province of Khorasan and its capital, Meshed, the area which bordered the British Indian province of Baluchistan as well as Afghanistan. In that area in the spring of 1926 there was an insurrection against the national Iranian govrenment led by a certain officer named Salar Djang, which revolt had a "definitely Bolshevist flavor."[62] The Soviet authorities in Tashkent wanted to intervene openly in this affair, but their interventionist plans were vetoed by Moscow, which apparently did not wish to antagonize the British who were well aware of the strategic nature of this area located as it was on an important road to India.[63]

During the years 1926 and 1927, Agabekov who had been transferred from Afghanistan was active in Eastern Persia. Under his aegis a number of agents were sent to the Persian-Indian boundary in Baluchistan. In fact, by the early spring of 1927 no fewer than fifty Soviet agents were operating on the Indian-Persian boundary. These agents were supposed to maintain an active liaison with Communists in the interior of India. The agents were especially charged to foment revolt on the Iranian-Indian frontier and even inside British Baluchistan, in event of an Anglo-Soviet war, the outbreak of which, it would seem, was really believed likely in Moscow.[64] It may be noted that at this time, the Soviets won the secret support of a certain Asoled Sultan, the Iranian governor of Bakharz, a strategic area south of Meshed and bordering on Afghanistan. The latter agreed that he would "pass across the frontier" Soviet men and arms "to any number and any quantity."[65]

Soviet interest in the strategic southern part of Iran continued during the course of the year, 1928, especially in view of the decision of the Executive Committee of the Communist International as well as of the Sixth Congress of that body which had stressed the importance of this region, as well as that of India in the furtherance of the World Revolution. During this time Soviet agents were even ordered to pay subsidies to the chiefs of strategically located South Persian tribes.[66]

In 1929 and after, Soviet influence, other than commercial, in Iran waned, owing to the growing power of the central Iranian Government under Shah Riza Pahlevi and the apparent desire on the part of the Kremlin, not to carry on moves of a provocative nature against this borderland of India which might offend the British Government. Moreover, after the middle of the 'thirties Soviet trade with Iran markedly diminished. Indeed, in the summer of 1939 the position of the Soviet Union in Iran was far weaker than it had been in the spring of 1921 when parts of Northern Persia were actually under Communist rule.

Thanks to the determination of the redoubtable governor of Chinese Turkestan, Yen Tsen-hsian, who was virtually an autonomous ruler, other than being able to establish consulates in Kashgar and Urumchi,[67] the Soviets were unable to gain any influence in this northern borderland of India.[68]

In Sinkiang in 1930 this old war-lord was assassinated after having ruled that land for seventeen years. For the next few years thereafter, Chinese Turkestan was in a state of anarchy with several groups, among which, interestingly enough, was a White Russian party, under a certain Pappengut, struggling for power. As victor in the confused situation there emerged a certain General Ma Sheng, who was a protégé of the Soviets.[69] His victory meant an augmentation of Soviet influence in Sinkiang. Soon after he came into power in 1933 Ma Sheng promulgated a "Six Point Program," the first two points of which were "anti-imperialism" (an anti-British slogan) and "kinship to Sovietism."[70] In addition, in December 1933, a "comprehensive agreement" was concluded between the new Sinkiang government and Pogodin, the principal Soviet envoy to that government. By the terms of the agreement which were secret and which were "most comprehensive," Russia was promised mining, oil and gold concessions and the right to build a railway from Soviet Central Asia into the Sinkiang capital, Urumchi. Pro-Soviet officers were put in charge of the remnant of the former White forces and so, ironically enough, this anti-Bolshevik force was put under what amounted to a Soviet command. In addition, Soviet military assistance was promised to the Ma Sheng government.[71]

Japan, China and Britain were annoyed by the sudden accession of Soviet influence in Chinese Turkestan in 1933 and 1934. In Japan, Foreign Minister Hirota informed the Diet, with some asperity, of "reports of the Sovietization of Sinkiang,"[72] an area which Japan herself was possibly coveting. The Chinese Government protested against the use of Soviet "foreign advisers" and protested also against the proposed loans by the Soviets to the Sinkiang Government.[73] The fact that the Sinkiang Government continued to admit a purely formal relationship with the Chinese state, did not please at all the authorities in Nanking (later Chungking). Although not protesting openly, the British were likewise certainly not pleased by the turn of events in Sinkiang; they realized that Soviet agents could now cross directly into India by traversing the Himalayan passes, and thus assist the cause of the Communist Party of India.[74] Soviet influence in Chinese Turkestan had not diminished by September 1, 1939. That the Russians had not openly Sovietized the area was probably a result of their desire not to offend too openly Great Britain, and perhaps also the Nationalist Government of China.

The Soviets were also interested in that other northern borderland of India, like Sinkiang nominally a part of China, the mysterious land of Tibet. Communist emissaries began to visit the "forbidden city" of Lhasa as early as 1922.[75] In 1927 a large delegation consisting of Sovietized Mongols arrived in Lhasa. They spent six months in Tibet, taking photographs of all strategic passes and fortified positions and they even promised the Tibetan authorities military aid in case the latter should come into conflict with Great Britain, or China, the nominal suzerain of Tibet. The Mongol Communists left behind a clever Red Mongol agent, a certain Dorjiev, who become friendly with many leading Tibetan dignataries including the Dalai Lama himself.[76]

In 1930 it was "decided to instruct the I.K.K.I. to take steps to combine the existing revolutionary groups in Tibet into a national party and to nominate Comrade Dorjiev as President of the Central Committee of the proposed new party," and a sum of money equivalent to £20,000 was assigned for these activities.[77] Besides, when in 1932 a war broke out between the Dalai Lama and his rival of East Tibet, the Panchen Lama (who was supported by the Chinese Nationalists), "Pravda" in its issue of July 27, 1932, saw fit to comment upon the situation by accusing the Dalai Lama of being a British agent who would aid "English imperialism" in strengthening "its influence over the western provinces of China and in particular over Chinese Turkestan."[78]

This statement indicates that the growing influence of the Soviets in Sinkiang was causing them to cast a glance at Tibet. However, nothing concrete was done by the Soviets between 1932 and 1939 to improve their position in "the roof of the world."

In addition to their attempts to infiltrate India's borderlands the Soviets also endeavored to send agents into India to form liaison with the C.P.I. Active in this work was Rattan Singh, who, as we have noted, represented the California members of the Ghadr Party at the Fourth Congress of the Comintern, and another agent named Teja Singh Swatanatar. These two men were able to bring about an arrangement by which an annual number of the recruits of the Ghadr Party were sent to Moscow for one year's training in sabotage and espionage. In 1934, according to British intelligence in India, there were about sixty ex-Ghadr Sikh students in training in Moscow in addition to those who had completed their course in espionage.[79] Besides, in the early 'thirties the Soviets utilized the services of Haidar Khan, Roy's former associate in Germany who, unlike the latter, had remained loyal to Moscow. Haidar Khan established himself in business in Madras and engaged in correspondence with Communist groups in various parts of the Indian peninsula.[80] These operations supplemented those of the British Communist Party which endeavored to subvert Indian youths in Britain. These operations in the 'thirties were carried on under the supervision of R. Palme Dutt who had completely displaced Saklatvala, his earlier rival, as the principal tutor of India's Communists,[81] probably owing to the latter's defeat in the general British elections of 1929.

* * * * *

Since the foreign policy of Great Britain and India was one during the years under survey, relations between Russia and India were obviously vitally affected by Anglo-Soviet relations. Commercial relations between the two powers resulting in the de facto establishment of Anglo-Soviet relations took place on March 16, 1921[82] and the establishment of de jure relations was established by the first MacDonald Cabinet on February 1, 1924.[83] But the course of these relations were not smooth. In September, 1924, the "Zinoviev letter" was disclosed in which "letter" (the authenticity of which has been questioned) the General Secretary Zinoviev of the Communist International allegedly ordered the "Central Committee" of the "British Communist Party" to form "cells" in the British army, in order to bring about an eventual "armed insurrection" against His Majesty's Government. The disclosure of the "Zinoviev letter" was largely instrumental in the victory of the Tories in the general election of October 1924.[84]

Anglo-Soviet relations were strained after this new Government, headed by Stanley Baldwin, came into power. The alleged sending of £250,000 by Soviet trade unions to British labor during the time of the General Strike of May, 1926, resulted in the exchange of acrimonious British and Russian notes.[85] Of greater direct significance to India in March, 1927, when Soviet influence along the Indo-Persian and Afghan-Persian frontiers was considerable, and at about the time when British officials in India and British writers were playing up the "Soviet menace" to the sub-continent,[86] Foreign Minister Sir Austen Chamberlain sent a "very energetic note" to Moscow demanding the complete cessation of all Communist propaganda in British territory and threatening to break off diplomatic relations in the event of non-compliance. Since the Soviets did not desist from their program, but decided instead to intensify their propaganda work in Iran in 1927 with particular interest in that part of Persia bordering India,[87] the British were further ired and action against the Soviets appeared inevitable.[88]

That action occurred on May 12, 1927, when a force of 200 plainclothes and uniformed policemen brusquely invaded the headquarters of the Soviet Trade Delegation and the premises occupied by Arcos, the corporation handling Anglo-Russian commerce in London. It was officially stated that the police, operating under orders of Home Secretary Joynson-Hicks, were searching for a "State document" which had mysteriously disappeared some months previously and which was thought to be in the custody of the Soviets' agents in London,[89] and it was unofficially reported that this document was one which contained information dealing with Britain's military policy in the North-West Frontier Province area of India, adjacent to the Afghan frontier. But though the British police searched the Soviet premises high and low, they could not find the mysterious document.[90] The upshot of the affair was another angry exchange of notes between Moscow and London which culminated in the official breaking of diplomatic relations by Britain with the Soviet Government on May 26, 1927,[91] an act which prompted the Chancellor of the Exchequer (the then Mr.) Winston Churchill to opine exultantly: "We have proclaimed them—the Soviet Representatives—treacherous, incorrigible, and unfit for civilised intercourse."[92] In a more temperate vein, his superior, Prime Minister Stanley Baldwin informed the House of Commons that the action "does not in any way mean or imply war against Russia" and would not even bar "the pursuit of legitimate trade between the two countries."[93]

The first effect of the diplomatic break was to arouse the British to reorganize and reinforce their army in India, and the rupture with Moscow is alleged to have induced the British to concentrate troops in the region of Peshawar in the vicinity of the Afghan frontier.[94] Contemporaneously, within India, the news of the diplomatic rupture was received with a definite measure of interest, particularly from Indian nationalists whose sympathies had been with Russia in her diplomatic dispute with Britain. It is significant that the Nehrus, père and fils, undertook their journey to Moscow in November, 1927, only a few months after the rupture, a visit which resulted in the younger Nehru's extolling of the Communist regime in his book, "Soviet Russia." It is likewise noteworthy that in the following month, the National Congress, at Jawaharlal Nehru's suggestion, enacted resolutions favorable to Russia, especially that which affiliated that body with the League Against Imperialism.

Following the Sixth Comintern Congress, the Soviet Government in its official journals as well as the E.C.C.I. inaugurated a scurrilous campaign against the British rulers of India as well as the native bourgeoisie of the Peninsula. Thus on April 28, 1929, "Pravda" made much over the textile strike in Bombay which was then getting under way, by declaring proudly that conservative labor leaders such as N. M. Joshi, had no influence over Indian workers whatsoever and that the latter must expose the "treason" of the labor leaders.[95] Then on June 12, 1929, "Izvestia" duly noted the existence in India of a potentially revolutionary "industrial proletariat some 4,000,000 strong" and observed that the peasants of India could indeed be led by this proletariat.

"Izvestia" went on to state:

> The question at present is whether imperialism which employs ruthless terror and occasionally grants sops to the national bourgeoisie will succeed in disrupting the (Communist) movement and in isolating and destroying the proletariat before the peasant masses of India stage an insurrection. This (question) reacts on English policy in all countries adjacent to India and looked upon by London as buffer states: Persia Afghanistan and Tibet.[96]

The article in "Izvestia" went on to state that although Gandhi had successfully betrayed the Indian peasants to the British in 1921-1922, and that, as of 1929, the "bureaucratic machinery of English imperialism is working well and with precision," this did not contradict the fact that the Indian peasantry were on the verge of a great revolution against the British imperialists and their bourgeois accomplices.[97]

These provocative utterances in the official Soviet press were followed by the Second World Congress of the Communist controlled League Against Imperialism in Frankfurt, on July 21, 1929. No fewer than twenty-seven of the delegates were Indians. One of the speeches at this Communist sponsored gathering was one by a Soviet delegate named Melnit Shanki who bitterly criticized the British Labor government for prolonging the imprisonment of the Indian comrades, the conspirators of Meerut.[98]

A few months after this gathering the Executive Committee of the Communist International issued a formal manifesto to the people which informed the Indian workers and peasants to spurn any offers made by "the imperialist lackeys now posing as a Labour government in England" in respect to any possible proposals for dominion status in India. The workers and peasants, held the manifesto, should not supinely wait for what the "imperialists" had to offer them, but rather should take their own fate into their own hands, and should rise and overthrow British rule and set up a Soviet India in its place.[99]

This bold pronouncement was followed by a long article published in "Izvestia" on February 9, 1930, which stated that one of the best developments in India from the Communist point of view was the growth of the revolutionary activity of the petit bourgeois youth in the form of the terrorist movement. True, held "Izvestia," these young petty bourgeois terrorists suffered from the "taint" of nationalist ideas, but they could be brought round to a proper ideological position by the revolutionary proletariat and the Communist party. Therefore, it was held to be one of the most important duties for the Indian Communists

> . . . to wrest the Indian revolutionary petty bourgeoisie away from under the influence of opportunists and to direct their activities into the proper channels under the leadership of the working class.[100]

In addition, about this time, Dictator Stalin himself spoke knowingly of a revolution in India which would take place in spite of the use by the bourgeoisie of "police bayonets" or "people like Gandhi," for the employment of such means in Czarist Russia did not save that regime.[101]

All these provocative statements from the official Soviet press and the E.C.C.I. could hardly be unnoticed in Great Britain. The opposition Conservatives took a serious view of this matter. They had opposed the re-establishment of diplomatic relations with the Soviet Union in November 1929 by MacDonald's Labour Cabinet and had subsequently noted that this Soviet propaganda was contrary to the protocol signed at the time of the resumption of relations by the terms of which the Soviets promised that Communist propaganda would be banned throughout the Empire.

Consequently, in February, 1930, Foreign Minister Arthur Henderson was most closely interrogated by Tory members in the House of Commons in regard to inflammatory Soviet propaganda about India. All Henderson would say was that he would "examine" the situation or that he did "not consider that it calls for any action on my part."[102]

A few months later, in May, 1930, Tories interrogated Secretary of State for India, John Benn, on the part played by Communists in the insurrections at Sholapur and Peshawar, but the latter argued "there had been no evidence that Communist agents were responsible for any of the recent disturbances" although he admitted that "the use of red uniforms and hammer and sickle badges had been mentioned in some of the official Peshawar telegrams."[103]

At this time other questions were posed by Tories concerning provocative articles of Comintern origin advocating revolution and sedition in India which appeared in the London "Daily Worker" as well as the dissemination of Soviet propaganda from Tashkent into India, especially the North-West Frontier Province. Here again, the spokesmen for the MacDonald Government answered lamely and indicated that no diplomatic action by Great Britain against the Soviets on account of this propaganda was contemplated.[104]

Tory fears were further aroused by the disclosure in a communique by the Government of British India on May 5, 1930, of Red propaganda on the Northwest Frontier and this was not the only report of Communist activity in that strategic area which at that time was in turmoil owing to a revolt by the

Pathans.[105] Besides, in the early summer of 1930 at a Congress of the Executive Committee of the Communist International, important Soviet leaders paid attention to the situation in India. Indeed, it is likely that if a Conservative Cabinet had been in power at that time, Britain would once again have broken diplomatic relations with Soviet Russia because of the latter's threatening attitude towards India.

Although they were out of office, the agitation of the Tories appears to have had a sobering effect on the Russians who did not want a diplomatic rupture with Britain. In the latter part of May, 1930, leading Soviet journals published editorials "in which reports in the London press alleging propaganda abroad by Moscow, particularly in India are described as pure invention based largely on false information."[106] There was a lull in official statements in the Soviet press or by the Executive Committee of the Comintern in regard to India for almost all the remainder of the year 1930, not counting articles in Comintern journals such as "International Press Correspondence," and the "Communist International."

However, beginning in December, 1930, the Soviet government and the Comintern suddenly resumed where they had left off. In that month there appeared the "Draft Platform of Action" of the Communist Party in India which, quite apparently was formulated in Moscow. On January 4, 1931, V. M. Molotov, as Chairman of the People's Commissars and second only to Stalin in the party hierarchy, in his report to the Central Executive Committee of the Soviet government mocked the First Round Table Conference then in progress.[107] There followed on February 1st a declaration from the Comintern that the Indian Communist party should "attract and unite under its banner the terrorist elements" who had proved their mettle by "killing a number of police officers and wounding others" and had even made an attempt on the Viceroy himself and had wounded the Governor of the Punjab.[108] Furthermore, at a military festival in Moscow held on February 4, 1931, to honor the fiftieth birthday of General Klimenty E. Voroshilov, the Commissar of War (who is now nominally the present-day Chief of State in the U.S.S.R.) the government of the Soviet Republic of Tadjikistan, a territory which included the Pamirs just north of Kashmir, sent an assurance that it would stand firm in the organization of its section of the Red Army "at the gates of India."[109] In addition, on April 3, 1931 "Pravda" published an article which contained instructions for the Communist Party of India to start a general strike, an agrarian revolution and a general attack on the Anglo-Indian Government.[110]

To add fuel to the flames more inflammatory references to India were made at another Plenary Conference or Congress of the Executive Committee of the Comintern, which conference convened in Moscow in April, 1931. On April 23rd special greetings were sent to the Indian Communists.[111]

Besides, a statement concerning Communist organizational activity in India was made at this plenary session of the E.C.C.I. to the effect that the agents of the Comintern in the subcontinent should organize a revolutionary offensive among the oppressed classes against imperialism and the Indian National Congress, should stir up workers and peasants, should organize a mighty all-Indian Communist Party and Red Labour Union and should prepare a general political strike.[112]

That the Soviet Government was fully behind this declaration was evinced by the fact that among the 30 members elected at this plenary session to a new Presidium of the Executive Committee of the Communist International, was none other than Stalin himself.[113] It was manifest that he was just as much in control of the Comintern as he was in control of the Communist Party of the Soviet Union, and thus Stalin must have played a major role in the formulation of Russian policy towards India.

Once again, as had been the case in the previous year, Conservative members of Parliament sharply questioned the Liberal-supported Labour Government on Communist threats to India, both external and internal, and intimated that His Majesty's Government should adopt a "get tough" policy with Russia as a result of the Soviet threat to India. And, once again, as was the case in 1930, the spokesmen of the Labour Government adroitly brushed the questions aside making thereby no commitments whatsoever and thus implied that they would not undertake any kind of a decisive policy in regard to Anglo-Russian relations.[114] It may be noted that the debate on this question involved an exchange of views between Sir Austen Chamberlain, the former Conservative Foreign Secretary, and Prime Minister Ramsay MacDonald, in which the latter held that the Tories were "inclined to view with undue alarm" Comintern manifestoes in regard to India.[115]

However, on May 9, 1931, the Moscow press published a most provocative pronouncement in which the Communist Party of India was called upon to organize "revolutionary disturbances" in order to "overthrow British domination" with an especial emphasis on the "violent destruction of British authority"; the pronouncement also advocated a new Indian Mutiny through a revolt of the native Indian soldiers.[116] The tone of these articles was so violent that the MacDonald government actually inquired of the Soviet ambassador in London whether Russia really had designs on India. The ambassador's protestations to the contrary convinced the Labor government as to lack of a Russian threat to India and in a formal statement to the House of Commons, on May 17, 1931, the Prime Minister declared:

> The Ambassador replied that the only publication which took place (on India) was of extracts of a new programme of the Indian Communist Party which had appeared in 'Pravda' of May 9. It was not issued from Moscow and was not issued by 'Pravda.' It is just as though 'Pravda' were to copy some of the stuff issued by the British Communist Party. . . .[117]

After noting that "India is in an unsettled condition" and conceding that "that unsettlement may be increased by 'Pravda' articles," MacDonald averred:

> So far as Soviet influence is concerned . . . we do not indulge in protests . . . we pursue the methods of negotiations and exchange of views and statements made about what actually has happened, and there is no reason why

that (Anglo-Russian relationship) should be interrupted and the Trade Agreement broken by anything we do.[118]

The Conservatives were utterly dissatisfied with this attitude of the MacDonald Government. Accordingly, they moved a vote of no-confidence in this Liberal-supported Labour Ministry. In the ensuing division the Ministry won by the narrow margin of 243 to 223 votes.[119] This vote did not end the matter, for the ministers of the Labour Party were still subjected to sharp interrogation from the Tory benches over the Russian threat to India.[120]

As had been the case in 1930, there developed a lull in the vigor of Russian and high level Comintern propaganda about India immediately after the spring of 1931, excepting again material which appeared in Comintern journals. Even more than in 1930, a large segment of the British public had been aroused, and there was real danger to Russia of hostile action against her by Britain if the Soviets were to continue an openly provocative policy in regard to India. This would particularly be the case were a Tory Government to come into power. And, as a matter of fact the Tories did come into power. For later in 1931 a "National Government," consisting of a small number of right-wing Labourites, the "National Liberals" and the Conservatives came into power as a result of the general election of October, 1931. MacDonald remained as the Prime Minister of the new government, but his power was nominal in that the Tories were in the saddle. The Foreign Secretary was Sir John Simon, a Conservative, who was no admirer of the Soviet Union.

Consequently with the assumption to power of this rightist coalition, a firmer attitude was taken by the British Government concerning the Russian and Comintern attitude towards India. Simon held that "the Soviet Government and the Communist International cannot be disassociated" and British policy was now to make representations to the Soviet ambassador in London concerning Comintern pronouncements towards India.[121] The Soviets, now realizing that a public inflammatory policy towards Hindustan was dangerous, maintained officially a far more discreet policy. It is apparent that in spite of the bombast and blustering about an insurrection in India, the Soviet government did not desire a diplomatic break with Great Britain which would most likely have occurred if the official Soviet press and the Executive Committee of the Comintern had continued to stress the necessity for a Communist rebellion in India.[122]

In line with this modification of Soviet policy on November 13, 1932, "Izvestia" charged that the allegation Soviet Russia was engaged in "the preparation of civil war in India" was based on "fabricated" documents and materials prepared by agents of British Intelligence.[123]

In the following year, Anglo-Russian relations were again strained to a measurable extent on account of the apparent Soviet menacing gestures towards India. These relations which had been subjected to pressure owing to the arrest of six British engineers working in Russia in March, 1933,[124] were further strained when in October and November of that year the organs of the Comintern stepped up their campaign against "imperialist" rule over "Colonial peoples" in general and in India in particular. Thus on November 5, 1933, the Executive Committee of the Third International issued a long new "catechism" for Communist agents in India consisting of 52 questions and their answers in a publication which exceeded altogether 15,000 words. The "catechism" went into great details in instructing Indian Communists how they might better carry on their subversive activities in preparation for the inevitable Red revolution.[125] Furthermore, it was at this time that the "open letter" allegedly written by the Chinese Communist party to the Indian Communists appeared, and it was in that very month of November, 1933, that the Communist Party of India was officially, albeit clandestinely, born (or reborn) in Calcutta.

As a consequence of the appearance of this Communist "catechism," Anthony Eden, speaking as Parliamentary Undersecretary for Foreign Affairs, informed the House of Commons that a report on this matter from Moscow had been called for.[126] This bestirring of the British may have disturbed the Russians to a certain extent, for a writer in the November 24, 1933 issue of the "International Press Correspondence" claimed that

"British imperialism" is preparing "above all for intervention against the U.S.S.R."[127]

Once again the Soviets chose to follow a discreet policy and with the exception of the "political thesis" of the C.P.I. nothing of significance emerged from the Soviet press or the Comintern's press, during 1934 and articles on India definitely diminished in 1935.

During the late 'twenties and early 'thirties there is no evidence that Soviet Russia was making preparations for a military invasion of India, such as that which was actually initiated by the "mad" Czar Paul at the turn of the nineteenth century, which would "liberate" the Indians from the tyranny of the British and bestow upon them the blessings of Bolshevism. The small-scale filibustering expeditions into Afghanistan that have been noted above, were the only actual threatening military moves by Soviet Russia in the direction of India.

There was a marked lessening of interest in India by the Soviet Union in the late 'thirties as compared to the earlier years of the decade. Articles in the Soviet press on India were few, pronouncements by the Executive Committee of the Comintern on the coming armed revolution in India were absent and even the journals of the Comintern had less to say about India as compared to previous periods. It would appear that the threat of Nazi Germany and Japan on the opposite ends of the Soviet empire tended to deflect Soviet interest from India. Furthermore, the period from 1936 to 1939 coincided with the great "purge" trials which occupied the time and attention of Dictator Stalin and his minions.

The Indian Communists in Russia also played a small part in the Soviet purges of this time. In the spring of 1938, the Indian press reported that almost all of the Indian Communists in Moscow and Leningrad had been arrested on the charge of being "Trotskyite agents of Fascists," a common charge against the victims of Stalin's purges. Among those arrested was none other than Virendranath Chattopadhyaya, "the celebrated Indian revolutionary"[128] who had been converted to Communism along with his "Berlin Committee" comrade, Ferozdin Mansoor, by M. N. Roy when the latter was in

Germany. Unlike Mansoor, who had repaired to India and had actually appeared as a witness in the Meerut conspiracy case,[129] Chattopadhyaya had remained in Europe, making his headquarters in Berlin where, together with certain of Roy's former colleagues, he maintained an emigré Indian Communist center. However, the dissolution of the German Communist Party in 1933 by the Nazis compelled Chattopadhyaya to proceed to Russia.[130] There is no evidence that he had any influence on the Indian Communist movement comparable to that once enjoyed by M. N. Roy, not to speak of the British Communist Party. It is doubtful whether Chattopadhyaya, the Kaiser's designated leader of the Indian National Movement during the First World War, was really ever a sincere Communist; he probably joined the Communists because he saw in Soviet Russia the sole nation which could liberate India from the rule of the British Raj. The "liquidation" of Chattopadhyaya and his colleagues destroyed a link in the way of direct connection between Moscow and the Indian Communists, and thereby all the more bolstered the position of the British Communists as the immediate bosses of their "comrades" in Hindustan.

CHAPTER SEVEN

An "Imperialist War" Becomes A "People's War"

The Nazi-Soviet pact of August 23, 1939, and the subsequent outbreak of the Second World War with Russia becoming the ostensible friend rather than the sworn enemy of the Hitler regime, was as confusing to the Indian Comrades as it was confounding to the Communists in the rest of the world.[1] However, the new line was helpful to the Indian Communists in that the anti-British turn in Soviet foreign policy made it possible for the Indian Communists all the more bitterly to denounce the alleged machinations of British imperialism.

Consequently, when it broke out, the Indian Communists branded the war as an "imperialist" one and appealed to the Indian masses to carry on active demonstrations against the involvment of India in the conflict. For example, Communists were active in a mass demonstration against India's participation in the war, held in September, 1939, in Madras in which, it is said, 10,000 persons participated. They were also active in an anti-imperialist and anti-war conference held at Nagpur the following month,[2] which Red leader B. T. Ranadive "inaugurated" and in which Communist dominated or influenced groups such as the national Kisan Sabha and the All-India Students' Federation were very much in evidence.[3]

The Communists were not long able publicly to express their views, a right which they had partly been able to manifest under the Congress ministries before September, 1939. Soon after the inception of the conflict, the Communists' two leading journals, published in Bombay, the "National Front" and the "Kranti" were banned.[4] However, the Indian Communists continued furtively to publish their secret organ the "Communist."[5] The full blow of British suppressive force fell, however, in March, 1940. On the twenty-fifth of that month the Anglo-Indian government ordered "the detention of the principal Communist leaders in India."[6] It was indicated at the same time that the Communists had been carrying on subversive "underground" propaganda and had been doing their best to hinder the supply of men and materials in the furtherance of the war effort.[7]

As a consequence, all the most important leaders of Indian Communism such as Dange, Muzaffar Ahmad, Ranadive, Ghate, Mirajkar and Nimbkar were summarily incarcerated.[8] Arrests of Communists continued during the course of the year 1940,[9] and in February, 1941, Sir Reginald Maxwell, the Home Member of the Anglo-Indian Government in the National Legislative Assembly declared before that body that out of some 700 persons then being detained in jail without trial "about 480 persons were almost without exception Communists or else active supporters of the Communist programme of violent mass revolution."[10]

The arrest and detention of the above-mentioned Communist leaders was compensated to a certain extent by the joining to the Communist Party, late in 1939 and early in 1940, of a number of prominent members of the Congress and its autonomous branch, the Congress Socialist party. They included such future noteworthy Red leaders as A. K. Gopalan,[11] E. M. S. Namboodripad,[12] and Sajjad Zaheer.[13] It may be noted these and others were members of the A.I.C.C. Indeed, some fifty-nine important members of the Congress Socialist Party joined the Communists at this time.[14] However, they too were subject to arrest by the authorities.[15]

In spite of the repression from British officialdom, the Communist party continued to carry on its subversive activities. This was particularly true of the period from September, 1939, to March, 1940, when the leaders of Indian Communism were still at large. Thus in November, 1939, the Politburo of the Indian Communist party denounced the war and held the "revolutionary utilization of the war crisis for the attainment of National Independence" was the "central task" of the Communist party.[16] With this watchword before them the Comunists disseminated propaganda and organized demonstrations during the course of 1939 and 1940 against the war effort. In their propaganda they were held to have "explained the true cause of the victories of Hitler over European countries as the result of the English policy of isolating the Soviet Union."[17] In rural areas the Communists carried on their propaganda under the slogan of " Na ek Pai, Na ek Bhai" (not one penny, not one brother), that is they appealed to peasants neither to subscribe to war loans nor to permit their men folk to join the Indian armed forces.[18]

Communist activity in the trade union movement bore fruit at the eighteenth session of the A.I.T.U.C. which met at Bombay in November 1940. At this session the unification of the former with the National Federation of Trade Unions, was formally approved.[19] The Communists here played an important role in having this united trade union federation (known as the A.I.T.U.C.) pass an anti-war resolution over the opposition of the "Royists."[20] On the other hand, however, the "Royists" and other non-Communist elements in the A.I.T.U.C. succeeded in enacting a resolution to the effect that "political questions" and questions of "affiliation with any foreign organization" (such as the Red International of Labour Unions) would be decided by a "three-fourths majority," thus hindering the passage of Communist-sponsored resolutions.[21] The Communists "accepted" this provision very reluctantly in the "interest of unity."[22]

Besides supporting trade union "unity" for their own selfish purposes, the Communists between September, 1939 and June, 1941, did their best to further the strike movement, in order to enhance their influence in Indian labor, to hinder the war effort and to further revolutionary sentiments among the Indian proletariat. On October 2, 1939,[23] and a month later on that Communist holiday, November 7th,[24] the textile workers of Bombay were called out on one day strikes. During the autumn of 1939 there likewise were strikes in other industrial centers such as Allahabad, Cawnpore and Calcutta[25] as well as by sailors on Indian commercial vessels.[26]

An even greater number of strikes convulsed industrial India in the first half of 1940 as compared to the second half of 1939. Greatest of all the strikes was one conducted by the Bombay textile operatives, which was not merely a one-day political strike, but a prolonged walkout of forty days' duration from March 3 to April 13, 1940. Some 175,000 workers participated in this walkout.[27] It was this strike which probably precipitated the arrest of the leading Indian Communists.

Besides unleashing a one-day sympathy strike, called by the Red-infiltrated executive of the A.I.T.U.C., of India-wide scope and involving 350,000 workers, the Bombay strike heralded a rash of other strikes, notably that of jute workers of Bengal and Bihar, oil-well workers of Assam, coal miners of Jharia and iron and steel workers of Jamshedpur.[28] During 1940 some 452,000 workers struck as compared to 409,000 in 1939, and this in spite of the arrest of Communists and Congress Socialists who called for the strikes.[29] This repression by British authorities made for an enforced quiet in the Indian scene during the first half of 1941, only two large strikes occurring in the Nagpur district.[30] The Communists were active in the peasant movement in the Malabar and Andhra districts of the Madras Presidency and in Bengal.[31] The peasant movement, as encompassed in the Kisan Sabha movement, in May, 1940, was claimed to have one million members.[32] At this time, in addition to the usual Communist demands for reduction of rents and debts, anti-British, anti-war slogans and praise for the Soviet agricultural system played a prominent part in the Red agrarian line.[33]

The Communists were also active among the students. They were now dominant in the All-India Student's Federation. This organization, which had been founded in August, 1936, claimed early in 1940, that it had over 100,000 members "with sections in every province."[34] When the war broke out, the Students' Federation at once followed the line of the C.P.I., denounced the war in its news organ, the "Student Call" as "imperialistic" and conducted various demonstrations against it. In the Fifth Annual Convention of this organization at Delhi, January, 1940, pro-Communist slogans against the war as well as against the

British and the princes were passed.[35] Proving the complete subordination of the Students' Federation to the C.P.I., the former body passed a resolution lauding the Soviet attack on Finland, then in progress.[36] The repression of the C.P.I., however, diminished the effectiveness of this student front, which assisted Red inspired strikes,[37] in the spring of 1940.

The Communists maintained their pre-war policy of trying to secure influence in the National Congress. Those of their number who were members of the A.I.C.C. "unhesitatingly" supported the "National Demands" of the Congress and through the alleged consistency and energy of their work" came to hold "positions of trust and responsibility in the Congress organizations." This was supposedly confirmed by "police reports."[38] As before the war, the Congress between 1939 and 1941 took no action against the Communists within its ranks.

However, in that autonomous branch of the Congress, the Congress Socialist Party, a more realistic attitude towards the "Trojan horse" Communist policy was taken. Using as justification a more hostile attitude by the Communists taken towards them[39] after a left-wing conference of Communists, Socialists and the Forward Bloc Party (the latter a new leftist anti-war group headed by S. C. Bose who had broken with the Congress) at Lucknow in October, 1939, had agreed to left-wing collaboration,[40] the National Executive of the C.S.P., meeting at Ramgarh, in March, 1940, ordered the expulsion of the Communists from that party,[41] a move naturally received with wrath by the latter.[42]

Communist criticism between the summers of 1939 and 1941 was mainly directed against the British and their "imperialistic war."[43] The keynote of this line was sounded by the Politburo of the C.P.I. in its thesis on the war in November, 1939, which manifesto argued:

> The war that is raging in Europe today is NOT a war of Democracy against Fascism. It is an Imperialist War; Britain and France are not fighting in defence of freedom and Democracy. Their victory would not mean the destruction nor even the weakening of Fascism. Chamberlain and Daladier are making use of the anti-Fascist mood of the people

> in order to strengthen their imperialist designs in their own countries. They are assisting the spread of reaction in many European countries. They are destroying the democratic way of life in their own countries. They will strengthen political and economic exploitation in India.[44]

Moreover, in haranguing textile workers on their one-day strike of November 7, 1939, Ranadive averred:

> Today the British lion has fallen into a pit which he has dug himself. He had meant it for Soviet Russia, the land where Workers and Peasants rule. It is not our good fortune to claim that we have pushed him into the pit. But it is certainly our good fortune that he is in it. We are not going to help him to come out.[45]

To which remarks his audience cried "Victory to the Red Flag," and "Down with Imperialist War."[46]

Needless to say, the proposals of the British and of the Anglo-Indian Government, especially the "August offer" of 1940 which promised India eventual dominion status were greeted by sneers and jeers from the Communists.[47] On the other hand, the Defence of India Act (Emergency Powers Act) enacted by the Anglo-Indian Government, soon after the outbreak of the war, was bitterly castigated, and when under the terms of this act arrests and imprisonments without trial occurred, howls of Red protest were raised.[48]

Communist censure was not confined solely to the "imperialists." The "puppet princes" came in for their share of abuse[49] and the abolition of the native states was demanded.[50] The Indian bourgeoisie also came in for stern censure.[51] Thus in the February 1941 issue of the clandestine journal "The Communist" it was stated:

> The national movement under bourgeois leadership has entered a blind alley. They feared the masses and trusted Imperialism . . . They put their class above the nation . . . They hand over the national organisers to Imperialism for safe custody.[52]

The attitude of the Communists towards the National Congress during the period from 1939 to 1941 was somewhat ambiguous. There are several instances of Red praise for that organization.[53] For instance, the statement made by the Working Committee of the Congress on September 14, 1939, holding that if the war were "imperialistic," India would have nothing to do with it and simultaneously attacking Fascism as well, was duly lauded by the Communists.[54] Although the "individual civil disobedience" movement inaugurated by the Congress in the fall of 1940 to force Britain to grant India autonomy immediately, was not really militant enough to suit the Communists' tastes, still for them it was a step in the right direction and they saw in this development and the attendant arrest of India's leaders signs that a real struggle between "imperialism" and the Indian masses was now under way.[55] The high point in the Communists' favorable attitude towards Congress came in their manifesto celebrating the tenth anniversary of the proclamation of Indian independence (January 26, 1940) in which they went so far as to identify the Congress with themselves in the yearning for Indian's freedom.[56]

On the other hand, brickbats as well as bouquets were hurled at the Congress. Thus in its thesis of November 1939, the C.P.I. asserted:

> The ruling leadership of Congress does not wish to utilise the weapon of mass struggle. It wants to utilise the war crisis for carrying on dealings with the imperialists without a struggle.[57]

The particular butt of the Communists in Congress was Mahatma Gandhi. Of "Gandhism" an official statement by the Executive Committee of the Indian Communist Party, just before it was broken up by the action of the Anglo-Indian police, declared that it was absolutely indispensable to know that "struggle against settlement, struggle against compromise, means simultaneously struggle against Gandhism . . . In brief, all round and convincing political exposure of Gandhism."[58] In addition, in his "Review of Gandhism," published at about the same time Dr. G. M. Adhikari, one of the top leaders of the party, stated:

> Once Gandhism held the fate of British rule in its hands. To-day it pursues the logic of 'unconditional co-operation' with the same Government and that at a time when an unjust, imperialist and predatory war is raging in the world . . . Gandhi's line is (that of) the cowardly and compromising bourgeoisie. . . .[59]

Besides the harsh criticism of Gandhi[60] Nehru was subjected to censure, because the latter in turn had criticized Communists for denying the right of the Congress high command to depart from the "mandate of struggle" which had been given at the Congress' Ramgarh session of March, 1940.[61] This Communist criticism was manifestly at variance with the talk of "unity" in the contest with the British Raj.[62]

The Communists also vilified the Congress Socialists, especially after their expulsion from that party, and[63] they treated the "Royists" who were now known as the Radical Democratic Party who supported the war effort, with supercilious scorn.[64] An air of contemptuous bravado was also taken towards the formation by "Royist" labor leaders, Messrs. Aftab Ali and Karnik, of a new pro-war and anti-Communist labor federation, the Indian Federation of Labour, which endeavored to compete with the A.I.T.U.C.,[65] and which allegedly received a 13,000 rupees a month grant from the Anglo-Indian Government.[66] This attitude by the Communists on the Congress and Congress Socialists signified a partial, but not complete, departure from the policy of "united front from above."

A harsh attitude was taken by the Communists in regard to the Muslim League which was looming into vital significance between 1939 and 1941, having initiated its demand for Pakistan in 1940. The League was held to be mainly an "upper middle class" organization which had little support from the Muslim peasantry.[67] The League was deemed to be "pro-imperialist"[68] and the British, it was claimed, "in every way encouraged the separatist tendencies of the Muslim League."[69] The Hindu parallel to the latter organization, the Hindu

Mahasabha was also branded as being "extremely reactionary."[70] We may note that in their position on the communal and nationalities questions between the summers of 1939 and 1941, the Communists took the line that there should be a single united India. Hence, they had no sympathy for the particularism of the Muslim League.[71]

That this "independent India" would not be attained by peaceful means was well indicated by the Communists. Thus the principle of "no violence" was bitterly excoriated[72] whereas the raising of a "people's army" was praised, and it was held that a "mighty wave of revolt" which was already (somewhat exaggeratedly) "sweeping the country" would result in "complete victory over British imperialism."[73]

While dilating much on the necessity for the liberation of India from "imperialist rule," the Indian Communists had little to say about their economic plans between the summers of 1939 and 1941. A partial exception to this was found in the "Manifesto of the Communist Party of India" on the tenth anniversary of Indian Independence Day (January 26, 1940) which held that their goals were:

> For a democratic republic with a People's Army.
> For the eight-hour day and a living wage.
> For freedom from rack-renting and debt-slavery.[74]

The reticence of the Communists on their economic plans in this document, which was a grandiloquent series of statements extolling the Soviets' position in world affairs at the commencement of 1940 and the urgent need for Indian independence,[75] was probably in line with the Communists' policy of not antagonizing the Congress, so that they might better carry on subversion within it.

During the period under review, the Communists of India, as before, were under the direct tutelage of the British Communist party. This circumstance was all the more brought into being owing to the lack of contact between Russia and the rest of the world as a result of the war. As examples of British tutelage of the Indian Communists, we may cite the appearance of a volume in 1940 by R. Palme Dutt entitled "India To-Day." This work was really an elaboration of Dutt's earlier "Modern India," brought up to date both in regard to historical events and the correct party line. It featured a Marxist analysis of the British rule in India, the history of the Indian national movement and the political, social and economic situation from the Communist point of view.[76] Dutt also presented an economic program for the Indian comrades to follow which involved: (a) the confiscation of all British capital holdings in India to take place along with the attainment of independence, (b) the "liquidation of landlordism" and the "redivision of land" among the peasantry (collectivization is not specifically mentioned) together with the abolition of peasants' debts and the " modernisation of agriculture," and (c) the future "Independent Indian State" should own all "key industries" including the various modes of transport as well as banking and credit.[77]

Another example of British Communist tutelage is found in an article by Harry Pollitt, the leader of British Bolshevism in the "Labour Monthly" of June, 1941, on the eve of the Nazi-Soviet war in which once again the British rule over India is excoriated, the war is branded as an "imperialist" one and British solicitude for the liberation of the several countries occupied by the Germans, is contrasted with Britain's total disinterestedness in the aspirations of the people of India.[78]

* * * * *

The sudden Nazi onslaught upon Soviet Russia on June 22, 1941, was as stunning and shocking a blow to the Indian comrades as it was to Communists throughout the globe. But with the former, it was a source, not only of shock, but likewise of embarrassment. For now, and particularly with the signing of a wartime alliance pact between Britain and the U.S.S.R. on July 12, 1941, the hated "imperialists" and the beloved land where the "workers and peasants rule" were allied.

An immediate debate ensued among the Communists, both inside and outside of jail as to what course they should pursue.[79] In July, 1941, they came to a decision. It represented a compromise. They would support the Russian part of the war as a heroic people's battle against Fascism, but would continue to denounce England's part of the conflict as "imperialistic" and would maintain the policy of castigating Britain's rule in India. This view was stated in a clandestine manifesto which allegedly emanated from the Politburo of the C.P.I., most of whose members were in prison; consequently, it must have come from those Communists who were working underground.

The manifesto stated:

> The Communist Party declares that the only way in which the Indian people can help in the just war which the Soviet is waging, is by fighting all the more vigorously for their own emancipation from the imperialist yoke. Our attitude towards the British Government and the imperialist war remains what it was. . . . We can render really effective aid to the Soviet Union, only as a free people. That is why our campaign for the demonstration of our support and solidarity with the Soviet Union must be coupled with the exposure of the imperialist hypocrisy of the Churchills and Roosevelts with the demand for the intensification of our struggle for independence.[80]

The C.P.I. immediately swung behind this peculiar anti-British, pro-Soviet line.[81] One of the wildest of the Communist notions at this time was one circulated by certain confused comrades to the effect that Churchill had been instrumental in provoking Hitler to declare war on Russia![82] In the summer of 1941 the Communists organized rallies (which the authorities permitted, since, after all, they were indirectly supporting the British cause) in which reference was frequently made to the Soviet Union as "Fatherland," a term most painful to patriotic Indian ears.[83]

The Communists continued to prate their new ambiguous hodgepodge of confusing ideas in regard to the war during the summer and autumn of 1941. For example, a so-called "party letter" dated October 30, 1941, affirmed

> . . . that only in the measure the people gather the strength to assert themselves against imperialists and their rule . . . will they be able to line up in the international people's front for winning the war against fascism and for the Soviet people and the people of the world.[84]

It was time to take the erring comrades to task,[85] and this the Communist Party of Great Britain endeavored to do in an official resolution on the subject of "India" by asserting in October, 1941:

> The war on the Soviet Union has aroused the deepest feelings of all Colonial and oppressed peoples. That great country, where the people of all races and colours live in harmonious economic and cultural unity, has always been an inspiration to all of them in the struggle for freedom.[86]

From this it follows that Russia must be supported at all costs. After complimenting the Indians for the anti-Fascist policies which they have evinced in the past,[87] the resolution maintained that since the "British-Soviet Alliance has at last been established," a "world alliance of the people against Fascism is being built up."[88]

The British Communist leaders admonished their Indian comrades that this alliance must be supported, for "the victory of Nazi Germany and its Axis partners would mean not only the enslavement of the peoples of Europe, but also a worse slavery of the people of India than ever known before," whereas victory for the "alliance of the peoples in association with the Soviet Union" would lead to "the most favorable world condition for the liberation of the Indian people. . . ."[89]

In these circumstances, the leaders of British Communism expressed confidence

> . . . that the masses of the Indian people and all their most progressive leaders (the Communists) will recognise that to-day the path to Indian Independence lies through the victory of the Soviet Union and its allies over Fascism. . . . The Unity of the British, American, Soviet and Indian peoples. . . . this is the path of victory over Fascism. This is the path to the liberation of all peoples.[90]

The Indian Communists had thus received their orders. Even those in prison had received a letter from Harry Pollitt—a letter which the British authorities deliberately permitted the Indian

Communists, incarcerated in Deoli prison to receive—stating the new line.[91] This new line brought about "protracted discussion" amongst the comrades both behind bars and at large. It was probably the greatest debate within the Indian Communist Party in its history. If it should accept the new line, the party would be restored to the same relative freedom it had enjoyed in the summer of 1939 with the likelihood that it would be recognized by the Anglo-Indian authorities as a legitimate political party. On the other hand, were it to follow this course, the opprobrium of many Indians would have to be faced for its betrayal of the national struggle. But if the Indian Communists should refuse to obey orders and would maintain their anti-British line, they would continue to have the respect of militant Indian nationalists, as a group struggling valiantly for Indian liberty, but, on the other hand, they would then be disowned by the Communist International, and would become a small group without important international connections, such as was the case with the "Royists" a decade previously.

The leaders of Indian Communism, P. C. Joshi, Ranadive and Ghate chose the former course, a course which seemed to have become a more palatable one in view of the Japanese entry into the war on December 7, 1941, and the consequent Nipponese threat to India.[92] The result of the new Communist line appeared as a manifesto of December 15, 1941, from the leaders of Indian Communism, some of whom were already being released from detention. This manifesto which represented the official turning point of the Communist Party of India in regard to the war, declared in part:

> We are a practical party and in the new circumstances our tasks are to work out new tactics, to put forth new slogans, corresponding to the present world situation, and the new situation in the National Movement. The chief slogan of our party, which we now put forth, is "a People's Role in the People's War."[93]

This manifesto was followed up a little later, by a booklet written by P. C. Joshi, the General Secretary of the party, entitled "Forward to Freedom," which appeared in February, 1942.

This booklet presented in full details the official views and policies of the Indian Communist Party. Joshi, who was now for the first time since 1939 able to carry on a more open leadership of the C.P.I., contended:

> The Indian people recognize that the war waged jointly by the U.S.S.R., Great Britain, the U.S.A. and China against the Fascist Powers is a People's War. The Indian People must strive to win it in common with the other progressive peoples in order to secure the victory of the U.S.S.R. and of all other peoples, the annihilation of Fascism and to win a peace and new order which ensures the independence and democratic liberties of all peoples and involves no annexations.[94]

Therefore, held Joshi, "our support to the war has to be unqualified, whole-hearted and full-throated"[95] and "we must go into the People's War for all we are worth."[96] To this end the Indian Communists were urged to "take a positive attitude towards the war effort because it is our war and we declare that we want to build a Real People's War effort."[97] For this purpose, therefore, Joshi urged that an all-out effort be made to further the civilian defense or A.R.P. (air-raid precaution) by means of a "policy of full co-operation with the Official A.R.P."[98] He also urged the creation of a "popular Home Guard, a Citizens' Army, organised for the defence of cities and district towns" against "the imminent danger of a Japanese invasion," a force raised under the slogan of "arm the people."[99] Further, affirmed Joshi, recruitment for the Indian armed forces must be greatly encouraged: "We want to increase recruitment a thousand-fold."[100]

To win the "People's War," Joshi affirmed that "unity is indispensable and in order to secure it

> . . . the Communist Party works for the broadest possible mobilisation in a united front of the Congress, the Muslim League, the Trade Union Congress, the All-India Kisan Sabha and the All-Indian Students' Federation.[101]

In this policy-determining booklet, Joshi chided the British on the "loss of Malaya"[102] by their imperialistic policies and also chided them for retarding the industrialization of India, an industrialization which would contribute to the speedy downfall of the Axis Powers.[103]

However, this criticism of the British was mild, indeed, compared to that made by the Communists before June 22, 1941. We find nothing in Joshi's remarks which advocate any militant struggle for the attainment of the admittedly indispensable Indian freedom. Support of the United Nations came first with Joshi.[104]

The principal leaders of the C.P.I. accepted the new line. But neither all of the minor leaders nor many in the rank and file of the party could accept it. These formed a party bearing the provocative name of the "Bolshevik-Leninist Party of India" and claimed an affiliation with the Fourth or Trotskyite International. This party continued the old Communist opposition to the "imperialist war" and endeavored to inaugurate a "mass struggle against it."[105] However, it was a small group and had to remain underground.

The pro-war attitude of the Communists, albeit qualified by the demand for India's independence, during the spring of 1942 convinced the Anglo-Indian authorities that the Communists should be permitted to carry on their activities as a legal political organization. Hence many prominent Indian Communists were released from detention. The culmination of the new lenient British policy was the formal removal of the ban on the Communist Party of India on July 24, 1942, which had the effect of legalizing the party. The Government of India held it took this step because the "announcements and circulars to party members" termed the war "a People's War" and encouraged "cooperation with the war effort."[106]

This decision by the Central Anglo-Indian Government, which was followed as a matter of course by the provincial governments, was well-received by those elements in Congress, led by C. R. Rajagopalacharia who favored India's participation in the war effort, not conditioned by the granting of freedom,[107] but not by the Congress as a whole. It was also well received by some non-Communist elements in Indian labor,[108] and needless to say received a resounding cheer from the C.P.G.B.,[109] but was met with reserve by conservative British circles[110] and by silence from the Muslim League.

The Communist Party immediately set to work to increase its influence in India. In the latter part of September, 1942, the Central Committee of the party met in Bombay in the first open meeting of that body in the history of the party. At this meeting plans were drawn for the augmentation of the party's influence and special attention was paid to the necessity for dissemination of the party's propaganda.[111]

Early in 1943, the Central Committee decided that a national convention of the party should be held to draw attention to it throughout India. The "First National Congress of the Communist Party of India" took place between May 23rd and June 1st, 1943, in Bombay. Led by Joshi, Ranadive and Dange, the 139 delegates did their best to make a considerable impression. To a certain extent they were successful. On May 23rd they conducted a great mass meeting attended by 25,000 workers.[112] On May 24th a "festival of national culture" was presented and on the same day a "Communist Exhibition" was opened in a large hall which was allegedly attended by many.[113] The serious part of the affair, the meeting of the delegates, took place between May 23rd and June 1st.[114] This consisted of a number of harangues by Communist leaders who laid down the party line and the passage of resolutions, carefully worked out in advance by the party's Central Committee, all to the enthusiastic applause of the assembled delegates. It also "elected" (that is confirmed) P. C. Joshi as General Secretary and otherwise confirmed the leaders of the C.P.I. in its Central Committee.[115]

Another decision of the now legalized C.P.I. was to organize a party press, and it was not long before the greatest number of journals in the history of that party made their appearance. The leading dispenser of the Red line was the English-language "People's War," which from July 1942 to July 1943 was edited by Joshi, and after the latter date was edited by Adhikari. This paper appears to have had a considerable increase in its circulation between 1942 and 1943 and one Communist source claims it increased 124 per cent in ten months. There was also a Communist vernacular languages press throughout India. In Bombay alone there were three vernacular newspapers printed in the Hindi, Marathi and Urdu languages. In addition, newspapers in Indian languages were published under the auspices of provincial committees of the Communist Party in Bengal, Andhra, Tamilnad, Kerala, the Carnatic and Orissa.[116] The party line was thus disseminated on a virtually all-Indian scale. In addition, a large number of pamphlets, booklets, leaflets and feuilletons were published in the party's central headquarters in Bombay.

In view of the great extent of illiteracy in India it was necessary for the Communists to find ways to supplement the printed page in the dissemination of their propaganda. This was accomplished through the media of dances, songs and the spoken verse. For instance, in Andhra there had existed a custom for minstrels to perform the "Burra Katha" or the Ballad of Recitation—which was simply a recitation by a minstrel of a heroic tale in ballad form to the accompaniment of an assistant beating the "burra" or drum. Communists, therefore, disguised themselves as minstrels and went from village to village with their drummer assistants; they rendered their versified stories or "kathas," but these did not deal with the heroes of Indian folk-lore, but rather with the Communist heroes of Russia, China and India.[117]

From 1942 to 1945 a well-knit, centralized organization was built up in the C.P.I. which followed the pattern employed by Communist parties everywhere. At the base were local and district groups and cells, above them were the provincial committees which coordinated the work of the district committees and above the latter was the All-India Central Committee of the party, a segment of which was the Politburo which maintained headquarters in Bombay.[118] The latter body was the ruling body.[119] Authority in the party theoretically ran from bottom to top but in practice, of course, the reverse was the case.

Up until 1943 the full time party workers received no pay, but beginning in that year they received a pittance of forty rupees ($1.00) a month for which paltry sum they worked long hours every day. In order to solve their immediate economic problems, the Communist Party workers ran cooperatives through which food was made available to them at reasonable prices. However, very often "professional" Communists had to beg for supplementary food as well as for clothes from friends and sympathizers. Married Communists and Communists supporting children received a slight increase in the paltry pay which was really an allowance.[120]

The C.P.I. definitely registered an increase in enrolled members between the summer of 1942 and that of 1945. Starting from a figure of 5,000 when the party emerged from underground in July, 1942[121] (at that, probably an exaggerated figure) the party claimed a membership in the following February of 9,219 with some 8,886 "auxiliaries training towards membership."[122] By March, 1944, the number of active Communist party members had risen to 25,000.[123] Near the end of the war in 1945 the C.P.I. claimed that there were no fewer than 40,000 card-carrying Communists, but this figure may be taken as an exaggeration, the true number being somewhere between 25,000 and 40,000.[124] Nonetheless, there appears to have been truth in Joshi's boast that towards the end of the war the Communist was the leading political party in India after the Congress and the Muslim League.[125]

What accounted for this rapid growth of the C.P.I.? In the first place, the ban on the activities of the Congress in the fall of 1942 and its autonomous branch, the C.S.P., temporarily removed powerful competitors of the Communists from the field. The only political parties in India of note, besides the Communist, which could freely carry on political activity between 1942 and 1945, were the Muslim League, the Radical Democratic and the Liberal. But the former group had a strictly communal basis, and the latter body's support was derived from only a small group of wealthy Indians. Only the Radical Democrats of M. N. Roy were in a position to form a mass party with an All-India following, but owing to the vague policies of that party, it failed to make headway, losing, râther than gaining ground.[126]

In the second place, the policy of "negative" opposition on the part of the Congress to the war was not popular with certain elements in that body, notably among certain Congress Socialists.[127] The latter felt they could do more in the way of advancing the cause of socialism in a legal political organization than in an underground movement. Hence, "large numbers" of them, particularly from the South Indian areas of Andhra, Kerala and the Carnatic joined the C.P.I. in 1942 and after.[128]

In the third place action taken by the Central Committee of the C.P.I. facilitated the rapid growth of membership. In September, 1942, it put forth the slogan of a mass Communist party. As reported by the "People's War" of April 4, 1943,

> It was found that old inhibitions still prevented the Party from enrolling the best militant and active elements.[129]

As a result, entrance requirements to membership were lowered.

Finally, of course, "the legalization of the party lifted a bar against growth of membership" as it permitted the party to work openly and this factor "at the same time attracted to the party elements disinclined to enter an illegal organization."[130]

As for their communal backgrounds (in religion the Communists were actually atheists) the overwhelming majority of Communists were Hindus. Thus out of the 193 delegates present at the First Congress of the C.P.I. in May, 1943, there were only 13 Muslims, as well as eight Sikhs, two Parsees, one Christian, one Jain and three out-castes or Untouchables. The balance of the delegates were Hindus.[131]

From the vocational point of view on the basis of statistics gathered in the late spring of 1943, 36 per cent of the members of the C.P.I. were peasants, 26 per cent were workers, 22 per cent were intellectuals, 11 per cent were budding intellectuals, i.e., students, and 5 per cent were women, placed, oddly enough, in a special category. The disproportionately high percentage of intellectuals is noteworthy.[132]

The C.P.I. became a more truly national movement than heretofore, as its tentacles spread throughout the length and breadth of the sub-continent. The Communists between 1942 and 1945 made appreciable progress in the princely states which had been immune previously to large scale Communist penetration. Such penetration was noteworthy in Central Indian princely states such as Gwalior, Baroda and Indore and in such Southern Indian princely states as Travancore, Cochin and Hyderabad. The Communists were active both among the peasants and the textile workers of these states.[133]

The areas of British India in which the Communists were most influential during these years were Bengal, the Andhra and Kerala regions of the Madras Presidency and the Punjab. In Bengal the Communist Party reported that it had 3,000 members as of April, 1943[134] and that its membership there had risen in January, 1945 to no fewer than 9,000 members, many of them former terrorists.[135]

In its organizing activity the C.P.I. for the first time in its history was unhampered by the Anglo-Indian Government. Indeed, in a circular dated September 20, 1943, that government held the Communists were performing a real service, because they are "almost the only Party which fought for victory" of the United Nations cause.[136]

Communist members of the All-India Congress Committee in the spring of 1942[137] hailed the arrival of Sir Stafford Cripps who had come to break the stalemate between the British, the Congress and the Muslim League on the form of future freedom in the sub-continent. Like true Congressmen they were disappointed that the Cripps' "Draft Declaration" of March 29, 1942 deferred Indian freedom until after the war, but unlike the former, the Communists were willing to support the war effort.[138] Hence, in a proposed resolution before the A.I.C.C., its Red members suggested that "the Congress . . . take the initiative in the national resistance to the aggressors," that is, support the war effort. Needless to say, the Communist minority failed to secure agreement to its views from the majority of the A.I.C.C.[139]

The minority of Communists on the latter body most bitterly remonstrated against the "Quit India" resolution proposed by the Congress leadership of Gandhi and Nehru. They argued that the Congress should work for a temporary national government in collaboration with the Muslim League to make India an independent opponent of the Axis and permit self-determination to Muslim areas. They did not approve of merely ordering the British to "Quit India." But the remonstrances of the thirteen Communist A.I.C.C. members was in vain, for the "Quit India" resolution was duly enacted on August 8, 1942.[140] The Communists were not the only group to oppose the "Quit India" resolution of the Congress. The Hindu Mahasabha, the Muslim League, the Liberals, and Roy's Radical Democrats also opposed it.[141] Fine company for Communists!

The ensuing civil disobedience campaign occasioned riots between the British and the Congressmen which resulted in numerous casualties, the incarceration of Gandhi and Nehru and a ban on the National Congress. This seemingly perturbed the Communists. Both Congress and the British were the recipients of Communist censure. The action of the A.I.C.C. was deemed a "grave mistake" and the use of civil disobedience as a weapon was deplored. The Congress was held to have fallen into a "fatal trap" which was "suicidal to Indian freedom;"[142] Gandhi was blamed for the resolution and it was charged he was "ready to make peace with Japan."[143] At the same time Communist ire was aroused over "the stupid and clumsy provocative measures adopted by the British government."[144] Both parties were deprecated by the "People's War" of August 23, 1942, the British for "their REPRESSION," the struggle of the police against the people," and the Congress for "their sabotage."[145] In Britain Comrade Pollitt sent an appeal to Prime Minister Churchill to grant Indian freedom at once so that a free India might fight on the side of the United Nations, but his appeal was in vain.[146]

The circumstances surrounding the Communists' refusal to agree to the "Quit India" resolution did them harm among the now underground Congressmen. The latter felt anger that the Communists were safely preaching a pro-war program while their own leaders were moldering in prison for their advocacy of India's freedom. The Communists' weakened position with Congressmen was not improved after the release of Gandhi in May, 1944.

The Communists hoped, through flattery, to win over the Mahatma as an ally of their cause. Thus at the time of Gandhi's release, party boss P. C. Joshi declared:

> Gandhiji, the beloved leader of the greatest patriotic organisation of our people, the mighty Indian National Congress is back in our midst again. . . . We are anxious about his health . . . Every son and daughter of India, every patriotic organisation of our land, is looking to the greatest son of our nation to take it out of the bog in which none is safe.[147]

But the Mahatma was no more impressed by this solicitude and flattery by Joshi than he had been with the blandishments of Saklatvala in 1927. He addressed a letter on June 11, 1944 to Joshi which asked the latter the following pertinent questions:

> 1. What is the meaning of 'People' in 'People's War'? Does it mean war on behalf of India's millions or the Negroes in the East, South or West of Africa, or the Negroes of America or all of them? Are the allies engaged in such a war?
> 2. Are the finances of the Communist Party represented by you subject to public audit? If they are, may I see them?
> 3. It is stated that the Communist Party has actively helped the authorities to arrest leaders and organisers of our labour strikes during the last two years. (Is that true?)
> 4. The Communist party is said to have adopted the policy of infiltrating the Congress organisation with a hostile intent. (Is that true?)
> 5. Is . . . the policy of the Communist Party dictated from outside (India)?[148]

On June 14th Joshi endeavored to answer Gandhi's questions. To the first question the former argued that the People's War meant the war of all the peoples of the globe against the Fascist aggressors, among which peoples was that of the Soviet Union; to the second Joshi stated that Gandhi or his representatives were free to check the C.P.I.'s finances, if they so desired; to the third query Joshi maintained it was a "vile charge" easy to make "but difficult to prove" that Communists had assisted the authorities in the arrest of labor leaders; to the fourth question Joshi flatly and falsely asserted "there is no question of our 'adopting a policy of infiltrating the Congress organisation;' " and to the fifth interrogation Joshi stated that "The Communist Party decides its own policy as it understands the interests of its own people and of the people of the world."[149]

Replying on July 30, 1944, Gandhi informed the Red leader that according to reports received by him, the Communists did not believe in God, truth and non-violence and that they were opposed to the institutions of marriage and monogamy but rather advocated sexual anarchy in its place; that they were anti-Congress, anti-Khaddar, and that they considered himself and referred to him as the "Rasputin of India."[150] But, added Gandhi in a conciliatory vein, Joshi's answer on Communist Party financing was "completely satisfactory" to him, although the latter's answer in regard to the war had failed to convince him that it was truly a "people's war."[151]

Gandhi's reply irked Joshi and he answered the Mahatma in the following petulant tone on September 12, 1944:

> If my own father had written to me what you have written, I would NOT have answered his letter and would have never again gone to meet him. I am writing to you because you are the nation's Father, (and) it will be unpatriotic on my part to get angry with you, even when you insult and humiliate us.[152]

Joshi went on to suggest that Gandhi place his anti-Communist file before such seemingly unprejudiced Congress leaders as Mrs. Arojini Naidu, C. R. Rajagopalacharia and Bhulabhai Desai so that they might examine the role of the Communists in an objective fashion.[153]

This dare by Joshi was accepted by Gandhi and shortly thereafter, a committee under Desai was set up for the purpose of providing the Congress with a thorough examination of the role of the Communist Party of India. While material for this report was being compiled, an anti-Communist sentiment began to develop in the Congress.[154] Thus a manifesto which was put forth by a number of Congressmen in December, 1944, presented the following viewpoint:

> Members of the Communist Party . . . have questioned the leadership of the Mahatmaji and his basic principles like truth and non-violence . . . (They) have no scruples to adopt any policy and programme to attain their end . . . (They) have created a tradition itself in vulgarising the patriotic standpoints of the Congress.[155]

It may also be noted that a prominent Congress leader of Madras, P. S. Sane, "went on a twenty-day hunger strike as a penance over the sorry state of affairs in the (Red-dominated) labour movement,"[156] and that to meet the Communist challenge in this movement certain Congress workers began establishing trade unions in Bombay to compete with those of the Communists, early in 1945.[157]

Whereas the Communists failed to make any appreciable progress in the National Congress between 1942 and 1945, they did succeed in making some progress in infiltrating the Muslim League.[158] We have seen that in 1942 the Communists reversed their former hostile attitude towards the League as a mere "reactionary" communal association, and praised it, at times even more vigorously, than the National Congress. Between 1942 and 1945 a not inconsiderable number of Muslim Communists joined the ranks of the League (a novelty, for previously Communists of Muslim origin had invariably joined the Congress) and they came to have influence in the League Associations in the Punjab, Sind, Assam, the North-West Frontier Province and Bengal.[159] They became especially influential in the Punjab Provincial League Committee, in which Daniyal Latifi, a Punjabi Communist, was made the "Office Secretary" of this Committee as well as Secretary of the League Assembly Party.[160]

Certain elements in the Muslim League appreciated Communist support and maintained an amicable attitude towards India's Communists. Thus Liaquat Ali Khan, then the General

Secretary of the League and the leader of the League in the Central Legislative Assembly paid tribute to the Communist Party of India for its "ceaseless efforts to convince the Hindu masses of the justice of the demand for the rights of self-determination to Muslims."[161]

On the other hand, Muslim League leader Mohammed Ali Jinnah maintained a suspiciously hostile attitude towards the Communists. In March, 1944, while addressing a conference of the Punjab Muslim Students' Federation, Jinnah referred scornfully to Red propaganda. He held that even though admittedly the Communists had won some converts among Muslims in the past

> . . . The Mussulman of the last five or seven or ten years has changed and the Communists will not succeed in fooling us . . . We do not want any flag excepting the League flag of Crescent and Star.[162]

Besides, it may be noted that in February, 1945, a proposal was made that Communists should be ineligible to hold any office in the Muslim League.[163]

The Communists maintained their usual activity in the Indian labor movement during the war years. Their labor policy was two-fold; to rally labor behind the "people's war," and to halt sabotage and ensure industrial production. A manifestation of the Communists' desire to further the first aim was the December, 1941, resolution of the Bombay Provincial Trade Union Congress, which held that "the war which the Soviet Union and Great Britain are jointly waging against Hitler's fascism . . . can no longer be regarded by the working class or the people of India as an imperialist war."[164] Communist control of the A.I.T.U.C. was evidenced as the war proceeded in its plenary sessions in February, 1942,[165] May, 1943,[166] May, 1944,[167] and January, 1945.[168] In the May 1943 session, S. A. Dange was elected to the presidency of that organization. Besides, Communists were elected to the seventy-member General Council of the A.I.T.U.C. and nine to the twenty-one member Working Committee of that body.[169] However, thanks to a provision requiring a three-fourths majority vote to approve resolutions, the Communists were unable to secure a passage of a number of resolutions, notably a mandatory non-strike resolution in 1942,[170] but they did get the qualified majority to pass certain resolutions favorable to them, for example, at the May 1943 session they secured a resolution sending "May Day greetings to 'the first Socialist State'" and "warm greetings to the workers' and peasants' Red Army."[171] Although they did not have a monopoly in the A.I.T.U.C., the Communists had powerful positions within it. Incidentally, the latter were pleased that its membership rose from 337,695 in 1942 to 432,000 in 1945.[172]

The Communists were also able to obtain a measurable degree of influence in the All-India Railwaymen's Federation (A.I.R.F.) which since its foundation in 1922 had remained detached from the main stream of the Indian labor movement. Thus, early in 1945, a Communist was elected to one of the two vice-presidencies of that body and the newly elected president of that body, V. V. Giri was known to be pro-Communist.[173]

Offsetting this Communist progress in the labor movement, the A.I.T.U.C. suffered to an extent from the patronage which was bestowed upon its rival, M. N. Roy's Indian Federation of Labour by the Anglo-Indian Government.[174] Nonetheless, the former body remained dominant in the field of Indian labor.

In line with their pro-war policies the Indian Communists maintained an anti-strike and anti-sabotage policy. They refused to support the strike movement of August-September, 1942, which was in sympathy with the "Congress Rebellion" of that time following the "Quit India" resolution of the A.I.C.C., and they thus effected a "steadying influence" on Indian labor at that time.[175] Furthermore, in the First Congress of the Communist Party of May, 1943, it was resolved that "Communists should take a bold and open stand against strikes as they injure the defence of the country in holding up production."[176] And, in February, 1945, they partially offset their earlier failure in getting a three-fourths majority of the A.I.T.U.C. to agree to an anti-strike resolution, by securing approval by that qualified majority of a resolution demanding "the uninterrupted production of war material."[177] As a consequence of the Communists' slogan, "no strike under any circumstances,"[178] as well as the very positive anti-strike attitude of the Anglo-Indian Government, the strike movement definitely declined during the period from the autumn of 1942 to the summer of 1945.[179]

Communist influence in the All-India Kisan Sabha induced it to follow the Soviet line after the outbreak of the Russo-German war. As soon as that conflict broke out, the A.I.K.S. officially "advocated as much help to 'our (Soviet) Fatherland' as possible"[180] and held a big "Soviet Day" demonstration on July 2, 1941, at the Town Hall in Calcutta, in which the Soviet cause was extolled to the skies.[181] In addition the Central Council of the A.I.K.S. after lauding "the brave people of the Soviet Union who are valiantly meeting the Nazi hordes," expressed regret on the "mysterious passivity of a section of Indian nationalists on this vital issue."[182]

Dutifully following the Communist line, the Executive of the All-India Kisan Sabha at its Nagpur session of February 1942, officially resolved:

> The entry of the Soviet Union into the war has substantially changed the significance of the war for all the peoples of the world. . . . The Council, therefore, has no hesitation in calling upon Peasants to align themselves on the side of the Allies in waging a relentless war for the final extermination of Fascism.[183]

Communist control in the A.I.K.S. was intensified in 1942 and 1943 by the incarceration of Congress Socialists who steadfastly and militantly opposed the British Raj. Hence prominent Communist leaders of the C.P.I. also became leaders of the A.I.K.S. Prominent in this category were E. M. S. Namboodripad, Sajjad Zaheer, and Muzaffar Ahmad. Other peasants' leaders, such as N. G. Ranga, and Swami Sahajan, although they were non-Communists, nonetheless collaboroated with the C.P.I. in 1942 and 1943.[184]

Red control of the All-India Kisan Sabha in 1943 was manifested at the conference of that body in Bhakan, the Punjab, on April 4th of that year. At that session which met under the presidency of the Bengali Communist, Bankim Mukherjee, the common theme of all speakers was that the Communist Party had saved the people "from going astray after August 9th last."[185] Repeated shouts of "long live the Red Army" and prophetically "not only will Russia win but Hitler will be slain," were raised by the excited pro-Communist audience.[186]

As was the case with the Communist Party itself, the Kisan Sabha movement was found in all parts of India, but was concentrated in certain areas, notably East Bengal, Andhra together with the adjoining Telengana region of the princely state of Hyderabad and East Punjab. In these areas, the Communists were very active in the peasants' movement.[187] The Kisan Sabha movement was also influential in Bihar, the Kerala and Tamilnad areas of the Madras Presidency, and the United Provinces.[188] However, in these latter areas, non-Communist elements were dominant in the local organizations. In line with the Communists' pro-war policies, peasants' agitation for drastic land reform and even militant agitation for substantial reductions in rent and interest markedly diminished, except in those parts of India where the underground Socialists were active in the peasants' movement.

Communist control of the A.I.K.S. was violently shaken in 1944 when the previous fellow-traveling but non-Communist leaders of that organization, N. G. Ranga and Swami Sahajan broke with the Communists. Ranga's break with the Communists had occurred when Gandhi, having been released from prison, informed him that the landlord system should ultimately "be abolished and replaced by a system of trusteeship regulated by the state." Impressed by this statement, Ranga pledged allegiance to the still banned Congress and forsook the Communists.[189] Swami Sahajan broke with the Communists because the Bengal peasant leaders had carried on separatist propaganda, in keeping with the then Communist line.[190] As a result in 1944, the Central Committee of the A.I.K.S. instituted a three-fourths majority rule on resolutions which would balk future Red resolutions,[191] and the General Secretary and central office of the Communist-controlled Bengal Provincial Kisan Sabha was suspended.[192]

Thus the Communists faced stern opposition in the year

1945, in the A.I.K.S., the membership of which was now 825,000 as compared to only 285,000 in 1943.[193]

The All-India Students' Federation also followed the Red line, supporting the Russian, but not the British participation in the war from June till December, 1941, and in the later months, at its annual session amidst alleged "scenes of tempestuous enthusiasm" it "passed the resolution of the People's War" for full support to the Allies by 534 votes to 9.[194] The pro-Communist students kept up their pro-war agitation during the course of the year[195] and unlike the case with the peasants' movement, the C.P.I. maintained control of the Students' Federation, which claimed a membership of no fewer than 300,000 members in 1945, until the end of the conflict.[196]

The C.P.I. also formed and dominated other front organizations between 1942 and 1945. Thus Communists dominated the Progressive Writers' and Artists' Association and the Indian People's Theatre Association which groups included very many of the leading artists and authors of the sub-continent.[197] They also formed a Women's Association which claimed a membership of 41,000, various "volunteer" front groups numbering some 25,000 adherents, and even children's groups.[198] The Communists also formed a group known as the "Friends of the Soviet Union" which did its utmost to extol the Soviet cause and to disseminate Red propaganda.[199]

* * * * *

Communist propaganda in India between 1942 and 1945 generally followed the lines laid down in P. C. Joshi's booklet "Forward to Freedom" which appeared during the former year. In the Party Congress of May, 1943, the Indian army was praised,[200] and a resolution was passed which urged that the party popularize the army as the defender of India.[201]

In supporting the war, the C.P.I.'s propaganda emphasized certain features of the conflict. Naturally, the cause of Soviet Russia and the battle of the Chinese Communists against Japan were praised to the utmost.[202] In addition, the need for a Second Front against the Germans was continually demanded until it developed.[203]

Furthermore, the Communists emphasized certain aspects of the war effort to the neglect of others. They particularly stressed the food raising (the "grow more food" campaign) and the food and cloth rationing programs.[204] In keeping with this, Communists were active in organizing people's food committees and in famine relief work of various kinds. "No other group ha(d) done more to popularize the government measures in this respecct."[205] In this campaign Communists performed genuinely effective service in the famine-ridden areas in Bengal and Kerala.[206] On the other hand Communists did not serve on provincial War Front Committees or in Air Raid Precautions squads. Neither did they propound propaganda in support of the war loan program.[207]

The Communists also insisted on the independence of India. They bitterly decried the "stalemate" which existed as a result of the breakdown of the Cripps negotiations, the "Quit India" resolution and the imprisonment of the Congress leaders. They held that the granting of independence to India could break the stalemate, and[208] a resolution to this effect which simultaneously demanded the release of the Congress leaders, was enacted by the First Party Congress.[209] But this "independence" would in no way jeopardize the status of India as an ally of Great Britain and the Soviet Union in the great "people's war."

Indian Communist propaganda took a critical tone towards the British between 1942 and 1945, although it had none of the venomous character which it had possessed prior to the Soviet-German phase of the war. However, sharp sentiments were expressed regarding the unwillingness of the British to make concessions beyond those already proposed in the Cripps proposals and their consequent failure to take steps in granting immediate freedom to India. In this connection British Secretary of State for India, Leopold-Charles Amery, was a frequent target for criticism. The latter was charged with being a diehard Tory of the worst type who desired to perpetuate British imperialist rule over India.[210] In addition, the British were chided by the Communists for the continued detention of the leaders of the Congress as well as certain Communist leaders.[211] Indeed, it may be noted that on June 6, 1943, "People's War" charged that no fewer than 390 Communists had been jailed between August, 1942 and June 1943, in spite of the legalization of the Communist Party.[212]

The Communists maintained an amicable attitude towards the Congress from the summer of 1941 to that of 1945. Joshi hailed the decision of the latter's Working Committee of December, 1941, (The Bardoli Resolution) which evinced a more pro-Allied disposition on the part of Congress. The attitude of Nehru, which was qualifiedly pro-war and pro-United Nations (the qualification being Indian freedom) was particularly applauded.[213] The comrades maintained a pro-Congress position until 1945 in spite of the growing feeling against them in that body. The Communists campaigned "unceasingly" for the release of Congress leaders from prison. Even Mahatma Gandhi became a hero to the Communists and a manifesto of the party of 1943, prior to his release, went so far as to declare that "the future of the Indian nation depended on whether we get Gandhi out or not." On the other hand, the Communists sharply criticized the Congress position that India's stand in the war was conditioned on the policy of the British government in regard to India,[214] as well as the "Quit India" resolution of August 8, 1942. Thus on July 18, 1943, "People's War" held that "it will be suicidal blindness to celebrate August 9th . . . for August 9th (sic) is not patriotic mobilisation but treacherous provocation."[215] This was naturally in line with the C.P.I.'s pro-war policy.

The attitude of the Communists towards the Muslim League represented a startling change from their earlier attitude towards that body. In the past they had, as we have observed, deemed the Muslim League as only a "reactionary communal organisation." But now, suddenly everything was different. Joshi himself averred: "It would be wrong and unrealistic to dismiss the Muslim League as a 'reactionary communal organisation.' It exercises influences over a large section of the Muslim population." "Nor," argued Joshi, "is the Muslim League alone responsible for lack of communal unity," for the "policy of the Congress leadership also has some responsibility."[216] Joshi expressed the hope that "progressive elements" in both League and

Congress would make for a "nation-wide political unity" which would unite the country behind the war effort.[217] This unity would be brought about if Congress were to concede such demands "of the Muslim League . . . as representation of the Central (and) Joint ministries" in the provinces.[218]

The failure of the League to achieve "unity" with Congress did not prejudice the former organization in the Communists' eyes between 1942 and 1945. Thus the part which the Muslim League played in the alleviation of the famine misery was duly praised and the independence resolution of the League in 1937 which spoke of "the independence of India in the form of a federation of independent states" was recalled with favor.[219]

The Communists had much to say on the question of regionalism in the sub-continent on a communal basis. Early in 1942, Joshi sarcastically referred to "Mr. Jinnah's dreamland of Pakistan" as a concept which "leads nowhere except to stalemate and sitting tight."[220] The Communist view was officially enunciated in a booklet by Dr. G. M. Adhikari entitled "Pakistan and Indian National Unity." He argued that India was inhabited by a considerable number of nationalities, each with its own territory, language, culture and psychological make-up. Such groups, for example, were Sindhis, Gujeratis and Andhras along with a great many others. These several nationalities should form sovereign states which would unite in a "free Indian Union or Federation" but each state would have the right "to secede from it if it so desired."[221] The princely states would disappear, being parcelled out among the new ethnic states. Adhikari held this scheme would satisfy the Muslims in that those states in which Muslims were predominant would be autonomous with the right of secession if they desired to set up independent states.[222] In Bengal, Adhikari suggested that Muslim Bengalis might form an autonomous state within Bengal or set up a separate East Bengal state.[223] The Punjab could also be divided into a Muslim (West Punjab) and a Sikh (East Punjab) state.[224] This scheme, held Adhikari, was superior to the Pakistan plan, in that it would avoid dividing India arbitrarily into two nations but would give liberty to all peoples of the Peninsula.[225]

The line on the nationalities as presented by Adhikari was disseminated freely by the Communists in their propaganda. For example, his views were reproduced verbatim in a resolution of the First Communist Congress which also held that the Communists' principles in regard to nationalities would lay the groundwork for the much-desired Congress-League unity.[226] There was also a tendency on the part of the Communists to look with especial favor on the concept of Pakistan for a time, in spite of Adhikari's criticism of the narrowly "religious" basis of the concept. Thus no less important a Communist personage than B. T. Ranadive at a "Pakistan Day" meeting in March, 1944, averred that the record "showed that the League demand was a demand for democracy and freedom."[227] In addition, the party's General Secretary Joshi held in an official article in "People's War" of August 29, 1944:

> Acceptance of Pakistan, of course, implies a radical revision of our traditional concept of a united India. But India will thereby be stronger and not weaker. Independent strong and contented Muslim states on our North-Western and North-Eastern borders will constitute the best defence of India. Whether it be through membership in the common union or through treaty relationships, we cannot but have the best of relations with them.[228]

It may thus be seen that Joshi was here returning to the original Communist view as laid down by Adhikari that there should be not one but two Pakistans or Muslim states.

A further modification of the Communist view on this question was made by Adhikari himself in his capacity of editor of the "People's War." In the October 1, 1944 issue of this publication, Adhikari asserted that "Jinnah has to give up his theory that the Indian Muslims are a Nation," while simultaneously declaring that "Gandhi has to give up his theory that India is one nation."[229] What should take place, added P. C. Joshi one week later, is that the "independent States of Pakistan and Hindustan" should agree on a common policy of "mutual assistance in defence against aggressors and for economic reconstruction. . ."[230] Now in this modified line, the Indian

Communists held that India must remain united for certain purposes, namely defense and reconstruction, but otherwise each state would have sole competence over the powers of government. This was fairly obvious "fence straddling" between the concept of a united India and one divided into two independent countries. There is also here a return to the idea that there should be but a single Muslim state or Pakistan. But to confound the confusion, on October 29, 1944, Joshi writing in the "People's War" emphasized the view that several Muslim nationalities (such as Baluchis and Pathans) desire "autonomy" for their "homelands." This was in contrast, of course, to the idea that there should be but one or at most two Muslim states or (one in the Northwest, the other in the Northeast) "Pakistans."[231]

It is evident the comrades were in somewhat of a quandary in regards to just how to deal with the ticklish question of Pakistan. One thing, however, is quite certain. They were generally favorable to the idea that India should be divided in its internal structure on the basis of ethnological units in such a way as to destroy the princely states.

In considering the Communists' attitudes on the communal question in general, it may be noted that they evinced definite interest in the second largest minority of the sub-continent, the Depressed Classes, commonly known as Untouchables. The Communists prior to 1944 had shown surprisingly little interest in them, a sole exception being the 1934 thesis of the C.P.I. which had stated that the Untouchables should be informed that "their emancipation cannot be achieved by their being taken inside the fold of Hinduism,"[232] and from that time till 1944 little was said on this subject by the Communists. However, on December 3, 1944, Ranadive in an article in the "People's War" agreed to the demands of the Scheduled Castes' Federation for separate electorates for the Untouchables in elections to all legislative bodies. He also called upon Untouchables to join trade unions and peasants' organizations where they would be subjected to Red influence. Ranadive did not criticize the Federation or its leader, Dr. Ambedkar for their policy on

Untouchables, but he did criticize them for their alleged passive attitude in the struggle for Indian freedom.[233]

The plan of Adhikari represented the ultimate political plan for the future of India of the Communists, but for the immediate task of winning the war the C.P.I. advocated a Provisional National government encompassing a "Government of National Unity." This government could not be the monopoly of a single party, but rather would draw in all political groups which would cooperate on the broad common platform for the establishment and maintenance of freedom in the sub-continent and effective prosecution of the war against the "Fascist aggressors." This was the old line of the "united front from above" par-excellence.[234]

The Communists in line with their pro-war policies put forth a moderate economic program which Joshi summed up as follows:

> Promote a policy of rapid industrialization in order to supply the needs of defence and the needs of the masses.
>
> Grant the workers' immediate demands, ensuring that their living conditions are not curtailed.
>
> Grant the demands of the peasants—the amelioration of the burden of indebtedness, rents and taxes. Exercise price control in their interest and give generous term of rent-remission in flood and famine-stricken areas.[235]

It may also be noted that the "Bombay Plan" for Indian post-war economic development fabricated by right-wing Congress and Liberal elements was noted by Joshi as a "welcome step forward."[236]

The favorable attitude towards the Congress and the Muslim League was not extended by the Communists to the minor parties, the Congress Socialist, the Forward Bloc, whose leader S. C. Bose, fled from India in 1941, traveled through Afghanistan and Russia and became an Axis propagandist until his death in a plane crash in August 1945,[237] and Roy's Radical Democrats, whose policies were not unlike the Communists' own line. The first two groups obviously were disapproved of by the Communists, because they thought the "people's war" was an "imperialist" war. They were, then, for the Communists mere lackeys for the Fascists.[238] M. N. Roy was castigated as a "political adventurer" and a "renegade and a spy" who through his Indian Federation of Labour was guilty of "splitting the working class."[239]

* * * * *

The signing of the Nazi-Soviet non-aggression pact of August 23, 1939, marked a renewal of interest on the part of the Soviet Government in regards to India. On that very date, Stalin significantly stated that "it was ridiculous . . . that a few hundred British should dominate India."[240]

In his official report as Foreign Commissar before that puppet parliament, the Supreme Soviet, on October 31, 1939, Molotov, referring to the British war effort, averred that "you cannot give the name of a fight for democracy as . . . the unremitting national oppression in India."[241] Furthermore, in a speech a few days later on November 6th, Molotov bitterly castigated "colonial oppression" in India.[242]

Taking their cue from the Foreign Minister, the Soviet press in November, 1939 assailed British rule in India as well as "right-wing Indians" and dilated verbosely on the allegedly growing signs of revolt in India. It pictured in lurid terms the position of the benighted Indian peasants who groaned under the most acute kind of poverty and oppression.[243] Soviet and Comintern publications repeatedly stressed the opinion that Britain's protestations about the tribulation of Poland and other areas of Europe under the Nazi heel were mere cant of the worst order, in view of the fearsome oppression she herself was carrying on against the people of India.[244]

A moment of fear that these pronouncements of the Soviet press were more than mere palaver occurred at the end of 1939 when the Italian press claimed that a Soviet force of no fewer than 800,000 men was massing on the Soviet-Afghan border with the apparent intention of a march on India.[245] However, the Afghan legation in London denied the report[246] and a little later, on March 2, 1940, Molotov averred in an address to the Supreme Soviet:

> As to the fantastic plans attributed to the Soviet Union of a Red Army 'march on India. . . .' and the like, they are such obvious absurdities that one must completely lose his sense to believe such absurd lies.[247]

The negotiations between Nazi Germany and the Soviet Union in the fall of 1940, following the fall of France most definitely involved India. Prior to the signing of the infamous Tripartite Pact, of September 27, 1940, between Germany, Italy and Japan, high officials of the latter country at first considered and then dropped the idea of having India included in a future Japanese sphere of influence.[248] In an apparent effort to bring Soviet Russia into the Axis bloc, on the following October 13th, von Ribbentrop sent a dispatch to Stalin asking that the latter send Molotov, his Soviet counterpart to Berlin. Having arrived in Berlin on November 13th, Molotov told Hitler that Soviet Russia might share in the British Empire, "a world-wide estate in bankruptcy."[249] Specifically, von Ribbentrop informed Molotov that in regards to the Soviet share of the spoils

> . . . the focal points in the territorial aspirations of the Soviet Union would presumably be centered south of the territory of the Soviet Union in the direction of the Indian Ocean.[250]

And added the Nazi Foreign Minister:

> An agreement could also be reached on possible Soviet aspirations in the direction of British India, if an understanding were reached between the Soviet Union and the Tripartite Pact.[251]

The Germans indicated that the 90th meridian of longitude would separate the Soviet from the Japanese sphere.[252] This would leave the Indian province of Assam and a part of East Bengal to the Japanese, although it left most of Tibet and the rest of India in the Soviet sphere.

The Nazis then produced for Molotov's perusal a "Draft

Agreement" between the nations of the Tripartite Agreement and the Soviet Union which would have made the Soviet Union an Axis partner. It contained two secret protocols. The first dealt with the parcelling out of the Old World and held in its fourth point that "the Soviet Union declares that its territorial aspirations center South of the national territory of the Soviet Union in the direction of the Indian Ocean." Hence it repeated von Ribbentrop's proposal.[253]

On noting the "Draft Agreement," Molotov declared that he was very interested in it, but he "could not take a definite stand at this time, since he did not know the opinions of Stalin. . ."[254]

On Molotov's return to Moscow, Stalin and his associates thoroughly discussed the planned alliance of Communism and Fascism. On November 25, 1940, Molotov handed a note to German Ambassador von Schulenberg which demanded of Germany as the price for Russian accession to the Axis alliance, that German troops be withdrawn from Finland, that Bulgaria and Turkey be placed in the Russian sphere of influence and

> . . . provided that the area south of Batum and Baku in the general direction of the Persian Gulf is recognized as the center of the aspirations of the Soviet Union.[255]

Hitler must have become furious when intelligence of the Soviet reply reached him, for only one month later the Führer himself sent top secret Directive No. 21 which called upon the German armed forces to be prepared to "crush Russia in a quick campaign."[256] But ignorant of the Führer's decision, the Soviet Government demanded of the German ambassador on January 17, 1941 that his government answer the Soviet's note of the previous November 25th.[257] This indicates that the Soviets were still interested in the prospect of seizing control of India and its borderlands. The Nazi Government replied evasively to the Soviet note.[258] Five months later it launched "Operation Barbarossa."

The Soviet Union was so engrossed in its desperate war effort that it had little interest in India between 1941 and 1945, as compared to former years.[259] To Russia, India during those years represented only one thing—an important base of supplies to her from the other United Nations. It was that India might better serve as a base that the Kremlin through the C.P.G.B. demanded the Indian Communists to follow their pro-war line. Typical of the attitude the Soviet held towards India during this war period was that of a statement in the official organ of the Soviet Academy of Sciences, "World Economics and World Politics," of August 1, 1943 which urged India to mobilize all her resources to meet the "immediate danger of invasion" (presumably from Japan) and which falsely asserted that the Indian people were "becoming more and more eager to participate in the war," so that, correspondingly, the anti-war influence of Gandhi was waning.[260]

The Soviet press was highly sensitive of criticism of Russia which appeared in certain segments of the Indian press during the war years. Thus the official Russian organ, "War and the Working Class," viciously attacked in insulting language, various articles in the Indian press which criticized certain facets of Soviet policy in the past and present. For example, articles in the Indian press which criticized Soviet policy in Poland and Northern Iran came in for brutal censure.[261]

It may also be noted that during the earlier part of Russia's conflict with Germany, the Soviets had nothing to say about the independence of India per se. However, in the April 15, 1945 issue of "War and the Working Class," the chief Soviet expert on India, A. M. Dyakov, stated with approval that "the main sections of Indian society are uniting more and more closely for the struggle for India's independence."[262] After the failure of the Simla conference[263] from June 25th to July 14th, 1945 in which the Viceroy conferred with Indian leaders, Gandhi, Jinnah and Maulana Abul Kalam Azad, President of the Congress, Dyakov opined that Viceroy Lord Wavell's

> . . . proposals were very limited in character and involved only a few and seemingly by no means far-reaching changes in the structure of the executive organs of the Indian Government.[264]

In addition, observed Dyakov, the proposals had the "inherent defect . . . of constituting the (Viceroy's) Council on lines of religious communities rather than of political parties."[265]

Thus as the Second World War neared its end, the Soviets through this spokesman were evidencing that there would soon be greater Soviet interest in India.[266]

* * * * *

During the first two years of the war, when the Soviet Union was deemed a virtual non-belligerent ally of Nazi Germany, there was a certain amount of nervous apprehension concerning the security of India's Northwest Frontier on the part of Britons and Americans.[267] In the spring of 1940 the British press significantly spoke of declarations of loyalty on the part of certain tribesmen of the Northwest Frontier through whose territory a potential Soviet force might conduct an advance. In some of these declarations the determination "to resist any threat of Russian invasion" was affirmed.[268] But Anglo-Saxon apprehensions were allayed by "Operation Barbarossa."

The conclusion of the Anglo-Soviet agreement of July 12, 1941 according to which the two nations agreed to assist each other in the war against Germany and to conclude no separate peace with the latter,[269] was followed by the extension of the British-Indian railway system to the Persian town of Zahidan from which place Allied goods were sent across Iran to the Soviet frontier.[270]

Anglo-Soviet wartime cooperation was manifested in respect to the internal affairs of Iran (where Soviet influence had for several years past been meager) and Afghanistan, as well as in the transport of war goods to the embattled Soviet forces. The two nations had collaborated in their ultimata in respect to Iran of August 25, 1941, which claimed that Germans were carrying on dangerous intrigues in Iran and had joined together in the occupation of the country.[271] Britain and Russia also collaborated in the division of Persia into three zones, a northern or Soviet zone, a southern or British zone, and an intermediate zone in which the Iranians were to maintain autonomy.[272]

Anglo-Soviet relations were likewise harmonious in Afghanistan, once the Soviets whose influence there between 1929 and 1941 had markedly declined,[273] were compelled to enter the war. In October, 1941, parallel British and Soviet notes to Kabul demanded the ouster of German and Italian nationals.

Realizing their land would likely have to endure the same foreign occupation as that of Iran in event of non-compliance, the Afghan government saw fit to honor the request so that some 300 German and Italian nationals were forthwith deported.[274] Formal Afghan neutrality in the war was reaffirmed by King Mohammed Zahir Shah in July, 1942,[275] and as the tide of battle shifted thereafter to the side of the United Nations, Afghanistan became even friendlier to Britain and the Soviet Union alike. However, Afghanistan did not become a belligerent on the Allied side, but maintained a policy of benevolent neutrality towards it.

It may be noted that in relation to the northern borderland of Sinkiang, Soviet influence there remained powerful until the fateful summer of 1941. However, as a result of Soviet military reverses in the early phases of the "Great Patriotic War" with Germany, Russian influence in Chinese Turkestan perceptibly declined and Governor Ma Sheng Shi-tsai who had been a virtual Soviet puppet was able to assert his authority and simultaneously to place this territory under the over-all control of the Nationalist Government.[276] Although towards the end of the war the Soviets were able to use their war-time influence with the Nationalist Government to effect the removal of Ma Sheng who had, from their standpoint, betrayed them, they had lost control of Kashmir's northern borderland.[277]

The Soviets were unable to gain influence in India's borderland of Tibet in the years of the Second World War.

* * * * *

Deeply preoccupied in their struggle for freedom, and in communal questions, there was little interest in the Soviet Union on the part of non-Communist Indians between the summer of 1939 and that of 1941. Nor, for that matter, was there a great deal of opinion expressed in regard to the activities of the Indian Communists nor of Communism as an ideology. However, Mahatma Gandhi reiterated his former view that he disapproved of the "violent" element inherent in Communism, particularly in connection with the liberation of India,[278] and that he could not subscribe to the Communist philosophy per se.[279] On the other hand Sir Rabindranath

Tagore continued to manifest a friendly interest in the Russian experiment. Even in his deathbed message of 1941 the great Bengali poet referred to the "unsparing energy which Russia has tried to fight disease and illiteracy and succeeded in steadily liquidating ignorance and poverty. . . ."[280]

Jawaharlal Nehru also continued to maintain his interest in the Soviet Union and Marxism between 1939 and 1941. He admitted that it had been a "shock" to him that Soviet Russia had concluded its "non-aggression" pact with Germany on August 23, 1939, and had followed this up in the succeeding month with an invasion of Eastern Poland in September, 1939. However, he expressed the opinion that there was not going to be in the future any "real alliance" between Russia and Germany.[281]

Nehru also retained his favorable attitude towards Marxism at this time. On September 29, 1939, he noted that both Marxism and Leninism were theories which explained man's poverty and the ways in which the latter might be terminated.[282] In a much bolder fashion on March 8, 1940, Nehru held that, for his own part, he would like to see a "socialist economy" established throughout India and that he even believed that the Soviet form of government "with certain variations and adaptations" suited to India "might fit in here," for, held Nehru, he believed that the Soviet system was compatible with democracy. However, the Pandit indicated that the Soviet system should not be introduced into India "for some time," for otherwise there would be terrible conflicts."[283]

The attack on Russia by Germany aroused genuine interest and sympathy for the Soviet Union[284] on the part of many Indian non-Communists. For example, seventy leading intellectuals of Bengal Province, led by the well-known scientist, Sir P. C. Roy, F.R.S.C., extended their support to Russia, a land which they held had attained great "moral and material achievements and which had evinced friendship for the people of the East."[285] Subsequently, a demand was voiced in the Indian press that an envoy from Russia be allowed to come to India. It was pointed out that both the United States and China had sent semi-official envoys to India and that the Soviet

Union had actually sent an envoy to Australia. "Why then should not such an envoy be sent to India as well?"[286]

The question of the Soviet Union in relation to Indian freedom came up in the fateful summer of 1942. On July 31st, R. H. Parker, a European member of the Indian Council of State suggested that Gandhi and other members of the Congress Working Committee should meet with Premier Joseph Stalin as well as Generalissimo Chiang Kai-shek,[287] an interesting albeit abortive suggestion. On the same day Gandhi specifically declared that he would not "be appeased into a political truce" if the Soviet Union along with the United States and China would guarantee fulfillment of Britain's pledge to free India after the termination of the war.[288]

The disinterested attitude on the part of the Soviet Union towards India between 1941 and 1945 evoked not a little irritation from Indian Nationalists. Thus the official historian of the National Congress noted that the only book on India published in the Soviet Union in 1943 was pro-British. "It was as if the Russians decided to gaze at India through British eyes. . . ."[289]

By contrast, Nehru maintained a favorable view toward Russia. After his release from prison in December 1941, he took a pro-United Nations position and was largely responsible for the pro-Allied, and pro-Soviet position encompassed in the Bardoli Resolution at that time.[290] Early in 1942 he believed that with the intensification of the war resulting from the Japanese invasion of Burma, there should be a direct relationship of cooperation between India and the Soviet Union.[291] At this time he publicly declared his admiration for the Soviets. Speaking at Lucknow on February 22, 1942, the Pandit stated:

> Our problems in India to-day are the same as those that faced Russia some years ago; and they can be solved in the same manner in which the Russians solved theirs. We should draw a lesson from the U.S.S.R. in the way of industrialisation and educating our country.[292]

Nehru went on to hold that the Soviets had been able to withstand the Nazi hordes only because Russia had been free and because the Soviet economic structure had a very strong foundation. He concluded by holding that India and Russia, together with China, should, at a not distant date, be bound in closer ties of amity than had hitherto been the case in view of the fact that these lands possessed much in common and that their problems to a great extent were similar.[293]

Nehru also evinced a favorable view towards Soviet Russia in his "Autobiography" which appeared in 1942 and his "Discovery of India" written in prison between 1942 and 1945. In the former volume, Nehru held that with all her blunders, Russia had triumphed over enormous difficulties, and had made giant strides towards a new order.[294] In the latter work, Nehru complimented the Soviets for their brave and tenacious battle against the Nazis,[295] held that the Russians were a new rejuvenated and revitalized people which, in spite of wartime devastation, possessed tremendous potential,[296] and specifically praised the Soviets' nationalities' policy.[297] He implied Russia would not be aggressive after the war because she would be busy in repairing the war-wrought devastation within her frontiers.[298] However, Nehru reiterated his view that there had been developments in Russia in recent years which had come as a shock to many of that country's old admirers,[299] and that in following a national policy Russia had confounded her sympathizers.[300]

In both works Nehru praised Marxism as an ideology but in his later work he held he disliked the regimentation implied in Marxism and the lack of ethics also implied in that ideology.[301]

In both volumes, Nehru bitterly attacked India's Communists for having vilified Gandhi and the Congress, for their abuse rather than an attempt to explain the meaning of Communism,[302] for the fact they were absolutely divorced from as well as ignorant of the basic traditions of India and for the fact that for Indian Communists, the world's history began in 1917.[303]

These sentiments indicated that in the days to come Pandit Jawaharlal Nehru in spite of his theoretical sympathy for socialist ideology, would be no friend of the Communist Party of India.

CHAPTER EIGHT

Indian Communism on the Eve of Independence

The years from 1945 to 1947 represented a time of turmoil in India. The yearning of Indian Nationalists for freedom boiled over in near insurrections in Calcutta in November, 1945, and in Bombay the following February.[1] Recognizing the dangers inherent in the situation and honestly evidencing sympathy for Indian national aspirations, Labour Prime Minister Clement Attlee announced on February 19, 1946 that a Cabinet Mission headed by Lord Pethwick-Lawrence, Secretary of State for India and Sir Stafford Cripps would visit India and endeavor to work out a plan which would be satisfactory to the national aspirations of Indians in general and to the specific wishes of the National Congress and the Muslim League in particular.[2] The Mission which arrived in India on March 24, 1946 failed to reconcile differences between the Congress, which demanded a strong Central Indian government and the League, which, although abandoning its desire for Pakistan, demanded an Indian federation with a central government possessing little authority.[3] Endeavoring to break the impasse, on May 16, 1946 the Cabinet Mission presented its own plan, which provided that in a free India, the central government would maintain control in the fields of foreign affairs, defense and communications, but would leave all other powers of government to the provinces and to two intermediate "tiers" of government, one for Muslim India (the Northwest and Northeast) and the other for non-Muslim India.[4] Optimistic hopes that a united, free India would come into being under this plan were dashed when the Muslim League, late in July, 1946, denounced the

Cabinet Mission's Plan as unworkable and called anew for a free Pakistan.[5] The setting up in September, 1946 of an "interim" government by which the Viceroy's Council took on an all-Indian complexion with Nehru serving as a virtual Prime Minister under the over-all supervision of the Viceroy, the convening of a Constituent Assembly, elected the previous June, in December, 1946 and the mediation efforts of the British, did not heal the irreconcilable Congress-League division.[6] Finally, on February 4, 1947 Attlee informed the House of Commons that a "transference of power" to the Indians would take place not later than June, 1948.[7] Galvanized into action by this declaration, Lord Mountbatten, the successor to Lord Wavell as Governor-General, early in 1947, did his utmost to reconcile the Congress and League to participate together in a single Indian dominion. His efforts were in vain.[8] Consequently, on June 3, 1947 in a broadcast to the peoples of India, Mountbatten indicated that the sub-continent would be granted freedom shortly on the basis of two independent dominions, Pakistan, which would include the predominantly Muslim-populated area of Western and Northwestern India (including the western part of the Punjab) and East Bengal, and the Indian Union, which would comprise the balance of British India.[9] The native states would be given the right to "accede" to either dominion or even to become independent, but in practice owing to the small size and lack of resources of most of them, independence was out of the question.[10] In line with this "Mountbatten Plan," India and Pakistan became free dominions within the British Commonwealth of Nations on August 15, 1947.

This freedom for the Muslims and the non-Muslims in the Peninsula was not paid without a price. Communal rioting in Calcutta and elsewhere, ensuing from the Muslim League's denunciation of the Cabinet Mission's Plan, lead to the deaths of 12,000 and the wounding of many thousands more in the period between August, 1946 and February, 1947.[11]

* * * * *

The Communists paid the penalty for their non-support of the National Movement so far as the Congress was concerned. A portent of Congress sentiment was expressed by Nehru shortly after his release from prison in June, 1945. On the 22nd of that month he affirmed in an interview:

> The Communists missed the chance of a life-time in India during the last two or three years. They would have made themselves an enormously powerful party if they had functioned somewhat different. At a critical moment in India's history, it was difficult to be neutral, but they went to the other side. They may be right, but the approach was wrong.[12]

On the following July 8th the Pandit asserted of the Communists that

> . . . having opposed the general trend of the national movement, they have created a barrier between themselves and Indian nationalism which greatly lessens their influence outside their own sphere.[13]

Anti-Communist sentiments in the Congress were brought out all the more as a result of the disclosure on August 29, 1945, of the report of the committee headed by Bhulabhai Desai which had investigated the C.P.I. as a result of the Gandhi-Joshi correspondence. The report contended that "it does appear that the views and attitude of the Communist Party after the 9th August (1942) have been to carry on propaganda contrary to the views and policy of the Congress."[14] In addition, at this time, Nehru made it clear that in his opinion Communists should not hold office in the National Congress.[15]

On September 2, 1945, an anti-Communist riot took place in Bombay and on the following day it was announced that the Executive Committee of the Bombay Provincial Congress had expelled four Communist members of that committee on the grounds that "they have opposed almost every ofifcial measure of the Congress," "they do not believe in non-violence as a creed or policy," and above all, "they refused to obey the Congress" resolution to "Quit India" of August 8, 1942.[16] The ousted Communists felt highly aggrieved at these proceedings and complained that they had been removed not by any "concrete and specific charges" but only by "a vague and specious one," a contention manifestly contradictory to the facts.[17]

Also in September, 1945, the Congress Committee appointed a committee consisting of Pandit Nehru, Vallabhbhai Patel and Govind B. Pant to examine the charges of indiscipline on the part of the Communists towards the Congress.[18] Furthermore, a leading member of Congress, the historian of the body, Pattabhi Sitaramayya in a meeting castigated the Communists in the following terms:

> Russia is knocking at our doors and is hardly forty miles from our frontier. If the Russians should invade the country —and this is not a fantastic proposition—on whose side will these Communists of India fight? Will they side with their Mother Country of their birth, or with their Father country of their idea? This eccentric party whose centre of gravity is Leningrad, whose head, is, however, in the Himalayas, is a dangerous party to be reckoned with.[19]

On September 21, 1945 the Congress Working Committee published the charge-sheet prepared by the above-mentioned sub-committee and sent it to the Communist members of the All-India Congress Committee (A.I.C.C.) demanding of them why disciplinary action should not be taken against them for their opposition to Congress policies and programs since the summer of 1942.[20] Moreover, in the course of an A.I.C.C. meeting held later in the month of September, 1945 in Bombay, a number of Congress speakers lashed out at the Indian Communist Party for its hostile attitude towards the "1942 struggle" and its support of the war. When a Communist leader, Dr. Ashraf, himself a member of the A.I.C.C., tried to speak, he was drowned out by jeering Congressmen. So great was the hostility to the Communists at this time that the latter were compelled to deny a rumor they intended to burn the A.I.C.C. pavilion in a kind of "Reichstag fire."[21]

Aware that expulsion from the Congress was likely to come soon, Communist Party boss P. C. Joshi called upon all Communists to resign from the Congress except the Communist members of the A.I.C.C., against whom disciplinary action was pending. In a statement in this connection issued on October 5, 1945, the Red General Secretary censured the Congress for "raising its arms against our young Party which consistently defended it (Congress) against imperialist slander at home and abroad."[22]

Meanwhile, in October, 1945 the A.I.C.C. went on record in opposing to Communists the right to hold "positions of responsibility" within the Congress.[23] In addition, on October 23rd of that year, Nehru delivered a sharp attack on the Indian Communists. "The cause of Communism and the name of Russia have suffered most at the hands of the Communist Party of India," averred the Pandit. Alluding to the anti-patriotic role played by the Communists, he added:

> When lakhs (tens of thousands) of Indians staked their all for the country's cause, the Communists were in the opposite camp, which cannot be forgotten. The common man associates the Communist Party with Russia and Communism. But actions of the Communist Party of India have prejudiced both Russia and Communism.[24]

Furthermore, Sardar Vallabhbhai Patel, the right-wing leader of Congress known as the "sledgehammer" of that body, ordered the expulsion of Communists from various provincial Congress organizations.[25] Bitterly venting his feelings at this latest turn of events, Joshi asserted with acerbity:

> Instead of offering a concrete plan for Indian freedom they (the A.I.C.C.) have committed the Congress to a course of action that will only further divide and disrupt the freedom forces. . . . In the name of the unity of India . . . they are . . . refusing to build a united front for Indian freedom. . . .[26]

Adding that "our party cannot patiently hear slanders against itself repeated ad nauseum" and "our party cannot permit itself to be chained and gagged by a leadership that is leading our freedom movement to the rocks," Joshi justified the new Communist line of asking members of the Communist party who were also members of Congress to resign from the latter organization.[27] In addition, the Communists purported to answer the charges presented against them in a bombastic, blustering book in two volumes put out by Joshi on November 27, 1945 entitled "The Communist Reply to the Congress Working Committee." This work didactically justified in its entirety the devious course of the Communist Party line for the past several years, took an aggressively hostile attitude towards the Congress for daring to take measures against the C.P.I., and contended the C.P.I. was in complete accord with India's national interests[28] while the Congress was diametrically opposed to those interests.

Needless to say, the Congress was angered at the impertinence of the Communists. On December 13, 1945, meeting at Calcutta, the Congress Working Committee confirmed the expulsion of all Communists from the A.I.C.C. and gave strict orders that in the future no Communist could hold office in the Congress on the national or provincial level. The basis for this action of the Working Committee was a four-thousand word report of the special sub-committee of that body consisting of Nehru, Patel and Pant, which dealt with the role the Communists had played in India since the founding of their party. In addition, a "charge sheet" was drawn up by the special sub-committee which recommended the expulsion of Communists from the All-India Congress Committee.[29]

In tracing the growth of the C.P.I. the report noted that before 1936 the Communists had characterized the Congress as a mere "reactionary body."[30] It noted that the Communists had been "more friendly" to the Congress between 1936 and 1939, but even then, there had been "much friction" between the Communists and the Congress. It remarked that between 1939 and 1941 the Communists had opposed the Congress for launching individual civil disobedience rather than a "mass struggle."[31]

The report was particularly concerned with Communist activity between 1941 and 1945. It noted than in propounding their demands for Indian participation in the war, there were actual "conflicts" in public meetings, especially in Andhra in which the Communists employed "violence" to bolster their views and it also commented upon the Communists' vilification of the Congress for the August 8, 1942 resolution and the "disturbances" which followed. The report maintained:

> At a time when the country was passing through a reign of terror and the Congress was involved in a life and death struggle, no organisation allied with the Congress, could without committing serious outrage to the ordinary tenets of discipline, indulge in such hostile activities.[32]

As for the Communists' blustering "Reply," of November 27, 1945, the sub-committee's report curtly commented:

> Hardly any attempt has been made in it to meet the charges nor is there a word of regret in it. . . . The signatories have throughout pleaded justification and attacked the fundamental policy of the Congress in unmistakable terms. Their explanation is tantamount to a tirade against the Congress. . . .[33]

The "charge sheet" in stern terms called upon the Communists on the A.I.C.C. who then numbered only eight members to explain their course and "to show cause why such action (their expulsion from the A.I.C.C.) should not be taken against you."[34]

The truculent Communists refused to justify their course before the Congress so the Working Committee's decision of December 13, 1945 became final. On their own volition the Communists saw to it that none of their members remained in or entered the Congress. The rupture between the National Congress and the C.P.I. endured in spite of sentiment expressed by Indian Communists and particularly by their British Communist mentors that a reconciliation between the two bodies was feasible as well as desirable.[35] As a result of the rupture Communist influenced organizations such as the A.I.K.S. and the A.I.T.U.C. came in for a definite measure of censure by the Congress at this time.[36]

We have seen that the Communists had been able to acquire

a measure of influence within the ranks of the Muslim League in the years 1942 to 1945. However, in 1945 and 1946 the leaders of the League, Mohammed Ali Jinnah and Liaquat Ali Khan launched a purge of Communists within their organization and emphatically disavowed Communist support in all forms.[37]

The Anglo-Indian authorities likewise had reason to take a more jaundiced view towards the Communists than during the later war years in view of the latter's policy of fomenting strikes, riots, and peasants' uprisings. Thus on January 14, 1947 a sweeping search was made of the offices of the C.P.I. and of organizations influenced by the Communists such as the All-Indian Kisan Sabha, the Students' Federation and the "Friends of the Soviet Union."[38] The bulk of the raids were carried out in Bombay, the seat of Indian Communism, but raids were also conducted against provincial headquarters of the Communist Party in such representative Indian cities as Madras, Lahore, Benares, Allahabad, Cawnpore and Delhi. In several instances arrests were made as well as the carrying out of seizures of documents and papers of various kinds. Among those apprehended were Dr. G. N. Adhikari, the editor of "People's Age" (formerly "People's War," the name having been changed on November 25, 1945) and two leaders of the A.I.K.S., Biwanath Mukherjee and Abdullah Rassool. A number of Communist trade union ofifcials were arrested as well.[39] P. C. Joshi refering to the raids in Bombay querulously sputtered: "The whole party office is being ransacked. Residential rooms are being raided. . . . Even personal letters of Mrs. Joshi have been looked through."[40]

The immediate cause of the raids was held to have been the fact that "People's Age" had printed in the summer of 1946 a series of articles which purportedly disclosed the contexts of "top secret documents" of the General Army headquarters, known as "Operation Asylum" regarding methods the Indian Army should adopt in dealing with future manifestations of unrest.[41] However, the basic cause was the strike-fomenting policy of the Communists.[42]

On January 19, 1947, the C.P.I.'s chief mentor R. Palme Dutt sent a telegram to Pandit Nehru in his capacity of Vice-

President (in effect, Prime Minister) of the Interim Government protesting the raids, demanding release of the imprisoned Communists, and the return of the seized documents. Dutt's superior, C.P.G.B. boss, Harry Pollitt, sent a similar message to Lord Pethwick-Lawrence. Nehru replied that the raids on the Indian Communists

> . . . took place without the knowledge or authority of the Ministers and were due to police action in connection with the investigation of a case instituted against a newspaper in Bombay.[43]

This statement, which would seem to indicate the British were solely responsible for the raids, elicited a sceptical reception in certain sections of the non-Communist Indian press, and it was freely alleged that Sardar Patel, the Home Minister of the Interim Government and leader of the right-wing Congressmen, was the man who ordered the raids.[44]

The raids in January, 1947 did not terminate the anti-Communist activities of the authorities. In Madras Presidency under the auspices of the energetic Congress provincial prime minister, Premier Prakasam, a drastic "public safety" ordinance was enacted by which persons could be arrested and detained without bail, without charges being presented and without appeal "except to the arresting agents." As a consequence, some 200 Communist leaders throughout the Presidency were arrested between February and April, 1947.[45] Contemporaneously, early in 1947, drastic action was undertaken by the authorities against Communist-inspired strikes, notably in the Bombay area which action was featured by what the Communists claimed was a "bloody slaughter" of the workers.[46]

In spite of the repression increasingly directed against them and their activities between August of 1945 and that of 1947, the Communists, of course, did their utmost to augment their influence in the turbulent sub-continent. Their policy during this period involved two facets—the one, continuance of their line of a "National Front" with patriotic Indian groups, and thus maintenance of an ostensibly friendly attitude towards the Congress and the Muslim League—the other a militant campaign of mass agitation, not excluding violence, ostensibly for Indian independence. This latter facet involved the resumption of a marked and sharp attitude against authority in general which contrasted with the mild and well-behaved conduct of the Communists from 1941 till the end of the war. The new Red line favored strikes, demonstrations, riots and even peasant uprisings which manifestly invited the repression against the Communists just noted.

The first significant manifestation of the new Communist policy occurred during the anti-British riots in Calcutta, in November, 1945. There the Communists did their utmost to incite workers to shout "get out of India," "get out of Asia," and to take to the barricades, and they also fostered a general strike of public service employees in that city during this sanguinary affair in which forty persons were slain and over 300 were wounded. Although this virtual insurrection was supressed, the Communists were pleased in that they had apparently enhanced their influence among the masses of Bengal as a result of the riots.[47]

The Communists next transferred their attention to Bombay. They were active in riots there in connection with Independence Day Celebrations (January 26, 1946). At that time clashes occurred between the Communists and Congress elements in which the former were stoned and their headquarters set afire with damage amounting to 100,000 rupees according to Communist estimates.[48] But the greatest subversive activity for the Communists was in connection with the Bombay sailors' "mutiny" or "strike" of February 19th to 23rd of 1946. This "strike" which had been occasioned by the low pay (especially as compared to British sailors) and poor living conditions of the seamen, was exactly the thing the Communists needed to arouse revolutionary sentiments in the Bombay area. Communist agitators were busy among the 20,000 "striking" sailors who had seized a score of ships in Bombay harbor and they encouraged them to shout "Inquilab Zindabad" (Long live the Revolution!) and "Down with British Imperialism" and to hoist Red flags. That the movement was not exclusively Communist, however, was indicated by the fact that Congress and League flags were also raised by the striking seamen.[49]

The Communists on shore, in the meantime, endeavored to stir up the masses into a frenzy. Heeding their call, on the following day, some 200,000 workers struck and riotous meetings and demonstrations were carried on in the streets. But on February 22nd, the British-directed police and military struck back vigorously, engaging in a "bloody battle" of several hours' duration with the demonstrating workers and students. In the meantime the strike of sailors spread to other naval seaports of India, notably Madras, Vizagapatam, and Karachi and there were likewise sympathetic strikes and demonstrations in such inland cities as Madura and Trichinopoly.[50]

By February 22nd, 1946, the Congress high command realized that matters were getting out of hand. As a consequence, hasty consultations took place between notable Congress leaders, Gandhi, Nehru and Patel on one hand and the Anglo-Indian authorities on the other. As a result the Congress through Patel appealed to the sailors' strike committee to desist from the "mutiny" and therefore the strike committee, which was on the whole dominated by non-Communist elements, gave in stating "we surrender to India and not to Britain," a reference to the fact that it was the Congress' (and also the Muslim League's) appeal and not British pressure which ended the mutiny.[51]

The attitude of the Congress and the League towards the strike in endeavoring to quench the flames of a potentially violent revolution throughout India, manifestly came in for bitter condemnation by the Communists,[52] but it also drew the acknowledgement that, as of the winter of 1946, "faith in the leaders of the League and Congress among the masses . . . was still great."[53]

That the "mutiny" of the sailors and the attendant violent strikes and demonstrations were of Communist inspiration rather than that of responsible Indian organizations, the Congress and the League, was indicated by Prime Minister Attlee when he declared in the House of Commons on February 22, 1946 that

> . . . the Congress has officially disclaimed participation in the mutiny, but left-wing elements and Communists are trying to work up sympathy[54]

for the mutinous seamen.

Communists were also active in other riots and clashes in India early in 1946, notably a hartal (complete stoppage of work) in Delhi on March 8, 1946 during the course of which the Town Hall was set on fire,[55] a "mutiny" by Gurhka (Nepalese) soldiers in the Dehra Dun area of Bengal[56] and armed clashes and riots in Southern India early in April, 1946.[57]

At the same time, the Communists, to the limit of their abilities, carried on a strike program during the first half of 1946. All types and categories of Indian labor were involved, textile, chemical, and machine tool workers in Calcutta, textile workers in Dacca, and rail workers in various parts of India were among the many participants of the great strike movement.[58] In all, during the first quarter of 1946, there were no fewer than 426 strikes in which 580,000 participated.[59] The "strike fever" then sweeping India was the most violent since 1928 when again Communists had been most active.[60]

The strike wave roared on as the year 1946 proceeded. Bombay was especially hard hit, being beset by not only industrial strikes but by its being, in July, 1946, virtually cut off from the rest of India by postal and telegraph strikes. Even white collar workers such as Bombay bank clerks walked out and police and tax collectors went on strike in various parts of India.[61] Altogether, in the last nine months of 1946 there were throughout India, 1,466 strikes in which 1,737,000 workers participated, an unprecedented amount of labor unrest.[62]

In spite of the repression against their party, the Indian Communists maintained their policy of inciting strikes and agrarian disturbances in 1947 in the months prior to the freedom and partition of the Peninsula. Representative strikes at this time involved textile workers in the Central Provinces (now Madhya Pradesh), Gujerat and Madras, tramway workers and longshoremen in Calcutta and even teachers and state employees in the Central Provinces.[63] Indeed, the year 1947 was as noteworthy for strikes in India, as had been the previous year, an acknowledgement of the Communists' influence in the working class movement.[64]

This influence of the Communists' had been largely occasioned by their continued dominance which had now become outright control of the A.I.T.U.C., by far the most important of All-Indian labor federations, the "Royist" Indian Federation of Labour, having very heavily lost ground. Moreover, certain small unions set up by pro-Congress elements had not been successful.[65]

As a result, in the spring of 1947, the Congress leadership determined to break the Communists' near monopoly in the labor field. At an important meeting of the leaders of the Interim Government, Home Minister Patel pointed out that Communists were fomenting strikes throughout India, and that they had even succeeded in establishing pockets "in every Government organisation." It was high time their activities were terminated. The way this could best be done would be to establish a more effective Congress-controlled conservative labor movement on an All-Indian scale.[66] As a result, an All-Indian trade union federation known as the Indian National Trade Union Congress (I.N.T.U.C.) was inaugurated in May, 1947 under the nominal leadership of Acharya Kripalani, the bitterly anti-Communist President of the Congress with the behind-the-scenes leadership remaining with Patel.[67]

A further blow was struck against the Communist position in the trade union movement when other anti-Communist elements, predominantly Socialists, subsequently founded in 1948 another all-Indian labor association known as the Hind Mazdoor Sabha (Indian Labour Association).[68] Since many of the unions together with their memberships that had been affiliated with the A.I.T.U.C. joined the new labor federations, the Communists, on the eve of freedom and partition of the sub-continent now faced most strenuous competition in the labor movement instead of the virtual monopoly they had possessed when the A.I.T.U.C. dominated the labor scene.[69]

The Communists were also active in stirring up the Indian peasantry between the summers of 1945 and 1947. In British India they were particularly active in the rural areas of East

Bengal, where Communist-controlled peasant unions demanded peremptorily that landlords lower the rents by one third (hence the name of the movement, "Tebhaga," one third part). Other areas of Communist activity in the kisan sabha movement were in various parts of the Madras Presidency, particularly in Andhra, in the United Provinces, and in the rural regions of the Bombay Presidency where Communists were particularly interested in carrying on propaganda among the Varils, a small nationality of "wretched peasants and debtors."[70] However, from 1945 to 1947 Congress and Socialist peasant leagues were rising to challenge the power of the Communist-influenced All-India Kisan Sabha, and their influence did much to retard the growth of the Communists in the countryside.[71]

The Communists were busier than ever in the native states of India in the year 1946 in both the industrial and agrarian spheres of these still feudal territories. In the industrial sphere, in the latter part of 1946, no fewer than 25,000 textile workers struck in Hyderabad and Mysore and a palm leaf weavers' strike in Travancore state and neighboring areas involved some 130,000 workers in November, 1946.[72]

But it was in the agrarian areas of the princely states—they were after all, fundamentally rural regions—that the Communists made their greatest gains and brought about the greatest amount of rioting and virtual rebellion. Hyderabad was an especially important area of Communist agitation. The situation in that princely state in regard to land tenure presented a particularly unpleasant picture, for that state was the domain of extremely wealthy landlords—42 per cent of the land was owned by only 110 landlords—and the Nizam himself, as the leading landlord of the state owned no fewer that 8,014 square miles of territory, the rents of which brought for him an annual income of 60 million rupees.[73] Little wonder, then, that he was deemed to be one of the (if not the) wealthiest men in the world.[74] By contrast, the peasantry of Hyderabad lived in extreme squalor and misery which was intensified in the mid-forties by conditions of drought and famine. Taking advantage of the situation, the Communists in 1946 took command of one of the leading popular organizations in Hyderabad (founded in

1942) known as the Andhra Conference, which represented the Telegu speaking peasantry of the state and which numbered some 100,000 persons in the summer of 1946.[75] This Communist-controlled organization organized the peasants into "village committees" which made stern demands on the landowners, insisting that unpaid labor service to the latter, known as "begar," be abolished and that land which had recently been acquired by landlords should be returned forthwith to the peasants. When the landlords refused to yield to the demands, the Communist-led peasants rose up in rebellion, seized the landlords' lands, and divided them up among themselves, although, oddly enough, they permitted the landowners to retain about 100 to 200 acres for their own use. The center of this peasants' insurrection was in the Nalgonda and Warangal districts of the Telengana region, in eastern Hyderabad.[76]

Infuriated by these events, the Nizam hurled some 4,000 troops into the disaffected areas and a considerable number were slain as a result of clashes between the peasants and the troops. In addition, some 2,000 persons were arrested. So serious had the situation become that Lord Auchinleck, the Commander-in-Chief of the Anglo-Indian army arrived in Hyderabad in December, to assist in the quelling of the rural rebellion.[77] Hyderabad then remained relatively quiet until August, 1947.

Another instance in which the ruler's troops had to be called out to suppress Communist agitation occurred in Travancore where the Maharajah's forces towards the end of 1946 were called out to suppress an alleged "Communist uprising."[78]

The Communists also became active in an important way for the first time in the highly strategic state of Kashmir, located just south of the High Pamir territory of the Soviet Union, with only a thin wisp of Afghan territory lying between them. We have noted that in 1931 there was a peasants' rebellion in Kashmir, and out of this revolt emerged an organization known as the "National Conference." During the 'thirties this body, in spite of the Muslim faith of its followers (Kashmir is about 90 per cent Muslim in faith), maintained a friendly relationship with the National Congress rather than with the Muslim League. Up to 1946, the Kashmiri National Conference was dominated by relatively conservative "bourgeois" elements which maintained a certain affinity with right-wing Congress circles. However, in 1946 the Communists began infiltrating the National Conference. They and other leftists within it demanded in the spring of 1946 the removal of the Maharajah and the establishment of a democratic republican government and an extensive land reform program.[79] The aroused ruler on May 20, 1946, firmly suppressed the movement, not without some bloodshed, and arrested its leaders, in spite of the desperate efforts of the "battle committees" of this Communist-infiltrated organization.[80]

Communists were also active even in very small states between 1945 and 1947, for example in the tiny state of Tehri-Gahrwal in the Central Himalayas.[81] They also carried on an agitation among various primitive tribal peoples of India.[82]

The Communists also did their best to infiltrate the States' Peoples' Association, a body representing the people of the various princely states. Publicity was given this movement in its meeting in Gwalior between April 19th to 29th, 1947 at which approval was registered for the introduction of democratic government in the states and the election of states' delegates to the Legislative Assembly by popular vote and not by appointment by the rulers.[83]

As might have been expected, the Communists were as busy as ever in the students' movement. In its Nagpur session in 1946, the All-India Students' Federation passed the usual number of pro-Communist resolutions.[84] However, the Communists encountered powerful opposition in the students' movement in 1947. They admitted that even in their hitherto exclusive preserve, the All-India Students' Federation itself, "pro-Congress elements" had attained a "strong influence" over that body. Besides, other non-Communist students' bodies, first the Students' Congress and then the National Union of Students arose to challenge the position of the All-India Students' Federation. Thus the Communists became virtually "isolated . . . on the students' front."[85] It may also be noted that the authorities of several colleges and universities were commencing to dismiss Communist and pro-Communist students. This was hardly unnatural in view of the part which students had played in various Red-inspired strikes and demonstrations.[86]

The Communists also suffered a reverse in the organized women's movement when their influence in the All-India Women's Conference waned and that organization came to be controlled by non-Communist elements.[87]

On October 12, 1945, party boss P. C. Joshi announced that the Indian Communists would contest the elections of provincial legislatures to be held between November 1945 and April 1946. It was indicated that in those constituencies in which the C.P.I. did not put up its own candidates, it would support Congress candidates in the general constituencies and Muslim League candidates in special Muslim constituencies.[88] The Communists put forward a limited number of candidates in agricultural regions where they had attained influence such as in Bengal and Madras Provinces. The Communists charged that in the areas in which the Communists stood a chance to win seats, the Congress formed a bloc with small ultra-conservative parties such as the Justice and non-Brahmin parties of the Madras area and even with the Hindu Mahasabha in the case of Bengal.[89]

In spite of the coalitions against them, the Communists elected nine deputies to various provincial assemblies and amassed a vote of nearly 700,000,[90] a figure somewhat over ten times that of the then claimed card-carrying membership of the C.P.I. of 60,000.[91] The Communists evinced strength in Andhra, but otherwise their showing must have been disappointing to their leaders. In the workers' list in spite of their control of the then virtual trade union federation monopoly, the A.I.T.U.C., the Communists received only 28.3 per cent of the votes whereas the Congress (including Congress Socialists) received 65.2 per cent of the vote. In the village areas the Communists secured 17.3 per cent of the vote as compared to the 76.7 per cent received by the Congress, a better performance in view of the much greater number of peasants than workers among the Indian masses.[92] Of course, the number of seats gained by the Communists was infinitesimal as compared to the vote amassed by the League in Muslim regions and electoral lists and Congress voting power in non-Islamic areas.[93]

The Communists made no serious attempt to enter the elections for the Central Legislative Assembly held at the same time as the provincial election, nor for the elections to the Constituent Assembly held in June, 1946, both of these elections being held under the terms of the constitution of 1919, (in contrast to the provincial which operated under the more liberalized provisions of that of 1935) which provided for an exceedingly narrow electorate. However, in the latter case, among the few seats for which they contested, the comrades gained a single victory—they elected a delegate from Bengal.[94]

* * * * *

The Communist party line during the period from 1945 to 1947 was elaborately put forth in the election manifestoes of the party in the elections to the provincial legislatures and for the Constituent Assembly. In these manifestoes it was insisted upon, in no uncertain terms, that "Indian must not fight Indian," rather Indians must stand united in a "United Freedom Front,"[95] against British imperialism, and recognize that it has always been the policy of the British to maintain a "divide and rule policy," a policy which was now being manifested by their new diabolical plan of slavery" namely "to divide India into a Hindu majority Dominion and a Muslim Dominion," a plan which had been revealed in the Cripps Proposals of 1942 and the Wavell offer of the summer of 1945.[96] Realizing this, therefore, all good Indians must spurn all British overtures and "no freedom loving Indian party should seek a unilateral settlement with the British Government. . . ."[97]

The political planks of the Communist platform as revealed by the electoral manifestoes involved:

> Immediate declaration of Indian independence by the British Government.
>
> Transfer of power to a real All-India Constituent Assembly which will draft the terms of the "Quit India" treaty or to face the united struggle of all Indian peoples.[98]

This All-Indian Constituent Assembly would be elected by

seventeen smaller constituent assemblies of a like number of states, these states being predicated upon ethnic considerations following the lines of the plan laid down a few years previously by Dr. Adhikari. The states' constituent assemblies, which were to be elected by "universal adult franchise," would be the only sovereign instrumentalities in India, and consequently, then, "the delegates of the All-India Constituent Assembly shall have no more authority than that of plenipotentiaries."[99] The constituent assemblies of the states would possess "the unfettered right" to decide upon their mutual relations within an independent India. As for the right of any Indian state to secede, the manifestoes did not specifically confirm such a right, but neither did they deny it.[100] As regards the disputed provinces of the Punjab and Bengal, the manifestoes followed Adhikari in favoring the partition of the former on communal lines, that is between Muslims in the western part of the province and the Sikhs in the eastern, but unlike the plan of the editor of "People's Age," held that Bengal must remain a united province.[101] As for princely India the manifestoes made it clear that the party stood for absolute self-determination and adult franchise for the peoples of the princely states, and also looked forward to the "final liquidation" of the "Princely agents" of the British.[102]

The Communist manifestoes held that their program of "free homelands in a free India,"[103] met the basic desires of the League and the Congress alike, for

> . . . the League is free to plead for and get a separate sovereign Federation of Muslim-majority areas living in friendly alliance with a sovereign Federation of Hindu majority areas, but not inside a common Indian Union.[104]

while on the other hand "the Congress is free to plead for and to get a Federal Indian Union based on autonomous but not sovereign units."[105]

Evidencing the leftward turn of the party in economic matters, the election manifestoes of the Communist party attacked not only the "British rulers," "but Indian capitalists as well." It was charged that they had assumed the role of "profiteers" and "black marketeers" during the war, that they had "cheated" and exploited Indian labor,[106] that they were planning to make deals with the British capitalists which were entirely contrary to the interests of the peoples of India,[107] and that these "lovers of their own riches and bloodsuckers of their own people" were "getting inside" India's chief political organizations, the National Congress and the Muslim League "to ensure their interests would be safe when popular Ministries came to power."[108] Hence, in consideration of these circumstances and in view of the "unprecedented post-war industrial crisis" which was impending:

> . . . it will be a crime against our country's future to leave India's economy in the hands of Indian capitalists, not only in a free India, but even for one single day longer.[109]

Consequently, the Communist manifestoes stridently demanded the "nationalisation of all key industries, like chemicals, iron and steel and coal mines,"[110] and dominating state control over other branches of industry, as well as pushing forward with a program of industrialization. As an immediate step in the industrial field it was advocated that a popular Indian government should

> . . . seize all British capital, plantations, industrial concerns, (and) mercantile firms in view of the British Government's refusal to part with India's sterling balances.[111]

As further measures to be undertaken by such an Indian government, a complete "cradle to the grave" social security program was demanded[112] as were such immediate measures as the confiscation of the "illegal riches of the war profiteers," and "no return of the reserve fund of the profiteer capitalists."[113]

A like radical tone was taken in regard to Indian agriculture in the Communist election platforms. The misery of the peasants in "serf villages" was alluded to,[114] and there was a vigorous advocacy of the following agrarian program:

(1) Abolition of landlordism, nationalisation of land, redistribution of land to make the uneconomic holdings of the poor peasants into consolidated economic holdings and to make large-scale co-operative farming possible.
(2) Usury to be banned. All agricultural credit through co-operative sales basis.[115]
(3) Private trade in people's food banned.[116]

The manifestoes of the Communist Party also made special appeals to certain categories of the population, for example, "to Mothers and Sisters,"[117] "to the Youth,"[118] and to the "Freedom-loving Intelligentsia."[119]

Following the same line which was taken in the election platforms of the C.P.I., spokesmen of that party and their mentors in the British Communist Party raked the "imperialists" over the coals for not "quitting India" at once and without qualifications.[120] They were charged with pitting Hindus and Muslims against each other, so that Britain might thereby retain her control over India. For example, in a political tract entitled "For the Final Bid to Power," General Secretary Joshi succinctly stated:

> Their aim is simple enough; they have no intention to let India regain her independence. Their strategy is equally traditional; to play one Indian party against another. And they hope this way to stay on top in India.[121]

Joshi charged that the British were further endeavoring to maintain the division of India, in that they insisted that the representatives of the Princes participate in the Indian constitution-making body so as to bring about the creation of a British-controlled puppet princely States' Dominion.[122]

The British were once again the recipients of traditional Communist charges—for example, they were deliberately thwarting the development of Indian industry,[123] and some new ones—for example, they were purposely starving the Indians for news of the outside world as well as literally.[124] The Communists also held India was as much as ever subjected to the thralldom of British capital.[125]

In view of this sentiment it is only natural that much was made over nationalist anti-British rioting, most notably the "strike" or "mutiny" of the Bombay sailors in February, 1946.[126] On the other hand, however, British attempts to grant satisfaction to Indian national aspirations were greeted with hoots of derision from the Indian comrades and their British mentors.[127] Thus referring to the Cabinet Mission Plan, R. Palme Dutt held that "The Constitutional Plan of 1946" was only "a very slight step forward," complained that by it the Constituent Assembly was not to be elected by universal suffrage, but in an "undemocratic way," contended that the plan partitioned India into four zones, one Hindu, two Muslim and one for the Princes, and argued that the proposed interim government would only "be a reconstituted Viceroy's Council" leaving the Governor-General with "overriding powers."[128] In brief, the whole Cabinet Mission's Plan, for Dutt, was nothing more than an attempt to establish an alliance between the British "imperialists" and "the upper-class leadership in India" and as such was analogous to deals made between British and Indian capitalists.[129]

Anti-British sentiments on the part of Communists, both in India and in England, applied to Conservative and Labour Governments alike. Early in August, 1945, Joshi bitterly assailed the policy of Churchill and Amery in connection with the Simla conversations earlier in the summer of that year, charging that they wanted the "deadlock" in India "to continue" and attacked the Tory Government for retaining the "ban" on Congress activities and keeping "the remaining prisoners in jail."[130]

For a time an amicable attitude towards the new Labour Ministry of Clement Attlee was held by the Communists in the belief it would favor an immediate "Quit India" policy.[131] However, with the failure of that government to grant immediate independence to India and with the onset of the "cold war" in 1946, all semblance of friendliness by the Communists to the Attlee Cabinet disappeared, and the Labourites were branded as "imperialists" with the same venom as had been the case with their Tory predecessors.[132] However, this notwithstanding, the C.P.I. handed the Labour Government's Cabinet Mission, prior to the announcement by the latter of its "Constitutional Plan of 1946," a memorandum of that party demanding that independence and sovereignty be granted India based on the Communist plans noted above.[133] The Cabinet Mission ignored the Communists' proposals and this all the more contributed to their animus against the cabinet of Clement Attlee.

The formation of the Interim Government in September, 1946, drew no applause from the Indian Communists. Thus an editorial in "People's Age" categorically remarked: "The present Interim Government is meant to be a tool in the hands of the Imperialists."[134] In addition, the enactment of a number of acts on both the national and provincial level, ameliorating the position of the Indian worker, notably the Factories' Amendment Act of April, 1946, and the Workmen's Compensation Acts of 1946 and 1947, as enacted by the Central Indian Government, and such provincial measures as the Bombay Industrial Relations Act of 1946 were either hooted at or passed over in silence by the Communists.[135] In the years 1946 and 1947, government in India, for the Communists, still dominated by "imperialism," could do no good.

As might have been expected, the Communists were no more charitable to the Mountbatten Plan than they had been to the Cabinet Mission's Plan. Indeed, they had characterized the British Government's formal notification in February, 1947, of their desire to leave India not later than June, 1948, as "an imperialist manoeuvre intended to strengthen the rule of England in India, only by changing its form."[136] And when the Mountbatten Plan was announced early in June, 1947, the Central Committee of the C.P.I. made the wrathful assertion that this plan "does not give India real independence, but is the culmination of a double-faced imperial policy." The party's resolution on this subject added:

> The strategy of British imperialism is to exploit all weaknesses in our national and social life and forge new alliances with princes, landlords, and Indian big business, to be able to control through them the Indian state of the future and also India's economy.[137]

Their resolution called upon the leaders of the Congress to "implement an anti-imperialist and democratic policy" and assured them of the most complete cooperation of the Communist Party in this task.[138] In addition, at about the same time, the Communist Party's Central Committee spoke with particular acerbity against the partition of Bengal and the Punjab, which as noted above, they had formerly been inclined to favor.[139]

The Communists were now openly hostile to the Indian bourgeoisie. It was claimed that Indian "big capitalists have strengthened their position and piled up big profits from the War" as a result of "war-financed contracts, shortages and high prices, inflation and the black market."[140] It was also maintained that Indian capitalists had foreseen the possibility that in the post-war era there would be a "weakening of British imperialism" and also a possibility for them of "playing on" rivalry between American capital which was held to be penetrating into India, and the hitherto dominant British capital, and, as a result the Indian capitalists would be able to undertake "profitable" industrial development. Emphasis was placed on the assumption that Indian capitalism was of an especially oligarchial nature, as instanced by the many firms controlled by the interests of Tata and Birla. Through these firms, it was argued, a handful of individuals dominated the entire economic life of India as far as native Indian capital was concerned.[141]

Contemporaneously, Communist writers assailed with acerbity the landlords of India, the inequitable division of land in the Punjab, an area wherein Communist influence among the peasantry was growing, being particularly singled out in this connection.[142]

In view of the attacks upon the Indian bourgeoisie and landed class, it is surprising that the Communists maintained in their propaganda a basically amicable attitude towards the National Congress and the Muslim League in that these classes (especially in the case of landlords in the League) played a very important role in these organizations. Nonetheless, in keeping with their policy of supporting a "united front" against the British, and still perhaps hoping against hope that they might yet in the future be able to infiltrate into these bodies, the

Communists retained seemingly relatively amicable attitudes toward them, thus largely maintaining the tactic of "united front from above." Thus Joshi in his pamphlet, "For the Final Bid for Power" declared of the Congress that

> . . . we are one with the Congress in demanding immediate transfer of power from the British Government[143]

and of the Muslim League

> . . . we are one with the League in making a demand on the basis of self-determination among Indian peoples.[144]

As for both the Congress and the League taken together, the then leader of India's Communists averred that "we respect the Congress and the League as a younger member of the family respects the elder members" and he acknowledged that "it is the . . . irresistible urge for freedom in the Congress and League that is our capital, too."[145]

However, a measure of criticism was included with the praise for the leading bodies of the still undivided sub-continent. Referring to the Congress, Joshi contended that

> . . . the Congress demand for transfers of power combined with its refusal to extend it and share that power with other Indian peoples, its demand for freedom from British domination, without simultaneously the freedom of all peoples, lead it straight to seeking a unilateral settlement with the British Government and to fighting other Indian parties.[146]

At the same time Joshi held that the very "strength" of the Congress itself made for the "sectarianism" of its leaders' policy and he made it clear that "we do not support Congress' refusal to apply self-determination (of the various nationalities) to our own political future."[147] Joshi criticized Congress leaders for negotiations with the British Government and in so doing endeavoring to seek "a unilateral settlement" without consideration of other Indian elements, which was a "sectarian" policy.[148] In addition, the leader of the C.P.I. criticized leading

Congressmen for "demagogy" in relation to their self-praise in connection with the "Quit India" resolution of August 8, 1942 and with their denunciation of the Communists for the latter's course of conduct at that time.[149]

Joshi also had words of criticism for the Muslim League. Hence his assertion that

> . . . the demand of the League for the partition of the country in order to be able to win sovereignty for Muslim-majority homelands makes it also seek a unilateral settlement with the British Government. . . . The League fails to see the simple truth: Why should the imperialist power that denies self-determination to India as a whole, agree to unilateral self-determination for the Muslims?[150]

Furthermore, Joshi held the Indian Communist Party does not

> . . . support the League when it demands unjust boundaries, like six provinces, or in its demand for partition as the only guarantee of sovereignty for Muslim-majority homelands.[151]

Wholehearted support was registered by India's Communists for the National Conference Party of Kashmir. Sympathetic attention was also given by the Communist press to its leader, Sheikh Abdullah in his trial following the suppression of his movement in May, 1946. His ensuing three years' prison sentence made him a quasi-martyr in the eyes of the Communists who, as we have noted, had infiltrated into his organization.[152] Some sympathy was also registered by the Communists for the cause of the erstwhile leader of the "Red Shirts," Abdul Ghaffer Khan, in the North-West Frontier Province who opposed the Muslim League, although they did not go all out in support of the "frontier Gandhi's" demands for the creation of an independent "Pathanistan."[153]

The Communists maintained their hostility to the Socialists and Radical Democrats or "Royists" on the left and the Hindu Mahasabha and the Rashtriya Swayamsewak Sangh (R.S.S.) on the right. In regard to the Socialists, who were splitting away from the Congress altogether and were presenting a bold program of radical and economic rehabilitation based on the nationalization of industries and drastic land reform,[154] they were most consistently and bitterly attacked in the "Pravda" of Indian Communism, the "People's Age" in a regular column entitled "Where Stands the Left?" This column consistently castigated the alleged Socialist "appeasement" of the right wing of the Congress.[155] As for M. N. Roy and his Radical Democratic political party and his labor organization, the Indian Federation of Labour, the quondam follower of Lenin and his organizations were regarded more with contempt than with outright animosity.[156]

As for the R.S.S., Dange declared that it was the purpose of the Communists to "demolish" the influence of that extremist communal organization.[157] It may also be noted that the Forward Bloc, under a new leader, Sarat Chandra Bose, brother of the late Netaji, (leader) Subhas Chandra Bose, attempted to make a political comeback under the name of the Socialist Republic Party. This party threatened to steal the Communists' thunder, for it spoke of setting up "Socialist Republics" based on "linguistic" lines.[158] However, the party made little progress and was generally ignored by the Communists.

Between August 1945 and August of 1947, Communist propaganda was blared forth, not only by "People's Age" but also by leading "central" Indian languages papers printed in Bombay as well as by a number of journals located in the several provinces of India.[159] In spite of all this propaganda, however, it is evident that the Communists were, by and large, in an inferior position on August 15, 1947, as compared to that which they had held at the close of the Second World War.

* * * * *

In contrast to the war years, the Soviets manifested a noteworthy interest in India between August, 1945, and August, 1947. A harbinger of the new Soviet interest came in the "New Times" of January 1, 1946, in which the Soviet spokesman on India, Dyakov, attacked the statements on India of Attlee and

Viceroy Lord Wavell of September 19, 1945 as reiterations of the "proposals made by the Churchill government in 1942 through Sir Stafford Cripps."[160] The announcement of elections in India to central and provincial legislative bodies was jeered at by Dyakov on the ground of the narrow electorates involved and for the reason that they were based upon communal lists which "cannot but aggravate Hindu-Muslim animosities and hamper agreement between the National Congress and the Muslim League."[161] Dyakov also assailed the then use of Indian troops in Indonesia and Indo-China as parts of British Imperial contingents in support of the Dutch and French respectively.[162]

Following the line set by Dyakov, a Soviet radio commentator named Mikhail Mikhailov, broadcast from Moscow on March 22, 1946 a severe criticism of the Indian elections, wrathfully charging that less than one per cent of the Indian people were able to vote for representatives to the Central Legislative Assembly (as compared to only 14 per cent in the case of the provincial legislatures) and Mikhailov tied this in with the alleged designs of elements in Britain to "instigate war against the Soviet Union."[163]

Due note was taken in the Soviet press of the tumults in Calcutta and Bombay and the naval "mutiny" in the latter city, respectively in November, 1945 and February, 1946,[164] and it was claimed that it was these events which "compelled the British Government to hasten its decision" of furthering Indian freedom through the dispatch of the Cabinet Mission.[165] It may be noted, however, that when the plans to send that mission in February, 1946, were announced, the Soviet press remained significantly silent.[166] However, when that Mission produced its Plan of May 16, 1946 and it appeared that it would become the basis for a free, and united (albeit decentralized India) the Soviet press was compelled to comment. Thus another Soviet "expert" on India named Boris Izakov, declared in "Pravda" on July 15, 1946, in reference to the Cabinet Mission Plan:

> Behind the velvet curtain in India, the people are demanding the independence which has been repeatedly prom-

ised. . . . The British Government mission dispatched to India came with a plan treating all possible questions but the basic one, the withdrawal of British troops from India. Divide and rule is one of the most common methods behind this curtain.[167]

The term "velvet curtain" was manifestly a Russian retort to the term "iron curtain" already in vogue in the West.

In addition, Dyakov averred:

It should be remembered that the declaration began by rejecting the Muslim League's demand for the division of India into Hindustan and Pakistan, but went on to say that the British government shares the fears of the Muslims that in a united India, they run the risk of being overwhelmed by the Hindu majority. This assertion, which has no real facts to warrant it, was a scarcely concealed move to continue the fight for Pakistan and to fan Hindu-Muslim enmity.[168]

And in so doing "it served as a signal for the fratricidal bloodshed that is going on in India to this day."[169]

The formation of the Interim Government in September, 1946, also received a sour reception in Moscow. Writing in "Pravda" on October 21, 1946, Dyakov sharply censored this new government in India. Its formation, he contended, was simply a maneuver by the "imperialists," and it was "wholly unfounded optimism to consider that the creation of the new government is any guarantee of the granting of independence to India."[170] In a subsequent article in "New Times" Dyakov charged that the British, desirous of maintaining control in India, hindered Hindu-Muslim negotiations in the autumn of 1946. Besides, he contended an effort was made to "thwart" the work of the newly-elected Indian Constituent Assembly by the statement of the

. . . British Government that no constitution framed without participation of the Muslim League would be accepted.[171]

It may also be noted that during the course of the year 1946 attention was frequently drawn by Soviet writers to the conditions of famine which beset India as well as the severe poverty of the masses. That the British as well as the upper classes were responsible for all this was, of course, clearly indicated.[172]

In the meantime, what the Soviets deemed as a "tool" of "imperialism," the Interim Government, on its part, was genuinely anxious to establish relations with the Soviet Union. In his broadcast to the Indian people on assuming a post tantamount to the Prime Ministership in the Interim Government, on September 7, 1946, Pandit Nehru declared that India sent her "greetings" to the United States of America and significantly added:

> To that other great nation of the modern world, the Soviet Union, which also carried a vast responsibility for shaping world events, we send greetings. They are our neighbours in Asia and inevitably we shall have to undertake many common tasks and have much to do with each other.[173]

In a press conference held on the following September 26th, the Pandit stated that his Interim Government would like to have the same type of diplomatic relations with Russia as it already had with the United States and China, "but," added Nehru

> . . . for the moment we have none, and we have to explore, investigate, and then establish it after consultation with the Soviet Government.[174]

It may also be noted that in this news conference Nehru gave an exposition of that policy variously termed "neutralism" or "independence" which since that time has characterized Indian policy in relation to the "cold war." Hence he stated that

> . . . in the sphere of foreign affairs, India still follows an independent policy, keeping away from the power politics of groups aligned one against the other.[175]

and at the same time he indicated that India might be directly opposed to Great Britain in future international conferences.[176]

As to Indo-Russian relations, Nehru followed up his statements by taking action to bring them about. He sent a message to V. Krishna Menon, then Secretary of the India League in London, to get into contact with Soviet Foreign Minister V. M. Molotov, then in Paris for the Peace Conference dealing with the European Axis Satellites. Menon was an apt choice for dealing with the Communists for he had frequently contributed to Communist publications, notably the "Labour Monthly," and was affiliated with the extreme left wing of the British Labour party. Indeed, an Indian spokesman actually declared that "Pandit Nehru selected Mr. Menon on a secret mission to Mr. Molotov because of his Communist background."[177] As subsequently revealed by Nehru to the Central Legislative Assembly on November 12, 1946, Menon, who worked in an "honourary capacity" only, but with his traveling expenses being paid, brought Molotov a personal letter from Nehru himself. The conversations turned on the establishment of Indo-Russian diplomatic relations.[178]

However, it may be noted that at the time the conversations were held, on September 28, 1946, Menon denied that they had any "significance."[179] The conversations also made little impression in Moscow. In his "Pravda" article of October 21, 1946, Dyakov gave scant coverage to the Menon-Molotov meeting, but instead quoted the Soviet Foreign Minister's public declaration on the role of India at the Paris Peace Conference which was to the effect:

> We might have expected more objective voting on the part of India, but we have been confronted again with the impossible situation wherein the Indian delegation simply fulfills its colonial obligation to vote in accordance with the will of another country—according to the will of Great Britain.[180]

And to this Dyakov added that at this conference, "the Indian delegation conducted itself as a loyal vassal of British imperialism."[181]

However, an event which definitely made for improvement in Indo-Russian relations occurred at the end of October, 1946. At the meeting of the United Nations General Assembly in New York, the Soviet Union and its satellites supported a resolution censuring the Union of South Africa for her discrimination against Indians resident there. The Soviet Deputy Foreign Minister, Andrei Vyshinsky was especially eloquent in his attack on the discrimination of Indians in South Africa and he spoke knowingly of "actual ghettos" for Indians there. Moreover, on October 30th, Foreign Minister Molotov himself made a speech in which he vigorously supported the Indian position.[182] On the other hand, Great Britain supported the case of South Africa. The resolution condemning South Africa was approved by a vote of 32 to 15 with 7 abstentions, so that it was the vote of Russia and her five satellites (including the then satellite Yugoslavia) which made possible the necessary two-thirds vote of approval for the resolution.[183] The resolution was not binding, of course, and South Africa has continued to oppress her Indian minority to the present day, but it was of moral significance, and the fact that it was Russian votes which won the day was not lost to the Indian delegation at the United Nations nor at New Delhi.[184] Indeed, a few months later, Pandit Nehru in his capacity as Vice-President of the Indian Interim Government sent a formal letter to Foreign Minister Molotov, thanking him for the support rendered to the Indian delegation at the General Assembly session during the discussion of the persecution of the Indian population in South Africa.[185]

Pandit Nehru was therefore well-disposed towards the Russians when he was questioned on November 12, 1946 in the Central Legislative Assembly on the Menon-Molotov meeting by various League members. Nehru, as we have noted, revealed the "friendly" character of the conversations and when asked whether Menon had Communist views and was therefore the right person to negotiate for India, the Pandit boldly replied: "I myself hold Communist views on a great many matters."[186]

The Soviets (as contrasted with the domestic Indian Communists) became even more popular with Congress when on December 23, 1946, Dyakov in his capacity as Soviet spokesman for India, made an address on Radio Moscow in which he held that a division of India into two states, one Hindu and one Muslim would simply aggravate communal tensions and would simply give the "British . . . an excuse for perpetual interference in India's internal affairs" so that they "would thus be able to retain their hold on the country.[187]

This statement indicated that the Soviets were taking a more hostile attitude towards the Muslims than were their comrades in India who were, if anything, more amicable to Jinnah's organization than they were to the Congress.[188]

Shortly after the commencement of the new year, 1947, a milestone in Indo-Soviet relations was registered with the arrival of a delegation of Soviet scholars at the Indian Science Conference held at Delhi in the first week of January. The Soviets had been invited the previous October by Nehru himself in his capacity as Vice-President of the Interim Government to send a delegation and they eagerly responded. On January 7th, Nehru specifically addressed the Soviet delegation in the following terms:

> For many years past we have looked with very great interest towards the Soviet Union for many reasons, but more specifically because of the tremendous achievements of the Soviet Union during the last quarter of a century or so. Inevitably when we want to produce great changes in India, we want to learn from your example. We want to know what you have done and how you have done it.[189]

V. P. Volgin, Vice-President of the Soviet Academy of Science and Chairman of the Soviet delegation replied that "this occasion would lead to the strengthening of the scientific bonds of cultural intercourse and friendly relations between the people of our country and the peoples of India."[190]

Following the conclusion of the Indian Science Conference the Soviet delegates undertook a tour throughout India.[191] A considerable amount of publicity for this junket was given in the Soviet press.[192] In late March an "Inter-Asian Relations Conference" was held in Delhi in which thirty-two Asian countries participated. Among these were Azerbaijan, Armenia, Kazakhstan, Tadjikistan and Uzbekistan, all constituent Republics of the U.S.S.R.[193] In his message of greeting at the inauguration of the conference on March 23, 1947, Nehru singled out the several Soviet delegations with the following words of praise:

> We welcome you delegates and representatives . . . from the Soviet Republics of Asia which have advanced so rapidly in our generation and which have so many lessons to teach us.[194]

The Inter-Asian Conference in practice dealt with matters of pertinent interest to Asian countries. It stressed specific political, economic and social questions rather than controversial political topics such as colonialism. Thus the conference in several committees discussed such matters as qualifications for franchise, migrations from one Asian country to another, the rights of women and means of facilitating economic development and improvement of the standard of living in Asian countries.[195] The conference adjourned on April 2, 1947, with Pandit Nehru being elected head of a standing organization formed by the conference to strengthen ties between Asian countries.[196] The participation of the Soviets (their indirect representation notwithstanding) was a unique honor to a fundamentally non-Asian nation.

The logical outcome of the good relations which were developing between the Interim Government of India and the Soviet Union was manifested on April 14, 1947 with the official announcement of the establishment of diplomatic relations between the Soviet Union and India. In the words of the official announcement of the External Department of the Interim Government of India:

> Being desirous of maintaining and further strengthening the friendly relations existing between India and the Union of Soviet Socialist Republics, the Government of India and the Government of the U.S.S.R. have decided to exchange diplomatic missions at embassy level.[197]

Thus culminated a period of confidential diplomatic negotiations which had been initiated by the Menon-Molotov conversations.

Soviet reaction to the announcement was rendered in an editorial in the official journal, "New Times" which held:

> The establishment of diplomatic relations between India and the Soviet Union is an event of no mean international significance. The Soviet public welcomes it as evidence of the friendly sentiments the peoples of the two countries entertain for one another, and as a sign that India is moving towards an independent policy.[198]

The editorial went on to praise the struggle of the Indians for freedom, but it sternly asserted that "the emancipation of India . . . is . . . by no means completed." Besides, it was darkly noted, "British and Indian reactionaries" were endeavoring to "undermine" amicable Indo-Soviet relations.[199]

A hitch in these amicable relations between the Indian Interim Government and the U.S.S.R. developed in June, 1947, over the election of non-Permanent members of the United Nations Security Council. A contest developed between India and an integral part of the Soviet Union, the Ukrainian Soviet Republic, over one of the seats at stake. The leader of the Indian delegation to the General Assembly, Mrs. Vijaya Lakshmi Pandit, the sister of Jawaharal Nehru, argued that if "equitable geographical distribution were to prevail, India would surely be granted the seat." Besides, she argued, were India not to be granted representation on the Security Council, a half billion people in Southern Asia would be unrepresented on that vital body, a circumstance which the framers of the United Nations Charter had surely wanted to prevent.[200] However, because of a deal concluded by the Soviet Union with Great Britain and China, the Ukraine received the disputed seat, and all that Mrs. Pandit could do was to protest against such "previous arrangements" which made the election by the Assembly "practically a farce."[201]

That this affair did not unduly injure Indo-Soviet relations is evinced by the fact that on June 25, 1947, it was announced that Mrs. Pandit herself would be the first Ambassador of the Indian Union Dominion to the Soviet Union.[202] The naming of Mrs. Pandit perhaps was meant as a gesture of sportsmanship by the Indians to indicate to the Soviets that they bore no grudge for the seating of the Ukraine on the Security Council. On August 11, 1947, four days before the liberation and partition of India, Mrs. Pandit arrived at her post in Moscow and declared upon her arrival:

> India has a special link with the Soviet Union since both India and Russia have shown a capacity to blend and harmonize different races and nationalities.[203]

Not long after Mrs. Pandit's arrival, the first Soviet ambassador to the Indian Union arrived in the person of A. A. Novikov, a veteran Soviet career diplomat.[204]

Because of its displeasure over the partition of India, the Soviets made no immediate effort to establish diplomatic relations with Pakistan. Apparently the Soviets blamed the Muslims on the division. However, following a policy of "Realpolitik" the Soviets undertook negotiations with Pakistan in October, 1947[205] and announcement of the establishment of Soviet-Pakistan diplomatic relations was made in May, 1948.[206]

Soviet displeasure at the Mountbatten plan was reflected in Dyakov's article in "Izvestia" in which he averred:

> The realization of the English plan of June 3rd will transform India into a conglomeration of dominions and states which are formally independent, many of which will actually remain entirely under English control.[207]

The result of all this meant, for this Kremlin spokesman, that the British would retain economic and political control alike over the allegedly free and truly divided sub-continent.[208]

The United States as well as Great Britain was severely censured by the Soviets in respect to India. The fear that the Americans would effectuate a successful economic penetration of the sub-continent was expressed. Thus a commentator of Radio Moscow averred on June 3, 1947:

> What the American monopolists say is that they want to help India develop her industry and agriculture . . . but

concealed behind this altruistic formula are far-reaching plans for ousting British capital and making India an object of their own economic expansion.[209]

The broadcaster added:

> The Indian people are not fighting for their liberty and independence in order to open the way to their country's enslavement by American monopolists.[210]

Like their Indian comrades the Russian Communist propagandists maintained a fairly friendly attitude towards both the National Congress and the Muslim League. Thus in the spring of 1946, Dyakov noted that the League, like the Congress, correctly supported the need for independence on the part of the peoples of the Peninsula. In December, 1946, as noted above, Dyakov attacked the League's concept of Pakistan, but this was not followed by a Soviet denunciation of that organization as such. On the other hand it may be noted that the right wing of Congress was subjected to Soviet criticism.[211]

* * * * *

A definite measure of friendly interest in the Soviet Union was manifested by non-Communist Indians (of course, the C.P.I. as always had nothing but excessive paeans of praise for the U.S.S.R.) between the summers of 1945 and 1947. An extreme example of non-Communist support for Russia came on April 11, 1947, in a debate in the Indian Constituent Assembly in which a Congress member, Balkhrishna Sharma, during the debate on Indian ratification of the peace treaty with Italy and with Nazi Germany's former Balkan satellites, audaciously asserted:

> The question the country is faced with today is whether we shall side with one bloc or the other. I am very clear in my mind it shall be the bloc of Soviet Russia and not the so-called Western democracies who are doing all manner of things calculated to lead to a Third World War.[212]

Furthermore, the prominent Muslim League leader, Sir Firozhdin Khan Noon, declared during the summer of 1946 that if the Hindus and the British did not agree to the setting up of Pakistan as a separate Muslim state in the Indian peninsula, "the Muslim League would be compelled to turn for assistance to Russia."[213]

Serious discussion was begun in certain commercial Indian quarters on the establishment of a large-scale Indo-Soviet trade, a commerce which had been lacking in the past save for British supplies to Russia during the Second World War. It was even suggested that the creation of a vigorous Indo-Russian trade would be of benefit to India. It would aid Indian economy by forming "a check against rising British prices," it would develop the facilities of the northwestern border territory of India, especially if a railway could be built across Afghanistan from Soviet Central Asia, and it would bring to India Russian equipment and machinery needed in her own industrial development as well as "cheap products" from areas under Soviet influence and control such as Czechoslovakia, Latvia and Estonia. In addition, in view of the possibility of the "third world war," it would be well for India to develop terrestrial trade routes with the Soviet Union so that she might be ensured of receiving "essential commodities" which would otherwise be cut off from India through the blocking of "vulnerable" sea routes thither in event of that conflict.[214]

It may also be noted that in certain Indian quarters life in the Soviet Union was noted with approval. For example, Russia was even praised for the alleged freedom of conscience to religious and non-religious people alike, as guaranteed by her constitution; this being favorably contrasted with the undue emphasis on religion and religious differences as embodied in Anglo-Indian legal precepts.[215] And along with the extolling of the manifestation of Communism in practice in the Soviet Union, there was also praise in certain non-Communist Indian quarters for Communism as a theoretical ideology, an ideology which was held to be ethically superior to capitalism.[216]

On the other hand, the Soviet Union was the recipient for brickbats as well as bouquets. Thus the noted right-wing Congressman, C. R. Rajagolpalacharia, Prime Minister of the Madras Presidency, stated on June 3, 1946:

> . . . I must ask the young people (in India) not to be misled by what is now being written in Russian papers regarding Indian political afafirs. . . . Russia does not want an Indian settlement now, as that would mean added strength for Britain for a free . . . India will add to the power and prestige of Britain.[217]

An even more hostile tack towards Russia was taken by M. R. Masani, one of the founders of the Congress Socialist Party, who, at the opening of the Indian Agrarian Conference in Karachi, late in 1946, bitterly criticized the Soviet system of collectivized agriculture.[218]

Prominent Muslim League members also maintained a suspicious and hostile attitude towards Soviet Russia. Thus in September, 1946, Mohammed Ali Jinnah was revealed by a source "very close to him" to feel that the League "did not seek or expect any aid from the Soviet Union."[219]

Specific policies of the Soviet Union encountered censure from prominent Indians. Thus Nehru himself criticized Russian policy in endeavoring to maintain control of the Azerbaijan area of Iran in the winter of 1946 as well as Soviet threats to Turkey, at that time. Thus the Pandit declared that "Indian opinion as a whole will strongly resent any aggression on Iran and Turkey by any power." Nehru also indicated "there appears to be Russian aggression" in Iran.[220] The prompt action of the United Nations Security Council compelled Soviet evacuation of the affected area of Iran and removed the danger to the sub-continent from that important borderland.[221]

The Soviet-Afghan treaty of June 13, 1946, was viewed with apprehension, in this case unwarrantedly, in certain sections of the Indian press. Thus the "National Herald" of Lucknow speculated that the Soviets would receive the northern provinces of Afghanistan in return for a Soviet promise to aid the latter in regaining territories annexed in the past by the Anglo-Indian Empire (such as the North-West Frontier Province, and British

Baluchistan as well).[222] At the same time Soviet aggression in Rumania in 1945 was subjected to criticism.[223]

It was held that although Russian progress from 1917 to 1946 had made a considerable impression among Indians, notably among certain sections of the working class and the youth, there was "bound to be disillusionment" when the real truth of the "limitations of the Soviet system" were properly weighed. Although this would not lead to the "complete elimination" of the "ideas of the Russian revolution," it would mean that India would be "turned away from the leadership of the new Nationalist Russia."[224]

Apprehension of the Soviet threat to India was expressed by British sources. It was felt Britain should under no conditions leave India in "chaos" but should resist "pressures . . . which are coming from Russia." The British should not leave India as a "vacuum" into which the Russian bear could stride with ease. Similar apprehensions were expressed by Americans,[225] especially in connection with the activity of Indian Communists and their sympathizers. John Foster Dulles declared on January 20, 1947, that he saw a clear danger in the pro-Communist tendencies which he felt were evident in certain Congress leaders.[226]

* * * * *

On August 15, 1947, free India and free Pakistan came into being. This event marked the emergence of vastly augmented political relations between the Soviets and the sub-continent, particularly between the Soviets and the Indian Union. It ushered in the manifestation of the concept and doctrine of "neutralism" as preached and practiced by the Nehru government of India, as well as a policy oscillating between "neutralism" and outright adherence to the policies of the nations of the democratic camp as evinced in the foreign policy of Pakistan. How Communist Russia at first manifested an abhorrence of, and later professed admiration for, Indian foreign policy, whereas, by contrast, the Soviet Union evidenced to a large extent from the outset only disgust for the foreign policies of Pakistan, is one of the most vital and significant stories of recent diplomatic history.

August 15, 1947, also marked an intensification of the activities of the Communists in the Peninsula, although their general position was manifestly weakened in that their slogans advocating liberation of the peoples of the sub-continent from "imperialist" rule—which slogans were still maintained—possessed an empty ring with the passage of time and the emergence of both India and Pakistan as free nations in a new Asia. Nonetheless, the Communists in both India and Pakistan, insofar as they were able, and not altogether without success in the case of the former country, did their utmost to convert these nations of the sub-continent into new "people's democracies," or satellites of the Soviets. Such a state of affairs would mean the successful effectuation of the designs the Soviets have held on the sub-continent, which designs have been present since November, 1917 in the manifestation of Russia's relations with colonial India.

EPILOGUE

Soviet Russia and Indian Communism 1947-1959

Following the foundation of the free Dominion of India, the Communist Party of India maintained a "united front from above" policy. It pretended to support the government of Prime Minister Nehru and the liberal wing of the Congress party, although it sharply criticized the "reactionary right wing" of the Congress. So amicable was the policy of the C.P.I. towards the new Nehru regime, that slogans of "no strike" and "increase production" were raised. The pro-Nehru policy as practiced by the C.P.I. in the autumn of 1947 was likewise championed by R. P. Dutt on behalf of the Communist Party of Great Britain.

But the honeymoon between India's Communists and the Nehru government was destined to be a brief one. Already in June, 1947, at a conference of the Institute of Economics and Pacific Affairs in Moscow, important papers were presented by Soviet experts on India, A. M. Dyakov, and V. V. Balabushevich, as well as by the Director of the Far Eastern Institute, E. M. Zhukov, which reports castigated the role of the Indian bourgeoisie and its political agent, the National Congress. Then, in the following September, Andrei Zhdanov, the then second most important Russian Communist, addressed the first session of the revived Communist International, which had been dissolved on May 22, 1943, now known as the Communist Information Bureau or Cominform, in Poland. He sounded a bold call for total "cold war" 'round the world, by holding that the world was irrevocably divided into the "democratic" and "imperialist" camps. Of special significance to India, Zhdanov held that the bourgeoisie were everywhere bound to be allies of "imperialism." For India's Communists this simply meant that they could no longer support Nehru's "bourgeois" government and still remain loyal to Moscow.

As loyal adherents of the world Communist movement, in December, 1947, the Central Committee of the C.P.I. made a declaration which changed the party line to fit into the new global "cold war" pattern. The "C.C." bitterly excoriated the Indian bourgeoisie, castigated the Congress including Nehru personally as well as conservatives in its ranks as hostile to Indian people and boldly chartered a highly militant course for the Communists of the Dominion of India. As a sequel to the declaration of December, 1947, in the Second Party Congress held in Calcutta, from February 28th to March 6th, 1948, there was presented a Political Thesis which was a bold-faced exposition of Red revolution. Not only were the bourgeoisie and the National Congress, as well as the "feudalists" and the "imperialists," which latter two groups even in the former "united front" days were by no means exempt from Communist censure, vigorously condemned, but a frank appeal for a struggle which would take on a violent character was promulgated. By this declaration Communists were candidly endeavoring to carry out a "one-stage" revolution in which, the bourgeoisie and its political arm, the Congress, the former native state rulers, landlords, British and other foreign interests and rich and "middle" peasants were ruthlessly to be swept aside in the creation of a "people's democracy." This program represented a return to the militant and revolutionary tactics of the C.P.I. in the early 'thirties. In accordance with this new policy, P. C. Joshi, apostle of caution and the "united front" with the "revolutionary national" Indian bourgeoisie was summarily ejected from his post as General Secretary of the C.P.I. and was even driven out of the party's Central Committee. His successor was B. T. Ranadive who only a few months previously in December, 1947 had espoused the "united front" program of Joshi.

Another important event of the Calcutta Congress was the creation of the Communist Party of Pakistan. Since August, 1947, the C.P.I. had operated as such also in Pakistan, but since the Soviet Union was preparing to recognize the Muslim Dominion (recognition was formally effected several weeks subsequent to the Calcutta Congress, April, 1948) it was felt that a separate Communist party should be formed there. An old-line Indian Communist, Sajjad Zaheer, was named the General Secretary of the party. Briefly reviewing its history, from 1948 to 1958 the Communist Party of Pakistan operated as a technically legal organization, but it was constantly under close surveillance by the authorities and its leaders were subject to sudden arrest. In March, 1951, it was accused by the then Pakistani Prime Minister, Liaquat Ali Khan, of having endeavored to foment a Communist insurrection with the aid of certain high officers of the Pakistani Army. As a consequence, Sajjad Zaheer was tried along with General Akbar Khan who had been Chief of Staff of the Pakistani Army and other high officers and civilian Communists in a secret trial. This trial, held at Rawalpindi and known consequently as the Rawalpindi Conspiracy Case, resulted in the conviction of Zaheer, Akbar Khan and most of their associates in January, 1953. In July, 1954, the Communist party was banned throughout Pakistan. Prior to this ban, it had shown signs of growing strength in East Pakistan or East Bengal where there was political dissatisfaction owing to the alleged suppression of the Bengalis by the Sindhis, Punjabis and emigré Muslims from Central and Northern India who dominated the Pakistani government. In July, 1957, there was formed a so-called National Awami (People's) Party which showed strong signs of being a disguised Communist party. But it was weak in the summer of 1958 as compared to the dominant anti-Communist Muslim League and Awami parties.

Returning to the history of the Communist Party of India, to offset the previous "errors" of that party (and his own) of "revisionism," "reformism," and undue friendship to the "bourgeois enemies of the people of India," Ranadive ordered a program of terror in the towns and countryside of India, alike, to be commenced. Arson, assassination, bombings, kidnappings and robberies were to be committed with the hope that the terror involved would shake the Indian Government to its foundations. Desperate and dastardly deeds were duly carried out in pursuance of this order in the spring of 1948, particularly in West Bengal and in the Andhra district of Madras Province. But the authorities of the Indian Union were not caught napping. Hundreds of Communists, including key leaders such as S. A. Dange, were incarcerated. By August, 1949, some 8,500 comrades were in detention. Communist-fomented strikes, notably an attempted railway strike of national proportions, scheduled for March, 1949, were suppressed by prompt governmental action. The Communist party was formally banned in many regions; notably in West Bengal, and it is a wonder that the C.P.I. was not banned for good and all throughout India at that time; the behavior of the Communists would scarcely have merited otherwise.

One area where Communist ferment was particularly in evidence during the spring and summer of 1948, was in the princely state of Hyderabad whose ruler, the Nizam, had insisted that his state was a truly sovereign nation. In the Telegu or Andhra speaking area of Hyderabad, the Communists claimed, not without veracity, that they had "liberated" some 3,500 villages. The Reds' rule constituted a kind of "parallel government" in this area known as Telengana. But in September, 1948, the troops of the Indian Union invaded Hyderabad and destroyed that princely state's presumption to sovereignty. That this action was aimed as much against the Hyderabad Communists as against the pretentions of the Muslim Nizam is manifested by the thoroughly severe measures undertaken by the Indian Army against the Communist-infested areas. The Communists, of course, fought back, and a most vicious guerilla war ensued in the former princely state.

Indeed, the policy of Red violence persisted throughout the years, 1948 and 1949, and the now furtive Communist leadership continued to call for the manifestation of "the highest forms of struggle," that is, armed insurrection, and to arouse black hatred for the British, the bourgeoisie, landlords, "feudals," rich and "middle" peasants and even to engender suspicion in respect to elements of the petty bourgeoisie and poorer peasants. This policy was obviously a foolish one; the Communists were losing friends and influence in an ever increasing tempo. Before long it was evoking dissension within the party itself. So early as June, 1948, the Andhra branch of the party, taking its cue from the Chinese Communists, were advocating that the struggle against the bourgeoisie be confined to the "big bourgeoisie" only with the "middle" bourgeoisie exempted, and were holding that the armed part of the struggle be limited essentially to peasant guerilla warfare as opposed to insurrectionary activity in urban areas. In 1949 advocacy for such a program in India was made by Liu Shao-chi, a leading Chinese Communist theorist. For this intervention by the Chinese comrades in this matter, Ranadive assailed Mao Tse-tung as a colleague of those Communist "heretics," Tito and Earl Browder in the C.P.I.'s theoretical journal, "The Communist" of July, 1949.

But the success of the Chinese Communists in the latter half of 1949 certainly prejudiced Ranadive's case against them, and, combined with the failure of the C.P.I., led to stern Muscovite action to alter the course of that party. Following the lead taken in a World Federation of Trade Unions Congress in Peiping in November, 1949, the journal of the Cominform, "For Lasting Peace, For People's Democracy" in its issue of January 27, 1950 called upon the Indian and other Asian Communist parties to take heed that "the path by the Chinese people . . . is the path that should be taken by the people of many colonial and dependent countries in their struggle for national independence and people's democracy." Since the Chinese Communists had heretofore sought collaboration with that element of the bourgeoisie which was not "big" and had collaborated with groups willing to do battle with the "imperialists," this, manifestly, should be the party line in India as well. Indeed, in a section of the January 27 editorial, specifically mentioning India, it was held to be the task of the Communists of India to "struggle . . . against the Anglo-American imperialists oppressing it and against the big bourgeoisie and feudal bourgeoisie and feudal princes collaborating with them —(and) to unite all classes, parties, groups and organizations willing to defend the national independence of India." But China's Communists had seized the Chinese mainland by violence. Would this also entail the espousal of violence in India? By implication the answer of the editorial was negative for while the policy-formulating statement mentioned Vietnam, South Korea, Malaya, the Philippines, Indonesia and Burma as places where armed struggle might be carried on, India and Pakistan were significantly omitted.

Ranadive, desperately endeavoring to remain in charge of India's declining Communist movement, through C.P.I. Politburo statements on February 22nd and April 6th, 1950 endorsed the new line, but his lip service was without avail. In the following May and June, the party's Central Committee "reconstituted" the Politburo as well as itself. Ranadive was replaced as General Secretary by Rajeswar Rao, leader of the Communists in the Andhra and Telengana regions.

The new C.P.I. leadership, in contrast to the old, lavishly praised Communist China, giving the impression that Peiping, not Moscow, was the Mecca of Indian Communism. It followed the line of the Cominform editorial, paying attention to the need for a "united front" basically a "united front from below," and looked with favor upon the "middle" peasants as well as the petty bourgeoisie. But the Nehru Government continued to draw heavy fire from Communist organs, which, remarkably enough in view of the Communists' insurrectionary tactics, were allowed to be published. In addition, in apparent defiance to the editorial of January 27th, guerilla warfare was still waged by Communists in the Telengana area of Hyderabad and adjoining areas of Madras State. However, by contrast, acts of urban terrorism markedly decreased.

As a consequence of two and a half years of terror and insurrection the Communists' position had deteriorated, notably as the policy of violence led to no victories. According to an official statement put out by the C.P.I.'s Politburo in September, 1950 in the form of a "Circular No. 3," it was admitted that "a state of semi-paralysisisation (sic) leading to lack of mass activities is now a general picture in the Party, though exceptions are also there." Indeed, the A.I.T.U.C. had decreased in membership from 700,000 in 1947 to about 100,000 in 1950 while the Communists' peasants' and women's movements had virtually disappeared. It was evident that the Indian comrades needed a new party line.

The task of furnishing that line, it would seem, was devolved upon, through "channels" to R. P. Dutt who was not an illogical choice. In the shape of a reply to questions about India on December 20, 1950, this long-time mentor of the C.P.I. demanded that the Communists fulfill the Cominform directive of the previous January and that in particular they give up their policy of rural violence. He emphasized that the C.P.I. should stress the ideal of the "democratic front," a variant of the old "popular front" strategy, and that emphasis be also placed on the "peace front." This implied that the comrades should modify somewhat their hitherto excessive censure of Nehru's foreign policy as being one in line with the Anglo-American "imperialists."

This directive from Dutt took effect. The Central Committee met that very month of December, 1950. It agreed to stress the idea of a "united front" of all "left" parties, to emphasize the "peace movement" and to insist that the struggle for Indian "liberation" be carried on "by all anti-imperialist classes, sections and parties." At the same time the "C.C." itself was reorganized. One month later, in January, 1951, a statement in a Communist organ, "Cross Roads," to the effect that "Pandit Nehru has taken a firm and forthright stand on the steps necessary to ensure world peace" signified a milder approach in respect to the Indian Government.

In the meantime—it is alleged, although not proved—four principal Communist leaders, General Secretary Rao, S. A. Dange, Ajoy Ghosh and Basava Punniah, proceeded on a secret mission to Moscow from which city they brought early in 1951 a "tactical line" to be followed by the C.P.I. This secret document called for an eventual Communist revolution, first in the form of "partisan areas (which) will inevitably arise in various parts of the country" and which eventually will involve nation-wide revolution. The immediate tasks of the party in this clandestine directive were very similar to that of the published "Draft Programme" of the C.P.I. of April, 1951. This Program held that the "Communist Party is not demanding the establishment of Socialism," but rather was advocating the creation of "a new Government of People's Democracy, created on the basis of a coalition of all democratic and anti-feudal and anti-imperialist forces in the country." The party proposed not only a united front of workers, peasants and the petty bourgeoisie but also advocated collaboration with "small manufacturers," "traders," and "non-monopoly capitalists," and indeed the "middle classes" generally in "a mighty Democratic Front." Advocacy of this kind of "democratic front" has persisted in Communist propaganda to the present day. On the other hand, the "big" bourgeoisie, landlords, princes, and, of course, foreign "imperialism," were duly castigated as they have also been in C.P.I. declarations to this time. Other Communist pronouncements in 1951 including the "Electoral Manifesto" or election platform, adopted on August 6, 1951, followed the same approach. This "Electoral Manifesto" is especially interesting in its advocacy that India have a federal system based upon linguistically-determined states; thus following the line first propounded by Adhikari in 1942.

Meantime, in view of the new party line, two important events took place. In May, 1951, Rao was punished for his continued advocacy of violence in the Telengana area by being removed as General Secretary. He was replaced by Ajoy Ghosh, a party hack, who had been identified with the more moderate wing of the party. But P. C. Joshi was not brought back to an influential position, although the Central Committee had agreed in December, 1950 to reconsider his former "heresy" of rightist "revisionism." The second event, was the unconditional surrender of the Communists in Telengana on October 22, 1951 following negotiations which had begun the preceding July 18th. Thus violence was finally eschewed by the C.P.I. and the Communists have not resorted to it as a matter of policy (other than in participation in certain localized riots) to the present time.

The new non-violent approach made it possible for the Communists to put up candidates for national and state offices in all parts of India in the elections of 1952, except in the state of Indore where the ban on the party remained in effect. In addition, certain dangerous Communists accused of criminal activity remained in detention and could not participate in the campaign. The Communists waged a hard-hitting campaign. For example, in Hyderabad, Communist party workers would make lists of landless peasants and draw up an allotment of lands and houses to be given them in event of Red victory. Many peasants were deceived by such fair promises and a number of Communists, some still in jail, were thereby elected. The Communists formed electoral alliances with various small left-wing parties but no support was made, in general, to the Indian Socialist Party, which was now entirely distinct from the National Congress, having dropped the name "Congress" in the Party Congress at Cawnpore in March, 1947, by order of Ghosh himself. The Socialists, he held in a circular letter to party members, were generally reactionary, but support might be given to certain "democrats" in the Socialist Party who had manifested "suffering and sacrifice for the cause of the people."

As a result of the poll held in February and March, 1952, the Communists were able to elect only 23 seats out of 489 to the House of the People, the lower house of the Indian Parliament as established by the Constitution of January, 1950. In view of the fact that the Congress party won 362 seats and other seats were widely scattered among various minor parties, the Communists took second place in the voting, if an exceedingly poor second. Their victories in the national and local legislatures were mainly in the Andhra region of Madras State, and in the States of Hyderabad and Travancore-Cochin.

Although the Communists were handicapped by the merger of the Socialist Party and the Kisan Mazdoor Praja Party, (K.M.P.P.) an independent Socialist group, in September 1952, which challenged the Communists' position as the leading opposition to the Congress, they were now in a position for the first time to utilize the national legislature to espouse their views. For this purpose the Communists had effective spokesmen in the House of the People and the Council of States (the upper house as provided by the Constitution of 1950, its membership being elected by state legislatures) in A. K. Gopalan and P. Sundarayya respectively. Dexterity in parliamentary maneuvers by these leaders, however, has often been offset by undue boisterousness on the part of Communist MP's. Besides, evident prevarications by C.P.I. parliamentary leaders in relation to Indian foreign and (chiefly) domestic Indian policies have injured their cause. The importance of their new parliamentary position to the Communists was evinced by the moving of their party headquarters to Delhi from Madras (it had been moved thither in 1951 from Bombay) in September, 1952.

Encouraged by their modest success in the general elections of 1952 as well as by the evident improvement in their party's strength, some 300 delegates representing 70,000 card-carrying C.P.I. members, met at Madura in Madras State from December 27, 1953 to January 3, 1954. The meeting brought into the open a surprising fissiparous tendency within the C.P.I. In view of the notorious unity, at least superficially, which normally accompanies Communist confabulations, this fact was all the more remarkable. The issue involved was whether the principal oponent of the Indian Communists was American or British "imperialism." Doubtlessly inspired by Moscow and personally espoused at the conference by none other than the C.P.G.B. head, Harry Pollitt himself, the official line was that American "imperialism" was "The Enemy." However, a determined opposition group led by Rajeswar Rao, who in spite of his demotion had remained an influential Communist leader, and specifically, leader of the very pro-Mao Tse-tung faction, contended that British "imperialism" was "The Foe." This opposition group, the "Andhra faction," contended that since Britain still maintained a powerful economic influence in India and that American capital formed not more than three to four per cent of foreign investments in India, it was foolish to call America India's chief enemy. As might have been expected, the "Andhra" or "left" group led by Rao and Punniah was defeated by the majority faction led by Ghosh, Dange and E. M. S. Namboodripad who took their orders from Pollitt who in turn ultimately must have received his from Moscow. However, the fact that there had even been opposition to his viewpoint filled the British Communist leader with wrath and he berated the delegates and their leaders like an angry schoolmaster for letting such a debate be carried on, as well as on the allegedly poor organization of the conference. This Madura Communist Congress, as revealed in its declarations, followed the line formulated in the statements of 1951 and was concluded by a demonstration supposedly involving 200,000 people on January 3, 1954.

Commencing in 1951, the Communists endeavored to regain their former position and enhance their influence in the workers', peasants', students', youth, intellectuals' and women's movements. In addition, they have endeavored to make the so-called "peace movement" into a great India-wide phenomenon.

We have seen how the Communists' policy of violence disrupted the numerical strength of the A.I.T.U.C. This Red organization had also been seriously weakened by the formation of the Indian Trade Union Congress (I.N.T.U.C.) under National Congress auspices in May, 1947, the Hind Mazdoor Sabha (H.M.S.) under Socialist party inspiration in December, 1948 and the United Trade Union Congress (U.T.U.C.) in April, 1949, under independent Socialist direction. Beginning in the autumn of 1951, the Communists sought to attain two basic aims in the labor movement. The first was to strengthen the position of their A.I.T.U.C.; the second was to bring about "trade union unity," ultimately in the form of a merger of all Indian unions into a great trade union federation which the Communists could ultimately come to dominate. In the field of building up Communist led unions, the Communists, under Dange, their labor "expert" and leading force in the A.I.T.U.C., were successful in obtaining control of unions of white-collar workers such as employees of banks, insurance companies and even the poorer civil servants. Such workers were markedly susceptible to the Communist virus on account of their literacy in English. They could read Communist propaganda emanating from England and Russian English language publications such as "New Times." Besides, they were burdened with poor working conditions. The Communists who maintained their influence among the textile workers in the Bombay area also came to dominate workers' associations in the petroleum and air transport fields. They failed, however, in the railways when the Indian National Railway Workers' Federation affiliated to the I.N.T.U.C. in April, 1953.

Commencing with an appeal in October, 1952, in which the veteran labor leader, N. M. Joshi who had become a "fellow traveler" took part, Communists have insisted that there be "unity" in the trade union field. The I.N.T.U.C. has sternly held aloof from Communist overtures, the H.M.S. and U.T.U.C. have at times and for limited purposes—such as local rallies—collaborated with the A.I.T.U.C., but a natural suspicion of the Communists' motives, especially in view of Indian labor history before 1947, have prevented the Communists from carrying out their designs in regard to "labour unity."

Since 1951, as Communists have tried to make their party "respectable," they have endeavored to soft pedal the strike movement as compared to the late 'forties, while fomenting a sufficient amount of labor unrest to permit themselves to be regarded as militant in the labor movement. Notable Communist-fomented strikes since 1950 have been the tramways workers strike in Calcutta in July, 1953, the teachers' strike in Andhra, in September, 1955, and the strikes of textile workers in Bombay in January, 1956 and in Gujerat in August of that year, the latter disturbances being correlated with the question of linguistic provinces in the area of the former Bombay State.

The Communists also have tried, commencing in 1952, to build up on a national basis, their All-India Kisan Sabha or Peasants' Union. Indeed, in April, 1953, the All-India Kisan Federation was re-established and beginning at the end of 1953 with a National Conference in New Delhi, this organization has been active in promoting the Communist line among India's peasants. The movement has had its greatest strength in the new Kerala State in Southern India, formed from parts of the former Madras State and the State of Travancore-Cochin. Communists have also maintained a rather high degree of influence among peasants in the State of Andhra, formerly the northern part of the Madras State, and in the Telengana area of Hyderabad; and also to the north in the areas of Assam and East

Punjab. In the last-named region Communist pressure brought about a merger of the local Communists with the Lal ("Red") Party, a descendant of the Ghadr Party, in the summer of 1952.

The Communists have been busy with the students' and youth movement. Starting in the summer of 1951, preparations were made to enable the All-India Students' Federation (A.I.S.F.) to expand its activity, particularly by carrying on agitation in Indian universities. In August, 1951, the A.I.S.F. began anew its fortnightly periodical, "The Student," as well publishing a large quantity of bulletins and circulars. Among India's universities, it is interesting to note that Aligarh Muslim University was chosen for a great amount of Communist agitation. The A.I.S.F. has been divided into state associations and in turn is a component of the International Students' Federation with headquarters in Prague. Annual conferences of the A.I.S.F. as well as numerous conferences of its regional associations have been held now for the last several years. A great effort has also been made by the C.P.I. in conjunction with the requests of the International World Federation of Democratic Youth to establish various youth front groups. Activity for this purpose, which has not had the relative success of that attending the students' movement, has largely been concentrated among young salaried employees.

Efforts have also been made by the C.P.I. to establish front organizations in artistic and professional circles. Outstanding in the artistic and literary fields have been the "Indian People's Theatre Association," and the "Progressive Writers' Association." These organizations have done much to give the C.P.I. an importance amongst intellectuals out of proportion to its strength in the Republic of India as a whole. This significance is noteworthily marked in the film industry—the second largest in the world in terms of quantity—indeed, it has been held that Communist influence in this field is "dominant." Like art, science also has had its Red front in the form of the "Indian Association of Scientific Workers," affiliated to that international Communist front, the "World Federation of Scientific Workers." Communist groups have been formed in both the legal and medical professions, and even businessmen or small capitalists, in conformity with the Communist line initiated since 1951 espousing apparent favor for them (in January, 1953, the "C.C." even declared that "national industry must be protected against the competition of foreign goods and concerns,") have been subjected to Communist organizing tactics. But with businessmen, the previous record of Communists in India and elsewhere, not to speak of the evident ultimate purpose of Communism, has brought about no appreciable Red successes.

Organizing women's groups has also been carried on by the C.P.I. Commencing with the "National Preparatory Conference" of women's groups in June, 1953, efforts have been steadily made since then with fair success to inspire enthusiasm for Communism among India's women.

But the main front on which the Communists have carried on since 1950 has been the "peace" front. Needless to say true pacifist propaganda is ignored, but only caustic and virulent, often vicious, calumnies against Great Britain and, above all, the United States, are substituted in its place. As early as December, 1950 R. P. Dutt informed his Indian comrades that they must emphasize the "peace movement;" so did the alleged "tactical line" brought back by Comrades Rao, Ghosh, Dange and Punniah in their hegira to Moscow early in 1951. Indeed, even before the winter of 1950-1951, under the leadership of Rao, the Communists were commencing to exploit the "peace movement." In New Delhi on March 3-4, 1951, a National Peace Conference was held and in Calcutta on April 2-6, 1952, an All-India Conference for Peace was convened. These organizations laid great stress, while the Korean War was still in progress, on alleged American germ warfare and indeed on American "atrocities" in general. The anti-United States line persisted even after the armistice of July, 1953. Emphasis on alleged American intervention in the troublesome Kashmir dispute between India and Pakistan has also been evidenced in this movement. On the more positive side appeals have been made for "summit meetings" and for international bans on atomic weapons. The leader of this "peace movement" has been Dr. Saif-ud-din Kitchlew, who has been not only chairman of meetings of the All-India Peace Council, the big "peace" front, within

India, but has also participated in meetings held abroad in such cities as Peiping and Vienna. In January, 1953, he received the International Stalin Prize "for the promotion of peace among nations." President Kitchlew of the A.I.P.C. has been careful enough publicly to disassociate himself from outright Communist activities, but there is no doubt that the front which he has led, has done probably more to advance the cause of world Communism in India than any other organization, including the C.P.I. itself, in recent years. It has done much to mix an ingredient of harsh anti-Americanism (and also anti-British sentiment which in the historical circumstances is not unnatural) into the essentially neutralist and isolationist spirit of India. In this respect the A.I.P.C. has done more for the Soviet Union and Communist China than such obvious fronts as the "Friends of the Soviet Union" and the "Indo-China Friendship Association." Of course, not all who would be won over to the international Communist view of world affairs, would necessarily thereby become all-out advocates for Communism in India. It may be added that the work of these last mentioned groups have been supplemented by the visits of many "cultural" delegations from the U.S.S.R. and Red China, especially since 1953. Furthermore, the liberal dissemination of Soviet literature at cheap prices throughout India has aided the Communist cause.

In recent years there has been a marked growth in the overall membership of the C.P.I. stemming from its line adopted since 1950 and undoubtedly aided by the activity of front groups. From the low point of some 20,000 in 1950, the party had attained the number of 70,000 adherents by the summer of 1953; some 100,000 were members of the party at the time of its Palghat Congress in the spring of 1956 and nearly 230,000 were enrolled when the Amritsar Congress was convened in April, 1958.

In conformity with its growth in card-carrying adherents, the C.P.I. has shown ever greater eagerness to contest elections on the state and national level. In February, 1954, in conjunction with the Praja Socialist Party, the Communists succeeded in defeating the Congress Party in the State of Travancore-Cochin. The Socialists, however, came to govern the state alone for a year, when their ministry collapsed and the Congress resumed authority. The Communists suffered a severe electoral setback in the State of Andhra, the first linguistic state formed in India (in October, 1953) in the election of February, 1955 when they were badly swamped by the Congress Party and its allies. Among the Communist losers for a seat in the state parliament was Basava Punniah, one of the C.P.I.'s leading lights. In the National Elections held early in 1957, the Communists gained ground. Not only were they able to hold their own as the leading opponent of the Congress in the election for seats in the House of the People, but, by a narrow vote, the Communists secured a slender majority in the new linguistic State of Kerala and were able to form a Communist ministry there in the spring of 1957 under the premiership of Namboodripad. This ministry was still in existence in the spring of 1959, although it was under increasingly heavy political fire from the Congress, and its hold on the new state was tenuous indeed. Its most interesting legislative achievement to date has been the passage of an act strictly regulating education which was held to have been hostile to the interest of Christian schools; Christianity is a strong force in Kerala. The establishment of Kerala along with thirteen other states, mostly linguistically-based, on November 1, 1956, essentially fulfilled the long-held Communist view on the establishment of such states.

The Fourth Communist Congress held in the South Indian city of Palghat in April, 1956, in its pronouncements, was featured by the continued insistence of the line of the C.P.I.'s maintenance of a "united front" with various leftist groups. In addition, the idea of "united front" was to be in part extended to Congress committees because "the Congress has, among its members a vast number of democratic elements;" hence, "we must strive to forge united front with Congress committees as well, appealing to the Congress and its masses to hold hands with us." A policy of collaboration with the Socialist Party (formed by Dr. Ram Lohia late in 1955 who had seceded from the Praja Socialist Party) and the Praja Socialist Party was also advocated. Continued hostility to the "monopoly bourgeoisie," landlords, remnants of feudalism and British capital was manifested, but the relatively friendly attitude heretofore held towards the "middle bourgeoisie," (such as "small industrialists,") the petty bourgeoisie, and "middle" peasants was also maintained. On the foreign scene general approval of India's policies and harsh hostility toward American "imperialism" were featured.

The Fifth Communist Congress was held in Amritsar in the Punjab exactly two years later, in April, 1958. The holding of this conference for the first time in Northwest India was occasioned by the desire of the Communists to extend their influence into areas where the party was weak. The party although locally powerful in Kerala, Andhra (where it had recovered some ground since the spring of 1955), West Bengal and the city of Bombay (where the Communist, S. S. Mirajkar, was elected mayor in that very month of April, 1958,) was weak in other areas, especially in North Central India. The Congress was featured by the adoption of a very democratic-appearing party constitution which emphasized the allegedly peaceful purposes of the party and by resolutions which spoke only of government "control" rather than outright nationalization of certain great industries which thereby seemingly placed the Communist position close to that of the Congress on this issue. On other issues the line followed that laid down by the Madura and Palghat Congresses, in respect to domestic affairs and the Communists' attitude towards Indian classes. In this conference, as in previous Communist Congresses since 1953, general approval was given to the foreign as contrasted with the domestic policy of Nehru.

In the summer of 1958, therefore, the Communist Party of India was making itself appear as a kind of legitimate opposition party in respect to the National Congress, pledged to the peaceful establishment of socialism in India, while going further than many democratic opposition political parties in other countries, in supporting the ruling party's foreign policy. It was thus following a modified version of P. C. Joshi's "united front from above" strategy of 1947, and it is pertinent to note that Joshi himself was once again, after a period of several years' disgrace and even banishment from the C.P.I., a prominent member of the party's Central Committee. Actual leadership, however, remains in the hands of Ghosh. Namboodripad, however, by virtue of his success to date in Kerala, has come to the fore as a Communist leader and he may supplant Ghosh as the leader of the C.P.I.

That the Communists have truly foresworn violence, have become a party of "loyal opposition," and have abandoned close connection with the Soviets in recent years, however, is a matter real doubt. In late 1955 an interesting document came to light known as the "Shepilov letter," (Shepilov was the then Soviet Foreign Minister) or "Zukhov letter," (Zukhov was one of Shepilov's aides who allegedly carried the letter to Delhi for the Indian comrades) which missive was revealed to have contained the following points:

1. The Communist Party of India should do nothing that would act as an irritant to or interfere with the major diplomatic operations in which Soviet Russia and the world Communist movement are engaged.
2. The Indian Communist Party should not become unduly perturbed or panicy at the ardent courtship of the Indian Government by their mentors in Moscow and Peiping nor take their public professions at face value.
3. The Communist Party of India must prepare for the time which will inevitably come when it will be possible for Communists within and without India to settle scores with the present bourgeois Government of India.

Although Indian Communists, naturally enough, denied the validity of this letter, their bluster about it, in addition to the general history of the Soviets towards India since 1917, lends credence to its veracity. If this letter were valid it indicates that Russia's friendly attitude towards India as manifested by Khrushchev in his famous visit (together with the now discredited Bulganin) to India in the late autumn of 1955 as well as by his amiable attitude towards Nehru upon the latter's visit to Moscow in June, 1955, by the praise in regard to Indian foreign policy in the Soviet press since 1953, by Soviet trade pacts with India especially that of December 22, 1953, by Soviet economic assistance to India in the form of constructing various enterprises notably the Soviet construction of a one million ton steel plant at Bhilai which was first announced in October, 1954, is simply a facade. Consequently, the friendly gestures of the Soviets notwithstanding, the U.S.S.R. through the instrumentality of the C.P.I., still has designs on India. It may be added that Communist China's conquest of the sub-continent's borderlands, Sinkiang and Tibet between 1949 and 1951 manifestly enchanced the threat of Communism to the Peninsula. However, Iran and Afghanistan have remained free, the former being allied to the West.

That Pandit Nehru and his Government are not unaware of the Communist danger is plainly evident. The Prime Minister has frequently spoken out against the Indian Communists subsequent to, as well as prior to, the adoption of the peaceful tactics of the C.P.I. in 1951. In 1952 while campaigning in Travancore-Cochin in connection with the national elections of that year, he espied a hammer-and-sickle flag flying from a palm tree and thereupon caustically commented: "What is that foreign flag doing over Indian soil?" Five years later, in January, 1957, again campaigning for the Congress, the Pandit, while holding that India should eventually manifest a socialist society, severely censured the Communists for the "forceful measures" they had shown in the past. And so recently as May 12, 1958, Nehru bluntly assailed the Communists in a Congress Party conference. In addition, it may be noted that India's Minister of Economics, Krishnamachari in September, 1957 flatly held that Russia might well aid a Communist revolt in India. Thus the Nehru Government which early in its existence passed various severe "preventive detention" laws and amendments to the criminal code in order to curb Communist activity, remains aware of the potential Red menace. Moreover, the fact that India received at her request a $225,000,000 loan from the United States in June, 1958, indicates that she is showing no sign of subservience to the Communist bloc. While India remains neutral in the "cold war," by the same token she shows no sign of degenerating into a Soviet satellite in the conduct of her foreign policy as is witnessed by the outcry in Indian official quarters over the cruel execution of the Hungarian patriot, the former Premier, Imre Nagy in June, 1958, as well as over the ruthless Soviet suppression of Hungary twenty months previously. India is determined to remain an integral part of the "free world" at all costs and manifest the hard-won independence, attained in August, 1947, which made of her a great Asian power.

Notes

CHAPTER ONE

1. See Hans Kohn, *A History of Nationalism in the East* (New York, 1929), p. 142

2. Quoted *ibid.* For another Bolshevik view on India at this time see United States Congress, Senate, Committee on the Judiciary, *Bolshevik Propaganda,* Hearings: 65:3, Pursuant to S. Res. 439-469, February 11—March 10, 1919, Exhibit 15, p. 1187.

3. Russian Federated Socialist Soviet Republic, Kommissariat po inostrannim dielam (K. M. Troyanovsky, editor), *Sinyaya Kniga,* sbornik tainikh dokumentov izvlechevnikh iz arkhiva bishago ministerstva inostrannikh diel (Moscow, 1918), p. 6.

4. *Ibid.,* p. 8.

5. *Ibid.*

6. *Ibid.,* p. 11.

7. *Ibid.,* p. 12.

8. K. Cummings and Petit, W. W. (editors), *Russian-American Relations* (New York, 1920), pp. 258 ff.

9. Quoted in *The First Congress of the Third International* (Glascow, 1919), pp. 6-7.

10. Karl Marx and Engels, Friedrich, *Manifesto of the Communist Party* (New York, 1932), p. 10.

11. *New York Tribune,* July 11, 1853, p. 1.

12. *New York Tribune,* July 2, 1853, p. 1.

13. Karl Marx, *Capital,* Vol. II, Ch. XXV, Section 44. (The text and specific page references vary to a certain extent in the several editions of this work which are available in English).

14. Karl Marx, *Writings,* IX, 939. Official Russian edition as quoted in A. M. Dyakov, *Natsionalnii vopros i angliiskii imperializm v Indii* (Moscow, 1948), p. 7.

15. See *New York Tribune,* August 10, 1853, p. 2.

16. See *New York Tribune,* August 8, 1853, p. 2.

17. See Dyakov, *op. cit.,* p. 8. See also Karl Marx and Engels, Friedrich, *Korrespondentsia Karl Marksa i Friedrich Engelsa c rosskiimi politicheskiimi deatelam* (Moscow, 1947), p. 90.

18. See Dona Torr, editor, *The Correspondence of Marx and Engels* (New York, 1934), p. 399.

19. Vladimir I. Lenin, *Writings,* VI, 26, (Russian edition) as quoted in Dyakov, *op. cit.,* p. 31.

20. Vladimir I. Lenin, *Writings,* XVI, 383-384, (Russian edition) as quoted in Dyakov, *op. cit.,* p. 10.

21. See Government of India (L. F. Rushbrook Williams, editor), *India in 1919* (Delhi, 1920) pp. 7 ff; W. K. Fraser-Tytler, *Afghanistan* (London, 1953) pp. 192 ff., Louis Fischer, *Soviets in World Affairs* (Princeton, New Jersey, 1951), II, 285; and Joseph Castagne, "Soviet Imperialism in Afghanistan," *Foreign Affairs,* (Vol. XIII, No. 4, July, 1935), p. 689. For the Communist view see Fedor Raskolnikov, "The War in Afghanistan," *Labour Monthly* (Vol. I, No. 3, March, 1929), pp. 179 ff.

22. The news of the wireless message is recorded in the *New York Times* of May 10, 1919, p. 1. As to the reception of the Afghan envoy in Tashkent, see F. M. Bailey, *Mission to Tashkent* (London, 1946), p. 169.

23. Bailey, *op. cit.,* pp. 170 ff.

24. Raskolinkov, *loc. cit.,* p. 182.

25. Bailey, *op. cit.,* p. 175.

26. P. T. Etherton, *In the Heart of Asia* (London, 1925), pp. 227-228.

27. See Bailey, *op. cit.,* p. 194 and pp. 200 ff. See also Etherton, *op. cit.,* pp. 164, 228 and 233.

28. Kohn, *op. cit.,* p. 133.

29. For the complete text of the treaty ending the Third Anglo-Afghan War of 1919 see Government of India, *A Collection of Treaties, Engagements and Sanads,* (compiled by C. Aitchison) (Calcutta, 1933) XIII, 286-288.

30. See M. N. Roy, "Memoirs," *Radical Humanist* (Calcutta), (Vol. XVII, No. 45, November 8, 1953), pp. 534-535. See also Sir George MacMunn, *Turmoil and Tragedy in India, 1914 and After* (London, 1935), pp. 49 ff.

31. See A. R. Desai, *Social Background of Indian Nationalism* (Bombay, 1948), p. 308, D. P. Mukerji, *Views and Counter-Views* (Lucknow, 1946), p. 193, L. S. S. O'Malley, *Modern India and*

the West (London, 1941), p. 96, and T. Walter Wallbank, *India in the New Era* (New York, 1951), pp. 87 ff.

32. Bailey, *op. cit.*, pp. 7-8.

33. *Ibid.*, p. 223.

34. Roy, *loc. cit.*, p. 535.

35. See K. Fuse, *Soviet Policy in the Orient* (Peiping, 1927), p. 8.

36. Castagne, *loc. cit.*, p. 701, Etherton, *op. cit.*, p. 237.

37. *New York Times,* November 27, 1919, p. 4.

38. M. N. Roy, "Memoirs," *Amrita Bazar Patrika* (Calcutta), February 24, 1952, p. 10.

39. Paresh Nath, "M. N. Roy, India's One Man Party," *Asia,* (Vol. XLIII, No. 5, May, 1943), pp. 151 ff.

40. M. N. Roy, "Memoirs," *Radical Humanist,* (Vol. XVII, No. 6, February 8, 1953), pp. 365 ff.

41. Chandra Chakraberty, *New India* (Calcutta, 1951), p. 34.

42. M. N. Roy, "Memoirs," *Radical Humanist,* (Vol. XVII, No. 7, February 15, 1953), pp. 379-380. See also Evelyn Roy, "Indian Political Exiles in France," *Labour Monthly,* (Vol. VII, No. 4, April, 1925); p. 209; Haribur Rahman, "Communism in India," *Living Age,* (Vol. CCCIXL, No. 4430, November, 1935), p. 237; Nath, *loc. cit.*, pp. 151 ff.; an article entitled "A Pupil of the Soviet" in the *Times* (London), February 25, 1930, p. 15; and another article in the *Times* (London), entitled "A Communist Plot in India—the Activities of Roy," of January 12, 1925, p. 11.

43. M. N. Roy, "Memoirs," *Radical Humanist,* (Vol. XVII, No. 32, August 9, 1953), p. 379 and also see his "Memoirs," in *Radical Humanist,* (Vol. XVII, No. 45, November 8, 1953), p. 535.

44. M. N. Roy, "Memoirs," *Amrita Bazar Patrika,* May 18, 1952, pp. 9-10 and also see his "Memoirs," in *Amrita Bazar Patrika,* February 24, 1952, p. 10.

45. M. N. Roy, "Memoirs," *Amrita Bazar Patrika,* May 18, 1952, pp. 9-10.

46. See Bailey, *op. cit.*, p. 145.

47. Etherton, *op. cit.*, p. 160.

48. *Ibid.*

49. See United States Department of State, *Second Congress of the Third International* (as reported verbatim from the Russian press), (Washington D. C., 1920), pp. 41 ff.

50. M. N. Roy, "Memoirs," *Amrita Bazar Patrika,* April 6, 1952, p. 6.

51. United States Department of State, *op. cit.,* pp. 41 ff.

52. M. N. Roy, "Memoirs," *Amrita Bazar Patrika,* June 6, 1952, p. 9.

53. Leo Pasvolsky, *Russia in the Far East* (New York, 1922), p. 74; Robert Payne, *Red Storm over Asia* (New York, 1951), p. 12.

54. See A. Lobanov-Rostovsky, *Russia and Asia* (Ann Arbor, Michigan, 1951), p. 282 and see Payne, *op. cit.,* p. 8.

55. M. N. Roy, "Memoirs," *Amrita Bazar Patrika,* August 3, 1952, p. 1 (supplement).

56. M. N. Roy, "Memoirs," *Amrita Bazar Patrika,* June 3, 1952, p. 9.

57. See Pasvolsky, *op. cit.,* pp. 75 ff. and George Lenczowski, *Russia and the West in Iran, 1918-1948* (Ithaca, New York, 1948), p. 6.

58. Pasvolsky, *op. cit.,* pp. 93-94.

59. *Ibid.*

60. See Pasvolsky, *op. cit.,* pp. 76 ff. and Lenczowski, *op. cit.,* p. 7.

61. See Lenczowski, *op. cit.,* p. 7.

62. M. N. Roy, "Memoirs," *Amrita Bazar Patrika,* July 13, 1952, pp. 1 ff. (supplement).

63. M. N. Roy, "Memoirs," *Amrita Bazar Patrika,* June 29, 1952, pp. 9-10.

64. The defeat of Russia in Poland in the autumn of 1920 blocked the path of Communism to the West. Only the East remained as an area open to Soviet aggression. For details of Russia's defeat in thc West see A. J. Grant and Temperley, Harold, *Europe in the Nineteenth and Twentieth Centuries* (London, 1940), p. 561.

Lenin held that capitalism could only survive through the colonial system. Hence, were Britain to lose India through Roy's plan, British capitalism would suffer a very serious blow. On Lenin's thesis on capitalism and colonialism see his *Imperialism* (New York, 1926), *passim,* and especially pp. 65-66.

65. M. N. Roy, "Memoirs," *Amrita Bazar Patrika,* July 27, 1952, p. 1. ff. (supplement).

66. *Ibid.*

67. *Ibid.*

68. *The Times* (London), February 25, 1930, p. 15.

69. M. N. Roy, "Memoirs," *Amrita Bazar Patrika,* March 15, 1953, pp. 1 ff. (supplement). See also *The Times* (London), February 25, 1930, p. 15 in which is recounted the experiences of the Mujahir, Abdul Qadir Khan.

70. M. N. Roy, "Memoirs," *Amrita Bazar Patrika,* March 15, 1953, pp. 1 ff. (supplement); *The Times* (London), February 25, 1930, p. 15.

71. M. N. Roy, "Memoirs," *Amrita Bazar Patrika,* March 29, 1953, pp. 1 ff. (supplement); *The Times* (London), February 25, 1930, p. 15.

72. M. N. Roy, "Memoirs," *Amrita Bazar Patrika,* March 29, 1953, pp. 1 ff. (supplement).

73. M. N. Roy, "Memoirs," *Amrita Bazar Patrika,* April 12, 1953, pp. 1 ff. (supplement).

74. M. N. Roy, "Memoirs," *Amrita Bazar Patrika,* April 12, 1953, pp. 1 ff. (supplement). See also his "Memoirs," June 28, 1953, pp. ff. (supplement) in *ibid.*

75. As regards Fazl-I-Ilani Qurban see Minoo R. Masani, *The Communist Party of India* (New York, 1954) p. 22. Concerning Shaukat Usmani's view of Roy see Government of India, *Judgment Meerut Conspiracy Case* (Simla, 1932), I, 66.

76. *The Times* (London), February 4, 1921, p. 9.

77. M. N. Roy, "Memoirs," *Amrita Bazar Patrika,* August 31, 1952, p. 1 (supplement).

78. *The Times* (London), February 3, 1921, p. 9.

79. Etherton, *op. cit.,* pp. 187 ff.

80. Lenczowski, *op. cit.,* pp. 51, 81.

81. *Ibid.,* pp. 103 ff.

82. *Ibid.,* p. 59.

83. See Alexander Barmine, *Memoirs of a Soviet Diplomat* (London, 1936), p. 123.

84. *The Times* (London), September 21, 1921, p. 12.

85. The ratification occurred in August, 1921. See Fraser-Tytler, *op. cit.,* p. 199.

86. Lobanov-Rostovsky, *op. cit.,* p. 289.

87. *The Times* (London), September 21, 1921, p. 12.

88. See an article by Ikbal Ali Shah of a rather alarming and sensational character, "The Bolshevik Advance on India," *Independent* (Vol. CVIII. No. 3804, February 11, 1922), pp.

13 ff. See also M. N. Roy, "Memoirs," *Amrita Bazar Patrika,* August 10, 1952, pp. 11-12.

89. M. N. Roy, "Memoirs," *Amrita Bazar Patrika,* March 29, 1953, pp. 1 ff. (supplement). See also his "Memoirs," *Amrita Bazar Patrika,* April 12, 1953, pp. 1 ff. (supplement).

90. *The Times* (London), February 25, 1930, p. 15.

91. M. N. Roy, "Memoirs," *Amrita Bazar Patrika,* March 29, 1953, p. 1 (suplement). See also his "Memoirs," *Amrita Bazar Patrika,* April 26, 1953, p. 1. (supplement).

92. Etherton, *op. cit.,* pp. 161-162 and pp. 230 ff.

93. *Ibid.,* p. 239.

94. Lenczowski, *op. cit.,* pp. 59 ff.

95. *Ibid.,* p. 106.

96. Government of India, (J. Rushbrook Wiliams, editor) *India in 1920* (Delhi, 1921), pp. 5-6.

97. *Ibid.,* p. 5.

98. M. N. Roy, "Memoirs," *Amrita Bazar Patrika,* August 3, 1952, pp. 1-2. (supplement).

99. *The Times* (London), February 16, 1921, p. 9.

100. For details of the note of March 16, 1921, see *The Times* (London), March 17, 1921, p. 11.

101. *Ibid.*

102. Government of India (J. Rushbrook Williams, editor), *India in the Years 1922-1923* (Delhi, 1923), pp. 29-30.

103. M. N. Roy, "Memoirs," *Amrita Bazar Patrika,* May, 3, 1953, pp. 1 ff. (supplement).

104. For details see United Kingdom of Great Britain and Northern Ireland, Foreign Office, *A Selection of Papers Dealing with the Relations between H. M. Government and the Russian Government,* Cmd. 2895 (London, 1927), pp. 4-12.

105. See Government of India, *A Collection of Treaties, Engagements and Sanads,* XIII, pp. 288-296, especially see p. 296 in regard to Afghanistan's willingness not to admit establishment of Soviet consulates. This treaty was followed in the spring of 1922 by the formal exchange of diplomatic relations between London and Kabul (*India* in 1922-1923, p. 30). See also on this subject an article by Shaw Desmond, "India Pictured as a Radical Volcano," *New York Times,* February 24, 1924, Section VIII, p. 3.

106. See W. P. and Zelda Coates, *Soviets in Central Asia* (London, 1951), p. 20.

107. See M. N. Roy, "Memoirs," *Amrita Bazar Patrika,* April 12, 1953, pp. 1 ff. (supplement).

108. Government of India (J. Rushbrook Williams, editor), *India in 1921* (Delhi, 1922), p. 2. See also Lobanov-Rostovsky, *op. cit.,* p. 284.

109. Castagne, *loc. cit.,* p. 800.

110. M. N. Roy, "Memoirs," *Amrita Bazar Patrika,* August 31, 1952, pp. 1 ff. (supplement). See also Fuse, *op. cit.,* p. 121.

111. *India in 1921,* p. 3.

112. M. N. Roy, "Memoirs," *Amrita Bazar Patrika,* May 3, 1953, p. 1. (supplement).

113. Government of India (J. Rushbrook Williams, editor), *India in the Years 1923-1924* (New Dehli, 1924), p. 30.

114. *India in 1921,* p. 4.

115. W. P. and Zelda Coates, *A History of Anglo-Soviet Relations* (London, 1944), pp. 61 ff.

CHAPTER TWO

1. For details, see the text of the note in *The Times* (London), September 21, 1921, p. 12.

2. M. N. Roy, "Memoirs," *Amrita Bazar Patrika,* May 3, 1953, pp. 1 ff. (supplement). See also his "Memoirs," in *Radical Humanist* (Vol. XVII. No. 45, November 9, 1953), pp. 534 ff.

3. M. N. Roy, "Memoirs," *Amrita Bazar Patrika,* May 3, 1953, pp. 1 ff. (supplement).

4. Shaw Desmond in the *New York Times,* February 24, 1924, Section VIII, p. 3.

5. M. N. Roy, "Memoirs," *Amrita Bazar Patrika,* April 26, 1953, pp. 1 ff. (supplement).

6. M. N. Roy, "Memoirs," *Amrita Bazar Patrika,* May 3, 1953, pp. 1 ff. (supplement). See also *The Times* (London), February 25, 1930, p. 15.

7. M. N. Roy, "Memoirs," *Amrita Bazar Patrika,* April 26, 1953, pp. 1 ff. (supplement).

8. *Ibid.*

9. M. N. Roy, "Memoirs," *Amrita Bazar Patrika,* May 3, 1953, pp. 1 ff. (supplement).

10. *Ibid.*

11. *Third Congress of the Communist International,* June

22–July 12, 1921 (New York, 1921), p. 21.

12. *Ibid.*

13. M. N. Roy, "Memoirs," *Amrita Bazar Patrika,* June 28, 1953, pp. 1 ff. (supplement). See also Kohn, *op. cit.,* p. 149.

14. M. N. Roy, "Memoirs," *Amrita Bazar Patrika,* June 28, 1953, pp. 1 ff. (supplement).

15. *Ibid.*

16. *Ibid.*

17. *Ibid.*

18. M. N. Roy, "Memoirs," *Amrita Bazar Patrika,* April 12, 1953, pp. 1 ff. (suplement).

19. M. N. Roy, "Memoirs," *Amrita Bazar Patrika,* June 28, 1953, pp. 1 ff. (supplement).

20. M. N. Roy, "Memoirs," *Amrita Bazar Patrika,* July 19, 1953, pp. 1 ff. (supplement).

21. As quoted in R. Palme Dutt, *India To-day* (London, 1940), p. 321.

22. M. N. Roy, "Memoirs," *Amrita Bazar Patrika,* July 19, 1953, pp. 1 ff. (supplement).

23. M. N. Roy, "Memoirs," *Amrita Bazar Patrika,* July 19, 1953, pp. 1 ff. (supplement). See also Subhas C. Bose, *The Indian Struggle* (London, 1934), p. 86.

24. Evelyn Roy, "The Crisis in Indian Nationalism," *Labour Monthly,* (Vol. II, No. 2, February, 1922), pp. 354-355.

25. Quoted in S. D. Punekar, *Trade Unionism in India* (Bombay, 1948), p. 91.

26. M. N. Roy, "Memoirs," *Amrita Bazar Patrika,* July 26, 1953, pp. 1 ff. (supplement).

27. *The Times,* (London) February 26, 1930, p. 15.

28. *Ibid.*

29. *Ibid.*

30. *The Times,* (London) February 27, 1930, pp. 15-16.

31. *Ibid.*

32. M. N. Roy, "Memoirs," *Amrita Bazar Patrika,* August 23, 1953, pp. 1 ff. (supplement). See also *The Times* (London), February 26, 1930, p. 15.

33. See Abani Mukherji, "The Moplah Rising," *Communist Review,* (Vol. II, No. 5, March, 1922), p. 373 ff. See also *The Times* (London), October 13, 1922, p. 13.

34. M. N. Roy, *One Year of Non-Co-operation from Ahmedabad to Gaya* (Calcutta, 1923), p. 60.

35. M. N. Roy, "Memoirs," *Amrita Bazar Patrika,* April 26, 1953, pp. 1 ff. (supplement).

36. United States Government, Office of Strategic Services, Research and Analysis Branch (R & A) No. 2681, *The Communist Party of India* (Washington D. C., 1945), p. 65.

37. M. N. Roy, "Memoirs," *Amrita Bazar Patrika,* August 23, 1953, pp. 1 ff. (supplement).

38. O'Malley, *op. cit.,* p. 105.

39. A. M. Dyakov, *Indiya vo vremya i posle vtoroi mirovoi voini* (Moscow, 1952), p. 297.

40. See Government of the United Kingdom of Great Britain and Northern Ireland, *Judgment of the High Court of Judicature at Allahabad in the Revolutionary Conspiracy Case,* Cmd. 2309 (London, 1924), pp. 2 ff.

41. Raj Chadha Tilak, "Punjab Communists, an Analysis," *Thought,* (Vol. IV, No. 21, July 19, 1952), p. 5, and also *Thought,* (Vol. IV, No. 31, August 2, 1952), p. 7.

42. Communist Party of Great Britain, *The Fourth Congress of the Communist International,* November 7—December 3, 1922 (London, 1923), pp. 208 ff.

43. *Ibid.,* p. 223.

44. *Ibid.,* p. 296.

45. See Kohn, *op. cit.,* pp. 148-149.

46. See M. N. Roy, *One Year of Non-Co-operation from Ahmedabad to Gaya,* pp. 106-111.

47. *Times of India* (Bombay), December 22, 1922, p. 4.

48. *Amrita Bazar Patrika,* December 27, 1922, p. 4.

49. For details see an article in the Comintern organ, *International Press Correspondence,* (Vol. III, No. 31, April 5, 1923), p. 275. For another approach to the workers, see the article, "To the Workers of All Countries," *International Press Correspondence* (Vol. III, No. 24, March 11, 1923), p. 190.

50. *The Tribune* (Lahore), April 24, 1924, p. 9. See also *The Tribune* (Lahore), May 9, 1924, p. 2.

51. *The Tribune* (Lahore), April 24, 1924, pp. 3-4.

52. *The Tribune* (Lahore), March 24, 1924, p. 3.

53. *The Tribune* (Lahore), March 21, 1924, p. 3. Roy believed at this time that the "nationalist bourgeoisie" should be assisted in the battle against imperialism. See his article, "Anti-Imperialist Struggle in India," in the *Communist International,* (Vol. I, No. 6, 1923), p. 92.

54. *The Tribune* (Lahore), November 7, 1924, p. 2.

55. M. N. Roy, *One Year of Non-Co-operation from Ahmedabad to Gaya,* pp. 150 ff.

56. Bose, *op. cit.,* p. 106.

57. *The Tribune* (Lahore), April 26, 1924, p. 2.

58. *The Tribune* (Lahore), April 25, 1924, p. 2. Also see Government of India, (J. Rushbrook Williams, editor), *India in the Years 1923-1924,* (New Delhi, 1924), p. 80.

59. *The Tribune* (Lahore), April 25, 1924, p. 2.

60. *The Tribune* (Lahore), May 8, 1924, p. 2.

61. Government of India (J. Rushbrook Williams, editor), *India in the Years 1924-1925* (New Delhi, 1925), p. 100.

62. *India in the Years 1923-1924,* p. 80.

63. See an article in the *Literary Digest,* "The Bolshevik Menace to India" (Vol. LXXXVIII, No. 12, March 20, 1926), pp. 16-17.

64. *The Tribune* (Lahore), April 25, 1924, p. 2.

65. Philip Spratt, "The Indian Trade Union Movement," *Labour Monthly,* (Vol. IX, No. 10, October, 1927), p. 613.

66. *The Tribune* (Lahore), May 8, 1924, p. 2.

67. Joseph Stalin, *Marxism and the National Question* (New York, 1942), p. 151.

68. See *The Times* (London), May 13, 1923, p. 12, and May 16, 1923, p. 12.

69. Evelyn Roy, "Indian Political Exiles in France," *Labour Monthly,* (Vol. VII, No. 4, April, 1925), p. 209.

70. For details see W. P. and Zelda Coates, *A History of Anglo-Soviet Relations,* pp. 114 ff.

71. See Government of United Kingdom of Great Britain and Northern Ireland, *Blue Book: A Selection of Papers Dealing with the Relations of His Majesty's Government and the Soviet Government, 1923-1927,* cmd. 2895 (London, 1927), pp. 20-24. See also Fischer, *op. cit.,* I, 448.

72. *The Tribune* (Lahore), April 26, 1924, pp. 2-3.

73. *The Tribune* (Lahore), May 6, 1924, p. 2.

74. W. P. and Zelda Coates, *A History of Anglo-Soviet Relations,* pp. 130 ff. Replaced Tory Baldwin Govt., Jan., 1924.

75. Joseph Stalin, *Foundations of Leninism,* (New York, 1939) p. 37.

76. *The Tribune* (Lahore), March 21, 1924, p. 3.

77. *The Tribune* (Lahore), March 19, 1924, p. 3.

78. *The Times* (London), April 19, 1924, p. 11.
79. *The Tribune* (Lahore), March 19, 1924, p. 3.
80. *The Times* (London), March 19, 1924, p. 13.
81. *The Times* (London), April 24, 1924, p. 11, May 12, 1924, p. 13.
82. *The Times* (London), May 22, 1924, p. 15.
83. *The Tribune* (Lahore), May 22, 1924, p. 2.
84. *The Times* (London), May 20, 1924, p. 8. See also Fuse, *op. cit.*, p. 138.
85. *The Times* (London), November 22, 1924, p. 12.
86. For the text of M. N. Roy's tirade see his "An Open Letter to Prime Minister MacDonald," *Communist Review,* (Vol. V., No. 3, July, 1924), pp. 120 ff.
87. *Ibid.* This followed an earlier pronouncement by Roy in which he bitterly attacked the "betrayal of India by the Labour Government." See M. N. Roy, "India and the British Labour Government," *Labour Monthly,* (Vol. VI, No. 4, April, 1924), pp. 200 ff.
88. Communist Party of Great Britain (published for the Communist International) *From the Fourth to the Fifth World Congress,* (Report of the Executive Committee of the Communist International) (London, 1924), p. 69.
89. *Ibid.,* p. 68.
90. *Ibid.,* p. 103.
91. For the complete statement by Judges Measers and Piggott see "Government of Great Britain and Northern Ireland," *Judgment of the High Court of Judicature at Allahabad in the Revolutionary Conspiracy Case,* Cmd. 2309 (London, 1924), p. 2.

CHAPTER THREE

1. Payne, *op. cit.,* p. 113.
2. Communist Party of Great Britain, *Fifth Congress of the Communist International* (London, 1924), pp. 96-98.
3. *Ibid.*
4. *Ibid.* p. 49.
5. Executive Committee of the Communist International, "Resolution on the Oriental Question" (adopted by the E.C.C.I. March 4, 1922), *International Press Correspondence* (Vol. II, No. 29, April 25, 1922), p. 22.

6. *Fifth Congress of the Communist International,* p. 155.

7. Government of the United Kingdom of Great Britain and Northern Ireland, House of Commons, *Communist Papers,* Documents selected from those obtained on the Arrest of certain British Communist Leaders on October 14 and 21, 1925, Parliamentary Publications, 192, Vol. XXIII (Accounts and Papers) Cmd. 2682, (London, 1926) p. 96.

8. *Ibid.*

9. *Ibid.,* p. 81. See also *The Tribune* (Lahore), December 4, 1929, p. 2.

10. House of Commons, *op. cit.,* p. 96.

11. Office of Strategic Services, *op. cit.,* pp. 2-3.

12. *Ibid.,* p. 61.

13. For details of this strike see Radakamal Mukerjee, *The Indian Working Class* (Bombay, 1951), p. 375, and for Communist propaganda about it see Evelyn Roy, "Some Facts about the Bombay Strike," *Labour Monthly,* (Vol. VI, No. 5, May, 1924), pp. 293 ff, and an editorial entitled "Indian Textile Workers' Strike," *Labour Monthly,* (Vol. VII, No. 12, December, 1925), p. 761. In the latter article it is stated that to the strikers "the All-Russian Textile Union sent financial aid. . ."

14. *From the Fourth to the Fifth Congress,* p. 69.

15. Workers' and Peasants' Party of Bengal, *A Call to Action* (Calcutta, 1928) p. 39.

16. *Ibid.*

17. *Ibid.*

18. *Ibid.*

19. *Ibid.,* p. 50.

20. See R. Palme Dutt, "The Path to Proletarian Hegemony in the Indian Revolution," *Communist International,* (Vol. VII, No. 14, December 1, 1930), pp. 312 ff., and an article entitled "India—North-West Railway Strike," *Labour Monthly,* (Vol. VII, No. 8, August, 1925), pp. 504-505.

21. "India—North-West Railway Strike," *loc. cit.,* pp. 504-505.

22. R. Palme Dutt, "The Path to Proletarian Hegemony in the Indian Revolution," *loc. cit.,* p. 312.

23. See Government of India, *Judgment Meerut Conspiracy Case,* II, 76.

24. B. Pattabhi Sitaramayya, *The History of the Indian National Congress* Vol. I, (Madras, 1935), p. 228.

25. Unsigned article, "The Cawnpore Conference," *Near East*

and India, (Vol. XXIX, No. 765, January 14, 1926), pp. 43-44.

26. *Ibid.*

27. Unsigned article, "The Indian Communist Party," *Near East and India,* (Vol. XXIX, No. 768, February 4, 1926), p. 142.

28. Nripendra Nath Mitra, *The Indian Annual Register, 1925,* II, 371.

29. Government of India, *Judgment Meerut Conspiracy Case,* II, 76.

30. *The Tribune* (Lahore), December 4, 1929, p. 2.

31. *The Tribune* (Lahore), June 26, 1929, p. 1. See also *The Times* (London), January 12, 1926, p. 16.

32. *The Tribune* (Lahore), June 26, 1929, p. 1, *The Times* (London) December 4, 1929, p. 13.

33. *The Tribune* (Lahore), December 7, 1929, p. 1.

34. *Ibid.*

35. *The Times* (London), December 4, 1929, p. 13.

36. R. Palme Dutt, *Modern India* (London, 1927), pp. 9 ff.

37. *Ibid.*, p. 13.

38. *Ibid.*, pp. 15-16 and 75 ff.

39. *Ibid.*, p. 87.

40. *Ibid.*, pp. 133 ff.

41. *Ibid.*, pp. 145-146.

42. *Ibid.*, pp. 133 ff.

43. *Ibid.*

44. *The Tribune* (Lahore), December 4, 1929, p. 2. July 2, 1932, p. 2, *The Times* (London), December 4, 1929, p. 13.

45. *The Tribune* (Lahore), December 4, 1929, p. 2, July 2, 1932, p. 2.

46. *The Tribune* (Lahore), July 2, 1932, p. 2. Also see Government of India (John Coatman, editor) *India in the Years, 1926-1927,* (New Delhi, 1927) p. 289.

47. *The Tribune* (Lahore), July 2, 1932, p. 2. Also see R. Palme Dutt, *The Problem of India* (New York, 1943), p. 159 for the Communist chronology on the formation of the workers' and peasants' parties.

48. Workers' and Peasants' Party of Bengal, *op. cit.*, p. 47.

49. *Ibid.*, p. 50.

50. *Ibid.* See also *The Tribune,* (Lahore) February 2, 1930, p. 2.

51. Desai, *op. cit.*, p. 324.

52. Spratt, *loc. cit.*, p. 613.

53. A. M. Dyakov, *Indiya i Pakistan* (Moscow, 1950), p. 21.
54. Spratt, *loc. cit.*, p. 619.
55. Office of Strategic Services, *op. cit.*, p. 62.
56. *Judgment Meerut Conspiracy Case,* I, 88.
57. *The Times* (London), December 4, 1929, p. 3. Also see Government of India, (John Coatman, editor) *India in the Years, 1927-1928,* (New Delhi, 1928) p. 341.
58. *The Tribune* (Lahore), June 19, 1929, p. 1.
59. *The Tribune* (Lahore), July 2, 1932, p. 1, December 4, 1929, p. 2, December 7, 1929, p. 1.
60. *The Tribune* (Lahore), June 29, 1929, p. 2.
61. *Judgment Meerut Conspiracy Case,* I, 155.
62. *Ibid.*
63. *Ibid.*
64. *The Tribune* (Lahore), June 26, 1929, p. 1; December 4, 1929, p. 2; February 7, 1930, p. 1.
65. *The Tribune* (Lahore), December 7, 1929, p. 1.
66. *The Times* (London), January 16, 1930, p. 11.
67. *India in the Years 1926-1927,* p. 290.
68. R. Palme Dutt, *India To-day,* p. 373; Spratt, *loc. cit.,* pp. 619-620.
69. Mitra, *The Indian Annual Register,* (July-December, 1927) II, 94.
70. *Ibid.,* II, 416.
71. *The Times* (London), December 4, 1929, p. 13.
72. See *The Times* (London), November 29, 1927, p. 8.
73. Spratt, *loc. cit.*, p. 619.
74. For the history of the Indian Communist press, including that press at this time see *New Age,* the present-day leading English language Communist organ of October 4, 1953, pp. 3-4. For activities of the Bombay Workers' and Peasants' Party see, *The Tribune* (Lahore), December 7, 1929, p. 1. and R. Palme Dutt, *India To-day,* p. 378.
75. *The Times* (London), August 3, 1929, p. 9.
76. Workers' and Peasants' Party of Bengal, *op. cit.*, p. 50.
77. *Ibid.*
78. Office of Strategic Services, *op. cit.*, p. 62.
79. R. Palme Dutt, *India To-day,* p. 378.
80. *The Tribune* (Lahore), December 6, 1929, p. 1, R. Palme Dutt, *India To-day,* p. 378.

81. Workers' and Peasants' Party of Bengal, *op. cit.*, p. 50. See also *India in the Years 1926-1927,* p. 290.

82. Spratt, *loc. cit.*, p. 619.

83. *The Tribune* (Lahore), December 5, 1929, p. 1.

84. Office of Strategic Services, *op. cit.*, p. 61.

85. *The Tribune* (Lahore), December 7, 1929, p. 1.

86. *The Tribune* (Lahore), December 5, 1929, p. 1.

87. Government of India (John Coatman, editor), *India in the Years 1927-1928,* (New Delhi, 1928), p. 341.

88. Workers' and Peasants' Party of Bengal, *op. cit.*, pp. 3-4.

89. *Ibid.*, pp. 5-6.

90. *Ibid.*, pp. 6-7.

91. *Ibid.*, p. 10.

92. *Ibid.*, pp. 11 ff.

93. *Ibid.*, p. 23.

94. *Ibid.*, pp. 11 ff.

95. *Ibid.*, pp. 33 ff.

96. *Ibid.*, pp. 31-32.

97. *Ibid.*, pp. 36 ff.

98. *The Tribune* (Lahore), December 6, 1929, p. 1.

99. *The Times* (London), December 9, 1929, p. 11.

100. R. Palme Dutt, *India To-day,* p. 357.

101. *Ibid.*

102. *Judgment Meerut Conspiracy Case,* I, 177.

103. See Clement P. Dutt, "The Struggle for Independence," *Labour Monthly* (Vol. X, No. 3, March, 1928), pp. 155 ff. See also Desai, *op. cit.*, p. 194.

104. See the unsigned article, "All India Trade Union Congress," *Labour Monthly,* (Vol. IX, No. 17, July, 1927), pp. 443-445.

105. *Ibid.*

106. See the unsigned article, "All India Trade Union Congress," *Labour Monthly,* (Vol. X, No. 4, April, 1928), pp. 251-253.

107. *Ibid.*

108. See the message of "The R.I.L.U. to the Eighth All-India Congress of Trade Unions," *International Press Correspondence* (Vol. VII, No. 68, December 1, 1927), p. 1539.

109. Mitra, *The Indian Annual Register,* July-December, 1928, II, 150.

110. *India in the Years 1926-1927,* p. 289, Bose, *op. cit.,* p. 178.

111. "S," "Trial of Indian Revolutionaries," *Communist International,* (Vol. VI, No. 20, September 1, 1932), p. 789.

112. See Jack Ryan, "Report on Indian Trade Unionism," *Far Eastern Bulletin, Pan Pacific Trade Union Secretariat,* January 16, 1929, p. 5. See also Jawaharlal Nehru, *Toward Freedom,* the Autobiography of Jawaharlal Nehru (New York, 1942), p. 142.

113. See John Coatman, *Years of Destiny* (London, 1932), p. 200. See also Bose, *op. cit.,* p. 178.

114. Bose, *op. cit.,* p. 178.

115. *Ibid.*

116. K. S. Shelvankar, *The Problem of India* (London, 1940), p. 214.

117. See the unsigned articles, "South Indian Railway Strike," *Labour Monthly,* (Vol. X, No. 10, October, 1928), pp. 636-639; and "Lillooah Railway Strike," *Labour Monthly,* (Vol. X, No. 9, September, 1928), pp. 572-575.

118. Office of Strategic Services, *op. cit.,* p. 49.

119. See M. Singh, "The Struggle of the Indian Textile Workers," *Labour Monthly,* (Vol. XVI, No. 6, June, 1934), pp. 346 ff.; R. Palme Dutt, *India To-day,* pp. 384-385; Bose, *op. cit.,* p. 177; and an unsigned article, "The General Strike in the Bombay Textile Mills," *Labour Monthly,* (Vol. X, No. 11, November, 1928), pp. 698 ff.

120. Singh, *loc. cit.,* p. 349.

121. R. Palme Dutt, *India To-day,* p. 375.

122. Coatman, *op. cit.,* p. 200.

123. See Edward Thompson and Garatt, G. T., *Rise and Fulfilment of British Rule in India* (London, 1940), p. 629, *The Tribune* (Lahore), September 13, 1928, p. 4, and *The Times* (London), January 19, 1929, p. 11.

124. Shelvankar, *op. cit.,* p. 214.

125. R. Palme Dutt, *India To-day,* pp. 322, 374

126. See the articles by "Valia," "The Development of the Communist Movement in India," *Communist International,* (Vol. X, No. 3, February 1933), p. 80, and "W," "Prospects of the Labour Movement in India," *Communist International,* (Vol. VII, No. 12, October 15, 1930), p. 257. See also R. Palme Dutt, *The Problem of India,* p. 160.

127. *The Tribune* (Lahore), December 6, 1929, p. 1.

128. Shelvankar, *op. cit.,* p. 221.

129. Office of Strategic Services, *op. cit.,* p. 51.

130. See Lester Hutchinson, *Conspiracy at Meerut* (London, 1935), pp. 7 ff.

131. *The Times* (London), December 9, 1929, p. 11.

132. See Jawaharlal Nehru, *The Discovery of India* (New York, 1936), p. 342, and Edward Thompson, *Ethical Ideas in India To-day* (London, 1942), pp. 22, 32-33.

133. Wilfred C. Smith, *Modern Islam in India,* (Lahore, 1943) pp. 104, 244.

134. Nehru, *Toward Freedom,* the Autobiography of Jawaharlal Nehru (New York, 1942), pp. 123 ff.

135. Jawaharlal Nehru, *Soviet Russia* (Bombay, 1929), pp. 25, 97.

136. *Ibid.,* pp. 2, 126, 129-131.

137. Sitaramayya, *op. cit.,* I, 51, Bose, *op. cit.,* p. 168.

138. As quoted in Nehru, *Soviet Russia,* pp. 131-132.

139. *Ibid.*

140. M. N. Roy, "Memoirs," *Radical Humanist,* (Vol. XVIII, No. 45, November 8, 1953), pp. 534-535.

141. See Evelyn Roy, "Indian Political Exiles in France," *loc. cit.,* p. 205.

142. *Ibid.,* p. 207.

143. *New York Times,* September 16, 1928, Section III, p. 7.

144. *The Times* (London), May 27, 1925, p. 15.

145. *Ibid.*

146. House of Commons, *op. cit.,* pp. 81, 84 ff.

147. M. N. Roy, *The Future of Indian Politics,* (London, 1926), pp. 15 ff.

148. *Ibid.* It may be noted on this question Roy succinctly stated in an article, "New Economic Policy of British Imperialism—its Effect on Indian Nationalism," *Communist International,* (Vol. 11, No. 21, 1926), p. 70. "Bourgeois nationalism of India has ended in a complete compromise with imperialism, as was predicted by those who judged the situation with Marxian realism."

149. M. N. Roy, *The Future of Indian Politics,* p. 117.

150. *Ibid.,* p. 98.

151. See M. N. Roy, *My Experience in China* (Calcutta, 1945), pp. 35 ff.

152. *India in the Years 1926-1927,* p. 290.

153. See *New York Times,* March 1, 1927, p. 4.

154. See Shelvankar, *op. cit.,* p. 48.

155. *India in the Years 1926-1927,* p. 290.

156. *Ibid.*

157. Mitra, *The Indian Annual Register, July-December, 1928,* II, 171 ff.

158. *Judgment Meerut Conspiracy Case,* I, 189.

159. *Ibid.*

160. Royal Institute of International Affairs, *Soviet Documents on Foreign Policy,* (London, 1952) II, 48.

161. *Ibid.*

162. *Ibid.,* II, 96 ff.

163. *India in the Years 1927-1928,* p. 543.

164. See the unsigned article, "The General Strike in the Bombay Textile Mills," *Labour Monthly,* (Vol. X, No. 11, November, 1928), pp. 698 ff. See also Masani, *op. cit.,* p. 28.

165. See the unsigned article, "Soviet Aid for Indian Strikers," *Literary Digest* (Vol. XCVIII, No. 5, August 4, 1928), p. 19. See also Masani, *op. cit.,* p. 28.

166. S. D. Punekar *op. cit.,* pp. 209-210.

167. A. Kuusinen, "Imperialisticheskii gnet i problemi revolutzionnogo dvizheniya v kolonialnikh stranakh," *Novii Vostok,* (Vol. VI, No. 23-24, October, 1928), pp. VII-XXX; Safdar, "India no VI Kongress Kominterna," *Ibid.,* pp. L-LXII; M. Rafail, "Problemi indiiskoi revolutzii," *Ibid.,* pp. 1-24; T. Rink "Problemi oboroni Indii," *Ibid.,* pp. 25-34.

Thus there were in this issue of *Novii Vostok* no fewer than four articles on the Communists in India.

See also Safdar, "Hindu-Mussulman Strife," *Communist International,* (Vol. IV, No. 5, March 30, 1927), pp. 68-71.

168. *The Tribune* (Lahore), July 2, 1932, p. 2.

169. Communist International, *The Communist International between the Fifth and Sixth World Congress, 1924-1928* published for the Communist International by the Communist Party of Great Britain (London, July, 1928), p. 476.

170. Grigorii Agabekov, *OGPU, the Russian Secret Terror,* (New York, 1931), pp. 201-202.

171. See Communist International, "Sixth Congress of the Communist International," in *International Press Correspondence* (Vol. VIII, No. 32, September 1, 1928), p. 1200. See also

Communist Party of France, *La Correspondence Internationale Compte Rendu stenographique du VI ieme Congress de L'Internationale communiste* (Paris, 1928), p. 43.

172. *Judgment Meerut Conspiracy Case,* I, 235.

173. *Ibid.*

174. *New York Times,* August 17, 1928, p. 23.

175. Communist International, "Thesis on the Revolutionary Movement in the Colonies and Semi-Colonies," *International Press Correspondence,* (Vol. VIII, No. 49, December 12, 1928), p. 1659.

176. *Ibid.,* p. 1661.

177. *Ibid.,* pp. 1664-1666.

178. *Ibid.,* p. 1668.

179. *Ibid.,* p. 1670.

180. *Ibid.,* p. 1671.

181. *Judgment Meerut Conspiracy Case,* I, 238.

182. *Ibid.* The acceptance of the new line on India by Britain's Communists is indicated by Clement P. Dutt's article, "The Indian League for Independence," *Labour Monthly,* (Vol. XI, No. 1, January, 1929), pp. 22 ff.

183. Mohan Das, *Communist Activity in India, 1925-1950* (Bombay, 1951), p. 4. See also R. Palme Dutt, *India To-day,* p. 373.

184. For details see Workers' and Peasants' Party, "The Political Situation in India," *Labour Monthly,* (Vol. XI, No. 3, March, 1929), pp. 152 ff.

185. Bose, *op. cit.,* pp. 179-180.

186. Workers' and Peasants' Party, "The Political Situation in India," *loc. cit.,* p. 161.

187. *Ibid.,* pp. 161-162.

188. *The Tribune* (Lahore), December 5, 1929, p. 1.

189. *New York Times,* September 16, 1928, Sec. III, p. 7.

190. *The Tribune* (Lahore), December 5, 1929, p. 1.

191. *The Tribune* (Lahore), June 27, 1929, p. 2.

192. *Judgment Meerut Conspiracy Case,* I, 141.

193. See the unsigned article, "The Indian Labour Problem," *International Press Correspondence,* (Vol. XIII, No. 22, May 19, 1933), p. 619. See also Dyakov, *Indiya i Pakistan,* p. 21.

194. Masani, *op. cit.,* p. 34. For the attitude of Communists in India at this time, see the article by Philip Spratt, "India on

the Eve of Revolt," *Labour Monthly,* (Vol. XI, No. 5, May, 1929), pp. 285 ff. written just before his arrest for conspiracy.

195. See *Pravda,* May 27, 1929, p. 1.

196. *New York Times,* May 16, 1925, p. 2.

197. As cited in R. Palme Dutt, *India To-day,* p. 378.

198. Gandhi's hostility to Communism is well evinced in his correspondence with the Indian Communist M. P. in Westminster, Shapurji Saklatvala. See Shapurji Saklatvala *Is India Different?* (London, 1927), pp. 19 ff.

199. *The Times,* (London) January 31, 1925, p. 11.

200. *India in the Years 1927-1928,* p. 289.

201. For the text see *The Tribune* (Lahore), August 26, 1928, p. 1, September 12, 1928, p. 2, *The Times* (London), August 27, 1928, p. 12.

202. See the *Modern Review* (Calcutta), (Vol. XLIV, No. 261, October, 1928, p. 370, and the *Mahratta* (Poona), September 2, 1928, p. 448.

203. For details, see Government of India, *Legislative Assembly Debates,* III, 467 (1928) September 10, 1928, and III, 1354, September 24, 1928. Also see *The Tribune* (Lahore), September 9, 1928, pp. 12, September 1928, p. 2, September 26, 1928, p. 1.

204. *The Times* (London), January 22, 1929, p. 15.

205. *The Times* (London), January 29, 1929, p. 13.

206. Mitra, *The Indian Annual Register,* January-June, 1929, I, 173. See also *The Tribune* (Lahore), February 6, 1929, p. 1, February 7, 1929, p. 1, February 8, 1929, p. 1.

207. For details see *The Tribune* (Lahore), March 23, 1929, p. 1.

208. R. Palme Dutt, *India To-day,* p. 378.

209. Hutchinson, *op. cit.,* pp. 51 ff.

210. R. Palme Dutt, *India, To-day,* p. 378.

211. *The Tribune* (Lahore), April 14, 1929, p. 1.

212. For details of this law see Shelvankar, *op. cit.,* p. 210 and the *New York Times,* July 28, 1929, Sec. III, p. 8.

CHAPTER FOUR

1. *The Times* (London), April 4, 1929, p. 10, April 5, 1929, p. 14.

2. *The Times* (London), August 26, 1929, p. 11.

3. See *The Times* (London), May 30, 1930, p. 18 and also H. N. Brailsford, *Subject India* (London, 1943), p. 178.

4. See Muzaffar Ahmad, "Meerut Communist Conspiracy," *Amrita Bazar Patrika,* (Independence Number) August 15, 1947, p. 225.

5. See *The Times* (London), April 4, 1929, p. 10; April 5, 1929, p. 11; April 19, 1929, p. 16; and April 24, 1929, p. 15.

6. For details see *The Tribune* (Lahore), January 18, 1933, p. 1.

7. For details see *The Tribune* (Lahore), April 19, 1929, p. 1. and *The Times* (London), March 23, 1929, p. 14.

8. *The Times* (London), April 9, 1929, p. 15.

9. *Ibid.*

10. *Ibid.*

11. *Ibid.*

12. *Ibid.*

13. *Ibid.* See also Clement P. Dutt, "The Class Struggle in India," *Labour Monthly,* (Vol. XI, No. 7, July, 1929), pp. 404 ff. and "S," "The Trial of the Indian Revolutionaries," *Communist International,* (Vol. VI, No. 14, September 1, 1929), p. 781.

14. See Brailsford, *op. cit.,* pp. 177-178 and 257-258. Also see H. S. L. Polak, Brailsford, H. N. and Lord Pethwick-Lawrence in their *Mahatma Gandhi* (London, 1948), p. 352.

15. For the effect of the Labour Party's victory on Anglo-Soviet relations see W. P. and Zelda Coates, *A History of Anglo-Soviet Relations,* pp. 321 ff.

16. R. Palme Dutt, *India To-day,* pp. 380-381.

17. *The Times* (London), March 22, 1929, p. 16, *New York Times,* March 21, 1929, p. 10.

18. *The Tribune* (Lahore), March 23, 1929, p. 1.

19. See an editorial in the *Modern Review,* (Vol. XLV, No. 269, May, 1929), p. 630.

20. See *The Tribune* (Lahore), March 23, 1929, p. 8; the *Mahratta* (Poona), April 7, 1929, p. 7; and the *Modern Review,* (Vol. XLV, No. 268, April, 1929) p. 524.

21. See especially the *Mahratta,* April 14, 1929, p. 205.

22. *Ibid.*

23. Nehru, *Toward Freedom,* p. 142.

24. A. C. Underwood, *Contemporary Thought in India* (London, 1930), p. 91.

25. *The Times* (London), August 31, 1929, p. 9.
26. Hutchinson, *op. cit.,* p. 106.
27. *The Tribune* (Lahore), June 27, 1929, p. 1.
28. *The Tribune* (Lahore), December 3, 1929, p. 9.
29. *The Tribune* (Lahore), December 4, 1929, p. 2.
30. See "The Speech of the Prosecutor in the Meerut Case," Part 2, in *Labour Monthly* (Vol. XII, No. 2, February, 1930), p. 105.
31. *Ibid.,* p. 104.
32. "S," "Trial of the Indian Revolutionaries," *loc. cit.,* p. 787.
33. *Ibid.,* p. 788.
34. *Ibid.*
35. *Ibid.*
36. *Ibid.*
37. See "The Speech of the Prosecutor in the Meerut Case," Part 1 in *Labour Monthly,* (Vol. XII, No. 1, January, 1930), p. 26.
38. See "S," "Trial of the Indian Revolutionaries," *loc. cit.,* p. 786 and "The Speech of the Prosecutor in the Meerut Case," Part 1, *loc. cit.,* p. 27.
39. See *The Times* (London), December 2, 1929, p. 11.
40. *The Tribune* (Lahore), December 11, 1929, p. 1.
41. *The Tribune* (Lahore), December 10, 1929, p. 2.
42. *The Tribune* (Lahore), December 2, 1929, p. 2.
43. See *The Times* (London), July 10, 1929, p. 15; September 16, 1929, p. 11; and September 25, 1929, p. 11.
44. As quoted in K. L. Gauba, *Famous and Historic Trials* (Lahore, 1946), p. 15.
45. *Ibid.,* p. 16.
46. *Ibid.* For a similarly brazen utterance by Communist leader, Mirajkar, see the unsigned article, "Accused's Speeches at Meerut," *International Press Correspondence,* (Vol. XI, No. 21, April 23, 1931), p. 402.
47. Hutchinson, *op. cit.,* p. 99.
48. *Ibid.,* p. 104.
49. For details see *The Tribune* (Lahore), January 16, 1930, p. 2, and *The Times* (London), January 15, 1930, p. 13.
50. *The Times* (London), January 28, 1930, p. 14.
51. *The Tribune* (Lahore), January 18, 1933, p. 2.
52. See R. Palme Dutt, *India To-day,* p. 379 and Dyakov, *Indiya i Pakistan,* p. 22.
53. *The Tribune* (Lahore), January 18, 1933, p. 2.

54. *Ibid.*

55. For details see the unsigned article in the *Modern Review*, "Some Meerut Accused Give up Defence," (Vol. LI, No. 2, February, 1932), p. 239.

56. See *The Tribune* (Lahore), January 18, 1933, p. 2.

57. *Ibid.*

58. *The Times* (London), January 17, 1933, p. 17; *The Tribune* (Lahore), January 18, 1933, pp. 1-2.

59. For details of the sentences of the other accused see *Ibid.*

60. See Soumyendranath Tagore, "Meerut," *International Press Correspondence,* (Vol. XIV, No. 34, August 4, 1933), p. 748.

61. See R. Palme Dutt, *India To-day,* pp. 379-381.

62. N. Somin, "Meerut Trial in India and the Colonial Policy of the Labourites," *Communist,* (Vol. II, No. 3, July-August, 1950), p. 67.

63. *The Tribune* (Lahore), January 19, 1933, p. 8.

64. See the editorial in the *Mahratta,* January 22, 1933, p. 6.

65. Hutchinson, *op. cit.,* p. 81. For an American view sympathetic to the prisoners see the editorial captioned "Convict 29 of Red Conspiracy," in the *Christian Century,* (Vol. L, No. 8, February 22, 1933), p. 267.

66. R. Palme Dutt, *India To-day,* pp. 380-381.

67. See Brailsford, *op. cit.,* p. 258. It may be noted that in an earlier work, *Rebel India* (New York, 1931), pp. 82-83, he had also taken a marked interest in the Communist conspiracy case.

68. See *The Times* (London), January 17, 1933, p. 13.

69. *Ibid.*

70. *The Times* (London), April 12, 1933, p. 11.

71. *The Tribune* (Lahore), July 2, 1933, p. 2, *The Times,* (London) July 18, 1933, p. 8.

72. For details of the commutations of the sentences see *The Tribune* (Lahore), August 5, 1933, p. 1.

73. *Ibid.*

74. Office of Strategic Services, *op. cit.,* p. ii.

75. *The Times* (London), August 4, 1933, p. 9.

76. Dyakov, *Indiya i Pakistan,* p. 22.

77. The *Mahratta,* August 13, 1933, p. 6.

78. *The Tribune* (Lahore), August 6, 1933, p. 8.

79. Bose, *op. cit.,* pp. 180 ff.; Sitaramayya, *op. cit.,* I, 603 ff.

80. R. Palme Dutt, *India To-day,* p. 33; Bose, *op. cit.,* p. 217.

81. Mohammed Ali, "India in 1930," *Communist International,* (Vol. VIII, No. 34, February 1, 1934), pp. 106-107.

82. Bose, *op. cit.,* p. 287, Dyakov, *Indiya i Pakistan,* p. 17.

83. Mohammed Ali, *loc. cit.,* p. 105.

84. For details see Government of India (John Coatman editor), *India in 1931-1932,* (New Delhi, 1932) pp. 72-73; *India in 1932-1933,* (New Delhi, 1933) p. 52; and *India in 1934-1935* (New Delhi, 1935) p. 109.

85. *New York Times,* June 21, 1930, p. 9.

86. *India in 1931-1932,* p. 8.

87. *Ibid.*

88. See MacMunn, *op. cit.,* p. 269; an unsigned article "Crushing India's Red Shirts," *Literary Digest,* (Vol. CXII, No. 13, March 26, 1932), p. 18; *New York Times,* June 21, 1930, p. 9; and Patrick Lacey, *Fascist India,* (London, 1946), p. 96.

89. Bose, *op. cit.,* p. 267.

90. *Ibid.*

91. Sitaramayya, *op. cit.,* I, 849; see also *ibid.,* I, 709.

92. See Mohammed Ali, *loc. cit.,* p. 106, and R. Palme Dutt, *The Problem of India,* p. 146.

93. Agabekov, *op. cit.,* p. 191.

94. *Ibid.,* p. 192.

95. M. N. Roy. *Letters from Jail,* (Bombay, 1943) III, 283, and by the same author, *Revolution and Counter-Revolution in China,* (Calcutta, 1946), p. 538.

96. See Communist Party of France, *op. cit.,* p. 43.

97. *The Times* (London), December 5, 1929, p. 14.

98. Young Workers' League (of) Madras, "Mr. Roy's Services to Counter Revolution," *International Press Correspondence,* (Vol. XI, No. 55, October 29, 1931), p. 996.

99. This is acknowledged by M. N. Roy himself in the Preface to his unpublished manuscript *Alternative to Communism* (Calcutta, 1953).

100. *Ibid.*

101. See the unsigned article, "Mr. Roy in the Service of British Imperialism and the National Congress," *Communist International,* (Vol. VIII, No. 20, November 15, 1931), pp. 649 ff.

102. M. N. Roy, *I Accuse* (with introduction by Aswami Kurma Sharma) (New York, 1932), p. 6.

103. *Ibid.* (Sharma in Roy) p. 7.

104. *Ibid.*

105. *The Times* (London), July 22, 1931, p. 15.
106. Sharma in Roy, *op. cit.,* p. 7.
107. *Ibid.*
108. *Bombay Chronicle,* October 22, 1931, p. 1.
109. See the editorial, "The Conviction of M. N. Roy," *Modern Review,* (Vol. LI, No. 2, February, 1932), p. 239.
110. See the editorial, "Jawaharlal Nehru on M. N. Roy," *Modern Review,* (Vol. LIV, No. 5, November, 1933), p. 605.
111. "Mr. Roy in the Service of British Imperialism and the National Congress," *loc. cit.,* p. 649.
112. Jay Prakash Narayan, *Towards Struggle* (Bombay, 1946), pp. 164 ff.
113. Ralph Linton, editor, *Most of the World,* selection, "India and Pakistan" by Ralph Linton, (New York, 1949), p. 621.
114. Clare and Harris Wofford, *India Afire* (New York, 1951), pp. 255-256.
115. *Ibid.*
116. N. V. Rajkumar, *Indian Political Parties* (New Delhi, 1948), pp. 61-62.
117. Sitaramayya, *op. cit.,* I, 961.
118. Rajkumar, *op. cit.,* p. 62.
119. Payne, *op. cit.,* p. 114.
120. Lawrence K. Rosinger, editor, *The State of Asia,* selection "India" by Lawrence K. Rosinger, (New York, 1951), p. 475.
121. Rajkumar, *op. cit.,* p. 68.
122. Bose, *op. cit.,* p. 300.
123. See the editorial, "The Congress Socialist Party," in the *Modern Review,* (Vol. LVI, No. 1, July, 1934), p. 114.
124. For the general policy of the Congress towards the Congress Socialist movement, see Rajkumar, *op. cit.,* p. 63. See also *The Tribune* (Lahore), July 29, 1934, p. 1.
125. "The Congress Socialist Party," *loc. cit.,* pp. 113-114.
126. Rajkumar, *op. cit.,* p. 68.
127. *Ibid.,* p. 62.
128. Narayan, *op. cit.,* p. 160.
129. *Ibid.,* p. 162.
130. The *Mahratta,* June 12, 1935, p. 1.
131. Office of Strategic Services, *op. cit.,* p. 64.
132. Valiya, "The Struggle of the Working Class for the Leadership of the National Movement in India," *Communist International,* (Vol. VIII, No. 17, October 1, 1931), p. 521.

133. *Ibid.*

134. *Ibid.,* p. 525.

135. *Kranti,* June 16, 1929, p. 1.

136. See the unsigned article, "The Indian National Revolution," *Labour Monthly,* (Vol. XII, No. 6, June, 1930), p. 333. See also *Workers' Weekly,* May 20, 1929, p. 1.

137. K. S. Bhat, "The Workers' Welfare League of India," *Labour Monthly,* (Vol. III, No. 12, December, 1931), pp. 777-779.

138. Nehru, *Toward Freedom,* p. 127.

139. Central Committee, Communist Party of India, "Draft Platform of Action of the Communist Party of India," *International Press Correspondence,* (Vol. X, No. 58, December 18, 1930), pp. 1218 ff.

140. *Ibid.,* p. 1222.

141. Central Committee of the Communist Parties of China, Great Britain and Germany, "Open Letter to the Indian Communists," *Communist International,* (Vol. XI, No. 10, June 1, 1932), p. 349.

142. *Ibid.*

143. *Ibid.,* p. 353.

144. *Ibid.,* p. 350.

145. *Ibid.,* pp. 351, 353.

146. *Ibid.,* pp. 350-351.

147. *Ibid.,* p. 352.

148. *Ibid.,* p. 354.

149. *Ibid.,* pp. 354-357.

150. *Ibid.,* pp. 351, 357.

151. *Ibid.,* pp. 357-358.

152. See R. Palme Dutt, "The Path to Proletarian Hegenomy in the Indian Revolution," *Communist International,* (Vol. VII, No. 14, December 1, 1930), p. 315; Valiya, "The Struggle for Indian State Independence," *Communist International,* (Vol. XVIII, No. 20, November, 1931), p. 697; R. Page Arnot, "Report of the Simon Commission," *Labour Monthly,* (Vol. XII, No. 7, July, 1930), pp. 388 ff.; and Shapurji Saklatvala, "The Indian Round Table Conference," *Labour Monthly,* (Vol. XII, No. 12, December, 1930), pp. 720 ff.

153. See Hugo Rathbone, "The Place of the Peasantry in the Indian Revolution," *Labour Monthly,* (Vol. XII, No. 7, July, 1930), pp. 418 ff.; Shapurji Saklatvala, "The Second Round Table Conference," *Labour Monthly,* (Vol. XIII, No. 10, October,

1931), pp. 636 ff.; R. Palme Dutt, "India," *Labour Monthly,* (Vol. XIII, No. 5, May, 1931), pp. 259 ff.; R. Palme Dutt, "The Path to Proletarian Hegenomy in the Indian Revolution," *loc. cit.,* p. 315; Clemens P. Dutt, "The Class Struggle in India," *loc. cit.,* pp. 404 ff.; and an article by G. Safarov "The Present Moment in India," *Communist International,* (Vol. XV, No. 26, December 1, 1929), p. 1053. The latter had been Roy's colleague in Soviet Turkestan.

154. A particularly savage attack on the Mahatma was made by Shapurji Saklatvala, the Indian Communist member of the British Parliament who, however, was defeated in 1929 for reelection, in his article, "Who Is This Gandhi,?" *Labour Monthly,* (Vol. XII, No. 7, July, 1930), pp. 413 ff.

155. See Clemens P. Dutt, "The Role and Leadership of the Indian Working Class," *Labour Monthly,* (Vol. XI, No. 12, December, 1929), pp. 741 ff.; D. P. R. Gunawardena, "The Indian Masses Come Forward," *Labour Monthly,* (Vol. XIV, No. 2, February 1932), p. 92; Safarov, "The World Economic Crisis in Imperialism and the Development of the Revolutionary Ferment in the Colonies," *Communist International,* (Vol. VI, No. 3, February 15, 1930), p. 1233; Safarov, "The Treachery of the Indian National Congress and the Revolutionary Upsurge in India," *Communist International,* (Vol. VIII, No. 9, May 1, 1931), p. 264; Safarov, "The Present Moment in India," *loc. cit.,* p. 250; Valiya, "Prospects of the Labour Movement in India," *Communist International,* (Vol. VII, No. 12, October 15, 1930), p. 260; Valiya, "The Round Table Congress and the Indian National Congress," *Communist International,* (Vol. VIII, No. 2, January 15, 1931), pp. 105.

156. See Valiya, "The Strength of the Working Class for the Leadership of the National Movement in India," *Communist International,* (Vol. VIII, No. 17, October 1, 1931), p. 523; Gunawardena, *loc cit.,* p. 52; unsigned article, "The Treachery of the Indian National Congress and the Revolutionary Upsurge in India," *loc. cit.,* p. 263, and the unsigned article, "Mr. Roy in the Service of British Imperialism and the Indian National Congress," *Communist International,* (Vol. VIII, No. 20, November 15, 1931), p. 649.

157. Mohammed Ali, *loc. cit.,* p. 108.

158. See R. Page Arnot, "Notes on British Imperialism," *Communist International,* (Vol. VIII, No. 5, February 15, 1931), p.

125; R. Palme Dutt, "The Path to Proletarian Hegenomy in the Indian Revolution," *loc. cit.,* p. 315 and Saklatvala, "The Round Table Conference," *loc. cit.,* p. 723.

159. Bose, *op. cit.,* p. 192.

160. Office of Strategic Services, *op. cit.,* p. 47; Bose, *op. cit.,* p. 42.

161. All India Trade Union Congress, "Manifesto of the All-India Trade Union Congress," *Labour Monthly,* (Vol. XII, No. 3, March, 1930), p. 187.

162. See Sitaramayya, *op. cit.,* I, 583; Shelvankar, *op. cit.,* p. 214; Government of India (John Coatman, editor), *India in 1929-1930,* (New Delhi, 1930) p. 11, *The Tribune* (Lahore), June 16, 1929, p. 3; June 28, 1929, p. 4.

163. Clemens P. Dutt, "The Role and Leadership of the Indian Working Class, *loc. cit.,* p. 742; Safarov, "The Present Moment in India," *loc. cit.,* p. 1052.

164. Sitaramayya, *op. cit.,* I, 583, Shelvankar, *op. cit.,* p. 214.

165. R. Palme Dutt, *India To-day,* pp. 372-374, Desai, *op. cit.,* p. 327.

166. "W," "Prospects of the Labour Movement in India," *Communist International,* (Vol. XII, No. 7, October 15, 1930), pp. 257-258.

167. R. Palme Dutt, "The Path to Proletarian Hegenomy in the Indian Revolution," *loc. cit.,* p. 313; Valiya, "The Round Table Conference and the Indian National Congress," *loc. cit.,* p. 48; Safarov, "The Treachery of the National Congress and the Revolutionary Upsurge in India," *loc. cit.,* p. 261; and unsigned article, "The Split in the All-India Trade Union Congress," *Communist International,* (Vol. VIII, No. 18, October 15, 1931) p. 583.

168. Office of Strategic Services, *op. cit.,* p. 47; Bose *op. cit.,* pp. 42, 263-264.

169. Bose, *op. cit.,* p. 264.

170. For details see Communist International, Executive Committee, "The XI Plenum of the E.C.C.I." *International Press Correspondence,* (Vol. XI, No. 30, June 10, 1931), p. 552.

171. R. Palme Dutt, *India To-day,* pp. 372; "W," "Prospects of the Labour Movement in India," *loc. cit.,* pp. 258 ff.

172. Office of Strategic Services, *op. cit.,* p. 52.

173. Young Communist League of India, "Draft Platform of

Action of the Young Communist League of India," *International Press Correspondence,* (Vol. XII, No. 2, March 10, 1932), p. 231.

174. *Ibid.,* p. 228.

175. Orgwald, "A Conversation with Indian Comrades," *International Press Correspondence,* (Vol. XIV, No. 20, March 29, 1934), pp. 519 ff.

176. Communist Party of China, Central Committee, "Open Letter to the Indian Communists," *International Press Correspondence,* (Vol. XIII, No. 51, November 24, 1933), p. 1153.

177. *Ibid.,* pp. 1154-1155.

178. *Ibid.,* p. 1155.

179. See Madhu Limaye, *Communist Party; Facts and Fiction,* (Hyderabad, India, 1951), p. 23; and Office of Strategic Services, *op. cit.,* p. 4.

180. Office of Strategic Services, p. ix.

181. *Ibid.*

182. Dyakov, *Indiya vo vremya i posle vtoroi mirovoi voine,* p. 33.

183. Communist Party of India, Central Committee, "Abridged Draft of the Political Thesis of the Central Committee of the Communist Party of India," *International Press Correspondence,* (Vol. XIV, No. 40, July 20, 1934), p. 1024.

184. *Ibid.,* p. 1025.

185. *Ibid.,* p. 1026.

186. *Ibid.,* p. 1028.

187. *Ibid.,* p. 1029.

188. *Ibid.,* pp. 1029-1030.

189. *Ibid.,* p. 1031.

190. *Ibid.*

191. See *Bombay Chronicle,* May 30, 1934, and League Against Imperialism, "Crushing the Working Classes in India," *International Press Correspondence,* (Vol. XIV, No. 44, August 17, 1934), p. 1139.

192. See *The Tribune* (Lahore), July 29, 1934, p. 1. for the official notification in full as published in the "Gazette of India."

193. R. Palme Dutt, *The Problem of India,* p. 393.

194. League Against Imperialism, *loc. cit.,* p. 1139.

195. *The Times of India* (Bombay), July 31, 1934, p. 8.

196. The *Mahratta,* August 5, 1934, p. 8.

197. *Ibid.*

198. 292 H. C. Deb. 5s, pp. 2253-2254.

199. See R. Palme Dutt, "The Meaning of the Indian Constitutional Proposals," *International Press Correspondence,* (Vol. XIV, No. 60, December 1, 1934), pp. 1597-1599; R. Page Arnot, "The Sham Constitution of India," *International Press Correspondence,* (Vol. XIII, No. 31, July 14, 1933), p. 683; Reginald Bridgeman, "The New Deal for India," *Labour Monthly,* (Vol. XVII, No. 1, January, 1935), pp. 20 ff.; Lester Hutchinson, "The New Imperialist Strategy in India," *Labour Monthly,* (Vol. XVII, No. 2, February, 1935), pp. 107 ff.; V. Basak, "The Present Situation in India," Part I, *International Press Correspondence,* (Vol. XIII, No. 39, September 8, 1933), pp. 853-854; Part II, *Ibid.,* (Vol. XIII, No. 41, September 15, 1933), p. 896; Part III, *Ibid.,* (Vol. XIII, No. 43, September 29, 1933), p. 946; Valiya, "The Constitution for the Enslavement of the Indian People and the Policy of the Indian Bourgeoisie," *Communist International,* (Vol. X, No. 11, June 15, 1933), pp. 385 ff; and a contribution from the just released from prison Ben Bradley, "The Background in India," *Labour Monthly,* (Vol. XVI, No. 3, March, 1934), pp. 173 ff.

200. See V. Basak, "A Few Remarks on the Communist Movement," *International Press Correspondence,* (Vol. XIV, No. 32, June 1, 1934), pp. 846-848.

201. See Ben Bradley, "What the Congress Socialists Want," *International Press Correspondence,* (Vol. XIV, No. 63, December 15, 1934), pp. 1694 ff. For Comintern attacks upon the "Royists," see the unsigned article, "India, a Few Facts of History," *International Press Correspondence,* (Vol. XIV, No. 8, February 9, 1934), p. 225.

202. See the unsigned article, "Problems of the Anti-Imperialist Struggle in India," *International Press Correspondence,* (Vol. XV, No. 10, March 9, 1935), p. 289.

203. D. F. Karaka, *Betrayal in India* (London, 1950), p. 238.

204. Puran Chandra Joshi, *For the Final Bid to Power* (Bombay, 1947), p. 122.

205. The *Mahratta,* June 12, 1935, p. 1.

206. See *New Age* (Delhi), October 4, 1953, p. 3.

207. See *The Times* (London), September 19, 1935, p. 11.

208. *The Times* (London), November 28, 1935, p. 8.

209. Office of Strategic Services, *op. cit.,* p. 48.

210. *India in 1933-1934,* pp. 10-11; Bose, *op. cit.,* p. 308.

211. See R. Palme Dutt, *The Problem of India,* p. 393; and Bose, *op. cit.,* p. 308.

212. R. Palme Dutt, *India To-day,* pp. 371-373.

213. M. Muzaffar, "India's Fight Against the India Bill," *Labour Monthly,* (Vol. XVII, No. 5, May, 1935), p. 305; Office of Strategic Services, *op. cit.,* p. 48.

CHAPTER FIVE

1. Communist International, *VII Congress of the Communist International* (Moscow, 1936), p. 299.

2. *Ibid.*

3. *Ibid.*

4. Georgi Dimitrov, *The United Front Against War and Fascism,* (address delivered at the Seventh World Congress July 25–August 20, 1935) (New York, 1936), p. 67.

5. Georgi Dimitrov, "The Offensive of Fascism and the Tasks of the C. I. in the Struggle for the Unity of the Working Class against Fascism," *International Press Correspondence,* (Vol. XV, No. 43, September 7, 1935), pp. 1221 ff.

6. R. Palme Dutt and Bradley, Ben "The Anti-Imperialist People's Front," *International Press Correspondence,* (Vol. XVI, No. 11, February 29, 1936), p. 297.

7. *Ibid.*

8. Harry Pollitt, Dutt, R. Palme and Bradley, Ben for the Communist Party of Great Britain, Central Committee, "Letter to the Indian Communists," *International Press Correspondence,* (Vol. XVI, No. 50, November 17, 1936), p. 1342.

9. *Ibid.*

10. *Ibid.*

11. *Ibid.*

12. *Ibid.,* pp. 1342-1343.

13. Dutt and Bradley, "The Anti-Imperialist Front," *loc. cit.,* p. 299.

14. *Ibid.*

15. For details see S. Krishna, "After the Lucknow Conference," *International Press Correspondence,* (Vol. XVI, No. 30, June 27, 1936), p. 804.

16. Ben Bradley, "Indian National Congress—Tripuri Session,"

World News and Views, (Vol. XIX, No. 18, April 1, 1939), p. 366.

17. V. K. Krishna Menon, "India and World Peace," *Labour Monthly,* (Vol. XX, No. 6, June, 1938), pp. 375 ff. This is the first but not the last article by this noted Indian in Communist publications to be noted here.

18. Statement: "Indian Communists Greet Haripura," in Ben Bradley, "India—the Haripura Session," *Labour Monthly,* (Vol. XX, No. 4, April, 1938), pp. 243-244.

19. Ben Bradley, Dutt, R. Palme and Pollitt, Harry (for the Communist Party of Great Britain), "Greetings to the Indian National Congress, Haripura Session," *International Press Correspondence,* (Vol. XVIII, No. 6, February 1, 1938), p. 113.

20. Communist Party of Great Britain, Central Committee, "Greetings to the Indian National Congress," *World News and Views,* (Vol. XIX, No. 10, March 11, 1939), p. 199.

21. Montagu Slater, "The Indian National Congress," *International Press Correspondence,* (Vol. XVI, No. 1, January 4, 1936), p. 14.

22. See *Labour Monthly* (Vol. XVIII, No. 5, May, 1936), pp. 282 ff. for the complete text of Nehru's presidential address at the Lucknow session of the Congress and *ibid.,* (Vol. XIX, No. 2, February, 1937), pp. 980 ff. for the complete text of his presidential address at the Faizpur session of the Congress.

23. See Montagu Slater, "The Indian National Congress and the Future," *International Press Correspondence,* (Vol. XVI, No. 2, February 8, 1936), p. 218.

24. Krishna, *loc. cit.,* p. 804.

25. Jawaharlal Nehru, "Nationalism and the Mass Struggle in India," *Labour Monthly,* (Vol. XX, No. 8, August, 1938), pp. 476 ff.

26. For criticism of Gandhi see, "A. R." "The Congress Movement without the Assemblies," *International Press Correspondence,* (Vol. XVIII, No. 46, October 30, 1937), p. 1059, and Ben Bradley, "The Indian National Congress—Tripuri Session, (*loc. cit.*), p. 367. For criticism of Bose see *ibid.,* and also Ben Bradley, "Indian Nationalism after Tripuri," *Labour Monthly,* (Vol. XXI, No. 5, May, 1939), p. 301.

27. Dutt and Bradley, "The Anti-Imperialist Front," *loc. cit.,* p. 299.

28. *Ibid.,* p. 300.

29. See Ben Bradley and Dutt, R. Palme, "Towards Trade

Union Unity in India," *International Press Correspondence,* (Vol. XVI, No. 12, March 7, 1936), pp. 325 ff.

30. See Montagu Slater, "India after the Elections," *International Press Correspondence,* (Vol. XVII, No. 10, March 6, 1937), p. 266. See also Ben Bradley, "A New Phase in the Struggle for Freedom," *International Press Correspondence,* (Vol. XVII, No. 16, April 10, 1937), pp. 400-401.

31. Dutt and Bradley, "The Anti-Imperialist Front," *loc. cit.,* p. 299.

32. *Ibid.,* p. 300.

33. See R. Bishop, "The Present Situation in India," *International Press Correspondence,* (Vol. XVI, No. 54, December 5, 1936), p. 1444, and Bradley, "Indian Nationalism after Tripuri," *loc. cit.,* p. 297.

34. Ben Bradley, "The Indian Elections," *Labour Monthly,* (Vol. XIX, No. 4, April, 1937), p. 240.

35. Acharya Narendra Deva, *Socialism and the National Revolution* (Bombay, 1946), p. 151.

36. See Ajoy K. Ghosh, "Indian States' Repressive Rule," *World News and Views,* (Vol. XIX, No. 4, January 28, 1939), pp. 82-83; "A. R." "Civil and Personal Liberties in Native States," *International Press Correspondence,* (Vol. XVIII, No. 4, January 29, 1938), pp. 78-79.

37. B. Singh, "The Position of the Working People," *World News and Views,* (Vol. XIX, No. 20, April 5, 1939), p. 448.

38. See Dutt and Bradley, "The Anti-Imperialist Front," *loc. cit.,* p. 297.

39. K. Tilak, *Rise and Fall of the Comintern,* (Bombay, 1947), p. 121.

40. Minoo R. Masani, "The Communists in India," *Pacific Affairs,* (Vol. XXIV, No. 1, March, 1951), p. 22.

41. Linton, *op. cit.,* p. 22, Masani, "The Communists in India," *loc. cit.,* p. 22.

42. Office of Strategic Services, *op. cit.,* pp. 59 ff.

43. Masani, *The Communist Party of India,* p. 74.

44. Office of Strategic Services, *op. cit.,* p. 24.

45. Narayan, *op. cit., p.* 143.

46. *Ibid.*

47. Ajoy K. Ghosh, "Before the Tripuri Conference," *World News and Views,* (Vol. XIX, No. 10, March 1, 1939), pp. 192-193.

48. Office of Strategic Services, *op. cit.,* p. 26.

49. Narayan, *op. cit.,* p. 143.

50. *Ibid.*

51. Narayan, *op. cit.,* p. 170.

52. See Masani, "The Communists in India," *loc. cit.,* p. 22.

53. *Ibid.*

54. Narayan, *op. cit.,* p. 171.

55. Narayan, *op. cit.,* pp. 170-171, Masani, "The Communists in India," *loc. cit.,* p. 22.

56. Narayan, *op. cit.,* p. 171.

57. Modan Gopal, "Leftism in Indian Politics," *Current History,* (Vol. XIII, No. 72, August, 1947), p. 88.

58. See Narayan, *op. cit.,* p. 171.

59. *Ibid.,* p. 172.

60. *Ibid.,* p. 174.

61. See Minoo R. Masani, *Socialism Reconsidered* (Bombay, 1944), pp. 28-29, and Narayan, *op. cit.,* pp. 175-176.

62. Narayan, *op. cit.,* pp. 176-178.

63. Masani, "The Communists in India," *loc. cit.,* p. 22.

64. R. Palme Dutt, *India To-day,* p. 472.

65. "Indian Correspondent," "Russia's Grip on India," *Saturday Review* (London), (Vol. XLXII, No. 4237, December 18, 1936), p. 783.

66. Nath, *loc. cit.,* p. 152.

67. "A. R." "The Annual Session of the All-India Trade Union Congress," *International Press Correspondence,* (Vol. XVIII, No. 7, February 14, 1938), p. 134.

68. *Indian Year Book, 1939-1940,* (Bombay, 1940), p. 575.

69. For details see Office of Strategic Services, *op. cit.,* p. 48.

70. Ramesh C. Majumdar, Raychaudhuri, H. C., Dutta, Kalikinkar, *An Advanced History of India* (London, 1948), p. 955.

71. See Krishnalal Shridharani, *War Without Violence* (New York, 1939), p. 17, and International Labor Organization, *Industrial Labour in India,* (Geneva, 1938) p. 134.

72. R. Palme Dutt, *India To-day,* pp. 371-372.

73. For details see L. Burns, "The Strike Struggle in India," *Communist International,* (Vol. XV, No. 1-2, January-February, 1938), pp. 95-96.

74. Burns, *loc. cit.,* p. 96.

75. Michael Carritt, "India Before the Storm," *Labour Monthly,* (Vol. XXII, No. 5, May, 1940), p. 299; Bradley, "Indian Nationalism after Tripuri," *loc. cit.,* p. 197; Burns, *loc. cit.,* p. 97.

76. R. Palme Dutt, *India To-day,* p. 384; Bradley, "Indian Nationalism after Tripuri," *loc. cit.,* p. 197.

77. Ben Bradley, "India's Workers' Great One Day Strike," *Labour Monthly,* (Vol. XXI, No. 1, January, 1939), pp. 46 ff., R. Palme Dutt, *India To-day,* p. 468.

78. See Burns, *loc. cit.,* p. 98.

79. Office of Strategic Services, *op. cit.,* p. 53.

80. Shelvankar, *op. cit.,* p. 223.

81. Masani, *The Communist Party of India,* p. 68.

82. See B. Shiva Rao, "New Social Forces in India," *Foreign Affairs,* (Vol. XXIII, No. 4, July, 1945), p. 639. See also Shelvankar, *op. cit.,* pp. 219 ff.

83. Shelvankar, *op. cit.,* p. 224.

84. Karaka, *op. cit.,* p. 239.

85. Office of Strategic Services, *op. cit.,* p. 54.

86. Karaka, *op. cit.,* p. 239.

87. Akademiya Nauk, S.S.S.R., *Krizis kolonialnoi systema* (Moscow, 1951), p. 92; Dyakov, *Indiya i Pakistan,* p. 27; O'Malley, *op. cit.,* p. 106; Karaka, *op. cit.,* p. 239.

88. Karaka, *op. cit.,* p. 239.

89. O'Malley, *op. cit.,* p. 196.

90. Shelvankar, *op. cit.,* p. 239.

91. Office of Strategic Services, *op. cit.,* p. 54.

92. Indian National Congress, *Report of the General Secretary* (New Delhi, 1936), p. 8.

93. Burns, *loc. cit.,* pp. 97-98.

94. Masani, *The Communist Party of India,* pp. 71-72.

95. Puran Chandra Joshi, *The Indian Communist Party,* (Foreword by Harry Pollitt) (London, 1942), p. 1.

96. Burns, *loc. cit.,* p. 97.

97. Montagu Slater, "Government Frames up Another Communist Conspiracy," *International Press Correspondence,* (Vol. XVI, No. 14, March 14, 1936), p. 376.

98. *Bombay Chronicle,* February 6, 1936, p. 1.

99. *The Times* (London), February 14, 1936, p. 13.

100. *The Times* (London), June 5, 1936, p. 11.

101. *Ibid.*

102. See "Indian Correspondent," "The Soviet Hand in India," *Saturday Review* (London), (Vol. CLXII, No. 4235, December 5, 1936), p. 725.

103. *Ibid.*

104. See R. Bishop, "Imperialism's Handiwork in India," *International Press Correspondence,* (Vol. XVI, No. 42, September 12, 1936), pp. 1153-1154. See also his article, "The Present Situation in India," *loc. cit.,* p. 1444.

105. Ben Bradley, "The Indian National Congress and Ministries," *International Press Correspondence,* (Vol. XVII, No. 41, September 25, 1937), p. 926.

106. "A. R." "The Situation in India," *loc. cit.,* p. 1385.

107. *New Age* (Delhi), October 4, 1953, p. 2.

108. *Ibid.*

109. Rabindranath Tagore, "The Soviet System," *Modern Review,* (Vol. L, No. 3, September, 1931), pp. 252-253.

110. Rabindranath Tagore, "On Russia," *Modern Review,* (Vol. LV, No. 6, June, 1934), p. 617.

111. Unsigned article in *Modern Review,* (Vol. XLVIII, No. 5, November, 1930), p. 534.

112. *Ibid.*

113. Rabindranath Tagore, "On Russia," *loc. cit.,* p. 620.

114. Sitaramayya, *op. cit.,* I, 620.

115. *Ibid.,* I, 782.

116. As quoted in Bose, *op. cit.,* p. 346.

117. As cited in Patricia Kendall, *India and the British* (London, 1931), p. 426.

118. Taraknath Das, "Indian Nationalism and Bolshevism," *Calcutta Review,* (Vol. XXXV, No. 3, June, 1930), p. 326.

119. Jawaharlal Nehru, *Important Speeches,* Being a Collection of Most Significant Speeches Delivered by Jawaharlal Nehru from 1922 to 1946, edited by J. S. Bright (Lahore, 1946), p. 94.

120. *Ibid.,* pp. 94-95.

121. *Ibid.,* pp. 102, 311.

122. *Communist,* (Vol. I, No. 12, December, 1936), p. 16.

123. Nehru, *Toward Freedom,* (appendix) p. 402.

124. *Ibid.,* p. 424.

125. *Ibid.*

126. Jawaharlal Nehru, *The Unity of India,* Collected Writings, (New York, 1948), essay—"From Lucknow to Tripuri, A Survey of Congress Politics," p. 117; essay—"The Choice Before Us," p. 296.

127. Nehru, "From Lucknow to Tripuri, A Survey of Congress Politics," *loc. cit.,* pp. 119 ff.

128. Nehru, *The Discovery of India,* pp. 401 ff.

129. Nehru, "From Lucknow to Tripuri, A Survey of Congress Politics," *loc. cit.*, p. 116.

130. *Ibid.*, p. 113.

131. As quoted in Menon, *loc. cit.*, p. 377.

132. See Iqbal Singh, *India's Foreign Policy,* (Bombay, 1946), p. 21.

133. *The Tribune* (Lahore), March 13, 1939, pp. 1, 16.

134. Mitra, *The Indian Annual Register,* July-December, 1936, II, 384.

135. As quoted in Menon, *loc. cit.*, p. 377.

136. Jagadisan M. Kumarappa, "Russia on the March," *Modern Review,* (Vol. XLIX, No. 6, June, 1931), p. 656.

137. Nitya N. Banerjee, "My First Day in Leningrad," *Modern Review,* (Vol. LIV, No. 6, December, 1933), p. 689.

138. Nitya N. Banerjee, "Russia Today," *Modern Review,* (Vol. LV, No. 2, February, 1934), p. 144. By the same writer, "Art and Literature in Russia Today," *Modern Review,* (Vol. LV, No. 5, May, 1934), pp. 567 ff.

139. G. S. Khair, "Liquidation of Illiteracy in Soviet Russia," *Modern Review,* (Vol. LV, No. 4, April, 1934), p. 419.

140. "C. A." "Russia and the Five Year Plan," *Modern Review,* (Vol. L, No. 6, December, 1931), pp. 621-622.

141. Prafulla C. Mukherjee, "Russia and Opportunities for Technical Men from India," *Modern Review,* (Vol. LIII, No. 3, March, 1933), p. 277.

142. N. I. Tcelyapov, "Higher Schools of the Soviet Union," *Modern Review,* (Vol. XLVI, No. 11, November, 1929), pp. 554 ff.

143. For example, see Mahmud Husan, "Soviet Policy, Old and New," *Calcutta Review,* (Vol. LV, No. 1, May, 1935), pp. 180-182.

144. Editorial, "The New Peril in India," *Feudatory and Zamindary Review,* (Vol. VI, No. 9, May, 1936), p. 456.

145. *The Tribune* (Lahore), October 10, 1937, p. 2.

146. *Young India,* May 1, 1920, p. 18; *Young India,* November 24, 1921, p. 510.

147. *Young India,* October 11, 1924, p. 406.

148. Saklatvala, *Is India Different?* p. 19.

149. *Ibid.*, pp. 21 ff.

150. *Young India,* March 26, 1931, p. 53.

151. *Harijan,* February 13, 1937, p. 45.

152. *Harijan,* January 28, 1939, p. 438.

153. *Young India,* March 26, 1931, p. 35. See also the work on this subject by Gandhi's disciple, Richard B. Gregg, *Gandhism and Socialism* (Madras, 1931) p. 36, who considered Gandhism "more effective than Socialism."

154. *Harijan,* February 13, 1937, p. 45.

155. *Harijan,* March 13, 1937, p. 152.

156. See Orgwald, *loc. cit.,* p. 532.

157. *Ibid.*

158. *Young India,* July 2, 1932, p. 251.

159. *Young India,* March 26, 1931, p. 53. See also Louis Fischer, *Gandhi* (New York, 1954), p. 88. and an article in the *Literary Digest,* (Vol. CVIII, No. 12, March 21, 1931), p. 13.

160. Werner Levi, *Free India in Asia* (Minneapolis, 1952), p. 82.

161. *Servant of India,* November 10, 1938, p. 555.

162. Bradley, "The Indian National Congress and Ministries," *loc. cit.,* p. 296; "A. R." "The Congress Movement without the Assemblies," *loc. cit.,* p. 1059.

163. Bradley, "Indian Workers' Great One-Day Strike," *loc. cit.,* p. 46; Bradley, "The Indian National Congress and Ministries," *loc. cit.,* p. 46.

CHAPTER SIX

1. *India in the Years 1922-1923,* p. 30.
2. *Ibid.*
3. Fuse, *op. cit.,* p. 123.
4. For details see *India in the Years 1923-1924,* pp. 27-28; *New York Times,* December 20, 1923, p. 3; Fraser-Tytler, *op. cit.,* p. 204.
5. *New York Times,* December 20, 1923, p. 3.
6. *New York Times,* December 21, 1923 p. 5.
7. *India in the Years 1923-1924,* p. 29.
8. See *Izvestia,* April 20, 1924, p. 2.
9. Agabekov, *op. cit.,* p. 42.
10. *Ibid.,* pp. 45 ff.
11. *Ibid.,* p. 55.
12. *Ibid.,* pp. 44 ff.
13. *Ibid.,* p. 56.

14. Masani, *The Communist Party of India,* p. 22.
15. Agabekov, *op. cit.,* pp. 59 ff.
16. *Ibid.*
17. *Ibid.,* pp. 66-68.
18. *India in the Years 1924-1925,* p. 12; Fraser-Tytler, *op. cit.,* pp. 204-205.
19. *India in the Years 1924-1925,* p. 12.
20. For details of this island incident, see Agabekov, *op. cit.,* pp. 69 ff., Fraser-Tytler, *op. cit.,* p. 219; *The Times* (London), December 28, 1925, p. 12; December 29, 1925, p. 13; March 5, 1926, p. 13; March 6, 1926, p. 13; March 30, 1926, p. 13.
21. Agabekov, *op. cit.,* p. 66.
22. See the unsigned article in *Literary Digest,* "The Bolshevik Menace to India," (Vol. LXXXVIII, No. 12, March 20, 1926), pp. 16-17.
23. Agabekov, *op. cit.,* p. 66.
24. *Ibid.*
25. See "The Bolshevik Menace to India," *loc. cit.,* pp. 16-17.
26. Agabekov, *op. cit.,* p. 158.
27. For details of the treaty see *New York Times,* October 10, 1925, p. X. 13.
28. See Fraser-Tytler, *op. cit.,* p. 221. See also *The Times* (London), September 14, 1926, p. 13.
29. *The Times* (London), November 7, 1926, p. 8.
30. *The Times* (London), May 9, 1927, p. 15; June 10, 1927, p. 14.
31. Agabekov, *op. cit.,* p. 158.
32. *The Times* (London), March 7, 1928, p. 15.
33. *New York Times,* May 4, 1928, p. 6; May 7, 1928, p. II, 3.
34. *Izvestia,* May 3, 1928, p. 3.
35. Agabekov, *op. cit.,* p. 162.
36. Agabekov, *op. cit.,* p. 164; Fraser-Tytler, *op. cit.,* pp. 213-215.
37. See Felix Howland, "Afghanistan Has no Frontiers," *Asia,* (Vol. XL, No. 12, December, 1940), p. 634.
38. Castagne, *loc. cit.,* p. 701.
39. Agabekov, *op. cit.,* pp. 164-165.
40. *Ibid.,* p. 166.
41. Fraser-Tytler, *op. cit.,* p. 217.
42. Agabekov, *op. cit.,* pp. 166-167.
43. *Ibid.,* pp. 167-168.

44. For details see Fraser-Tytler, *op. cit.,* p. 217; see also *New York Times,* May 24, 1929, p. 5.
45. Agabekov, *op. cit.,* p. 168.
46. Castagne, *loc. cit.,* p. 702.
47. Agabekov, *op. cit.,* p. 168.
48. Fedor Raskolnikov, "The War in Afghanistan," *Labour Monthly,* (Vol. XI, No. 3, March 1929), pp. 181 ff.
49. *New York Times,* October 10, 1929, p. 4; October 24, 1929, p. 10; November 3, 1929, p. 1; Fraser-Tytler, *op. cit.,* p. 222, unsigned article, "No Buffer—Afghans Play Both Ends Against the Middle," *Literary Digest,* (Vol. CXXIII, No. 2, July 10, 1937), pp. 13-14.
50. Agabekov, *op. cit.,* pp. 169-170.
51. *Ibid.*
52. Fraser-Tytler, *op. cit.,* p. 230.
53. *Ibid.*
54. *Ibid.* See also *The Times* (London), July 9, 1931, p. 13.
55. Fraser-Tytler, *op. cit.,* p. 227; Castagne, *loc. cit.,* p. 703.
56. Howland, *loc. cit.,* p. 634; *New York Times,* November 9, 1933, p. 1.
57. Howland, *loc. cit.,* p. 635.
58. *Ibid.*
59. Castagne, *loc. cit.,* p. 703.
60. *India in the Years 1922-1923,* p. 30.
61. Lenczowski, *op. cit.,* pp. 95-96.
62. For details of this intrigue, see Agabekov, *op. cit.,* pp. 73-74.
63. *Ibid.*
64. *Ibid.,* p. 90.
65. *Ibid.,* p. 88.
66. *Ibid.,* pp. 140 ff.
67. See "The Bolshevik Menace to India," *loc. cit.,* p. 17.
68. David J. Dallin, *Soviet Russia and the Far East,* (New Haven, Connecticut, 1943), p. 193; Wilbur Burton, "Tug of War in Central Asia," *Asia,* (Vol. VI, No. 9, September, 1935), pp. 517-520.
69. Dallin, *op. cit.,* pp. 93 ff.; Barmine, *op. cit.,* p. 231; and Burton, *loc. cit.,* p. 519.
70. Dallin, *op. cit.,* p. 97.
71. *Ibid.,* pp. 97-98.
72. *Ibid.,* p. 100.
73. *Ibid.*

74. See Burton, *loc. cit.*, p. 517.
75. Masani, *The Communist Party of India,* p. 23.
76. Amaury de Riencourt, *Roof of the World,* (New York, 1950), pp. 185-186.
77. Masani, *The Communist Party of India,* p. 23.
78. *Pravda,* July 27, 1932, p. 2.
79. Masani, *The Communist Party of India,* p. 273.
80. *Ibid.*, p. 46.
81. *Ibid.*, p. 47.
82. *The Times* (London), March 17, 1921, p. 11.
83. *The Times* (London), February 2, 1924, p. 10.
84. See J. A. R. Marriott, *Anglo-Russian Relations, 1689-1943* (London, 1943), p. 191 and Foreign Office, *Blue Book,* pp. 28-33.
85. W. P. and Zelda Coates, *A History of Anglo-Soviet Relations,* pp. 228 ff.
86. See Sir Stanley Reed and Cadell, P. R. *India, the New Phase* (London, 1928), p. 72; *New York Times,* July 9, 1926, p. 21. For an American view of the Soviet threat to India see Katherine Mayo, *Mother India* (New York, 1927), pp. 322-323.
87. Agabekov, *op. cit.*, pp. 92 ff.
88. Foreign Office, *Blue Book,* pp. 45-50, especially p. 47. Agabekov (*op. cit.*, p. 93) observes the Soviet Government was "much troubled" by the British representations.
89. W. B. Middleton, *Britain and Russia* (London, 1946), p. 129; W. P. and Zelda Coates, *A History of Anglo-Soviet Relations,* p. 268.
90. See *New York Times,* June 30, 1927, p. 15; and W. P. and Zelda Coates, *A History of Anglo-Soviet Relations,* p. 268.
91. Foreign Office, *Blue Book,* pp. 69 ff.
92. As quoted in W. P. and Zelda Coates, *A History of Anglo-Soviet Relations,* p. 299.
93. 206 H. C., deb. 5s, pp. 2171 and 2197 ff.
94. *New York Times,* June 30, 1927, p. 15.
95. *Pravda,* April 28, 1929, p. 4.
96. *Izvestia,* June 12, 1929, p. 3.
97. *Ibid.*
98. Unsigned article, "League against Imperialism," *Modern Review,* (Vol. XLVI, No. 2, August, 1929), p. 230.
99. Communist International, Executive Committee, "Manifesto to India," *International Press Correspondence,* (Vol. IX, No. 57, November 1, 1929), pp. 1485-1488.

100. *Izvestia,* February 9, 1930, p. 3.

101. Joseph Stalin, *Political Report to the Sixteenth Party Congress of the Russian Communist Party* (London, 1930), p. 19.

102. See 234 H. C. Deb. 5s, p. 1478.

103. See 235 H. C. Deb. 5s, p. 899.

104. See 238 H. C. Deb. 5s, pp. 1428-1429 and 239 H. C. Deb. 5s, pp. 830-831 and pp. 1478-1479.

105. See *The Times* (London), June 19, 1930, p. 14 regarding alleged Communist activity in the Peshawar area.

106. See *The Times* (London), May 22, 1930, p. 15; June 18, 1930, p. 13, and August 19, 1930, p. 12.

107. For details of Molotov's report see Royal Institute of International Affairs, *op. cit.,* II, 465. In 1930 Molotov announced "it is essential to form a Communist Party of India for none has ever existed," obviously an insult to M. N. Roy who had been a short time before expelled from the Comintern. (Payne, *op. cit.,* p. 113).

108. *The Times* (London), February 2, 1931, p. 12.

109. *The Times* (London), February 5, 1931, p. 11.

110. *Pravda,* April 3, 1931, p. 3.

111. *The Times* (London), April 25, 1931, p. 12.

112. *The Times* (London), April 28, 1931, p. 16.

113. *Ibid.*

114. See 248 H. C. Deb. 5s, p. 1734; and 251 H. C. Deb. 5s, pp. 1356 and 1612.

115. For full details of the discussion see 252 H. C. Deb. 5s, p. 1356.

116. For details of this program which called for the "violent destruction of the British political and economic power" in India see *Pravda,* May 9, 1931, p. 3.

117. See 252 H. C. Deb. 5s, pp. 1619 ff., especially p. 1630.

118. *Ibid.*

119. *Ibid.*

120. *Ibid.* See also 253 H. C. Deb. 5s, p. 602.

121. See 257 H. C. Deb. 5s, pp. 783, 1882.

122. See *Pravda,* August 16, 1931, p. 3. For concern over Soviet radio propaganda beamed to India see *The Times* (London), January 25, 1932, p. 13.

123. See *Izvestia,* November 15, 1932, p. 1.

124. See W. P. and Zelda Coates, *A History of Anglo-Soviet Relations,* p. 504.

125. For details of the Soviet "catechism" intended for the benefit of Indian Communists, see *The Times* (London), November 9, 1953, p. 11.

126. See 281 H. C. Deb. 5s, p. 551.

127. See *The Times* (London), June 2, 1934, p. 13.

128. See the leading article, "Moscow Indians Rounded Up," *Calcutta Review,* (Vol. LXVII, No. 3, June, 1938), p. 338.

It may be noted that Chattopadhyaya had been a contributor to Communist publications. See his articles, "The Capitulation of the Indian Bourgeoisie," in *International Press Correspondence,* (Vol. XI, No. 15, March 19, 1931), p. 285, and "The Indian National Congress," *Labour Monthly,* (Vol. XIII, No. 5, May, 1931), pp. 303.

129. *The Times* (London), September 13, 1929, p. 16.

130. "Moscow Indians Rounded Up," *op. cit.,* p. 338.

CHAPTER SEVEN

1. Masani, "The Communists in India," *loc. cit.,* p. 23.

2. Dyakov, *Indiya vo vremya i posle vtoroi mirovoi voini,* p. 15. He claims that "the leading role in this conference was played by the Indian Communists."

3. B. Ashe, "The Anti-War Movement in India," *World News and Views,* (Vol. XIX, No. 58, December 16, 1939), p. 111.

4. Dyakov, *Indiya vo vremya i posle vtoroi mirovoi voini,* p. 17; R. Palme Dutt, *India Today,* (Bombay, 1949), p. 399.

5. Dyakov, *Indiya vo vremya i posle vtoroi mirovoi voini,* p. 18.

6. *The Times* (London), March 26, 1940, p. 7.

7. For details see *ibid.*

8. B. Ashe, "Increased Tension in the Indian Situation," *World News and Views,* (Vol. XX, No. 13, April 6, 1940), p. 216; Carritt, "India Before the Storm, *loc. cit.,* p. 301.

9. See *The Hindu,* (Madras) September 3, 1940, p. 5. Also see *The Times* (London), September 3, 1940, p. 3.

10. Government of India, *Legislative Assembly Debates,* (February, 1941) I, 121. See also the unsigned article, "Mobilising India," *World News and Views,* (Vol. XXI, No. 2, January 11, 1941), p. 23.

11. For details about Gopalan, see V. P. Johar, "Gopalan, the

Darling of the Kerala Reds," *Amrita Bazar Patrika,* July 27, 1952, p. 2. (supplement).

12. For details about Namboodripad see Office of Strategic Services, *op. cit.,* p. 63.

13. For details about Zaheer, see *ibid.,* p. 66.

14. *Ibid.,* p. 55.

15. Johar, *loc. cit.,* p. 2.

16. For the Communist position see Puran Chandra Joshi, *Communist Reply to Congress Working Committee's Charges,* (Bombay, 1945) I, 36.

17. Dyakov, *Indiya vo vremya i posle vtoroi mirovoi voini,* p. 19.

18. *Ibid.*

19. Ashe, "The Political Situation in India," *loc. cit.,* p. 689.

20. *Ibid.*

21. R. Palme Dutt, *India Today,* (1949 ed.) p. 400.

22. *Ibid.*

23. For complete details of the strike of October 2, 1939 see S. S. Batiwala, "The Bombay Strike," in the still tolerated Indian Communist journal, the *National Front,* of October 8, 1939, p. 1. See also Carritt, "India Before the Storm," *loc. cit.,* p. 299; Ashe, "The Anti-War Movement in India," *loc. cit.,* p. 1151; R. Palme Dutt, *India Today,* (1949 ed) p. 399; and Shelvankar, *op. cit.,* p. 242.

24. Dyakov, *Indiya vo vremya i posle vtoroi mirovoi voini,* p. 15.

25. Carritt, "India Before the Storm," *loc. cit.,* p. 299.

26. Dyakov, *Indiya vo vremya i posle vtoroi mirovoi voini,* p. 15.

27. *Ibid.,* pp. 16-17.

28. R. Palme Dutt, *India Today,* (1949 ed.) pp. 398-399; Dyakov, *Indiya vo vremya i posle vtoroi mirovoi voini,* p. 15.

29. Dyakov. *Indiya vo vremya i posle vtoroi mirovoi voini,* p. 17.

30. For details see the unsigned article, "News from India," *World News and Views,* (Vol. XXI, No. 13, March 29, 1941), pp. 204-205.

31. Dyakov, *Indiya vo vremya i posle vtoroi mirovoi voini,* pp. 16 ff.

32. Carritt, "India Before the Storm," *loc. cit.,* p. 299.

33. B. Ashe, "Political Parties in India," *World News and*

Views, (Vol. XIX, No. 60. December 30, 1939), p. 1174; Dyakov, *Indiya vo vremya i posle vtoroi mirovoi voini,* pp. 16 ff; Carritt, "India Before the Storm," *loc. cit.,* p. 299.

34. James Gordon, "Indian Students Against the Imperialist War," *World News and Views,* (Vol. XX, No. 18, February 24, 1940), p. 121.

35. *Ibid.*

36. *Ibid.,* p. 122.

37. *Ibid.,* p. 121. See also Dyakov, *Indiya vo vremya i posle vtoroi mirovoi voini,* pp. 16-17.

38. Michael Carritt, "The Crisis in India," *Labour Monthly,* (Vol. XXIII, No. 2, February, 1941), p. 82.

39. Narayan, *op. cit.,* pp. 180-181.

40. *Ibid.,* pp. 179-180.

41. *Ibid.,* p. 181.

42. R. Palme Dutt, *India Today,* (1949 ed.) p. 399.

43. Dolores Ibarruri, "The Struggle of the Indian People against Imperialist War and for National Independence," *World News and Views,* (Vol. XX, No. 4, January 27, 1940), p. 53; V. K. Krishna Menon, "Labour and India," *World News and Views,* (Vol. XXI, No. 1, January 4, 1941), pp. 4-5; B. Ashe, "India and World Opinion," *World News and Views* (Vol. XX, No. 5, February 3, 1940), pp. 67-68; Michael Carritt, "India Before the Storm," *loc. cit.,* pp. 294-295.

44. Joshi, *Communist Reply to Congress Working Committee's Charges,* I, 37.

45. Batiwala, *loc. cit.,* p. 1.

46. *Ibid.*

47. See R. Page Arnot, "India To-day," *Labour Monthly,* (Vol. XXII, No. 9, September, 1940), pp. 495, and B. Ashe, "The Viceroy's Offer to India," *World News and Views,* (Vol. XX, No. 33, August 17, 1940), pp. 447-448.

48. See B. Ashe, "The Underground Struggle in India," *World News and Views,* (Vol. XX, No. 43, October 26, 1940), p. 597. See also his article, "India and World Opinion" *loc. cit.,* pp. 67-68.

49. See B. Ashe, "Who Are the Indian Princes?" *World News and Views,* (Vol. XX, No. 6. February 10, 1940), p. 89.

50. R. Palme Dutt, *India To-day,* (1940 ed.) p. 405.

51. B. Ashe, "Non-Violence or a People's Army," *World News and Views,* (Vol. XX, No. 27, July 6, 1940), p. 15.

52. *Communist,* (Vol. II, No. 7, February, 1941), p. 15.

53. See Communist Party of India, Central Committee, "Manifesto of the Communist Party of India," *World News and Views,* (Vol. XX, No. 11, March 16, 1940), p. 166; Communist Party of Great Britain, Central Committee, "Stand by the Indian People," *World News and Views,* (Vol. XIX, No. 53, November 1, 1939), p. 1087. See also the articles by Ashe, "Increasing Tension in the Indian Situation," *World News and Views,* (Vol. XX, No. 13, April 6, 1940), p. 216; Carritt, "India Before the Storm," *loc. cit.,* p. 301; and Arnot, "India To-day," *loc. cit.,* p. 496; and an unsigned article "The Working Committee on the War Situation," *World News and Views,* (Vol. XIX, No. 50, October 21, 1939), p. 1040.

54. See the unsigned article, "India and the War," *Labour Monthly,* (Vol. XXI, No. 10, October, 1939), pp. 626 ff.

55. See V. K. Krishna Menon, "Amritsar," *World News and Views,* (Vol. XXI, No. 15, April 12, 1941), pp. 231-232. See also Ashe, "The Political Situation in India," *loc. cit.,* p. 689, and Carritt, "The Crisis in India," *loc. cit.,* p. 82.

56. See Communist Party of India, Central Committee, "Manifesto of the Communist Party of India," *loc. cit.,* p. 166.

57. Joshi, *Communist Reply to Congress Working Committee's Charges,* I, 83.

58. Quoted in Ashe, "The Underground Struggle in India," *loc. cit.,* p. 599.

59. Mitra, *The Indian Annual Register,* (July-December, 1945) II, 114-115.

60. See Carritt, "India Before the Storm," *loc. cit.,* p. 300, and an unsigned article, "Letter from India," *World News and Views,* (Vol. XX, No. 32, August 10, 1940), p. 439.

61. B. Ashe, "The Viceroy's Offer to India," *World News and Views,* (Vol. XX, No. 33, August 17, 1940), p. 448.

62. See Narayan, *op. cit.,* p. 142.

63. Acharya Narendra Deva, *Socialism and the National Revolution* (Bombay, 1946), pp. 132-133. See also Narayan, *op. cit.,* p. 187.

64. Ashe, "The Underground Struggle in India," *loc. cit.,* p. 559.

65. R. Palme Dutt, *India Today,* (1949 ed.) p. 402.

66. See R. Palme Dutt, *India Today,* (1949 ed.) p. 403, and Ashe, "The Political Situation in India," *loc. cit.,* p. 689.

67. Ashe, "Political Parties in India," *loc. cit.*, p. 1173.

68. *Ibid.*

69. Dyakov, *Indiya i Pakistan,* p. 17.

70. Ashe, "Political Parties in India," *loc. cit.*, p. 1173.

71. See R. Palme Dutt, *India Today,* (1949 ed.) pp. 529 ff.

72. See Ashe, "Non-Violence or a People's Army," *loc. cit.*, p. 439.

73. Harry Pollitt, "India, a Call to the British People," *Labour Monthly,* (Vol. XXIII, No. 6, June, 1941), p. 265.

74. Communist Party of India, Central Committee, "Manifesto of the Communist Party of India," *loc. cit.*, p. 167.

75. For full details of the manifesto, see *ibid.*, pp. 166-167.

76. R. Palme Dutt in the 1940 edition of his *India To-day* went great details (pp. 3-16) in arguing that India was a wealthy country. Following Marx, he then went into detail to show that Britain had ruined India (pp. 16-27). He then attacked the zamindary (landlord) and other systems of land tenure (pp. 21-23). Dutt then went into the history of the Indian national movement, praised Tilak and Das, was relatively friendly to Jawaharlal Nehru and Bose, but scorned Gandhi (pp. 24-36). This leading mentor of India's Communists dealt with (pp. 37-47) the history of the Indian labor movement up to 1940 and also (pp. 48-60) made particular reference to the government and politics of India as of 1940, criticizing the government structure of India, but showing an amicable attitude towards the National Congress.

77. *Ibid.*, p. 535. Dutt insisted that British concessions be confiscated and held that "key industries" should be owned by the Indian state.

78. Pollitt, *loc. cit.*, pp. 263-265.

79. For the Communists' attitude before the Second World War as applied to an Anglo-Soviet alliance against the Fascist powers see the article in *National Front* (Bombay) of April 3, 1938, p. 4 in which a rising Communist leader, P. Sundarayya, argued that "the immediate issue before us in India is not the fight against fascism, but the fight for a true democracy in our country. India's part in the coming international struggle for power is the struggle for her own freedom. Only in so far as she consistently pursues this will she be able to weaken the forces of reaction in the world."

80. Quoted in Deva, *op. cit.*, pp. 152-153.

81. B. Pattabhi Sitaramayya, *The History of the Indian National Congress* (Bombay, 1947), II, 241.

82. Deva, *op. cit.*, p. 142.

83. Sitamarayya, *op. cit.*, II, 241.

84. Quoted in Deva, *op. cit.*, pp. 152-153.

85. An ambiguous line was taken in respect to India and the war between June and October, 1941 by British Communists and their fellow travelers as shown by the following articles: V. K. Krishna Menon, "Freedom's Battle," *Labour Monthly* (Vol. XXIII, No. 8, August, 1941), pp. 364 ff.; "The Change in India," *World News and Views,* (Vol. XXI, No. 31, August 2, 1941), p. 484; "India—a Conference," *World News and Views,* (Vol. XXI, No. 32, August 9, 1941), p. 507; Bill Keats, "Release the Indian Prisoners," *World News and Views,* (Vol. XXI, No. 33, August 16, 1941), p. 552. The change in the line of the C.P.G.B. came with the publication of an article by "An Indian Resident in London," who held that India must participate in the war on the Allied side. See *World News and Views,* (Vol. XXI, No. 40, October 4, 1941), p. 637.

86. Communist Party of Great Britain, Central Committee, "India," *World News and Views,* (Vol. XXI, No. 42, October 18, 1941), p. 668.

87. *Ibid.*

88. *Ibid.*

89. *Ibid.*

90. *Ibid.*

91. Mohan Das, *op. cit.*, pp. 7-8.

92. See Office of Strategic Services, *op. cit.*, p. 6, Linton, *op. cit.*, p. 639.

93. Joshi, *Communist Reply to Congress Working Committee's Charges,* I, 5.

94. Joshi, *The Indian Communist Party* (also referred to as *Forward to Freedom*) p. 18.

95. *Ibid.*

96. *Ibid.*, p. 12.

97. *Ibid.*, p. 21.

98. *Ibid.*, p. 22.

99. *Ibid.*

100. *Ibid.*, p. 23.

101. *Ibid.*, pp. 16, 18.

102. *Ibid.*, pp. 10-11.

103. *Ibid.*, pp. 23-24.

104. See Akademiya Nauk, *op. cit.*, pp. 95-96.

105. Tilak, *op. cit.*, p. 122.

106. For the official Government of India announcement in full see *The Hindu* (Madras), July 24, 1942, p. 6.

107. *Ibid.*

108. *Ibid.*, pp. 4, 6.

109. See Harry Pollitt, "Greetings to India," *World News and Views,* (Vol. XXII, No. 31, August 1, 1942), p. 326, and Ben Bradley, "A Great Step Forward in India," *World News and Views,* (Vol. XXII, No. 31, August 1, 1942), p. 326.

110. *The Times* (London), July 24, 1942, p. 3.

111. Ben Bradley, "Stabbing Our Allies in the Back," *World News and Views,* (Vol. XXIII, No. 3, January 16, 1943), p. 22.

112. *People's War,* (Bombay) May 16, 1943, p. 6. See also unsigned article, "First National Convention of the Communist Party of India," *World News and Views,* (Vol. XXIII, No. 26, June 29, 1943), p. 285.

113. *Ibid.*

114. *Ibid.*

115. *The Hindu,* June 2, 1943, p. 2.

116. See *New Age,* October 4, 1953, p. 2.

117. See Khwaja Ahmad Abbas, "Moscow Comes to India," *Asia,* (Vol. XL, No. 8, August, 1944), p. 350.

118. Office of Strategic Services, *op. cit.*, p. 7. See also Karaka, *op. cit.*, p. 240.

119. Office of Strategic Services, *op. cit.*, p. 7.

120. Karaka, *op. cit.*, p. 240.

121. Office of Strategic Services, *op. cit.*, pp. 5, 7.

122. Unsigned article, "The Growth of the Communist Party of India," *World News and Views,* (Vol. XXIII, No. 18, May 1, 1943), p. 142.

123. For details of the C.P.I.'s membership at this time see *ibid.* See also Office of Strategic Services, *op. cit.*, p. 8, and *People's War,* March 7, 1943, p. 1.

124. Office of Strategic Services, *op. cit.*, p. 8.

125. Bradley "Stabbing Our Allies in the Back," *loc. cit.*, p. 22.

126. See Sitaramayya, *op. cit.*, II, 114 ff.

127. Office of Strategic Services, *op. cit.*, p. 10.

128. *Ibid.*

129. *People's War,* April 4, 1943, p. 3.

130. Office of Strategic Services, *op. cit.*, p. 10.
131. *People's War,* June 13, 1943, p. 1.
132. *Ibid.*
133. Office of Strategic Services, *op. cit.*, p. 13.
134. *People's War,* April 4, 1943, p. 3.
135. *People's War,* June 13, 1943, p. 1, January 7, 1945, p. 2.
136. Mitra, *The Indian Annual Register,* July-December, 1945, II, 117.
137. D. N. Pritt, "India," *Labour Monthly,* (Vol. XXIV, No. 4, April, 1942), p. 105.
138. See *New York Times,* April 1, 1942, p. 4. For the British Communist view see Ben Bradley, "India Threatened," *Labour Monthly,* (Vol. XXIV, No. 5, May, 1942), p. 45.
139. Joshi, *Communist Reply to Congress Working Committee's Charges,* I, 77.
140. *Ibid.*, I, 95-96. See also Linton, *op. cit.*, p. 639, and R. Palme Dutt, *The Problem of India,* p. 206.
141. Sir Reginald Coupland, *India, a Re-Statement* (Oxford, 1945), p. 22.
142. See R. Palme Dutt, "India and the Second Front," *Labour Monthly,* (Vol. XXIV, No. 8, August, 1942), p. 231; unsigned article, "India—What Must Be Done," *Labour Monthly,* (Vol. XXIV, No. 9, September, 1942), pp. 259 ff; and another unsigned article, "The Only Solution for India," *World News and Views,* (Vol. XXII, No. 44, August 15, 1942), p. 337. See also *People's War,* August 23, 1942, p. 1.
143. Unsigned article, "India—What Must Be Done," *loc. cit.*, p. 264.
144. Harry Pollitt for the Communist Party of Great Britain, Central Committee, "Statement by the Communist Party of Great Britain on India," *World News and Views,* (Vol. XXII, No. 33, August 15, 1942), p. 339.
145. *People's War,* August 23, 1942, p. 1.
146. Harry Pollitt, "India, the Communist Party's Call to the Prime Minister," *World News and Views,* (Vol. XXII, No. 35, August 29, 1942), p. 357.
147. *People's War,* May 14, 1944, p. 1.
148. Puran Chandra Joshi, *Correspondence between Mahatma Gandhi and P. C. Joshi,* (Bombay, 1945), p. 2.
149. *Ibid.*, pp. 4 ff.
150. *Ibid.*, p. 21.

151. *Ibid.*

152. *Ibid.*, p. 23.

153. Mitra, *The Indian Annual Register,* July-December, 1945, II, 117-118.

154. *Ibid.*

155. *People's War,* December 17, 1944, p. 2.

156. *Amrita Bazar Patrika* (Calcutta), December 22, 1944, p. 2.

157. *The Hindu,* January 1, 1945, p. 8.

158. Office of Strategic Services, *op. cit.,* p. 33.

159. Modan Gopal, *loc. cit.,* p. 90.

160. *Amrita Bazar Patrika,* February 5, 1945, p. 4.

161. *Star of India,* June 11, 1945, p. 2.

162. *The Tribune* (Lahore), March 21, 1944, p. 8.

163. *Amrita Bazar Patrika,* February 15, 1945, p. 3.

164. R. Palme Dutt, *The Problem of India,* p. 192.

165. Dyakov, *Indiya vo vremya i posle vtoroi mirovoi voini,* p. 27; R. Palme Dutt, *India Today,* (1949 ed.) p. 400.

166. Masani, "The Communists in India," *loc. cit.,* p. 24.

167. See Office of Strategic Services, *op. cit.,* p. 33, and Mitra, *The Indian Annual Register,* January-June, 1943, I, 312.

168. Office of Strategic Services, *op. cit.,* p. 50.

169. *Ibid.,* pp. 32-33.

170. See All-India Trade Union Congress, *Report, Twentieth Session, Nagpur, 1943* (Bombay, 1943), p. 27. See also, Dyakov, *Indiya vo vremya i posle vtoroi mirovoi voini,* pp. 29, 400, and Office of Strategic Services, *op. cit.,* p. 50.

171. All-India Trade Union Congress, *Report, Twentieth Session, Nagpur,* p. 27.

172. Desai, *op. cit.,* p. 195, Office of Strategic Services, *op. cit.,* p. 50, Dyakov, *Indiya vo vremya i posle vtoroi mirovoi voini,* p. 29.

173. Office of Strategic Services, *op. cit.,* p. 51.

174. See Lawrence K. Rosinger, *Restless India,* (New York, 1946), p. 39 and George Raleigh Parkin, *India Today*—an Introduction to Indian Politics, (New York, 1946), p. 36.

175. Linton, *op. cit.,* p. 639.

176. *The Hindu,* June 2, 1943, p. 2.

177. Dyakov, *Indiya vo vremya i posle vtoroi mirovoi voini,* p. 28.

178. Mohan Das, *op. cit.,* p. 8.

179. Dyakov, *Indiya vo vremya i posle vtoroi mirovoi voini,*

p. 28. For another Soviet analysis emphasizing the miserable condition of Indian workers during the war period see V. V. Balabushevich, *Rabochii klass i rabochii dvizhenie v Indii* (Moscow, 1949), pp. 10-11.

180. Sitaramayya, *op. cit.*, II, 241.

181. Unsigned article, "India and the Soviet Union," *World News and Views,* (Vol. XXI, No. 51, December 19, 1941), p. 813.

182. All-India Kisan Sabha, Central Kisan Council' "Indian Peasants Call for Aid to the Soviet," *World News and Views,* (Vol. XXI, No. 41, October 11, 1941), p. 653.

183. Quoted in Joshi, *The Indian Communist Party* (*Forward to Freedom*) p. 29.

184. Office of Strategic Services, *op. cit.*, p. 55.

185. Mitra, *The Indian Annual Register,* January-June, 1943, I, 313.

186. *Ibid.*, I, 314. For additional information about this session see also Puran Chandra Joshi, "The Peasants of India," *World News and Views,* (Vol. XXIII, No. 20, May, 1943), p. 159. Also see the latter's work in connection with the peasants' movement, *Among Kisan Patriots,* (Bombay, 1946), pp. 1 ff. and *passim*.

187. Dyakov, *Indiya vo vremya i posle vtoroi mirovoi voini,* p. 1.

188. *Ibid.*

189. See *The Leader,* December 8, 1944, p. 2, and *The Hindu,* December 9, 1944, p. 5.

190. Office of Strategic Services, *op. cit.*, p. 58.

191. *Ibid.*, p. 59.

192. *Ibid.*, p. 58.

193. For detailed statistics of the peasants' movement at this time see Dyakov, *Indiya vo vremya i posle vtoroi mirovoi voini,* p. 30.

194. Quoted in Joshi, *The Indian Communist Party* (*Forward to Freedom*), p. 326.

195. Bradley, "A Great Step Forward in India," *loc. cit.*, p. 326.

196. See *People's War,* March 14, 1945, p. 3 and Dyakov, *Indiya vo vremya i posle vtoroi mirovoi voini,* p. 34.

197. Office of Strategic Services, *op. cit.*, p. 16; Limaye, *op. cit.*, p. 55. The latter author gives P. C. Joshi full credit for building up these cultural front organizations.

198. Modan Gopal, *loc. cit.*, p. 90. Dyakov, *Indiya vo vremya*

i posle vtoroi mirovoi voini, p. 34; *People's War,* March 21, 1943, p. 3, April 18, 1943, p. 3, May 9, 1943, p. 6.

199. Office of Strategic Services, *op. cit.,* p. 16.

200. *The Hindu,* June 1, 1943, p. 2.

201. *Ibid.*

202. *People's War,* June 6, 1943, pp. 1, 3.

203. Tilak, *op. cit.,* p. 122.

204. *People's War,* April 25, 1943, p. 1.

205. Office of Strategic Services, *op. cit.,* p. 19. For the Indian Communist view see Puran Chandra Joshi's article, "How to End Hoarding in India," *World News and Views,* (Vol. XXIII, No. 33, October 30, 1943), p. 351.

206. Office of Strategic Services, *op. cit.,* p. 19.

207. *Ibid.*

208. Ben Bradley, "India Must be Freed," *Labour Monthly,* (Vol. XXIV, No. 10, October, 1942), p. 307.

209. *The Hindu,* June 1, 1943, p. 2.

210. See R. Palme Dutt, "India," *Labour Monthly,* (Vol. XXV, No. 1, January, 1943), p. 5; Emile Burns, "Amery Must Go," *World News and Views,* (Vol. XXIII, No. 18, May 1, 1943), p. 141; Ben Bradley, "Indian Crisis," *Labour Monthly,* (Vol. XXV, No. 5, May, 1943) pp. 153 ff; and the unsigned article, "Amery," *World News and Views,* (Vol. XXII, No. 40, October 3, 1942), p. 395.

211. See S. A. Dange, "India and the British Elections," *Labour Monthly,* (Vol. XXVII, No. 6, June, 1945), p. 183; Bradley, "Indian Crisis," *loc. cit.,* p. 154; and the unsigned article, "Gandhi," *World News and Views,* (Vol. XXIII, No. 9. February 27, 1943), p. 68.

212. *People's War,* June 6, 1943, p. 4.

213. Joshi, *The Indian Communist Party* (*Forward to Freedom*), p. 26.

214. *Ibid.,* pp. 26-27.

215. *People's* War, July 18, 1943, p. 1.

216. Joshi, *The Indian Communist Party* (*Forward to Freedom*), p. 27.

217. *Ibid.,* p. 28.

218. *Ibid.* In spite of Joshi's favorable attitude towards the League certain British Communist mentors of the C.P.I. remained critical of it. See Ben Bradley, "India Threatened,"

Labour Monthly, (Vol. XXIV, No. 5, May, 1942), p. 146, and Pritt, *loc. cit.,* p. 107.

219. See E. M. S Namboodripad, "Eighteen Months of Famine," *World News and Views,* (Vol. XXIV, No. 32, August 5, 1944), p. 254, and *People's War,* October 1, 1944, p. 2.

220. Joshi, *The Indian Communist Party (Forward to Freedom),* p. 27.

221. G. M. Adhikari, *Pakistan and Indian National Unity* (London, 1943), pp. 117 ff.

222. *Ibid.*

223. *Ibid.*

224. *Ibid.*

225. *Ibid. See* also G. M. Adhikari, "Pakistan and National Unity," *Labour Monthly,* (Vol. XXV, No. 3, March, 1943), pp. 88-89. Note the analogy with Stalin's professed theory of nationalities, see his *On the National Question,* p. 7.

226. *The Hindu,* June 2, 1943, p. 2.

227. *People's War,* March 26, 1944, p. 2.

228. *People's War,* August 29, 1944, p. 2.

229. *People's War,* October 1, 1944, p. 1.

230. *People's War,* October 8, 1944, p. 2.

231. *People's War,* October 29, 1944, p. 2.

232. Communist Party of India, Central Committee, "Abridged Draft of the Political Thesis of the Central Committee of the Communist Party of India," *loc. cit.,* p. 1031.

233. For details see *People's War,* December 3, 1944, p. 1.

234. Bradley, "Indian Crisis," *loc. cit.,* p. 156; R. Palme Dutt, *The Problem of India,* p. 216.

235. Joshi, *The Indian Communist Party (Forward to Freedom),* p. 17.

236. Puran Chandra Joshi, "India's Post War Plan," *World News and Views,* (Vol. XXIV, No. 16, April 15, 1944), p. 123. See also R. Palme Dutt, "Planning for India," *Labour Monthly,* (Vol. XXVI, No. 9, September, 1944), pp. 286-287.

237. See Clare and Harris Wofford, *op. cit.,* pp. 201 ff.; Rosinger, *Restless India,* p. 68; Wallbank, *op. cit.,* p. 156.

238. See Joshi, *The Indian Communist Party (Forward to Freedom),* p. 19; R. Palme Dutt, "India Faces Japan," *Labour Monthly,* (Vol. XXVI, No. 5, May, 1944), p. 134; Dyakov, *Indiya vo vremya i posle vtoroi mirovoi voini,* p. 35.

239. See V. K. Krishna Menon, "India for Action," *Labour Monthly,* (Vol. XXIV, No. 6, June, 1942) pp. 185-188.

Other topical articles dealing with India at wartime include that of Clemens P. Dutt, "India and Freedom," *Labour Monthly,* (Vol. XXIV, No. 8, August, 1942), pp. 247, and those of V. K. Krishna Menon, "India and the War," *Labour Monthly,* (Vol. XXIV, No. 1, January, 1942), pp. 22 ff., and "Egypt and India," *World News and Views,* (Vol. XXII, No. 28, July 11, 1942), p. 300.

240. United States Government, Department of State, *Nazi-Soviet Relations, 1939-1941* (edited by Raymond J. Sontag and James C. Beddie), (Washington, D. C., 1948), p. 74.

241. *New York Times,* November 1, 1939, p. 8.

242. *New York Times,* November 7, 1939, p. 1.

243. See *Trud,* November 11, 1939, p. 2, and *Pravda,* November 16, 1939, p. 5.

244. Unsigned article, "The Indian People Ask," *Communist International,* (Vol. XVI, No. 10, October, 1939), pp. 1045-1046.

245. See *New York Times,* December 28, 1939, p. 1, December 29, 1939, p. 3. and January 1, 1940, p. 3.

246. *The Times,* (London) January 9, 1940, p. 7.

247. *New York Times,* March 3, 1940, p. 3.

248. For details see Herbert Feis, *The Road to Pearl Harbor* (Princeton, New Jersey, 1950), pp. 114 ff.; United States Department of State, *op. cit.,* p. 213; Dallin, *op. cit.,* p. 155.

249. United States Department of State, *op. cit.,* pp. 243-244.

250. *Ibid.,* p. 250.

251. *Ibid.,* p. 251.

252. *Ibid.*

253. For details of the Draft Agreement see *ibid.,* pp. 255 ff.

254. *Ibid.,* p. 254.

255. For the text of the Soviet note in reply to the German memorandum see *ibid.,* pp. 258 ff.

256. *Ibid.,* p. 260.

257. *Ibid.,* p. 270.

258. Dallin, *op. cit.,* p. 159.

259. But, this notwithstanding, Russia was held to have "sympathy" for the Indians. See Frances Gunther, *Revolution in India* (New York, 1944), p. 44.

260. *New York Times,* August 2, 1942, p. 7.

261. See the unsigned articles entitled "Obtash Chetelam,"

Voina i Rabochii Klass, (No. 8, September 15, 1943), pp. 25-26, dealing with alleged anti-Papal activity on the part of the Soviets; "Fascisti agenti na uperami Gangi," *Voina i Rabochii Klass,* (No. 13, July 1, 1933), pp. 23-24, complaining about some Indian criticism of Russia's Polish policy, and "Nebitnii Opastnost," *Voina i Rabochii Klass,* (No. 21, November 1, 1944), pp. 19-20, denouncing the criticism by the *Bombay Chronicle* of Soviet policy in Northern Iran.

262. A. M. Dyakov,"The Political Situation in India," *War and the Working Class,* (No. 7, April 1, 1945), p. 13.

263. See George Raleigh Parkin, *India Today*—an Introduction to Indian Politics (New York, 1946), pp. 296 ff.

264. A. M. Dyakov, "After the Failure of the Simla Conference," *War and the Working Class,* (No. 13, July 1, 1945), p. 1.

265. *Ibid.*

266. Y. Mikneyev, "A Journey to Australia," *War and the Working Class,* (No. 12, June 15, 1945), p. 2. See also an unsigned article, "Famine in India," *War and the Working Class,* (No. 11, June 1, 1945), p. 20.

267. See, W. E. Lucas, "Russia's Threat to India," *The Nation* (New York), (Vol. CLII, No. 22, May 31, 1941), pp. 632-633.

268. See *The Times* (London), May 18, 1940, p. 5, June 7, 1940, p. 5, June 17, 1940, p. 5.

269. See W. P. and Zelda Coates, *A History of Anglo-Soviet Relations,* pp. 681 and 775-776.

270. For details, see *The Times* (London), October 4, 1941, p. 3.

271. For details, see Lenczowski, *op. cit.,* pp. 166 ff.

272. *Ibid.,* p. 174.

273. See Elizabeth Bacon and Hudson, Alfred E., "Afghanistan Waits," *Asia,* (Vol. XLI, No. 1, January, 1941), p. 32; Donald N. Wilber, "Afghanistan, Independent and Encircled," *Foreign Affairs,* (Vol. XXXI, No. 3, April, 1935), p. 490; Howland, *loc. cit.,* p. 635; and Fraser-Tytler, *op. cit.,* 252 ff. For a Communist view, see Ben Bradley, "Unrest in the North-West Frontier," *International Press Correspondence,* Vol. XVII, No. 17, April 17, 1937), pp. 421-422.

274. See *The Times* (London), October 21, 1941, p. 5; Fraser-Tytler, *op. cit.,* pp. 254-255. For Communist views see the unsigned articles "Afghanistan Expels Fascists," *World News and Views,* (Vol. XXI, No. 44, November 1, 1941), p. 702, and

"Afghanistan," *World News and Views,* (Vol. XXI, No. 48, November 29, 1941), p. 748. For a historical review of the situation see *New York Times,* July 6, 1946, p. 3.

275. *The Times,* (London) July 3, 1942, p. 3.

276. See Harriett L. Moore, *Soviet Far Eastern Policy* (Princeton, New Jersey, 1945), pp. 131 ff., and Dallin, *op. cit.,* pp. 361-362.

277. Dallin, *op. cit.,* p. 363.

278. See the *Harijan,* December 19, 1939, p. 351; January 26, 1941, p. 376.

279. See the *Harijan,* January 26, 1941, p. 376; April 13, 1940, p. 92.

280. Nehru, *The Discovery of India,* p. 376.

281. Nehru, *The Unity of India,* essay "War Aims and Peace Aims," p. 309.

282. Nehru, *Important Speeches,* p. 164.

283. Nehru, *The Unity of India,* essay, "The Constituent Assembly," p. 370.

284. *The Times* (London), June 25, 1941, p. 5.

285. See unsigned article, "India and the Soviet Union," *loc. cit.,* p. 813.

286. See the unsigned articles, Anglo-Soviet Alliance," *Calcutta Review,* (Vol. LXXXIII, No. 3, May. 1942), pp. 299 ff., and "Relations with Soviet Russia," *Calcutta Review,* (Vol. LXXXV, No. 3, December, 1942), pp. 270-271.

287. *New York Times,* August 1, 1942, p. 5.

288. *Ibid.*

289. Sitaramayya, *op. cit.,* II, 747.

290. Parkin, *op. cit.,* p. 214.

291. John S. Howland, *Indian Crisis* (New York, 1943), p. 182.

292. Nehru, *Important Speeches,* p. 213.

293. Nehru, *Towards Freedom,* pp. 229-230, 348-349.

294. Nehru, *Important Speeches,* p. 214.

295. Nehru, *The Discovery of India,* p. 480.

296. *Ibid.,* pp. 44, 553.

297. *Ibid.,* pp. 247-248.

298. *Ibid.,* p. 569.

299. *Ibid.,* p. 553.

300. *Ibid.,* p. 425.

301. Nehru, *Towards Freedom,* pp. 229-230, 348-349. See also his *The Discovery of India,* p. 18.

302. Nehru, *Towards Freedom,* p. 233.
303. Nehru, *The Discovery of India,* pp. 441, 528.

CHAPTER EIGHT

1. See George E. Jones, *Tumult in India* (New York, 1948), pp. 14-16; Dyakov, *Indiya vo vremya i posle vtoroi mirovoi voini,* p. 65; *The Hindu,* November 23, 1945, p. 4.
2. 434 H. C. Deb. 5s, pp. 964-965.
3. Wallbank, *op. cit.,* p. 162.
4. *The Hindu,* May 13, 1946, p. 3; May 17, 1946, p. 4.
5. Wallbank, *op. cit.,* pp. 164-165.
6. 434 H. C. Deb. 5s, 663 ff.
7. Rosinger, *The State of Asia,* p. 455; Wallbank, *op. cit.,* pp. 165-166.
8. *Ibid.*
9. For details see *The Tribune* (Lahore), June 4, 1947, p. 1.
10. See unsigned article "Paramountcy and the States," *Feudatory and Zamindary Review,* (Vol. XXVII, No. 10, June, 1947), p. 527; unsigned article, "Sovereign Status for Hyderabad," *Feudatory and Zamindary Review,* (Vol. XXVII, No. 11, July, 1947), p. 595; and unsigned article, "The States and Accession," *Feudatory and Zamindary Review,* (Vol. XXVII, No. 12, August, 1945), p. 647.
11. Wallbank, *op. cit.,* p. 165.
12. Nehru, *Important Speeches,* p. 86.
13. *Ibid.,* p. 291.
14. Mitra, *The Indian Annual Register,* July-December, 1945, II, 117-118.
15. *The Times* (London), September 4, 1945, p. 3.
16. *The Hindu,* September 4, 1945, p. 3.
17. *The Hindu,* September 5, 1945, p. 3.
18. Mitra, *The Indian Annual Register,* July-December, 1945, II, 118-119.
19. Quoted in Martin Ebon, *World Communism Today* (Toronto, 1948), p. 403.
20. Mitra, *The Indian Annual Register,* July-December, 1945, II, 118-119.
21. *The Hindu,* September 21, 1945, p. 4.
22. Mitra, *The Indian Annual Register,* II, 120.

23. R. Palme Dutt, "India and Pakistan," *Labour Monthly,* (Vol. XXVIII, No. 3), March, 1946, pp. 91-92.

24. Mitra, *The Indian Annual Register,* July-December, 1945, II, 122.

25. Modan Gopal, *loc. cit.,* p. 91.

26. P. C. Joshi quoted in unsigned article, "Indian Communists and the Congress," *World News and Views,* (Vol. XXV, No. 45, November 17, 1945), p. 362.

27. *Ibid.*

28. See Joshi, *Communist Reply to Congress Working Committee's Charges,* I, 1 and *passim.*

29. *The Hindu,* December 14, 1945, p. 4.

30. *Ibid.*

31. *Ibid.*

32. *Ibid.*

33. Mitra, *The Indian Annual Register,* July-December, 1945, II, 119.

34. *The Hindu,* December 14, 1945, p. 4.

35. See R. Palme Dutt, "Travel Notes," *Labour Monthly,* (Vol. XXVIII, No. 6, June, 1946), p. 188; "Travel Notes," *Labour Monthly,* (Vol. XXVIII, No. 9, September, 1946), p. 285; "India and Pakistan," *loc. cit.,* pp. 91, 92, and Michael Carritt, "A Constituent Assembly," *Labour Monthly,* (Vol. XXVII, No. 11, November, 1945), pp. 344-345.

36. Linton, *op. cit.,* p. 643.

37. Jones, *op. cit.,* p. 179.

38. *The Hindu,* January 15, 1947, p. 4.

39. *Ibid.*

40. *Ibid.*

41. *Ibid.*

42. *The Times* (London), January 15, 1947, p. 3.

43. *The Times* (London), January 20, 1947, p. 2. See also Harry Pollitt (For the Communist Party of Great Britain, Executive Committee,) "Free the Communist Leaders," *World News and Views,* (Vol. XXVII, No. 4, January 25, 1947), p. 40.

44. *The Tribune* (Lahore), January 16, 1947, p. 4.

45. *The Tribune* (Lahore), January 30, 1947, p. 1, *New York Times,* April 13, 1947, p. 32, "Bombay Correspondent," "Communism in India," *Economist,* (Vol. CLIII, No. 5439), November 22, 1947), p. 846.

46. For details of clashes between strikers and the authorities see Dyakov, *Indiya vo vremya i posle vtoroi mirovoi voini,* p. 97.

47. See *ibid.,* pp. 65-66.

48. *The Hindu,* January 27, 1946, p. 3.

49. Dyakov, *Indiya vo vremya i posle vtoroi mirovoi voini,* p. 68.

50. A full account of these proceedings from the Communist point of view is given in a volume put out by the Communist Party of India, entitled *Strike,* (Bombay, 1946) pp. 13 ff. and *passim.* Also see the C. P. I.'s publication, *People's Age* of February, 24, and March 3, 1946 which issues are full of excited propaganda about the affair. Also note Dyakov, *Indiya vo vremya i posle vtoroi mirovoi voini,* p. 70, and Akademiya Nauk, *op. cit.,* p. 101, for the Russian Communist, and R. Palme Dutt, *India Today,* (1949 ed.) pp. 537-538 for the British Communist views on this affair. *The Times of India* and *Bombay Chronicle* as well as other Indian newspapers also give copious accounts from a non-Communist standpoint.

51. See *Strike,* pp. 13 ff. and *passim,* and R. Palme Dutt, *India Today,* (1949 ed.) p. 539.

52. See *People's Age,* March 10, 1946, pp. 2, 11.

53. Dyakov, *Indiya vo vremya i posle vtoroi mirovoi voini,* p. 73.

54. 434 H. C. Deb. 5s, pp. 1441-1442.

55. Communist Party of India, *Political Thesis Adopted at the Second Congress, February 29—March 6, 1948* (Calcutta, 1948), p. 28.

56. *Ibid.*

57. See *New York Times,* April 4, 1946, p. 3.

58. Dyakov, *Indiya vo vremya i posle vtoroi mirovoi voini,* pp. 68, 74.

59. *Ibid.,* p. 74. See also *Political Thesis,* p. 28.

60. Dyakov, *Indiya vo vremya i posle vtoroi mirovoi voini,* pp. 68, 74.

61. See *People's Age,* September 1, 1946, pp. 1, 4; September 8, 1946, pp. 1, 8; September 15, 1946, p. 1; September 22, 1946, pp. 4, 8.

62. *People's Age,* February 16, 1947, p. 1.

63. For details of the strikes, riots and arrests see *People's Age,* January 9, 1947, p. 1; February 16, 1947, p. 2; March 30, 1947, p. 3; and June 29, 1947, p. 2.

64. See Andrew Mellor, *India Since Partition* (New York, 1951), p. 127.

65. See Dyakov, *Indiya vo vremya i posle vtoroi mirovoi voini,* p. 76. See also *People's War,* March 18, 1945, p. 2.

66. Mellor, *op. cit.,* p. 127.

67. *Ibid.*

68. Masani, "The Communists in India," *loc. cit.,* p. 25.

69. *Ibid.*

70. See *People's Age,* September 15, 1946, p. 5; September 22, 1946, pp. 5, 7; and Dyakov, *Indiya vo vremya i posle vtoroi mirovoi voini,* pp. 77, 101.

71. Dyakov, *Indiya vo vremya i posle vtoroi mirovoi voini,* p. 101.

72. See *People's Age,* November 10, 1946, p. 1.

73. See Alexander Roth as quoted in the unsigned article, "Peasant Revolt in Hyderabad," *Modern Review,* (Vol. LXXXII, No. 3, September, 1947), p. 81.

74. See the unsigned article, "Fabulous Wealth of the Nizam," *Feudatory and Zamindary Review,* (Vol. XXV, No. 1, September, 1944), p. 14.

75. *People's Age,* October 20, 1946, pp. 6-7.

76. Roth, *loc. cit.,* p. 182. See also *People's Age,* October 20, 1946, pp. 6-7 for a laudation of Red activities in Hyderabad.

77. Dyakov, *Indiya vo vremya i posle vtoroi mirovoi voini,* p. 102.

78. *People's Age,* May 18, 1947, p. 9.

79. Dyakov, *Natsionalnii vopros i angliiski imperializm v Indii,* p. 195. See also his *Indiya i Pakistan,* p. 10.

80. Dyakov, *Indiya vo vremya i posle vtoroi mirovoi voini,* p. 103.

81. *People's Age,* September 1, 1946, pp. 6-7.

82. Payne, *op. cit.,* p. 115.

83. Dyakov, *Indiya vo vremya i posle vtoroi mirovoi voini,* p. 104.

84. *Ibid.*

85. Limaye, *op. cit.,* p. 55. He claims between 1945 and 1947 the All-India Students' Federation became a mere "paper organisation."

86. Dyakov, *Indiya vo vremya i posle vtoroi mirovoi voini,* p. 76.

87. Limaye, *op. cit.,* p. 55.

88. Mitra, *The Indian Annual Register,* July-December, 1945, II, 121.

89. Akademiya Nauk, *op. cit.,* p. 101, Dyakov, *India vo vremya i posle vtoroi mirovoi voini,* p. 79.

90. Unsigned article, "Communist Progress in India," *World News and Views,* (Vol. XXI, No. 19, May 11, 1946), p. 145; Dyakov, *Indiya vo vremya i posle vtoroi mirovoi voini,* p. 79. The Communists gained seven seats from the workers' electoral list, one from the Untouchables' list and one, oddly enough, from the Christian communal list.

91. Ramesh Sanghvi, "The New Upsurge," *World News and Views,* (Vol. XXVII, No. 5, February 1, 1947), p. 60. Scc also *New York Times,* January 8, 1947, p. 5.

92. Unsigned article "Communist Progress in India," *loc. cit.,* p. 145; Dyakov, *Indiya vo vremya i posle vtoroi mirovoi voini,* p. 79.

93. R. Palme Dutt, *India Today,* (1949 ed.) p. 543; Dyakov, *Indiya vo vremya i posle vtoroi mirovoi voini,* p. 79; unsigned article "Communist Progress in India," *loc. cit.,* p. 145.

94. Dyakov, *Indiya vo vremya i posle vtoroi mirovoi voini,* pp. 86-87.

95. On October 12, 1945 Communist party leader P. C. Joshi declared that the C.P.I. would contest the elections for provincial legislatures. For details of his statement see Mitra, *The Indian Annual Register,* July-December, 1945, II, 121.

96. Communist Party of India, *Election Manifesto of the Communist Party of India,* in appendix of P. C. Joshi's *For the Final Bid to Power,* (Bombay, 1947), pp. 100-101.

97. *Ibid.,* p. 105.

98. *Ibid.*

99. *Ibid.,* p. 106.

100. *Ibid.*

101. *Ibid.,* pp. 106-107.

102. *Ibid.,* p. 106.

103. *Ibid.,* p. 108.

104. *Ibid.,* p. 111.

105. *Ibid.*

106. *Ibid.,* p. 110.

107. *Ibid.*

108. *Ibid.,* pp. 110-111.

109. *Ibid.,* p. 117.

110. *Ibid.,* p. 111.
111. *Ibid.,* p. 112.
112. *Ibid.*
113. *Ibid.*
114. *Ibid.,* pp. 114-115.
115. *Ibid.,* p. 116.
116. *Ibid.,* pp. 117-118.
117. *Ibid.,* p. 120.
118. *Ibid.*
119. *Ibid.,* pp. 120-121.
120. See R. Palme Dutt, "Quitting India," *Labour Monthly,* (Vol. XXVIII, No. 10, October, 1946), p. 300; James Spedding, "Stop Interfering in India," *World News and Views,* (Vol. XXVI, No. 27, July 6, 1946), p. 211; Michael Carritt, "The Failure of a Mission," *World News and Views,* (Vol. XXVI, No. 32, August 10, 1946), pp. 249-250; and unsigned article, "Conscription for What," *Labour Monthly,* (Vol. XXVIII, No. 12, December, 1946), p. 362. The latter article held peace-time conscription had been introduced in Britain to hold down the hapless Indians.
121. Joshi, *For the Final Bid to Power,* pp. 54-55.
122. *Ibid.,* pp. 60 ff.
123. "A. G." "India's Food Problem," *Labour Monthly,* (Vol. XXVIII, No. 5, May, 1946), p. 160.
124. R. Palme Dutt, "Travel Notes," *Labour Monthly,* (Vol. XXVIII, No. 6, June, 1946), pp. 185-186.
125. For details see R. Palme Dutt, *India Today,* (1949 ed.), pp. 178 ff.
126. R. Palme Dutt, "India—No Time to Lose," *World News and Views,* (Vol. XXVI, No. 9, March 2, 1946), p. 65.
127. R. Palme Dutt, "Independence for India," *Labour Monthly,* (Vol. XXVIII, No. 8, August, 1946), pp. 246-247.
128. *Ibid.,* pp. 247-248.
129. *Ibid.,* p. 249.
130. Puran Chandra Joshi, "India, What Now?" *World News and Views,* (Vol. XXV, No. 31, August 11, 1945), p. 243.
131. Communist Party of Great Britain, (Central Committee), "India," *World News and Views,* (Vol. XXV, No. 40, October 13, 1945), p. 316; Michael Carritt, "Labour and India," *World News and Views,* (Vol. XXV, No. 38, September 28, 1945), p. 299; and Joshi, "India, What Now?" *loc. cit.,* p. 243.

132. R. Palme Dutt, "Independence for India," *loc. cit.,* p. 247; unsigned article, "Plan for India," *World News and Views,* (Vol. XXVI, No. 21, May 25, 1946), p. 161.
133. Unsigned article, *New Times,* (Moscow) (No. 9, May 1, 1946), p. 32.
134. *People's Age,* September 1, 1946, p. 5.
135. For details see *ibid.*
136. Dyakov, *Indiya vo vremya i posle vtoroi mirovoi voini,* p. 109.
137. *People's Age,* June 29, 1947, p. 6.
138. *Ibid.* For hostile British Communist reaction to the plan see Harry Pollitt (for the Communist Party of Great Britain, Executive Committee) "India," *World News and Views,* (Vol. XXVII, No. 23, June 21, 1947), pp. 265-266, and R. Palme Dutt, "The Mountbatten Plan for India," *Labour Monthly,* (Vol. XXIX, No. 7, July, 1947), pp. 210 ff.
139. See *People's Age,* June 22, 1947, p. 7 in reference to the attitude of the C.P.I. as regards the partition of Bengal, and March 30, 1947, p. 2 in respect to the partition of the Punjab.
140. R. Palme Dutt, "India and Pakistan," *loc. cit.,* p. 90.
141. *Ibid.*
142. R. Palme Dutt, "Travel Notes," *Labour Monthly,* (Vol. XXVIII, No. 10, October, 1946), p. 319.
143. Joshi, *For the Final Bid to Power,* p. 84.
144. *Ibid.*
145. Communist Party of India, "Election Manifesto of the Communist Party of India," *World News and Views,* (Vol. XXVI, No. 10, March 9, 1946), p. 78.
146. Joshi, *For the Final Bid to Power,* p. 81.
147. *Ibid.,* p. 84.
148. *Ibid.,* p. 5.
149. *Ibid.,* p. 70.
150. *Ibid.,* pp. 81-82
151. *Ibid.,* p. 84.
152. See the article on the defense of Sheikh Abdullah, "Not Guilty." *Labour Monthly,* (Vol. XXVIII, No. 10, October, 1946), p. 311. See also Dyakov, *Indiya vo vremya i posle vtoroi mirovoi voini,* p. 79.
153. Dyakov, *Indiya vo vremya i posle vtoroi mirovoi voini,* p. 224.

154. See Narayan, *op. cit.*, pp. 225 ff.; Jones, *op. cit.*, p. 178, Rajkumar, *op. cit.*, pp. 63-64; and Mellor, *op. cit.*, p. 72.

155. For example, see *People's Age,* February 9, 1947, p. 9.

156. Unsigned article, "Communist Progress in India," *World News and Views,* (Vol. XXVI, No. 19, May 11, 1946), p. 145.

157. "Bombay Correspondent," "Communism in India," *loc. cit.*, p. 846.

158. See Mohan Singh, *Congress Unmasked* (Ludhiana, India, 1947), pp. 24, 36 ff.

159. For details see *New Age,* October 4, 1953, p. 3.

160. A. M. Dyakov, "India after the War," *New Times,* (No. 2, January 15, 1946), pp. 10 ff.

161. *Ibid.*, pp. 10-11.

162. *Ibid.* For a generalized criticism of British rule in India, see also Dyakov's article, "India and her Peoples," *New Times,* (No. 5, March 1, 1946), pp. 25 ff. See also A. Bolshakov, "Life in India as It Really Is," *New Times,* (No. 7, April 1, 1946), pp. 29-30, and V. Borisov, "The British Colonial Empire as It Really Is," *New Times,* (No. 22, November 15, 1946), pp. 25-28.

163. *New York Times,* March 26, 1946, p. 2.

164. Unsigned article, *New Times,* (No. 6, March 15, 1946), p. 13, and news item, *New Times,* (No. 7, April 1, 1946), p. 32.

165. Unsigned article, "The Indian Problem," *New Times,* (No. 6, March 15, 1946), pp. 17-18.

166. But this did not apply to the comrades in England, the immediate supervisors of India's Communists. See R. Palme Dutt, "India—No Time to Lose," *loc. cit.*, p. 65.

167. *Pravda,* July 15, 1946, p. 3.

168. A. M. Dyakov, "The Events in India," *New Times,* (No. 24, December 15, 1946), p. 15.

169. *Ibid.*

170. *Pravda,* October 21, 1946, p. 4.

171. Dyakov, "The Events in India," *loc. cit.*, p. 15.

172. Dyakov, "India after the War," *loc. cit.*, p. 13.

173. As quoted in Sitaramayya, *op. cit.*, II, ccxliii.

174. *The Hindu,* September 27, 1946, p. 4.

175. Jawaharlal Nehru, *Before and After Independence,* Speeches, 1922-1950, J. S. Bright, editor (New Delhi, 1950), p. 400.

176. *The Hindu,* September 27, 1946, p. 4.

177. *New York Times,* September 26, 1946, p. 34.

178. *The Times* (London), November 13, 1946, p. 5.
179. *New York Times,* October 1, 1946, p. 15.
180. *Pravda,* October 21, 1946, p. 4.
181. *Ibid.*
182. For full details see United Nations General Assembly, *Plenary Meetings of the General Assembly, 23 October–16 December, 1946;* Documents A/205 and A/205, Add: 1. *Treatment of Indians in the Union of South Africa,* pp. 1006 ff., especially pp. 1041-1046.
183. *Ibid.,* p. 1061.
184. *Pravda,* October 21, 1946, p. 4.
185. See *New Times,* (No. 10, March 7, 1946), p. 31.
186. *The Hindu,* November 13, 1946, p. 4.
187. As quoted in unsigned article, "Soviet Comment on Pakistan," *Modern Review,* (Vol. LXXXI, No. 1, January, 1947), p. 9.
188. *Ibid.*
189. See A. Volgin, "Our Trip to India," *New Times,* (No. 12, March 21, 1947), p. 20, and unsigned article, "India and Russia," *Calcutta Review,* (Vol. XII, No. 1, January, 1947), pp. 52-53.
190. Unsigned article, "India and Russia," *loc. cit.,* pp. 52-53.
191. *Ibid.*
192. For details see Volgin, *loc. cit.,* pp. 21 ff.
193. *New Times,* (No. 13, March 28, 1947), p. 32.
194. Nehru, *Before and After Independence,* p. 425.
195. Unsigned article, "The Inter-Asian Relations Conference," *Calcutta Review,* (Vol. CII, No. 2, February, 1947), p. 154.
196. *New Times,* (No. 15, April 11, 1947), p. 31.
197. *The Hindu,* April 16, 1947, p. 7.
198. Leading article, "Establishment of Soviet-Indian Diplomatic Relations," *New Times,* (No. 16, April 18, 1947), p. 31.
199. *Ibid.* The theme of the editorial was: "The machinations of the foes of international peace and friendship were unable to prevent the establishment of diplomatic relations between India and the Soviet Union."
200. Unsigned article, "The Security Council and India," *Calcutta Review,* (Vol. CIV, No. 1, January, 1947), p. 47.
201. *Ibid.*
202. *The Hindu,* June 27, 1947, p. 4.
203. *New York Times,* August 12, 1947, p. 3.

204. *The Times* (London), October 22, 1947, p. 3.

205. *The Times* (London), December 18, 1947, p. 3.

206. *The Times* (London), May 13, 1948, p. 3.

207. *Izvestia,* July 5, 1947, p. 3.

208. *Ibid.* The Soviet view in brief was that the Mountbatten plan for the sub-continent, by partitioning it, "gives England an opportunity to retain to a maximum degree her economic and political position there."

209. *New York Times,* June 4, 1947, p. 14.

210. *Ibid.*

211. See the unsigned articles, "Spotlight on Slander," *New Times,* (No. 12, June 15, 1946), p. 19 and "Anti-Soviet Slander in India," (No. 10, March 7, 1947), p. 26.

212. *Times of India* (Bombay), April 12, 1947, p. 4.

213. Unsigned article, "Different Voices but One Choir Leader," *New Times,* (No. 18, September 15, 1946), p. 28.

214. See the unsigned article, "Indo-Russian Trade Prospects," *Modern Review,* (Vol. LXXX, No. 2, August, 1946), p. 101.

215. See the unsigned article, "Religion in Russia and India," *Modern Review,* (Vol. LXXXI, No. 2, February, 1947), p. 180.

216. "B. K." "Communism and Indian Communism," *Modern Review,* (Vol. LXXXIX, No. 4, April, 1946), p. 292.

217. Unsigned article, "Spotlight on Slander," *loc. cit.,* p. 19.

218. Unsigned article, "Anti-Soviet Slander in India," *loc. cit.,* p. 26. For critical views of Soviet policy see also D. P. Mukherji, "Views and Counter-Views," (Lucknow, 1946), p. 188, and Iqbal Singh, *op. cit.,* pp. 71-72.

219. *New York Times,* September 25, 1946, p. 11. The statement was made in connection with a reported attempt by a Muslim League member in September, 1946 to interview Foreign Minister Molotov in Paris in regard to possible Soviet aid to the League. The rumor, however, was denied.

220. Nehru, *Important Speeches,* p. 358.

221. For the story of the Soviet retreat from Northern Iran in 1945-1946, see Lenczowski, *op. cit.,* pp. 284 ff.

222. See the unsigned articles in the *New Times,* "Diverting Attention," (No. 17, September 1, 1946), p. 24, and "Different Voices but One Choir Leader," *loc. cit.,* p. 28. As for Afghanistan, it may be noted that the Soviets made little progress there between August, 1945 and August, 1947. Neither did they make any progress in Chinese Turkestan nor Tibet during that period.

223. "B. K." "Communism and Indian Communism," *loc. cit.*, p. 294.

224. *Ibid.*, pp. 292-295.

225. *New York Times*, March 3, 1946, p. IV, 5. See also Robert A. Smith, *Divided India* (New York, 1947), p. 25.

226. *New York Times*, January 21, 1947, p. 11.

Bibliography

A. *Books and Pamphlets*

Adhikari, Gangadhar M., *Pakistan and Indian National Unity,* London, Labour Monthly, 1943, 32 pp.

Agabekov, Georgii (Grigorii), *OGPU, the Russian Secret Terror,* New York, Brentano's, 1931, 277 pp.

Akademiia Nauk, S.S.S.R., *Krizis kolonialnoi systemi,* Moscow, Akademiia Nauk, 1951, 289 pp.

Bailey, Frederick M., *Mission to Tashkent,* London, Jonathan Cape, 1946, 308 pp.

Balabushevich, V. V., *Rabochii klass i rabochee dvizhenie v Indii,* Moscow, Uchenie zapiski Tikhookeanskogo instituta AN SSSR, (Vol. II) 1949, 226 pp.

Barmine, Alexandre, *Memoirs of a Soviet Diplomat,* L. Dickson, London, 1938, 360 pp.

Beauchamp, Joan, *British Imperialism in India,* London, Martin Lawrence, 1934, 135 pp.

Bose, Subhas C., *The Indian Struggle, 1920-1934,* London, Wishart & Co., 1934, 349 pp.

Brailsford, Henry Noel, *Rebel India,* New York, New Republic Co., 1931, 262 pp.

————, *Subject India,* New York, the John Day Co., 1943, 223 pp.

Cambridge University, *Cambridge History of India;* the Indian Empire, 1858-1918, H. H. Dodwell, editor; Cambridge, (England) (Cambridge) University Press, 1932, Vol. VI, 660 pp.

Chakraberty, Chandra, *New India,* Calcutta, Vijayakhrishna Press, 1951, 125 pp.

Coates, W. P. and Zelda K., *A History of Anglo-Soviet Relations,* London, Lawrence & Wishart, 1944, 816 pp.

————, *Soviets in Central Asia,* London, Lawrence & Wishart, 1951, 288 pp.

Coatman, John, *Years of Destiny;* India, 1926-1932, London, Jonathan Cape, 1932, 384 pp.

Coupland, Sir Reginald, *India: a Re-Statement,* Oxford, Oxford University Press, 1945, 311 pp.

———, *The Indian Problem; Report on the Constitutional Problem in India,* New York, London, Oxford University Press, 1944, 711 pp.

Cummings, K. and W. W. Petit, (editors) *Russian-American Relations;* Documents and Papers, prepared for the Foreign Policy Association, New York, Harcourt, Brace & Howe, 1920, 375 pp.

Dallin, David J., *Soviet Russia and the Far East,* New Haven, Connecticut, Yale University Press, 1943, 398 pp.

Das, Mohan, *Communist Activity in India, 1925-1950,* Bombay, the Democratic Research Service, 1951, 16 pp.

Das, Rajani Kanta, *The Labour Movement in India,* Berlin, Leipzig, Walter De Gruyter Co., 1923, 112 pp.

Desai, A. R., *Social Background of Indian Nationalism,* Bombay, Oxford University Press, 1948, 415 pp.

Deva, Acharya Narendra, *Socialism and the National Revolution,* Bombay, Padma Publications, 1946, 208 pp.

Dutt, Rajani Palme, *India To-day,* London, Victor Gollancz Ltd., 1940, 544 pp.

———, *India Today,* (revised edition) Bombay, People's Publishing House, 1949, 581 pp.

———, *Modern India,* London, Communist Party of Great Britain, 1927, 174 pp.

———, *The Problem of India,* New York, International Publishers, 1943, 224 pp.

Dyakov, A. M., *Indiya i Pakistan,* Moscow, Pravda, 1950, 71 pp.

———, *Indiya vo vremya i posle vtoroi mirovoi voini, 1939-1949,* Moscow, Akademiya Nauk, 1952, 258 pp.

———, *Natsionalnii vopros i angliiskii imperializm v Indii,* Moscow, Gos-izd. vv pol-litri., 1948, 328 pp.

Ebon, Martin, *World Communism Today,* New York and Toronto, McGraw-Hill Book Co., 1948, 536 pp.

Etherton, Percy T., *In the Heart of Asia,* London, Constable & Co., 1925, 205 pp.

Feis, Herbert, *The Road to Pearl Harbor,* Princeton, New Jersey, Princeton University Press, 1950, 356 pp.

Fischer, Louis, *Gandhi and Stalin,* Madras, Rajkamal Publications, 1947, 147 pp.

———, *The Soviets in World Affairs,* Princeton, New Jersey, Princeton University Press, 1951, 2 Vols.

Fraser-Tytler, Sir William K., *Afghanistan;* a Study of Political Developments in Central Asia, London, Oxford University Press, 1953, (second edition) 348 pp.

Fulop-Millar, René, *Lenin and Gandhi,* London & New York, G. P. Putnam's Sons, 1927, 343 pp.

Fuse, K., *Soviet Policy in the Orient,* Peiping (Peking), Enjinsha, 1927, 409 pp.

Gauba, K. L., *Famous and Historic Trials,* Lahore, Lion Press, 1946, 423 pp.

Grant, A. J. and Harold Temperly, *Europe in the Nineteenth and Twentieth Centuries,* London, Longmans, Green & Co., 1940, 716 pp.

Gregg, Richard B., *Gandhism and Socialism,* Madras, S. Ganesan, 1931, 400 pp.

Gunther, Frances, *Revolution in India,* New York, Island Press, 1944, 122 pp.

Howland, John S., *Indian Crisis,* New York, the Macmillan Co., 1943, 193 pp.

Hutchinson, Lester, *Conspiracy at Meerut,* London, George Allen & Unwin, Ltd., 1935, 190 pp.

Joshi, Puran Chandra, *Among Kisan Patriots,* Bombay, People's Publishing House, 1946, 16 pp.

———, *The Indian Communist Party;* Forward to Freedom, with introduction by Harry Pollitt, London, Communist Party of Great Britain, 1942, 33 pp.

Jones, George E., *Tumult in India,* New York, Dodd, Mead & Co., 1948, 277 pp.

Karaka, D. F., *Betrayal in India,* London, Victor Gollancz Ltd., 1950, 253 pp.

Kendall, Patricia, *India and the British,* London, Charles Scribners' Sons, 1931, 467 pp.

Kohn, Hans, *A History of Nationalism in the East,* New York, Harcourt Brace & Co., 1929, 476 pp.

Lacey, Patrick, *Fascist India,* London, Nicholson and Watson, 1946, 150 pp.

Lenczowski, George, *Russia and the West in Iran, 1918-1948,* Ithaca, New York, Cornell University Press, 1948, 383 pp.

Lenin, Nikolai, *Imperialism,* New York, Vanguard Press, 1926, 108 pp.

Levi, Werner, *Free India in Asia,* Minneaoplis, University of Minnesota Press, 1952, 161 pp.

Limaye, Madhu, *Communist Party; Facts and Fiction,* Hyderabad, (India) Chetana Prakashan, 1951, 100 pp.

Linton, Ralph, editor, *Most of the World,* New York, Columbia University Press, 1949, 917 pp.

Lobanov-Rostovsky, Prince A., *Russia and Asia,* Ann Arbor, Michigan, the G. Wahr Publishing Co., 1951, 342 pp.

Lyons, Gervais, (James) *Afghanistan, the Buffer State,* Madras, Higginbothan & Co., 1910, 232 pp.

MacMunn, Sir George, *Turmoil and Tragedy in India;* 1914 and After, Jarrolds, 1935, 294 pp.

Majumdar, Ramesh Chandra, H. C. Raychaudhuri, Kalikinkar Dutta, *An Advanced History of India,* London, Macmillan Co., 1948, 1081 pp.

Marx, Karl, *Capital;* a Critique of Political Economy, Chicago, C. H. Kerr & Co., 1909-1921, 3 Vols.

———, *Correspondence,* New York, International Publishers, 1934, 551 pp.

Marx, Karl and Friedrich Engels, *Korrespondentsia Karl Marksa i Friedrich Engelsa c rosskiimi politicheskiimi deatelami,* Moscow, Goz-iz., 1947, 687 pp.

———, *Manifesto of the Communist Party,* New York, International Publishers, 1932, 48 pp.

Marriott, J. A. R., *Anglo-Russian Relations, 1689-1943,* London, Methuen & Co., 1943, 227 pp.

Masani, Minoo R., *The Communist Party of India,* New York, the Macmillan Co., 1954, 302 pp.

———, *Socialism Reconsidered,* Bombay, Padma Publications, 1944, 70 pp.

Mayo, Katherine, *Mother India,* New York, Harcourt Brace & Co., 1927, 440 pp.

Middleton, W. B., *Britain and Russia,* London, Hutchinson & Co., 1946, 238 pp.

Mellor, Andrew, *India since Partition,* New York, Frederick A. Praeger, 1951, 156 pp.

Moore, Harriet L., *Soviet Far Eastern Policy, 1931-1945,* Princeton, New Jersey, Princeton University Press, 1945, 285 pp.

Mukerjee, Radakamal, *The Indian Working Class,* Bombay, Hind Kitabas, 1951, 407 pp.

Mukerji, Dhurjati Prasad, *Views and Counter-Views,* Lucknow, Universal Publishers, 1946, 196 pp.

Mukhtar, Ahmed, *Trade Unionism and Labour Disputes in India,* Calcutta, Longmans, Green & Co., 1935, 251 pp.

Narayan, Jay Prakash, *Towards Struggle,* Bombay, Padma Publications, 1946, 244 pp.

Nehru, Jawaharlal, *Before and After Independence;* Speeches, 1922-1950, edited by J. S. Bright, New Delhi, the Indian Printing Works, 1950, 612 pp.

———, *The Discovery of India,* New York, the John Day Co., 1946, 595 pp.

———, *Important Speeches,* Being a Collection of Most Significant Speeches Delivered by Jawaharlal Nehru from 1922 to 1946, edited by J. S. Bright, Lahore, the Indian Printing Works, 396 pp.

———, *Mahatma Gandhi,* Calcutta, Signet Press, 1948, 169 pp.

———, *Soviet Russia,* Bombay, Chetena, 1929, 132 pp.

———, *Toward Freedom,* the Autobiography of Jawaharlal Nehru, New York, the John Day Co., 1942, 438 pp.

———, *The Unity of India,* Collected Writings 1937-1946, the John Day Co., 1948, 432 pp.

O'Malley, L. S. S., *Modern India and the West,* London, Oxford University Press, 1941, 834 pp.

Parkin, George Raleigh, *India Today*—an Introduction to Indian Politics, New York, Toronto, Longmans, Green & Co., 1946, 387 pp.

Pasvolski, Leo, *Russia in the Far East,* New York, the Macmillan Co., 1922, 181 pp.

Payne, Robert, *Red Storm over Asia,* New York, the Macmilan Co., 1951, 309 pp.

Polak, H. S. L., Henry Noel Brailsford, Lord Pethwick-Lawrence, *Mahatma Gandhi,* London, Odham Press Ltd., 1948, 320 pp.

Punekar, S. D., *Trade Unionism in India,* Bombay, New Book Co., 1948, 407 pp.

Rajkumar, N. V., *Indian Political Parties,* New Delhi, All-India Congress Committee, 1948, 139 pp.

Raman, T. A., *Report on India,* New York, Oxford University Press, 1943, 231 pp.

Reed, Sir Stanley and P. R. Cadell, *India, the New Phase,* London, Phillip Alan & Co., 1928, 175 pp.

Riencourt, Amaury de, *Roof of the World, Tibet, Key to Asia,* New York, Rinehart, 1950, 322 pp.

Rosinger, Lawrence K., *Restless India,* New York, Henry Holt & Co., 1946, 113 pp.

Rosinger, Lawrence K., and Associates, *The State of Asia,* New York, Henry Holt & Co., 1946, 113 pp.

Roy, Manabendra Nath, *The Future of Indian Politics,* London, R. Bishop, 1926, 118 pp.

————, *I Accuse,* New York, Roy Defense Committee of India, 1932, 30 pp.

————, *Letters from Jail,* Bombay, Renaissance Publishers, 1943, Vol. III, 284 pp.

————, *My Experience in China,* Calcutta, Renaissance Publishers, 1945, 70 pp.

————, *New Orientation,* Calcutta, Renaissance Publishers, 1946, 27 pp.

————, *Revolution and Counter-Revolution in China,* Calcutta, Renaissance Publishers, 1946, 631 pp.

Roy, Manabendra Nath and Evelyn, *One Year of Non-Cooperation from Ahmedabad to Gaya,* Calcutta, Communist Party of India, 1923, 184 pp.

Saklatvala, Shapurji, *Is India Different?,* London, Communist Party of Great Britain, 1927, 35 pp.

Shelvankar, Krishnarao Shivarao, *The Problem of India,* London, Penguin Books, 1940, 254 pp.

Shridharani, Krishnalal, *War Without Violence,* New York, Harcourt, Brace & Co., 1939, 351 pp.

Singh, Mohan, *Congress Unmasked,* Ludhiana, India, 1947, Desh Sewak Sanehwal, 1947, 199 pp.

Sitaramayya, B. Pattabhi, *The History of the Indian National Congress,* Vol. I, Madras, Law Printing House, 1935, 1164 pp.; Vol. II, Bombay, Padma Publications, 1947, 1098 pp.

Smith, Robert A., *Divided India,* New York, Whittlesey House, McGraw-Hill, 1947, 259 pp.

Smith, Wilfred C., *Modern Islam in India,* Lahore, Minerva Book Shop, 1943, 399 pp.

Spratt, Phillip, *The Communist Peace Appeal—its Real Character,* Bombay, Democratic Research Society, 1951, 46 pp.

Stalin, Joseph, *Foundations of Leninism,* New York, International Publishers, 1939, 127 pp.

———, *Marxism and the National Question,* New York, International Publishers, 1942, 222 pp.

———, *On the National Question,* London, Lawrence & Wishart, 1943, 32 pp.

Steiger, G. Nye, *A History of the Far East,* Boston, Ginn & Co., 1936, 928 pp.

Tendulkar, Dinanath Gopal, M. C. Rau, M. Sarabhai, U. K. Jaseri, *Gandhiji, His Life and Work,* Bombay, Jhaveri, Karnatak Publishing House, 1944, 501 pp.

Thompson, Edward John, *Ethical Ideas in India To-day,* London, Watts & Co., 1942, 39 pp.

Thompson, Edward John and G. T. Garratt, *The Rise and Fulfilment of British Rule in India,* London, Macmillan & Co., 1934, 690 pp.

Tilak, K., *Rise and Fall of the Comintern,* Bombay, Spark Syndicate, 1947, 157 pp.

Underwood, A. C., *Contemporary Thought of India,* London, Williams & Norgate Ltd., 1930, 235 pp.

Wallbank, T. Walter, *India in the New Era,* New York, Scott, Foresman & Co., 1951, 204 pp.

Wofford, Clare and Harris, *India Afire,* New York, the John Day Co., 1951, 343 pp.

B. *Documents*

All India Kisan Sabha, General Kisan Council, "Indian Peasants Call for Aid to the Soviet," *World News and Views,* Vol. XXI, No. 41, October 11, 1941, p. 653.

All India Trade Union Congress, "An Appeal to Indian Labour," an Address Delivered by D. Chaman Lal, General Secretary of the A.I.T.U.C., *Labour Monthly,* Vol. I, No. 2, September 1921, pp. 181-182.

———, *Report, Twentieth Session, Nagpur,* Bombay, Model House, 1943, 82 pp.

———, "Resolutions," Seventh Annual Session held in Delhi, March, 1927, *Labour Monthly,* Vol. IX, No. 7, July, 1927, pp. 443-444.

———, "Resolutions," Eighth Annual Session, held in Cawnpore, November, 1927, *Labour Monthly,* Vol. X, No. 4, April, 1928, pp. 251-253.

Bradley, Ben (jamin), Rajani Palme Dutt and Harry Pollitt, (for the Central Committee, Communist Party of Great Britain) "Greetings to the Indian National Congress, Haripura Session," *International Press Correspondence,* Vol. XVIII, No. 6, February 1, 1938, pp. 113-114.

Communist International, *The Communist International between the Fifth and Sixth Congress,* published for the Communist International by the Communist Party of Great Britain, London, Communist Party of Great Britain, 1928, 508 pp.

———, *From the Fourth to the Fifth World Congress,* Reports of the Executive Committee of the Communist International, London, Communist Party of Great Britain, 1924, 122 pp.

———, *First Congress of the Third International, March, 1919,* edited by William Paul, Glascow, Socialist Labour Press, 1919, 12 pp.

———, *Second Congress of the Third International, July 19–August 7, 1920,* (As reported verbatim from the Russian press for the United States Department of State) Washington, D. C., United States Government Printing Office, 1920, 137 pp.

———, *Third Congress of the Third International, June 22–July 12, 1921,* Theses and Resolutions, New York, the Contemporary Publishing Association, 1921, 199 pp.

———, *Fourth Congress of the Communist International, November 7–December 3, 1922,* London, Communist Party of Great Britain, 1922, 297 pp.

———, *Fifth Congress of the Communist International, June 17–July 8, 1924,* London, Communist Party of Great Britain, 1924, 294 pp.

———, *Compte-rendu stenographique du VIieme Congress de L'internationale Communiste,* July 17–August 28, 1928, Paris, Communist Party of France, 1928, 287 pp.

———, *Seventh Congress of the Communist International, July 25–August 20, 1935,* Moscow, Foreign Language Publishing House, 1939, 604 pp.

———, "Thesis on the Revolutionary Movement in the

Colonies and Semi-Colonies,"—Adopted at the Sixth Congress of the Communist International, *International Press Correspondence,* Vol. VIII, No. 49, December 12, 1928, pp. 1659-1676.

———, Executive Committee, "The XI Plenum of the E.C.C.I." *International Press Correspondence,* Vol. XI, No. 30, June 10, 1931 (special number), p. 552.

———, ———, "Report of the Meeting of the Executive Committee of the Communist International," *Communist Review,* Vol. I, No. 1, May, 1921, p. 21.

———, ———, "Resolution on the Oriental Question," (as adopted by the E.C.C.I. on March 4, 1922), *International Press Correspondence,* Vol. II, No. 29, April 25, 1922, p. 225.

———, ———, "To the Workers of all Countries," *International Press Correspondence,* Vol. III, No. 24, March 11, 1923, (Political Prisoners' Week) p. 190.

Communist Party of China, Central Committee, "Open Letter to the Indian Communists," from the C.C. of the Communist Party of China, *International Press Correspondence,* Vol. XIII, No. 51, November 24, 1933, pp. 1153-1158.

Communist Parties of China, Great Britain and Germany, Central Committees, "Open Letter to the Indian Communists," from the C.C.'s of the Communist Parties of China, Great Britain and Germany, *Communist International,* Vol. XI, No. 10, June 1, 1932, pp. 347-358.

Communist Party of Great Britain, Central Committee, "Communist Views," (on the Cripps Proposals) *World News and Views,* Vol. XXII, No. 14, April 4, 1942, p. 203.

———, ———, "Greetings to the Indian National Congress," *World News and Views,* Vol. XIX, No. 10, March 11, 1939, p. 199.

———, ———, "India," *World News and Views,* Vol. XXI, No. 42, October 18, 1941, p. 668.

———, ———, "India," *World News and Views,* Vol. XXV, No. 40, October 13, 1945, p. 316.

———, ———, "Stand by the Indian People," *World News and Views,* Vol. XIX, No. 53, November 1, 1939, pp. 1087-1089.

Communist Party of India, Central Committee, "Abridged Draft of the Political Thesis of the Communist Party of India," *International Press Correspondence,* Vol. XIV, No. 40, July 20, 1934, pp. 1024-1034.

———, ———, "Draft Platform of Action of the Communist Party of India," *International Press Correspondence,* Vol. X, No. 58, December 18, 1930, pp. 1218-1222.

———, ———, "Election Manifesto of the Communist Party of India," *World News and Views,* Vol. XXVI, No. 10, March 9, 1946, p. 78.

———, ———, "For a Free and Happy India," (Election Manifesto) *World News and Views,* Vol. XXV, No. 47, December 1, 1945, p. 391.

———, ———, "Manifesto of the Communist Party of India," *World News and Views,* Vol. XV, No. 11, March 16, 1940, pp. 166-167.

———, ———, *Strike;* the Story of the Strike in the Indian Navy, Bombay, People's Publishing House, 1946, 42 pp.

———, Second Congress, *Political Thesis Passed by the Second Congress, February 28—March 6, 1948,* Calcutta, published by M. Kaul for the Communist Party of India, 1949, 65 pp.

Dimitrov, Georgi, "The Offensive of Fascism and the Tasks of the C. I. in the Struggle for the Unity of the Working Class against Fascism," *International Press Correspondence,* Vol. XV, No. 43, September 7, 1935, pp. 1121-1128.

———, *The United Front against War and Fascism,* (Speeches delivered at the Seventh Congress of the Communist International, July 25—August 20, 1935) New York, International Publishers, 1936, 258 pp.

India, Government of, (L. F. Rushbrook Williams, editor), *India in 1919,* Calcutta, Superintendent of Government Printing, 1920, 281 pp.

———, (———, ———), *India in 1920,* Calcutta, Superintendent of Government Printing, 1921, 275 pp.

———, (———, ———), *India in 1921-1922,* Calcutta, Superintendent of Government Printing, 1922, 368 pp.

———, (———, ———), *India in 1922-1923,* Calcutta, Superintendent of Government Printing, 1923, 358 pp.

———, (———, ———), *India in 1923-1924,* Calcutta, Superintendent of Government Printing, 1924, 448 pp.

———, (———, ———), *India in 1924-1925,* Calcutta, Superintendent of Government Printing, 1925, 435 pp.

———, (John Coatman, editor,) *India in 1925-1926,* Calcutta, Superintendent of Government Printing, 1926, 463 pp.

———, (———, ———,) *India in 1926-1927,* Calcutta, Superintendent of Government Printing, 1927, 377 pp.

———, (———, ———,) *India in 1927-1928,* Calcutta, Superintendent of Government Printing, 1928, 461 pp.

———, (———, ———,) *India in 1928-1929,* Calcutta, Superintendent of Government Printing, 1929, 416 pp.

———, (———, ———,) *India in 1929-1930,* Calcutta, Superintendent of Government Printing, 1930, 494 pp.

———, (———, ———,) *India in 1930-1931,* Calcutta, Superintendent of Government Printing, 1931, 752 pp.

———, (———, ———,) *India in 1931-1932,* Calcutta, Superintendent of Government Printing, 1932, 238 pp.

———, (———, ———,) *India in 1932-1933,* Calcutta, Superintendent of Government Printing, 1933, 197 pp.

———, (———, ———,) *India in 1933-1934,* Calcutta, Superintendent of Government Printing, 1934, 196 pp.

———, (———, ———,) *India in 1934-1935,* Calcutta, Superintendent of Government Printing, 1935, 145 pp.

———, *Judgment Meerut Conspiracy Case,* Simla, Government of India Press, 1932, 2 Vols.

———, *The Legislative Assembly Debates,* Vol. III, September, 1928, Simla, Government of India Press, 1928.

———, ———, Vol. I, February, 1941, Simla, Government of India Press, 1941.

Indian National Congress, *Report of the General Secretary,* New Delhi, 1936, Indian National Congress, 40 pp.

Indian Year Book, a Statistical and Historical Annual of the Indian Empire with an Explanation of the Principal Topics of the Day, Vol. XXVI, 1939-1940, Bombay, Bennett & Coleman & Co., Ltd., 1940, 1265 pp.

International Labor Office, *Industrial Labour in India,* Studies and Reports—Industrial Relations, Geneva, International Labor Office, 1938, 335 pp.

Joshi, Puran Chandra, *Communist Reply to Congress Working Committee's Charges,* Bombay, People's Publishing House, 1945, 2 Vols.

———, *Correspondence between Mahatma Gandhi and P. C. Joshi,* Bombay, People's Publishing House, 1945, 68 pp.

———, *For the Final Bid to Power,* Bombay, People's Publishing House, 1947, 122 pp.

———, "An Indian Appeal to the British People," *World News and Views,* Vol. XXII, No. 34, August 22, 1942, p. 348.

Labour Monthly, "The Speech of the Prosecutor in the Meerut Case," Part I, *Labour Monthly,* Vol. XII, January, 1930, pp. 24-29, Part II, *ibid.,* Vol XII, No. 2, February, 1930, pp. 97-105, Part III, *ibid.,* Vol. XII, No. 3, March, 1930, pp. 177-183.

League Against Imperialism, "Crushing the Working Classes in India," *International Press Correspondence,* Vol. XIV, No. 44, August 17, 1934, p. 1139.

Mitra, Nripendra Nath, *The Indian Quarterly Register,* (later issued on an annual basis and called *The Indian Annual Register*), Calcutta, The Annual Register Office:

A. *The Indian Annual Register* for 1922, Calcutta, the Annual Register Office, 1923, 1012 pp.

B. *The Indian Annual Register* for 1925 (Vol. II, July-December), Calcutta, the Annual Register Office, 1926, 407 pp.

C. *The Indian Annual Register* for 1928 (Vol. II, July-December), Calcutta, the Annual Register Office, 1929, 516 pp.

D. *The Indian Annual Register* for 1936 (Vol. II, July-December), Calcutta, the Annual Register Office, 1937, 512 pp.

E. *The Indian Annual Register* for 1943 (Vol. I, January-June), Calcutta, the Annual Register Office, 1944, 436 pp.

F. *The Indian Annual Register* for 1945 (Vol. II, July-December), Calcutta, the Annual Register Office, 1946, 474 pp.

Orgwald, "A Conversation with Indian Comrades," (An analysis of the then policies of Indian Communism as ascertained by an interview by the author with leading

Indian Communists) *International Press Correspondence,* Vol. XIV, No. 20, March 29, 1934, pp. 517-522.

Pollitt, Harry, (for the Central Committee, Communist Party of Great Britain) "The Communist Party's Call to the Prime Minister," *World News and Views,* Vol. XXII, No. 35, August 29, 1942, p. 357.

———, (—————) "Free the Indian Communist Leaders," *World News and Views,* Vol. XXVII, No. 4, January 25, 1947, p. 40.

———, (—————) "Greeting to India," *World News and Views,* Vol. XXII, No. 31, August 1, 1942, p. 326.

———, (—————) "India," *World News and Views,* Vol. XXVII, No. 23, June 21, 1947, pp. 265-266.

———, (—————) "India, a Call to the British People," *Labour Monthly,* Vol. XXIII, No. 6, June, 1941, pp. 263-265.

———, (—————) "Statement by the Communist Party of Great Britain on India," *World News and Views,* Vol. XXII, No. 33, August 15, 1942, p. 330.

Pollitt, Harry, Rajani Palme Dutt and Ben (jamin) Bradley for the Central Committee, Communist Party of Great Britain, "Letter to the Indian Communists," *International Press Correspondence,* Vol. XVI, No. 50, November 7, 1936, pp. 1342-1344.

Red International of Labour Unions (R.I.L.U.) "The R.I.L.U. to the Eight All-India Congress of Trade Unions," *International Press Correspondence,* Vol. VII, No. 68, December 1, 1927, p. 1539.

Royal Institute of Internal Affairs, Jane Tabrisky Degras compiler, *Soviet Documents on Foreign Policy,* London, New York, Oxford University Press, 1951-1953, 3 vols.

Russian Federated Soviet Socialist Republic, Commissariat of Foreign Affairs, *Sinyaya Kniga,* Sbornik tainikh dokumentov izvlechevnikh iz arkhiva bishago Ministerstav inostrannikh diel Moscow, izdanie narodnago kommissariata po inostrannim dielam, 1918, 115 pp.

United Kingdom of Great Britain and Northern Ireland, Foreign Office, *Blue Book,* a Selection of Papers dealing with the Relations of His Majesty's Government with the Soviet Government, Cmd., 2895, London, His Majesty's Stationery Office, 1927, 72 pp.

——————, House of Commons, *Communist Papers and Documents Selected from those Obtained on the Arrest of Certain British Communist Leaders on October 14 and 21, 1925,* Parliamentary Publications, 192, Vol. XXIII (Accounts and Papers) Cmd. 2682, London, His Majesty's Stationery Office, 1926, 135 pp.

——————, India Office, *Judgment of the High Court of Judicature of Allahabad in the Revolutionary Conspiracy Case,* Cmd. 2309, London, His Majesty's Stationery Office, 1924, 16 pp.

——————, Parliament, (House of Commons), (Parliamentary) *Debates,* (Hansard) London, His Majesty's Stationery Office

A. 292 H. C. Deb. 5s (1927)
B. 234 H. C. Deb. 5s (1930)
C. 235 H. C. Deb. 5s (1930)
D. 238 H. C. Deb. 5s (1930)
E. 239 H. C. Deb. 5s (1930)
F. 248 H. C. Deb. 5s (1931)
G. 251 H. C. Deb. 5s (1931)
H. 252 H. C. Deb. 5s (1931)
I. 253 H. C. Deb. 5s (1931)
J. 257 H. C. Deb. 5s (1931)
K. 265 H. C. Deb. 5s (1932)
L. 281 H. C. Deb. 5s (1933)
M. 284 H. C. Deb. 5s (1933)
N. 292 H. C. Deb. 5s (1934)
O. 404 H. C. Deb. 5s (1944)
P. 419 H. C. Deb. 5s (1946)
Q. 434 H. C. Deb. 5s (1947)

United Nations, General Assembly, Plenary Meeting of the General Assembly, 23 October–16 December, 1946, Docs. A/205 and A/205, Add. 1, *Treatment of Indians in the Union of South Africa,* New York, United Nations, 1947, pp. 1006-1061.

United States Government, Department of State, *Nazi-Soviet Relations,* edited by Raymond J. Sontag and James C.

Beddie, Washington D. C., United States Government Printing Office, 1948, 362 pp.

———, Office of Strategic Services, *The Communist Party of India,* (at one time placed in the Confidential Center) R. & A. No. 2681, Washington, D. C. 1945, United States Government Printing Office, 82 pp.

United States Senate, Committee on the Judiciary, *Bolshevik Propaganda,* hearings 65:3, pursuant to S. Res. 439 and 469, February 11–March 10, 1919, Washington D.C., United States Government Printing Office, 1919, 1265 pp.

Workers' and Peasants' Party of Bengal, *A Call to Action,* being the Resolutions, Theses and Report Presented to the Third Annual Conference of the Workers' and Peasants' Party of Bengal, Calcutta, Workers' and Peasants' Party of Bengal, 1928, 58 pp.

Workers' and Peasants' Party of India, "The Political Situation in India," (the Party Thesis) *Labour Monthly,* Vol. XI, No. 3, March, 1929, pp. 151-162.

Young Communist League of India, "Draft Platform of Action of the Young Communist League of India," *International Press Correspondence,* Vol. XII, No. 10, March 10, 1932, pp. 228-232.

Zinoviev, G., "Survey of the Class War," (Report of the President of the Communist International at the Fourth Congress of the Communist International) *Communist Review,* Vol. III, No. 9, January, 1923, pp. 474-503.

C. *Selected Periodical Articles*

Abbas, Khwaja Ahmad, "Moscow Comes to India," *Asia,* Vol. XI, No. 8, August, 1944, pp. 350-351.

Adhikari, Gangadhar M., "Pakistan and National Unity," *Labour Monthly,* Vol. XXV, No. 3, March, 1943, pp. 87-91.

Ahmad, Muzaffar, "Meerut Communist Conspiracy," *Amrita Bazar Patrika,* (Independence Number) August 15, 1947, pp. 223-226.

Ali, Mohammed, "India in 1930," *Communist International,* Vol. VIII, Nos. 3-4, February 1, 1931, pp. 105-113.

Arnot, R. Page, "The Meerut Sentences," *Labour Monthly,* Vol. XV, No. 1, January, 1933, pp. 96-101.

———, "Notes on British Imperialism," *Communist International,* Vol. VIII, No. 5, February 15, 1931, pp. 125-131.

———, "Report on the Simon Commission," *Labour Monthly,* Vol. XII, No. 7, July, 1930, pp. 388-403.

———, "The Sham Constitution of India," *International Press Correspondence,* Vol. XIII, No. 31, July 14, 1933, pp. 683-687.

Ashe, B., "The Anti-War Movement in India," *World News and Views,* Vol. XIX, No. 58, December 16, 1939, p. 1151.

———, "Britain and the North-West Frontier," *World News and Views,* Vol. XX, No. 20, May 18, 1940, p. 291.

———, "Increased Tension in the Indian Situation," *World News and Views,* Vol. XX, No. 13, April 6, 1940, p. 216.

———, "India and World Opinion," *World News and Views,* Vol. XX, No. 5, February 3, 1940, pp. 67-68.

———, "Non-Violence or a People's Army," *World News and Views,* Vol. XX, No. 27, July 6, 1940, p. 379. 1173-1174.

———, "Political Parties in India," *World News and Views,* Vol. XIX, No. 60, December 30, 1939, pp. 1173-1174.

———, "The Political Situation in India," *World News and Views,* Vol. XX, No. 49, November 30, 1940, pp. 689-690.

———, "The Underground Struggle in India," *World News and Views,* Vol. XX, No. 43, October 26, 1940, pp. 597-599.

———, "Who Are the Indian Princes?," *World News and Views,* Vol. XX, No. 6, February 10, 1940, p. 89.

———, "The Viceroy's Offer to India," *World News and Views,* Vol. XX, No. 33, August 17, 1940, pp. 447-448.

Bacon, Elizabeth and Alfred E. Hudson, "Afghanistan Waits," *Asia,* Vol. XVI, No. 1, January, 1941, pp. 31-36.

Bannerjee, Nitya, N., "Art and Literature in Russia," *Modern Review,* Vol. LV, No. 5, May, 1934, pp. 567-570.

———., "My First Day in Leningrad," *Modern Review,* Vol. LIV, No. 12, December, 1933, pp. 683-689.

———., "Russia Today," *Modern Review,* Vol. LV, No. 2, February, 1934, pp. 140-144.

Basak, V., "A Few Remarks on the Indian Communist Movement," *International Press Correspondence,* Vol. XIV, No. 32, June 1, 1934, pp. 845-849.

————, "The Situation in India," Part I, *International Press Correspondence,* Vol. XIII, No. 39, September 8, 1933, pp. 853-854, Part II, *ibid.,* Vol. XIII, No. 40, September 15, 1933, pp. 896-897 and *ibid.,* Vol. XIII, No. 41, September 22, 1933, pp. 927-928, Part III, *ibid.,* Vol. XIII, No. 43, September 29, 1933, pp. 946-948.

Basu, Tara, "India's Famine," *Labour Monthly,* Vol. XXVI, No. 1, January, 1944, p. 32.

Beauchamp, Joan, "The Sixty-Six Per Cent Background to the India Bill," *Labour Monthly,* Vol. XVII, No. 3, March, 1935, pp. 171-176.

Bernard, Theos, "The Peril of Tibet," *Asia,* Vol. XL, No. 9, September, 1940, pp. 500-504.

Bhat, K. S., "The Workers' Welfare League of India," *Labour Monthly,* Vol. XIII, No. 12, December, 1931, pp. 777-779.

Bishop, R., "Imperialism's Handiwork in India," *International Press Correspondence,* Vol. XVI, No. 42, September 12, 1936, pp. 1153-1154.

————., "Industrial Ferment in India," *International Press Correspondence,* Vol. XVIII, No. 1, January 8, 1938, pp. 15-16.

————., "The Present Situation in India," *International Press Correspondence,* Vol. XVI, No. 64, December 5, 1936, pp. 1444-1445.

Blair, Hamish, "Communism in the Open—the Meaning of the Bombay Riots," *Saturday Review,* (London) Vol. CLVII, No. 4101, June 2, 1934, p. 633.

Bolshakov, A., "Life in India as It Really Is," *New Times,* No. 7, April 1, 1946, pp. 29-30.

Borisov, V., "The British Colonial Empire as It Really Is," *New Times,* No. 22, November 15, 1946, pp. 25-28.

Bradley, Ben (jamin), "The Background in India," *Labour Monthly,* Vol. XVI, No. 3, March, 1934, pp. 173-177.

————, "A Great Step Forward in India," *World News and Views,* Vol. XXII, No. 31, August 1, 1942, p. 326.

————, "India, the Haripura Session, *Labour Monthly,* Vol. XX, No. 4, April, 1938, pp. 237-244.

———, "India Must Be Freed," *Labour Monthly,* Vol. XXIV, No. 10, October, 1942, pp. 306-307.

———, "India Threatened," *Labour Monthly,* Vol. XXIV, No. 5, May, 1942, pp. 144-148.

———, "India's Workers' Great One Day Strike," *Labour Monthly,* Vol. XXI, No. 1, January, 1939, pp. 46-52.

———, "Indian Crisis," *Labour Monthly,* Vol. XXV, No. 5, May, 1943, pp. 153-158.

———, "The Indian Elections," *Labour Monthly,* Vol. XIX, No. 4, April, 1937, pp. 229-240.

———, "The Indian National Congress," *International Press Correspondence,* Vol. XVIII, No. 6, February 6, 1938, pp. 126-127.

———, "The Indian National Congress and Ministries," *International Press Correspondence,* Vol. XVII, No. 41, September 25, 1937, pp. 925-927.

———, "Indian National Congress—Tripuri Session," *World News and Views,* Vol. XIX, No. 18, April 1, 1939, pp. 365-366.

———, "A New Phase in the Struggle for Freedom," *International Press Corespondence,* Vol. XVII, No. 16, April 14, 1937, pp. 400-401.

———, "Stabbing Our Alies in the Back," *World News and Views,* Vol. XXIII, No. 3, January 16, 1943, p. 22.

———, "Unrest in the North-West Frontier," *International Press Correspondence,* Vol. XVII, No. 17, April 17, 1937, pp. 421-422.

———, "The Urgency of India," *World News and Views,* Vol. XXII, No. 29, July 18, 1942, p. 312.

———, "What the Congress Socialists Want," *International Press Correspondence,* Vol. XIV, No. 60, December 15, 1934, pp. 1694-1698.

Bradley, Ben (jamin) and Rajani Palme Dutt, "Towards Trade Union Unity in India," *International Press Correspondence,* Vol. XXI, No. 12, March 7, 1936, pp. 325-328.

Bridgeman, Reginald, "The New Deal for India," *Labour Monthly,* Vol. XVII, No. 1, January, 1935, pp. 20-29.

Burns, Emile, "Amery Must Go," *World News and Views,* Vol. XXIII, No. 18, May 1, 1943, p. 142.

Burns, L., "The Strike Struggle in India," *Communist Inter-*

national, Vol. XV, No. 1-2, January-February, 1938, pp. 95-98.

Burton, Wilbur, "Tug of War in Central Asia," *Asia,* Vol. XXXV, No. 9, September, 1935, p. 517.

Carritt, Michael, "Britain and India," *World News and Views,* Vol. XXV, No. 24, June 23, 1945, p. 187.

———, "A Constituent Assembly," *Labour Monthly,* Vol. XXVII, No. 11, November, 1945, pp. 342-345.

———, "The Crisis in India," *Labour Monthly,* Vol. XXIII, No. 2, February, 1941, pp. 75-82.

———, "The Failure of a Mission," *World News and Views,* Vol. XXVI, No. 32, August 10, 1946, pp. 249-250.

———, "India before the Storm," *Labour Monthly,* Vol. XXII, No. 5, May, 1940, pp. 294-303.

———, "The Indian Conspiracy Case," *World News and Views,* Vol. XXI, No. 23, June 7, 1941, pp. 366-367.

———, "Labour and India," *World News and Views,* Vol. XXV, No. 38, September 28, 1945, p. 299.

———, "A Tense Situation in India," *World News and Views,* Vol. XXV, No. 20, May 26, 1945, pp. 156-157.

Castagne, Joseph, "Soviet Imperialism in Afghanistan," *Foreign Affairs,* Vol. XIII, No. 4, July, 1935, pp. 698-705.

Chattopadhyaya, Virendranath, "The Capitulation of the Indian Bourgeoisie," *International Press Corespondence,* Vol. XI, No. 15, March 19, 1931, pp. 285-286.

———, "The Indian National Congress," *Labour Monthly,* Vol. XIII, No. 5, May, 1931, pp. 303-307.

Dange, S. A., "Danger Signals in Indian Economy," *Labour Monthly,* Vol. XXVI, No. 8, August, 1944, pp. 181-183.

———, "India and the British Elections," *Labour Monthly,* Vol. XXVII, No. 6, June, 1945, pp. 181-183.

Das, Taraknath, "Indian Nationalism and Bolshevism," *Calcutta Review,* Vol. LXX, No. 2, February, 1939, pp. 137-143.

———, "Realities in World Politics of the Pacific," *Calcutta Review,* Vol. XLIV, No. 2, February, 1939, pp. 137-143.

———, "War or Peace in the Far East," *Calcutta Review,* Vol. XLII, No. 1, January, 1937, pp. 87-89.

Dutt, Clemens, P., "The Class Struggle in India," *Labour Monthly,* Vol. XI, No. 7, July, 1929, pp. 404-416.

———, "India and Freedom," *Labour Monthly,* Vol. XXIV, No. 8, August, 1942, pp. 247-250.

———, "The Indian League for Independence," *Labour Monthly,* Vol. XI, No. 1, January, 1929, pp. 22-28.

———, "Indian Politics, an Analysis," *Labour Monthly,* Vol. VII, No. 7, July, 1925, pp. 399-410.

———, "The Role and Leadership of the Indian Working Class," *Labour Monthly,* Vol. XI, No. 12, December, 1929, pp. 741-752.

———, "The Struggle for India," *Labour Monthly,* Vol. X, No. 3, March, 1938, pp. 155-162.

Dutt, Rajani Palme, "Independence for India," *Labour Monthly,* Vol. XXVIII, No. 8, August, 1946, pp. 245-249.

———, "India," *Labour Monthly,* Vol. XIII, No. 5, May, 1931, pp. 259-274.

———, "India Faces Japan," *Labour Monthly,* Vol. XXVI, No. 5, May, 1944, p. 134.

———, "India, No Time to Lose," *World News and Views,* Vol. XXVI, No. 9, March 2, 1946, pp. 65-66.

———, "India and Pakistan," *Labour Monthly,* Vol. XXVIII, No. 3, March, 1946, pp. 83-93.

———, "The Meaning of the Indian Constitutional Proposals," *International Press Correspondence,* Vol. XIV, No. 60, December 1, 1934, pp. 1597-1599.

———, "The Mountbatten Plan for India," *Labour Monthly,* Vol. XXIX, No. 7, July, 1947, pp. 210-219.

———, "The Path to Proletarian Hegemony in the Indian Revolution," *Communist International,* Vol. VII, No. 14, December 1, 1930, pp. 312-318.

———, "Planning for India," *Labour Monthly,* Vol. XXVI, No. 9, September, 1944, pp. 286-287.

———, "Quitting India," *Labour Monthly,* Vol. XXVIII, No. 10, October, 1946, p. 299.

Dutt, Rajani Palme and Ben (jamin) Bradley, "The Anti-Imperialist People's Front," *International Press Correspondence,* Vol. XVI, No. 11, February 29, 1936, pp. 297-300.

Dyakov, A. M., "After the Failure of the Simla Conference," *War and the Working Class,* No. 13, July 1, 1945, pp. 11-14.

———, "India after the War," *New Times,* No. 2, January 15, 1946, pp. 10-13.

———, "India and Her Peoples," *New Times,* No. 5, March 1, 1946, pp. 25-31.

———, "The Indian Problem," *War and the Working Class,* No. 2, January 15, 1945, pp. 12-17.

———, "The Political Situation in India," *War and the Working Class,* No. 9, April 1, 1945, pp. 10-12.

Ghosh, Ajoy K., "Before the Tripuri Conference," *World News and Views,* Vol. XIX, No. 10, March 11, 1939, pp. 198-199.

———, "Indian States' Repressive Rule," *World News and Views,* Vol. XIX, No. 4, January 29, 1939, pp. 82-83.

Gopal, "The Peasants' Struggle for Debt Cancellation," *International Press Correspondence,* Vol. XVII, No. 25, May 14, 1938, p. 617.

Gopal, Modan, "Leftism in Indian Politics," *Current History,* Vol. XIII, No. 72, August, 1947, pp. 88-91.

Gordon, James, "Indian Students Against the Imperialist War," *World News and Views,* Vol. XX, No. 18, February 24, 1940, pp. 121-123.

Gunawardena, D. P. R., "The Indian Masses Come Forward," *Labour Monthly,* Vol. XI, No. 2, February, 1931, pp. 87-92.

Howland, Felix, "Afghanistan Has No Frontiers," *Asia,* Vol. XL, No. 2, December, 1940, pp. 633-636.

Husan, Mahmud "Soviet Policy Old and New," *Calcutta Review,* Vol. XL, No. 5, May, 1935, pp. 180-182.

Hutchinson, Lester, "The New Imperialist Strategy in India," *Labour Monthly,* Vol. XVII, No. 2, February, 1935, pp. 107-113.

Ibarruri, Dolores, "The Struggle of the Indian People against Imperialist War and for National Independence," *World News and Views,* Vol. XX, No. 4, January 27, 1940, p. 53.

Joshi, Puran Chandra, "How to End Hoarding in India," *World News and Views,* Vol. XXIII, No. 33, October 30, 1943, p. 351.

———, "India—What Now?" *World News and Views,* Vol. XXV, No. 31, August 11, 1945, p. 1243.

———, "India's Post-War Plan," *World News and Views,* Vol. XXIV, No. 16, April 16, 1944, p. 123.

———, "The Peasants of India," *World News and Views,* Vol. XXIII, No. 20, May 15, 1943, p. 159.

Kambagal, "The Expropriation of the Peasants and the Duties of the Communists in India," *International Press Correspondence,* Vol. XIII, No. 54, December 8, 1933, pp. 1232-1235.

Keats, Bill, "Release the Indian Prisoners," *World News and Views,* Vol. XXI, No. 33, August 16, 1941, p. 522.

Khair, G. S., "Liquidation of Illiteracy in Soviet Russia," *Modern Review,* Vol. LV, No. 4, April, 1934, pp. 419-423.

Krishna, S., "After the Lucknow Conference," *International Press Correspondence,* Vol. XVI, No. 30, June 27, 1936, pp. 803-804.

Kumarappa, Jagadisan M., "Russia on the March," *Modern Review,* Vol. XLIX, No. 6, June, 1931, pp. 651-657.

Kuusinen, A., "Imperialisticheskii gnet i problemi revolutsionnogo dvizhenia v kolonialnikh stranakh," *Novii Vostok,* Vol. VI, No. 23-24, October, 1928, pp. VII-XXX.

Lucas, W. E., "Russia's Threat to India," *Nation* (New York) Vol. CLII, No. 22, May 31, 1941, pp. 632-633.

Masani, Minoo R., "The Communists in India," *Pacific Affairs,* Vol. XXIV, No. 1, March, 1951, pp. 13-18.

Menon, V. K. Krishna, "Amritsar," *World News and Views,* No. 5, April 12, 1941, pp. 231-232.

————, "The 'Change' in India," *World News and Views,* Vol. XXI, No. 31, August 2, 1941, p. 494.

————, "Egypt and India," *World News and Views,* Vol. XXII, No. 28, July 11, 1942, p. 300.

————, "Famine in India," *Labour Monthly,* Vol. XXV, No. 10, October, 1943, pp. 316-318.

————, "Freedom's Battle," *Labour Monthly,* Vol. XXIII, No. 8, August, 1941, pp. 364-366.

————, "India and China," *World News and Views,* Vol. XXII, No. 10, March 7, 1942, p. 149.

————, "India and World Peace," *Labour Monthly,* Vol. XX, No. 6, June, 1938, pp. 375-378.

————, "India—a Conference," *World News and Views,* Vol. XXI, No. 32, August 9, 1941, p. 507.

————, "India for Action," *Labour Monthly,* Vol. XXIV, No. 6, June, 1942, pp. 26-28.

————, "India in the War," *Labour Monthly,* Vol. XXIV, No. 1, January, 1942, pp. 26-28.

———, "Labour and India," *World News and Views,* Vol. XXI, No. 1, January 4, 1941, pp. 4-5.

Mikneyev, Y., "A Journey to Australia," *War and the Working Class,* No. 12, June 15, 1945, pp. 20-26.

Mukherji, Abani, "The Indian Labour Movement," *Communist Review,* Vol. III, No. 5, September, 1923, pp. 239-245.

———, "The Moplah Rising," *Communist Review,* Vol. II, No. 5, March, 1922, pp. 373-378.

Muzaffar, M., "India's Fight against the Indian Bill," *Labour Monthly,* Vol. XVII, No. 5, May, 1935, pp. 300-305.

Nair, Kusun, "India on the Fence," *Fortune,* Vol. XLIII, No. 1, January, 1951, pp. 61, 142-143.

Namboodripad, E. M. S., "Eighteen Months of Famine," *World News and Views,* Vol. XXIV, No. 32, April 15, 1944, p. 254.

Nath, Paresh, "M. N. Roy, India's One Man Party," *Asia,* Vol. XLIII, No. 5, May, 1943.

Nehru, Jawaharlal, "Nationalism and the Mass Struggle in India," *Labour Monthly,* Vol. XX, No. 8, August, 1938, p. 476-482.

Pritt, D. N., "India," *Labour Monthly,* Vol. XXIV, No. 4, April, 1942, pp. 105-108.

Rafail, M., "Problemi indiiskoi revolutsii," *Novii Vostok,* Vol. VI, No. 23-24, October, 1928, pp. 1-24.

Rahman, Haribur, "Communism in India," *Living Age,* Vol. CIXL, No. 4430, November, 1935, pp. 236-240.

Rao, B. Shiva, "New Social Forces in India," *Foreign Affairs,* Vol. XX, No. 4, July, 1945, pp. 635-643.

Raskolnikov, Fedor, "The War in Afghanistan," *Labour Monthly,* Vol. XI, No. 3, March, 1929, pp. 179-185.

Rathbone, Hugo, "The Place of the Peasantry in the Indian Revolution," *Labour Monthly,* Vol. XII, No. 7, July, 1930, pp. 418-428.

Rice, Stanley, "Communism in India," *Nineteenth Century and After,* Vol. CII, No. 605, July, 1927, pp. 38-47.

Rink, T., "Problemi oboroni Indii," *Novii Vostok,* Vol. VI, No. 23-24, October, 1928, pp. 25-34.

Roy, Evelyn, "The Crisis in Indian Nationalism," *Labour Monthly,* Vol. II, No. 2, February, 1922, pp. 146-157.

———, "Indian Political Exiles in France," *Labour Month-*

ly, Vol. VII, No. 4, April, 1925, pp. 205-209.

———, "Some Facts about the Bombay Strike," *Labour Monthly,* Vol. VI, No. 5, May, 1924, pp. 293-300.

Roy, Manabendra Nath, "The Anti-Imperialist Struggle in India," *Communist International,* Vol. I, No. 6, 1923, pp. 83-93.

———, "India and the British Labour Government," *Labour Monthly,* Vol. VI, No. 4, April, 1924, pp. 200-219.

———, "Memoirs," *Amrita Bazar Patrika,* 1952 and 1953, *passim, Radical Humanist,* Vols. XXI and XXXIII, 1953, *passim.*

———, "The New Economic Policy of British Imperialism —its Effect on Indian Nationalism," *Communist International,* Vol. II, No. 21, 1926, pp. 70-91.

———, "An Open Letter to Prime Minister MacDonald," *Communist Review,* Vol. V, No. 3, July, 1924, pp. 120-127.

Ryan, Jack, "Report on Indian Trade Unionism," *Far Eastern Bulletin,* (Pan Pacific Trade Union Secretariat), January 16, 1929, p. 5.

Safarov, G., "The Present Moment in India," *Communist International,* Vol. VI, No. 26, December 1, 1929, pp. 1052-1055.

———, "The Treachery of the Indian National Congress and the Revolutionary Upsurge in India," *Communist International,* Vol. VIII, No. 9, May 1, 1931, pp. 258-264.

———, "The World Economic Crisis in Imperialism and the Development of the Revolutionary Movement in the Colonies," *Communist International,* Vol. VI, No. 31, February 15, 1930, pp. 1233-1239.

Safdar, "Hindu-Mussulman Strife," *Communist International,* Vol. IV, No. 5, March 30, 1927, pp. 68-71.

———, "Indiya na Vi Kongress Kominterna," *Novii Vostok,* Vol. VI, No. 23-24, October, 1928, pp. L-LXII.

Saklatvala, Shapurji, "India in the Labour World," *Labour Monthly,* Vol. I, No. 5, November, 1921, pp. 440-451.

———, "The Indian Round Table Conference," *Labour Monthly,* Part I, Vol. XII, No. 12, December, 1930, pp. 720-723, Part II, *ibid.,* Vol. XIII, No. 2, February, 1931, pp. 86-92.

———, "The Second Round Table Conference," *Labour Monthly,* Vol. XIII, No. 10, October, 1931, pp. 636-642.

———, "Who Is This Gandhi?," *Labour Monthly,* Vol. XII, No. 7, July, 1930, pp. 413-417.

Shah, Ikbal Ali, "The Bolsheviks Advance on India," *Independent,* Vol. CCVIII, No. 3804, February 11, 1922, pp. 31-32.

Shcherbinovsky, N., "Independence Day for India, *New Times,* No. 5, January 31, 1947, pp. 29-30.

Singh, B., "The Position of the Working People," *World News and Views,* Vol. XIX, No. 20, April 5, 1939, p. 448.

———, "The Struggle of the Indian Textile Workers," *Labour Monthly,* Vol. XXI, No. 6, June, 1934, pp. 346-352.

Slater, Montagu, "Government Frames up another Communist Conspiracy," *International Press Correspondence,* Vol. XVII, No. 10, March 6, 1937, pp. 266-267.

———, "The Indian National Congress," *International Press Correspondence,* Vol. XVI, No. 1, January 4, 1936, pp. 13-14.

———, "The Indian National Congress and the Future," *International Press Correspondence,* Vol. XVI, No. 5, February 8, 1936, pp. 218-219.

Somin, N., "Meerut Trial in India and the Colonial Policy of the Labour Government," *Communist,* Vol. III, No. 3, July-August, 1950, pp. 62-87.

Spedding, James, "Stop Interfering in India," *World News and Views,* Vol. XXVI, No. 27, July 6, 1946, p. 211.

Spratt, Phillip, "India on the Eve of Revolt," *Labour Monthly,* Vol. XI, No. 5, May, 1929, pp. 285-288.

———, "The Indian Trade Union Movement, *Labour Monthly,* Vol. IX, No. 10, October, 1927, pp. 606-620.

Tagore, Sir Rabindranath, "On Russia," *Modern Review,* Vol. LV, No. 6, June, 1934, pp. 611-620.

———, "The Soviet System," *Modern Review,* Vol. L, No. 3, September 1931, pp. 251-253.

Tagore, Soumyendranath, "Meerut," *International Press Correspondence,* Vol. XIII, No. 34, August 4, 1933, p. 748.

Tcelyapov, N. I., "Higher Schools in the Soviet Union," *Modern Review,* Vol. XLVI, No. 11, November, 1929, pp. 554-557.

Tilak, Raj Chadha, "Punjab's Red and White Communists," *Thought,* Vol. IV, No. 24, June 14, 1952, p. 7; "Punjab's Communists, an Analysis," *ibid.,* Vol. IV, No. 24, July

19, 1952, p. 5, "Punjab's Communists, an Analysis," *ibid.*, Vol. IV, No. 31, August 2, 1952, p. 7.

Valiya, "The Constitution for the Enslavement of the Indian People and the Policy of the Indian Bourgeoisie," *Communist International,* Vol. X, No. 11, June 15, 1933, pp. 385-390.

———, "The Development of the Communist Movement in India," Part I, *Communist International,* pp. 79-84, Part II, *ibid.*, Vol. X, No. 7, April 15, 1933, pp. 230-235.

———, "The Economic Crisis and the Policy of British Imperialism in India," *Communist International,* Vol. IX, No. 9, May 15, 1932, pp. 317-325.

———, "The Round Table Congress and the Indian National Congress," *Communist International,* Vol. VIII, No. 2, January 15, 1931, pp. 106-113.

———, "The Struggle for Indian State Independence," *Communist International,* Vol. VIII, No. 20, November 15, 1931, pp. 694-699.

———, "The Struggle of the Working Class for the Leadership of the National Movement in India," *Communist International,* Vol. VIII, No. 17, October 1, 1931, pp. 516-526.

Volgin, A., "Our Trip to India," *New Times,* No. 12, March 21, 1947, pp. 19-24.

Wilber, Donald, "Afghanistan, Independent and Encircled," *Foreign Affairs,* Vol. XXXI, No. 3, April, 1953, pp. 486-494.

D. *Periodicals*

1. Reviews

Asia
Calcutta Review
Communist (Bombay)
Communist International (English edition)
Communist Review (London)
Current History
Economist
Feudatory and Zamindary Review (Madras)
Foreign Affairs
Fortune

Harijan (Ahmadabad)
Independent
International Press Correspondence
Labour Monthly
Literary Digest
Living Age
Mahratta (Poona)
Masses of India (Berlin)
Modern Review (Calcutta)
Nation (New York)
National Front (Bombay)
Near East and India
New Age (New Delhi)
New Times (English language edition)
Nineteenth Century and After
Novii Vostok (Moscow)
People's Age (Bombay)
People's War (Bombay)
Radical Humanist (Calcutta)
Saturday Review (London)
Servant of India (Poona)
Voina i Rabochii Klass, (Moscow)
War and the Working Class, (Moscow)
Workers' Weekly (London)
Young India (Ahmadabad)

2. Newspapers

Amrita Bazar Patrika (Calcutta)
Bombay Chronicle
Daily Herald (London)
Daily Worker (London)
Hindu (Madras)
Izvestia
Manchester Guardian
New York Daily Tribune
New York Times
Pravda
The Times (London)
Times of India (Bombay)
The Tribune (Lahore, now published at Ambala)

Index

Index